Gardner, B. Delworth,
1928-

Plowing ground in
Washington.

$29.95

DATE			

Plowing Ground in Washington

The Political Economy of U.S. Agriculture

Plowing Ground in Washington

The Political Economy of U.S. Agriculture

B. Delworth Gardner

Pacific Research Institute for Public Policy
San Francisco, CA

ISBN 0-936488-70-0

Printed in the United States of America
10 9 8 7 6 5 4 3 2 1

PACIFIC RESEARCH INSTITUTE FOR PUBLIC POLICY
755 Sansome Street, Suite 450
San Francisco, CA 94111
(415) 989-0833

Distributed to the trade by National Book Network, Lanham, MD.

Library of Congress Cataloging-in-Publication Data

Gardner, B. Delworth, [date]
Plowing ground in Washington : the political economy of U.S. agriculture / B. Delworth Gardner.
p. cm.
Includes bibliographical references and index.
ISBN 0-036488-70-0
1. Agriculture and state--United States. 2. Agriculture price supports--United States. 3. Agriculture--Environmental aspects--United States. I. Title.
HD1761.G244 1995
338.1'873--dc20 94-47984
CIP

Director of Publications: *Kay Mikel*
Cover Design: *Judith Haig*
Copy Editor: *Robert Racine*
Index: *Shirley Kessel, Primary Sources Research*
Printing and Binding: *Data Reproductions Corporation*

Contents

List of Tables

Preface

This book is about the political economy of the agricultural sector in the United States. "Political economy" suggests that the agricultural economy is, in part, political. The sector is governed by statutes and administrative regulations that importantly influence the conditions under which farmers produce and market agricultural products and what consumers pay for food and fiber. Policy also influences the choices available to farmers and thus affects the personal freedom so much cherished in a liberal society. The relevant legislation that sets policy guidelines is administered by the executive branch, mostly but not entirely under the supervision of the U.S. Department of Agriculture (USDA). There is scarcely a department or agency of the federal government, however, that does not affect farmers in some way. Particularly important are the Department of Interior, the Office of the Special Trade Negotiator, and the Environmental Protection Agency.

The purpose of this book is to give informed citizens a better understanding of the policies governing the agricultural sector and how these policies get formulated, enacted, and put into action. Why should average citizens care about agricultural policy? What is at stake for them? After all, American farmers are known the world over for their ability to produce food and fiber efficiently, and since the nation is well fed and well clothed, what is the problem? For several decades, productivity advances in agriculture have exceeded those for the economy as a whole. It was recently calculated that the average American farmer feeds his own family and seventy-eight other people. Moreover, there may be no other producers in the country who have as favorable a public image as does the American farmer, although this may be changing. Then what could be the problem that justifies another book on the subject of agricultural policy?

The answer is found in basic economics. A near consensus exists among economists who have studied agricultural policy that despite the accomplishments of farmers, farm policy as it exists today (1) distorts the economy and produces a significant efficiency loss that reduces average standards of living, (2) massively redistributes income and wealth from taxpayers and consumers to farmers, primarily landowners, who are now richer than average Americans, and (3) degrades and despoils the natural and physical environment in significant ways. The perverse efficiency, equity, and environmental impacts of subsidized agricultural policy are becoming increasingly onerous and will continue to be so if that policy is not reformed. In short, the agricultural sector could function much more efficiently than it does now to benefit both consumers and taxpayers, and probably even producers, if the current subsidies and regulations were modified or, even better, altogether abandoned. The most significant point about these policies is that, in aggregate, any gains to producers are much more than offset by the losses suffered by taxpayers and consumers. Agricultural policy is thus clearly a negative-sum operation for the economy as a whole.

The first four chapters provide evidence that agriculture is more inefficient and inequitable than it could be. The implications for efficient resource allocation are explored in Chapters 2 and 3. Chapter 4 is a special case study of the efficiency of credit markets in agriculture as reflected in the policies of the Farmers Home Administration. Chapter 5 deals with the effects of agricultural income support policies on income distribution, both within the sector and in relation to the rest of the economy.

But if the situation is as bad as inferred in these chapters, why has the U.S. body politic allowed this situation to arise and perpetuate itself? Chapter 6 discusses the various rationales offered to explain why agricultural policy has developed as it has. Special-interest politics is probably the most compelling explanation, although others also have some validity. The political decision-making model of Chapter 7 develops hypotheses that purport to explain how special interest groups demanding political favors and the politicians and bureaucrats supplying these favors interact to produce policy that harms the majority of us. Chapter 8 reviews some of the recent law and regulations that affect the demand for and supply of political pressure in its various forms. Chapter 9 then tests the hypotheses developed in earlier chapters by analyzing data on the contributions of political action committees and other forms of political influence peddling. This chapter is more technical and quantitative than the others, and those readers without some background in statistical analysis may have some difficulty in understanding the numbers in the regression tables. The chapter's concluding section, however, contains the important findings.

Chapters 10 and 11 analyze the impact of agricultural subsidies and other farm policies on the natural and physical environment. Chapter 12 does the same specifically for irrigation subsidies. Chapter 13 concludes and asks what can be done to produce a more efficient, equitable, and environmentally benign policy governing the agricultural sector of the economy.

It is well to keep in mind that the purpose of all economic production is to increase consumption and standards of living. The vast majority of Americans, as well as other world consumers, will reap significant benefits from reforms proposed here, particularly if similar actions are also undertaken in other developed countries, such as Canada, Japan, and the European Community.

Acknowledgments

This project was suggested to me by Professor Terry L. Anderson of the Political Economy Research Center and Montana State University, and he provided strong encouragement throughout. Dr. Anderson also read two drafts, and his suggestions, both substantive and editorial, were invaluable. His reminders that I was writing primarily for a noneconomist readership were frequent and much needed. Professor Lee Alston of the University of Illinois and Professor Wally Thurman of North Carolina State University also reviewed the manuscript and were helpful in suggesting additional sources and in identifying glitches in logic and fact. It is likely that the book would have been better if I had followed their counsel even more closely. Several student research assistants also made important contributions: Melissa Grant, Marshall Daneke, and especially Suzanne Amos Hyland, who spent coutless hours searching for references and preparing the Federal Election Commission data for analysis.

I received funding assistance from the Olin Foundation and from the College of Family, Home, and Social Sciences and the David M. Kennedy Center of International Affairs at Brigham Young University, which supported my efforts as a fellow for two years. Rulon D. Pope and Richard J. Butler, my department chairs in economics at Brigham Young University, cooperated in every way possible to facilitate completion of the project. I gratefully acknowledge the help and encouragement of all these parties.

The officers and staff of the Pacific Research Institute for Public Policy were a pleasure to work with throughout the project. Robert Racine provided editorial expertise that proved to be immensely helpful in improving the readability of the book and Kay Mikel took a very messy manuscript and converted it into final copy. Finally, a special debt of gratitude is owed my wife, Kathryn Christensen Gardner, for making it pleasant as well as productive to do much of the writing on our computer at home.

PART I

Agricultural Programs and their Welfare Impacts

1

Farmers and Farm Policy

It is not easy to define the agricultural sector of the U.S. economy, let alone analyze it. Sometimes the claim is made that agriculture is the largest sector of the economy in terms of the number of people employed. To validate the claim, the sector must be defined very broadly to include not only farmers (those identified by the census as producing some specified value of food and fiber) but also those who sell inputs (machinery, chemicals, veterinary services) to farmers and those who transport, finance, and process agricultural output beyond the farm gate. This study will focus on those policies that most directly affect farmers, those who till the land and manage livestock.

Income is one way of measuring the size or importance of an economic sector. Net farm income fluctuates markedly from year to year because of changes in yields and prices, and probably would be even more volatile were it not for government payments to farmers, which are structured to be higher when prices are lower, and vice versa. For example, net farm income rose from $46.7 billion in 1985 to $54.5 billion in 1989.[1] However, net farm income has been less than 2 percent of the gross national product (GNP) since 1975 and in recent years has fluctuated between 1.1 and 1.3 percent of GNP,[2] a very small part of the entire economy.

A common perception is that the farming population is rural while the nonfarming population is urban. This perception is simplistic and is increasingly wrong with the passage of time. In fact, farmers are now a small proportion even of *rural* Americans. The 1989 Current Population Survey indicated that about 25 percent of the U.S. population lived in rural areas, just over 66 million people. This compares with 64.8 million in 1988. Rural areas are defined as open countryside and communities with under 2,500 residents that are not considered to be suburbs of large cities. However, only about 9 percent of all rural Americans work on farms or ranches, and fewer than 19 percent derive their main livelihoods from activities associated broadly with agriculture.[3]

The number of people actually living on farms was only 1.9 percent of the nation's total population in 1989 and declined from 4,951,000 in 1988 to 4,801,000 in 1989.[4] The census defines farms as places that sold at least $1,000 in agricultural products during the preceding year, not a very useful definition for analyzing many problems of the farm sector since many people are included who depend on off-farm employment for the bulk of their incomes. Moreover, the farm population is based on residence only. Many people reside on farms but do no farm work, and some farmers and hired workers do not reside on farms.[5] However, for census purposes every farm has a designated farm operator, and hence the number of farms is identical to the number of farmers. Of course, some of these farm units may be owned by the same party and leased to tenant operators. In 1978, the number of farmers was 2,258,775, but by 1987 the number had fallen to 2,087,759.[6] However, it must be emphasized that many of these "farmers" are not significant producers of agricultural output.

Agriculture is one of the most regulated sectors of the U.S. economy and has been for many decades. Production of almost every commodity is affected by some governmental policy. These policies may be classified in generic terms rather than on a commodity-by-commodity basis,[7] but even then the list is long. Specifically, agricultural policy includes direct income transfers to farmers through price support and conservation payments; regulated production through acreage set-asides, marketing quotas and marketing orders, government-imposed quotas on imports and subsidization of exports, penalties imposed on producers for not adhering to mandated conservation measures, government sponsorship and funding of research and extension activities, direct subsidization of inputs such as irrigation water and electric power, and demand enhancement programs for agricultural commodities such as foreign food aid, food stamps, and school lunches. Even though this list is not complete, it indicates the array of policies that have an impact on farmers, taxpayers, and consumers.

Most of these policies are covered in the 1985 Food Security Act and its successor, the 1990 Food, Agriculture, Conservation, and Trade Act, the two most recent major pieces of legislation. These two acts will be extensively described and evaluated in the following chapters.

Agriculture is not only one of the most regulated sectors of the economy but also one of the most heavily subsidized. No attempt is made here, however, to compare the degree of subsidization with that of other economic sectors. A popular rationale for both regulation and subsidy is the alleged inferior bargaining position of agricultural firms in the economy. Because farm firms are so small in comparison with the firms that sell to and buy from them, it is contended that farmers are disadvantaged in their market transactions and, therefore, that government regulation and subsidy are required to put them on a "level playing field." There are good reasons for rejecting this assertion, however, as will be clear in the pages that follow.

The Watershed Year, 1985

Some students of agricultural policy, this author included, believed that the 1985 legislation would be different, finally breaking with the past going back at least to the Great Depression and taking strong steps to get the government out of agriculture. At least five reasons prompted such a prediction.

First, sharply rising taxpayer costs for existing programs were becoming increasingly burdensome. When the 1981 Agricultural and Food Act was passed, its anticipated annual budgetary costs were $1–2 billion. As commodity markets weakened in the early 1980s, however, support prices established in the 1981 act came into play and program costs increased sharply. The Commodity Credit Corporation (CCC) alone spent $9 billion in acquiring program-commodity surpluses in 1982, and even more surpluses were expected in 1983. Therefore, in an attempt to check the large budgetary costs of expected increased deficiency payments associated with falling market prices, the government initiated the payment-in-kind (PIK) program, which required farmers to divert huge tracts of cropland from production in exchange for some $9.5 billion worth of surplus CCC-owned commodities (Geoffrey Becker, 1986, 11). As expected, the PIK program reduced the CCC's direct monetary payments, but other program costs associated with farm policy rose rapidly. Federal outlays on farm programs totaled nearly $19 billion in 1983. Surely, it was supposed, the taxpayers were weary of carrying this heavy burden and would demand that support to agriculture be lowered in the 1985 act.

Second, many interest groups within agriculture itself were hurt by the 1981 legislation, especially the PIK program. For example, PIK penalized livestock producers who had to pay more for feed, harmed marketing and financial firms that had fewer products to handle, and imposed substantial losses on input suppliers, such as those who sell agricultural chemicals to farmers, because so much acreage was removed from production. All these groups lobbied vigorously for a more market-oriented 1985 act.

Third, the Gramm–Rudman–Hollings deficit-reduction legislation was being actively debated. If enacted, it appeared that the government would strongly resist any policy enlarging the already huge budget deficits, and large agricultural price support payments certainly qualified as such a policy.

Fourth, and perhaps most significant, for the first time in decades the political environment appeared to be propitious for reform. The voting power of the farm bloc had declined significantly since the 1930s as the number of farmers dwindled, and in fact, large commercial farmers influenced most by price supports had become less than 1 percent of the nation's population. A very popular conservative president, Ronald Reagan, had just been reelected, and the conservatives were riding high in their Washington saddles. The administration's rhetoric, at least, was against regulation, for free trade, and highly supportive of market allocations of resources.

Fifth, in preparation for the 1985 bill, academic think tanks across the country held conferences and published reports. The recommendations emanating from these forums were nearly unanimous that the nation's taxpayers and consumers would be well served if agricultural policy could be freed from government controls. In the long run, it was argued, even most farmers would benefit from pursuing such a course.

So what did Congress deliver in the Food Security Act (FSA) of 1985? For the most part simply an extension of agricultural programs that had existed since the 1930s, but that have turned out to be by far the most costly in the nation's history. It is true that some elements of the 1985 act tilted policy toward freer markets—a slight reduction in many support prices, a new marketing-loan program that permitted loan rates for cotton and rice to move in relation to world market price levels, and at least a start toward "decoupling" of farm output decisions from governmental income support payments. (These programs and their economic consequences will be described in some detail in Chapter 2.) But on the whole, these changes were quite insignificant, and the basic programmatic structure was largely unchanged from that of earlier legislation. After the disappointing congressional actions in 1985, the think tanks were much more cautious in predicting policy shifts toward freer markets in the 1990 bill.

In a sense, this book is an attempt to resolve the dilemma suggested by these seemingly inconsistent facts: Though there were strong theoretical and practical reasons for expecting revolutionary reform in agricultural policy in the 1985 farm bill, little change was made.

As a result of the provisions of the 1985 act continuing support prices at high levels and a concomitant weakening of world market prices, direct CCC payments to farmers soared to over $26 billion in 1986 and were only slightly lower in 1987.[8] The 1986 figure is approximately ten times higher than the one for 1980. While less than 30 percent of the 1980 corn acreage was enrolled in government programs, farmers responded to the attractive price support programs in the 1985 act, and perhaps to their worsening economic condition, by enrolling more than 70 percent of the 1986 acreage (Geoffrey Becker, 1986, 8).

In addition, other programs that did not involve direct payments to farmers but nevertheless increased government costs in 1986 amounted to about $14 billion. The largest single item in this list was $8 billion of Farmers Home Administration (FHA) loans to farmers (discussed in Chapter 4), many of which will never be paid back.

Still other agriculturally related programs and subsidies swelled the costs to the U.S. economy. In fiscal 1986, the value of commodities exported under Public Law 480, the Food for Peace Program, amounted to $1.4 billion; $2.5 billion of export guarantees were provided for exporting firms; and the Export Enhancement Program that subsidizes U.S. agricultural commercial sales abroad cost the government another $75 million. Not all of these outlays represented net losses to the government, however, since the CCC earned some revenues from the sale of commodities it acquired under government loan programs.[9] On the domestic side, food assistance programs cost $20.2 billion in 1986, the bulk of this in food stamps for the needy and in the Women, Infants, and Children Feeding Programs.

The 1985 act also continued and extended programs that do not involve direct government payments to farmers but that do benefit them while imposing losses on consumers. Noteworthy among these are the dairy, sugar, and peanut programs. The American consumer pays prices above, sometimes far above, world market levels because the government imposes quotas and other import controls that protect domestic producers. Significantly, these programs help farmers far less than they harm consumers (B.L. Gardner 1981).

Beyond the farm bills, other recent legislation has increased income support for the agricultural sector, including Congress's response to the 1980 grain embargo by President Carter and the drought legislation of 1988. Because of the disastrous effects of the grain embargo, legislation was later passed to make the farm sector essentially "embargo proof."[10] Of course, advocates of free markets may not regard this as altogether misguided since embargoes invite retaliation from trading partners and become a major impediment to free trade.

The 1989 Disaster Assistance Act provided benefits for producers who suffered losses in 1988 due to drought, hail, excessive moisture, or related conditions. This was the largest disaster relief measure in U.S. history up to that time and cost the taxpayers $3.9 billion. The rhetoric justifying this legislation is revealing:

> *It is the sense of Congress that disaster payments made to producers are intended to preserve each producer's livelihood and farming operation, to enable the producer to meet preexisting commitments and obligations, to protect the infrastructure of the U.S. agricultural production input,*

> *supply, marketing, and distribution systems, and to preserve the vitality and health of rural communities.*[11]

Nearly every major lobbying interest in the agricultural sector and derived industries brought weight to bear, and the favorable vote was unanimous in the Senate and nearly so in the House.

What a difference a century makes! In 1887, President Grover Cleveland vetoed a bill appropriating $25,000 to drought-stricken farmers saying, "It is not the duty of government to support the people" (Lee and McKenzie 1987, 53).

These agricultural policies were not initiated all at once. They evolved over time primarily as a natural consequence of two factors: perceived long-standing problems in the agricultural sector itself and the increasing tendency to use governmental power to tax and redistribute incomes. The historical antecedents of current policies go back several decades, and some understanding of them will help put the upcoming analysis of current programs in perspective.

A Brief History of the Development of Agricultural Policy

The bulk of the current structure of agricultural policy consisting of price supports, acreage allotments and set-asides, marketing quotas, loans to farmers, and marketing orders was initiated in the 1930s as an integral part of President Franklin D. Roosevelt's New Deal. Special attention was given to agriculture because of low farm incomes, falling commodity prices, and sharply diminishing land prices. Poverty in the agricultural sector was perceived to be acute. However, many previous attempts had been made by government to aid the agricultural sector, since difficult times did not begin in the 1930s. It has long been understood and accepted that the sector has certain characteristics that make it particularly vulnerable to sharp cyclical swings of good times and bad, with the bad times generally outnumbering and outlasting the good.

Paramount among these characteristics are low income elasticity and low price elasticity of demand. The former implies that when economic growth occurs and incomes are rising, the demand for agricultural products does not rise proportionately with the demand for other goods. A consequence is that agricultural incomes fall behind the remainder of the developing economy. This phenomenon is common to nearly all developing and developed countries. Low price elasticities mean that, when supply shifts, as is common in a sector where random weather strongly influences production, price changes are sharp and unpredictable, and incomes are therefore highly unstable over time.

This instability is dramatically illustrated in data provided by Theodore Lowi covering the period during which agricultural policy was emerging:

> *After the Civil War America's largest and most basic industry was never for long out of trouble. At the beginning of WW I, for example, net farm income was $3.6 billion. By 1919, it was $9.3 billion; but two years later it was back down to $3.7 billion. It rose slowly to $6.1 billion in 1920–30 and had fallen off to $1.9 billion by 1932. (Lowi 1979,70)*

The period from 1910 to 1914 has been called the "Golden Age" for agriculture because of the favorable relationship between the prices farmers received and their production costs. In fact, in later decades when the "parity" price support concept became popular, farmers and their supporters argued that parity be defined as the relationship between prices and costs that existed from 1910 to 1914. Naturally, this boosted prices farmers received. The implementation of parity pricing ultimately led to excess supplies, acquisition of surplus stocks by the government, and costly disposal programs that have plagued the agricultural economy periodically ever since.

Agriculture's good times generally continued through World War I, stimulated in part by increased demand because of the war. However, in 1921 grain prices fell sharply, and farmers who had paid high prices for land in anticipation of favorable commodity prices could not make their mortgage payments and were foreclosed on by their lenders.

Given the sharp fluctuations in farm income as well as per capita incomes that fell well below the average for their urban counterparts, it is understandable that agricultural producers would seek governmental aid in their behalf. However, before World War I this help was not granted in the direct government subsidies and price supports that were to characterize later programs. As the quotation above from President Cleveland indicates, it was not then customary for troubled sectors of the economy to expect direct government income transfers. Aid would be sought more indirectly through macroeconomic policies such as low interest rates and promotion of foreign sales of agricultural commodities.

During the nation's most rapid development in the 30 years following the Civil War, the agricultural sector was a net debtor to the rest of the economy. This meant that the sector's wealth position would be positively affected by unanticipated general price inflation. With rising prices, debt would be repaid with depreciated dollars conferring wealth gains on debtors. Since agriculture was a net debtor, the sector favored "easy money" policies that produced inflationary conditions in the economy. But since the three decades following the Civil War were not inflationary but deflationary, net debtor sectors lost out relative to their creditors. William Jennings Bryan, the famous orator-politician and presidential candidate, was only one of many spokespersons for cheaper money and easier credit.

There were other differences between agriculture and the remainder of the economy. As most industrial sectors concentrated into relatively fewer and larger firms to utilize economies of scale and maintain some control of their markets, agriculture remained relatively decentralized and geographically dispersed and hence was unable to control or even affect market prices. Moreover, as many other industries showed an increasing capacity to invent and absorb new technology and use it profitably, scattered and decentralized agriculture found any collective action to develop technology much more costly (Olson 1965). It therefore took on new technology hesitantly and only with net debt.[12]

During Abraham Lincoln's administration in the 1860s, agriculture made substantial progress in enlisting active governmental support. The land grant act of 1862 provided federal land for establishing state agricultural experiment stations and colleges of agriculture and mechanical arts. The homestead acts provided federal land to settlers who would bear the costs of homesteading and working the land. The USDA was established and governmental support services in research, quarantine, and vocational education soon followed (Lowi 1979, 70).

Still, this support was insufficient to remove agriculture's vulnerability to cyclical booms and busts. Therefore, farmers sought strong federal regulation of the economic forces they said caused their problems: tight money and restraints on trade. Their proposed solutions took two main forms: the organization of cooperatives to better control their domestic markets and international protection through tariffs on imports and even dumping excess domestic supplies on world markets.

The promotion of cooperatives led to the passage of the 1922 Capper–Volstead Act, the 1926 Cooperative Marketing Act, and the 1929 Agricultural Marketing Act (AMA). The Capper–Volstead Act provided broad exemptions for agricultural cooperatives from antitrust provisions of the Sherman and Clayton acts. Between 12,000 and 14,000 active cooperatives were supported by the Capper–Volstead Act (Hoffman and Libecap 1991). The Cooperative Marketing Act created the Division of Cooperative Marketing within the USDA. The AMA further promoted cooperatives and joint marketing efforts. Its aim was to extend the scope and strength of producer-owned and -controlled coops at a time when many were failing.

The AMA also created the Federal Farm Board, which was permitted to make loans to the coops for the purpose of stabilizing prices, the first direct government intervention that attempted to control supply getting to the market. These loans could be used to purchase and hold production off the market temporarily and to develop improved merchandising and distribution networks. Limited price insurance was also provided (Hoffman and Libecap 1991). The Federal Farm Board had a short life, however, because in a period of rapidly falling prices, it paid more for the stocks it acquired than they could be sold for and the board soon ran out of its appropriated capital (Luttrell 1989, 7–9). The effort was regarded largely as a failure although it set the precedent for later governmental programs to control prices.

Legislation of the 1920s also created marketing orders for many perishable commodities, such as milk, nuts, and fruits. These orders were supply controls imposed by the federal government to raise prices. Marketing orders were unworkable for nonperishable crops such as cotton, wheat, rice, and the feed grains, however. These commodities could be stored by farmers and released on the market when prices were going up, hence negating the beneficial effects of the short-run supply control produced by the marketing orders.[13]

But even these significant government actions were insufficient income supports to create parity between agricultural and nonagricultural incomes and to stabilize the farming sector. When the Great Depression arrived and the interventionist Roosevelt administration came to power in 1932, one of the first orders of business was massive income support to the agricultural sector via a myriad of federal programs of the kind that are still extant today.

Notes

1. National Center for Food and Agricultural Policy (1990), *Gleanings* 1 (3) (Washington, DC: Resources for the Future, Spring).
2. United States Department of Commerce, Bureau of the Census (1990), *Statistical Abstract of the United States* (Washington, DC), pp. 426 and 646.
3. United States Department of Agriculture, Office of Public Affairs, "Yeutter to the National Rural Electric Cooperative Association," *Selected Speeches and News Releases* (Washington, DC: February 1–8), p. 1.
4. United States Department of Agriculture, Office of Public Affairs (1992), *Selected Speeches and News Releases* (Washington, DC: June 4–10), p. 12.
5. United States Department of Agriculture, Office of Public Affairs (1990), "Census Shows Rural Population Increasing, Farm Population Also Reported," *Selected Speeches and News Releases* (Washington, DC: November 1–8), p. 11.
6. United States Department of Commerce, Bureau of the Census (1990), *Statistical Abstract.*
7. For example, the prices of the following commodities are supported in one way or another through activities of the Commodity Credit Corporation: cotton, wheat, rice, peanuts, tobacco, wool, mohair, honey, milk, corn, barley, oats, rye, sorghum, soybeans, and sugar.
8. Nearly 90 percent of the estimated $26 billion direct payments to farmers went for just five of the supported commodity groups: feed grains, cotton, wheat, rice, and milk. See Geoffrey Becker (1986, 9).
9. The CCC is a wholly government-owned corporation operating within the USDA. It has an authorized capital stock of $100 million, but can borrow up to $25 billion at any given time from the U.S. Treasury to carry out its activities. The borrowed funds must eventually be repaid, but since the CCC almost always spends more than it earns, appropriations must be requested from Congress to offset these losses. CCC programs have "entitlement" status in the federal budget, and the CCC has no choice but to make available its loans, payments, and related price support benefits to all farmers who qualify for them. See Geoffrey Becker (1986, 4).
10. Christopher Leman and Robert L. Paarlberg, "The Continued Power of Agricultural Interests," personal communication.
11. See *United States Code,* Title 2, Sections 431, 432, 439a, 441; Title 26, Section 170(c).
12. Lowi puts the issue this way: "the only things stable about agriculture have

been 1) its declining relative economic importance in the census and in the economy, 2) the reverence it enjoys in the American mythology, and 3) the political power it possesses despite (1) and largely because of (2)" (Lowi 1979, 69).

13. Marketing orders will be discussed further in the following chapter.

2

Why Agricultural Policy Wastes Resources and Reduces Standards of Living

Every American has a stake in agricultural policy and should be interested in how efficiently the farming sector works and what can be done to improve it. Food and clothing are important components of every family's consumption bundle, and how efficiently they are produced is a significant determinant of the average standard of living. This chapter will define economic efficiency and explain how it is measured. It will also discuss some of the rudiments of governmental programs and policies in the agricultural sector and explain how they waste resources and reduce standards of living. It will also discuss U.S. agriculture as part of the world economy and explain what is at stake in efforts to liberalize agricultural trade worldwide. More specific theoretical and empirical arguments for excessive resources and inefficiency in the sector will be presented in Chapter 3.

Efficiency Defined

"Efficiency" has a rather specific meaning in a number of technical fields.[1] To the engineer, for example, efficiency generally is measured as the ratio of output per unit of input—for example, units of horsepower per unit of energy consumed. Efficiency has a similar meaning in economics: the units of valuable output per unit of scarce inputs, with emphasis on the words "valuable" and "scarce" (Heyne 1980, 104; Sowell 1980, 52). That is, the greater the value of the output given the scarce input bundle used to produce it, the greater the efficiency.

Typically, in agricultural production, a combination of inputs or factors of production such as land, labor, machinery, fertilizer, and pesticides are combined simultaneously to produce outputs or products such as a bushel of corn and a number of pounds of cornstalk. If efficiency is to be evaluated on a farm or for a sector of the economy, however, both the inputs and outputs must be meaningfully aggregated in some fashion to make comparisons possible.

This task is normally accomplished by converting heterogeneous physical quantities of outputs and inputs into value or dollar terms by multiplying the physical units by their prices. These resulting values can then be aggregated by class of commodity into total output value and total input value. In fact, values can be aggregated all the way to the national income, and comparisons of efficiency can be made between different countries.

Efficiency is also known to economists as "allocative efficiency," which is achieved if and when the value of output from a given bundle of inputs (resources) is a maximum. Equivalently, an allocation of resources is efficient if all resources are employed in their highest-valued uses; that is, a unit cannot be transferred to any other use or time period and produce a greater value of output. Thus, an allocation of production factors is efficient when a given output is produced with the least costly bundle of inputs.

When viewed in the aggregate, an efficient allocation of available resources across the economy will maximize the national income, the annual flow of final goods and services. Thus, efficiency is one of the most important determinants of the average standard of living. Economic growth is simply the increase in the per capita national income through time corrected for inflation. When the word "efficiency" is used throughout this book, it will be in this sense of utilizing resources so as to maximize the aggregate economic product of the nation.

Recently, economic growth has been an important national goal that drives much of the economic policy rhetoric of the executive branch. The Bush administration often said it was actively promoting economic growth. President Bill Clinton's rhetoric of "getting the country moving again" is a euphemism for promoting growth policies. Tax, trade, monetary, energy, environmental, and many social policies are evaluated at least partially in terms of how they affect economic growth or, the same thing, economic efficiency.

Efficiency and Equity

But efficiency is not the only concern of politicians and most Americans, who also worry about how the national income is divided; that is, the "equity" of the economic system. The negotiations over the budget compromise late in 1990 clearly established this point as a political reality. Significantly, equity probably has a larger political constituency than does efficiency. Nearly all individuals are keenly aware of their *relative* income standings and thus have an incentive to obtain information on how a given policy or market outcome will affect them and what can be done to increase their share. But outcomes that represent a prospective gain in efficiency are often a "collective good"; that is, they will be shared among many individuals in the economy whether they contribute to its supply or not. Many of the prospective gainers from improvements in efficiency do not even know who they are. As a result, factors affecting efficiency are often subordinated to concerns over equity in the political arena (Thurow 1981).

But to argue that efficiency and equity represent two quite different notions affecting human welfare does not mean that they are independent of each other. How the economic pie is divided is a critical determinant of how large the pie is and is becoming increasingly so as more programs to achieve equity are introduced. The size of the bundle of resources committed to the production of output is not a given or constant. Nor is the quality of the inputs committed or the technology utilized. Inputs are owned by people, and in a free society the quantity and quality of inputs owners choose to supply the production process with will depend largely on the expected payoffs to themselves. Hence, the expected payoffs constitute the incentives for efficient production in the economy. Therefore, if the government is involved in many significant redistributive activities that impair incentives, such as subsidies, taxes, public services, trade barriers, and regulatory activities, efficiency will be reduced. This point was demonstrated forcefully by the "supply-siders" who came to Washington with the first Reagan administration. Their principal contention was that high marginal tax rates on income distort incentives to offer labor and capital productively. Therefore, resources would be either withheld from production by their owners or utilized less productively because of shirking or mismanagement due to high taxes and tax loopholes.[2] As will be demonstrated, incentives have an important effect on efficiency in the agricultural sector.

The Determinants of Efficiency

Efficient resource allocation in agriculture is significantly influenced by at least four factors: (1) the inherent productive quality of the land, labor, and capital resources utilized; (2) the burdensome nature of the rules and regulations imposed on agricultural producers; (3) the appropriateness of the technology utilized in farming; and (4) the freedom of both input and output prices to change and to reflect relative scarcity and thus to provide signals for efficient resource allocation. Enough has been said already to indicate the important role of points (1) and (2). Relative to point (3), obviously if opportunities for technical change are exploited that result in more value of output per unit of measured inputs, then efficiency will have been increased. It is point (4) that requires greater elaboration here. Prices are the key information in a capitalistic economy, and the late, great Austrian economist F. A. Hayek (1945) has provided the clearest exposition of the role of prices in a competitive economy. Essentially, Hayek argues that the most important economic problem society faces is how to utilize the relevant dispersed knowledge that exists only in the minds of discrete individuals. Fortunately, individuals need not know all the details of every other decision around them. All they need know is the price that encapsulates all these relevant details. Markets coordinate the separate actions of different people and prices represent the relevant knowledge. An important aspect of Hayek's model is the assertion that the price and market system is not the product of human design, but arises spontaneously to serve these indispensable coordination needs.

An implication of Hayek's logic is that the consumer must value the commodity at least as much as its price or there would be no trade. Sellers must receive at least their variable supply costs or they would not be interested in trading. Thus, at the margin in competitive markets, the market price roughly represents both consumer value and producer cost. If the price rises, a signal is sent to producers to supply more of the commodity, but consumers will wish to buy less of it. By the same token, if the price of an input rises, producers will employ less of it, and the quantity of output supplied will decline.

If either input or output prices are distorted by public policy and therefore do not represent the subjective market "values" and "costs" of consumers and producers, then these distorted prices will cause inefficiency. In other words, only in unfettered competitive markets are prices generated that can efficiently guide resource allocation.

Even in the absence of distortions, however, not all producers and consumers value units of output and inputs the same. This will depend on their unique and "subjective" valuation of various alternatives (Pasour 1990, 12). Therefore, economic efficiency is not "objective" in the sense that outside observers can definitively determine when production is economically efficient. Only the decision maker who has an endowment of resources and is given prices knows what the relevant alternative values of the employed inputs are (Buchanan 1959, 1125–1138). However, the outside observer can identify market imperfections and institutional constraints that might distort prices and thus impair efficiency.

Some Attempts to Combine Efficiency and Equity Criteria

It was argued that how the pie is divided affects efficiency if incentives or costs are distorted by redistributive devices such as taxes, subsidies, and welfare programs. But equity is important in its own right as a determinant of individual well-being. Most people behave as though they have an interest in the well-being of others, both in absolute terms and relative to themselves. Were it otherwise, philanthropy and altruism would not exist. Some people, however, are malevolent and obtain satisfaction from seeing others relatively worse off. What motivates this benevolent or malevolent interest in others is often unclear. What is important is that if people's level of well-being is interdependent with that of others, efficiency is inadequate as the sole criterion of well-being. To consider both efficiency and equity, the Pareto criterion was invented.[3]

Most changes in the status quo, including changes produced by public policy, involve some gainers and some losers. How are the welfare implications of these changes to be judged, since it has been demonstrated that interpersonal comparisons of well-being are scientifically inadmissible? (see L. Robbins 1932). The Pareto criterion provides one approach to this dilemma. To unambiguously indicate an improvement in aggregate welfare, the Pareto criterion requires that at least one person be better off because of a change in the status quo and that no individual be made worse off.

Two objections have been raised to the Pareto criterion. The first is that it is difficult to imagine any policy change that would make no one worse off and that could therefore meet the strict requirements of the criterion for an improvement in aggregate welfare. If a change benefits one person and if he knows about it, he will presumably make the change unless he is prevented from doing so by someone who opposes it? Hence, the Pareto criterion is quite useless as a guide to social policy since its conditions could never be met. The second objection is that the criterion is insensitive to the magnitude of the total gains produced by a policy change compared with the total losses. Thus, even if the gains were an order of magnitude larger than the losses, so long as there were any losers the Pareto criterion would be violated and no favorable verdict on the policy could be pronounced. Only those who believe that equity should completely dominate efficiency considerations would find such a conclusion desirable.

Occasionally equity will come into sharp conflict with efficiency if inefficient policies benefit poor people substantially at the expense of rich people. Given the egalitarian impulses of most Americans, the equity impacts might be so positive that the inefficiency would be tolerated, even though the verdict on such a policy would be negative on efficiency grounds.

Fortunately, inefficient agricultural subsidies are paid disproportionately to farmers that on average have far higher incomes and wealth than do the average taxpayers who foot the bill (see Chapter 5 discussion of equity issues). This means that both efficiency and equity criteria would be negative on the policy. Of course, focusing on income averages obscures the wide distribution of incomes that exist in both the farm and the taxpayer populations.

Economic theorists have devised the "compensation principle" for evaluating public policies that benefit some people at the expense of others. This criterion asserts that a policy represents an improvement in welfare when those who benefit evaluate their combined gains at a higher magnitude than the sum of aggregate losses. Thus, the winners *could* fully compensate the losers and still come out ahead. This principle is known as the Hicks–Kaldor criterion for a welfare improvement, named for the two British economists who first enunciated it.[4]

The Hicks–Kaldor criterion will be employed in the efficiency analysis of the agricultural sector undertaken here. If a given policy makes some people worse off and others better off, the gains and losses will simply be aggregated, and if the gains exceed the losses the policy will be considered efficient. There is ample precedent for this decision, since the Hicks–Kaldor criterion is commonly used by welfare economists.[5]

As a practical matter, efficiency and equity are often treated separately, both analytically and politically. Economic analysts can advise policy makers regarding which policies produce an efficient allocation of resources and what equity impacts might be expected, but the decision regarding whether income transfers are made to the losers is essentially a political issue.

I have argued that Americans place much importance on improving living standards, which are more easily achieved if resources are efficiently allocated. Paradoxically, however, it is also true that, in the political arena, economic efficiency has no major constituency to promote it, whereas almost every interest group seems to be willing to invest large quantities of resources to maintain or improve the income and wealth of its members.[6] Hence, policies that are demonstrably efficient are often sacrificed to transfer incomes to politically potent interest groups. The converse is equally true: Inefficient policies persist because they promote the narrow interests of the politically powerful.

What can explain this political outcome? Most efficiency benefits arise from superior *market* performance, and these gains are nearly always prospective and invisible before they occur. Producers of commodities that are expected to be profitable use their superior information, resources, and expertise to supply consumers more efficiently than do their competitors.

But until the commodities are available at observed prices, consumers are not likely to know (or care) about them. Efficient public policies are no different. For example, few would dispute the fact that lower marginal income tax rates have reduced distortions in the economy and therefore have made the economy work more efficiently. But if individual taxpayers were asked how much they have benefited from reduced rates, their answers would be couched in terms of lower taxes paid rather than gains in overall efficiency in the economy.

So it is with market efficiency gains that could be achieved in the agricultural sector if subsidies were removed. The consumers and taxpayers, who would be the principal gainers, have little hard information about how much they would gain, individually or collectively. Hence, they have little incentive to generate political pressure for removal of the subsidies. But farmers and landowners who might lose if the subsidies were removed know very well who they are and what their prospective losses might be. In the political arena, they can be expected to fight vigorously and spend generously to maintain their favored treatment. They have created institutions such as the USDA to provide a broad array of services, a system of land grant universities and colleges to provide research and extension services, and a multiplicity of farm and commodity organizations to look after their interests. In contrast, what governmental agencies, with the possible exceptions of the Council of Economic Advisors and the Office of Management and Budget in the White House, are looking after the interests of consumers and taxpayers? Probably none.

Two Approaches to Estimating Efficiency

The dominating intellectual interest of economics as a discipline is to elucidate what efficiency is and what gains can be captured by removing impediments to the functioning of efficient markets. For purposes of analysis, efficiency can be framed in two ways. The first is *a priori* and *theoretical:* to show in principle how certain policies immobilize resources and prevent them from moving to more efficient employments where they would have higher value. The second approach is *empirical:* a quantitative demonstration of what resources actually produce versus what they could produce under more conducive institutional arrangements.

Both approaches have limitations: the a priori because it is difficult to demonstrate the costs of inefficiency without empirical measurement, and the empirical because it is not always obvious what the alternatives to present employment are, what they are worth, and what the costs might be of transferring resources to the alternatives. Of course, the two approaches are not mutually exclusive, and it is desirable to combine them wherever feasible. An empirical test of a theoretical implication is ideal from a scientific viewpoint. Both approaches will be utilized here. Theoretical reasoning will be utilized, principally in this chapter, to indicate why present policies are inefficient in terms of increased or decreased agricultural output compared with the efficient level. Empirical studies that have attempted to quantify the inefficiency of given policies will be reported and evaluated, primarily in Chapters 3 and 4.

The importance of evaluating inefficiency cannot be overemphasized. Given the political potency of equity considerations and the inertia of the status quo, unless progress can be made in estimating what agricultural policies are costing in sacrificed standards of living, it is doubtful that a very persuasive case for reform can be made. Of course, there may be equity grounds for opposing agricultural policies as well, and some of those issues will be discussed in Chapter 5.

Some Theoretical Arguments for Economic Inefficiency in Agriculture

A near consensus exists among economists that government agricultural policies that support prices above equilibrium levels, and subsidize and regulate inputs, distort relative prices and cause inefficiency in the allocation of resources. High governmentally guaranteed prices, such as mandated target prices for wheat, the feed grains, rice, and cotton, and support prices for milk, sugar, peanuts, tobacco, wool, and mohair draw excessive quantities of resources into the sector. Input regulations mandated by government, such as acreage set-asides, that attempt to reduce supply will ensure that resources are inefficiently utilized by distorting the mix of inputs that would have been most efficient.

The reasons that price support programs are economically inefficient are not mysterious. In an economic system where farmers are paid a support price and consumers pay another lower, market-determined price, inefficiency is sure to exist. The only question is how serious the inefficiency is empirically. High guaranteed prices to farmers above market-clearing levels stimulate production that would otherwise not occur. Scarce labor and capital resources are utilized that have higher valued alternatives elsewhere in the economy. Production costs of the supported commodities, at the margin, are higher than the commodities' worth to consumers.

The efficiency problem is even more complex because of the way government loans are made available to farmers through nonrecourse loans.

Loan rates tend to serve as a floor below which consumer prices cannot fall.[7] This means that the latter often cannot move down to market-clearing levels, thus limiting gains to consumers.

It works this way. Government loans are available to farmers in advance of the growing season. Because the loans are nonrecourse loans, the farmer can forfeit the crop utilized as collateral on the loan to the government as full repayment of the loan. Therefore, if the market price at the time the crop is ready for market is above the loan rate, the farmer will ordinarily sell the crop and with some of the proceeds repay the loan. Conversely, if the market price is below the loan rate, the farmer is ahead by turning the crop over to the government to discharge the loan. If the government prevents its accumulated stocks from getting to the domestic market, this action will decrease supply to the market and increase market prices to the level of the loan rate, at which point the farmer will sell in the market. Hence, if loan rates are high, this floor to market prices will be high. In periods of heavy production when market prices normally would be low, farmers not enrolled in government programs will also benefit since they receive higher market prices than they would have in the absence of the program. And, of course, these higher prices will induce more output and thus contribute to the production of unsold stocks or surpluses.

Of course, unsold stocks of commodities accumulate in either private or government bins and must be stored at significant cost. To keep these storage costs at politically "acceptable" levels, pressures arise to draw down the surplus stocks. This is usually accomplished by subsidized disposal: making food aid available to foreign governments, subsidizing commercial sales to foreign consumers, conveying food to domestic consumers via subsidized food stamp and school lunch programs, and simply giving government stocks away to "deserving" recipients, all of which imply inefficiency because the value to consumers at the margin is less than production costs.

Price supports also misallocate resources among countries. The trade implications of domestic agricultural sector protection are explored in a later section of this chapter. Here the focus is on domestic price support and loan policy. In the period immediately before 1985, the loan rate was placed above world market prices and served as a floor under which domestic market prices choked off U.S. exports. Thus, high loan rates caused the loss of billions of dollars of revenues for American farmers. Foreign customers opted not to buy U.S.-produced commodities since cheaper supplies were available from international competitors. Primarily for this reason, the Food Security Act (FSA) of 1985 gave the secretary of agriculture discretion to lower loan rates as much as 20 percent if the statutory rate made U.S.

production uncompetitive in world markets.[8] Mostly because of this feature, the FSA was said to be more "market-oriented" in comparison with the 1981 farm act.

Significantly, foreign traders in rice and cotton were especially handicapped since world prices for these two crops were far below the loan rates mandated in the 1981 farm act. Therefore, a new deficiency payment program, called the marketing loan, was initiated for these two crops by the FSA.[9] This program allows rice and cotton farmers to repay their government loans at the level of world prices. Hence, domestic market prices were not supported at or above the loan rate by the nonrecourse loan, and traders could successfully compete with foreign suppliers in world markets. Of course, since the deficiency payments were very large, these marketing loans were immensely costly for taxpayers.

For the most part, the 1990 Food, Agriculture, Conservation, and Trade Act (FACTA) gives the secretary of agriculture less discretion in setting loan rates than the FSA did. The FACTA requires that any reduction in loan rates be related to stocks of the commodity on hand.[10] However, the secretary is empowered by the FACTA to implement marketing loans and offer loan deficiency payments to producers of wheat and the feed grains as was the case for cotton and rice under the 1985 act. The effect may be to make U.S. exports more competitive, but could even increase the cost of deficiency payments to the taxpayers. Potentially, this provision could sharply increase the costs of government programs if world market prices are low, partially because of the dumping proclivities of the European Community. At the very time when world production exceeds demand at prevailing prices and signals should be given to agricultural producers to reduce supply, the policy for supporting prices and subsidizing exports gives signals for maintaining supply at high levels to the detriment of taxpayers who foot the bill. It is difficult to find a stronger argument for the inefficiency of our current price support policies.

The FACTA also sharply departed from the FSA by instituting marketing-loan deficiency payments for oilseed crops.[11] The reason appears to be foreign competition, especially from Brazil and the EC. Producers of oilseeds will now have the option of obtaining or forgoing such a loan but will be eligible to receive loan deficiency payments anyway.[12]

Ordinary deficiency payments for wheat and the feed grains caused the budgetary costs of support programs to be very high in the early and mid-1980s, as pointed out in the preceding chapter. In the cases of cotton and rice, the budgetary costs of the mandatory marketing-loan deficiency payments for these crops have been huge, despite payment limitations to individual farmers (to be discussed in Chapter 5). As a consequence, the budgetary costs to the federal government were so high in the mid-1980s that pressures were brought by the Office of Management and Budget to reduce the output of program crops. Similar pressures also came from foreign competitors who regarded the income support policy, especially the marketing-loan feature, as subsidized and unfair protection of American farmers. But these pressures had little effect on actions taken by the congressional agriculture committees as they fashioned the 1990 FACTA. In fact, as already pointed out, the FACTA extended the marketing-loan feature to oilseeds and possibly to wheat and the feed grains at the discretion of the secretary of agriculture to make U.S. exports competitive. The budgetary costs could be enormous in the years ahead if the secretary exercises his options and the European Community continues to subsidize exports, keeping world market prices low.

It helps some that the Omnibus Budget Reconciliation Act of late 1990 reduced the acreage on which deficiency payments could be paid by 15 percent. It was estimated that this provision will reduce program costs by approximately $6.8 billion for the years 1991 through 1995.[13] Farmers are permitted to shift up to 25 percent of base acreage to nonprogram crops without jeopardizing their acreage bases in program crops. But whether this anticipated saving in budgetary costs ever materializes and will be enough to compensate for the extension of marketing-loan provisions that could increase program costs must await historical experience.

What conclusion can be drawn concerning the efficient use of resources when target and support prices are established above equilibrium levels? Resources will be attracted into the agricultural sector that would not be there in the absence of these programs. Moreover, because the budgetary costs of agricultural programs are very large, efforts to reduce these costs have been attempted by placing restrictions on input use such as acreage set-asides. Theoretically, while output may have been reduced (although this is far from obvious empirically), it has been produced at a greater cost than would have been the case if the input bundle had not been restricted. The magnitude of these inefficiencies, however, is an empirical matter that will be discussed in Chapters 3 and 4.

The Claim that Price Support Policy Stabilizes the Sector

Some defenders of agricultural policy argue that support prices and loan rates produce a more stable and efficient industry. Guaranteed prices are alleged to reduce an important source of risk to the farmer, and if the farmer is risk averse, the risk reduction can produce a more efficient commitment of resources, as elaborated by Chavas and Holt (1990, 529–538).

That farming is a risky business is beyond doubt. The demand for agricultural products is reasonably stable through time except when cataclysmic events such as war and severe pestilence occur. The two principal determinants of demand, consumer income and population, normally change slowly. However, farm revenues can change abruptly from year to year because of variation in both yields and prices. Yields are influenced by variations in weather and infestations of pests. Partial and even total crop failures occur occasionally in nearly all regions of the country and frequently in some. Prices of agricultural products are notoriously volatile in the absence of government programs, primarily because of inelastic demand curves and shifting supplies.[14]

The income instability problem for the individual farmer may be quite different than that for the whole industry, for which price and yield tend to move in opposite directions in the absence of government price supports. If yield is down, price will be up, as every fruit and vegetable grower knows. Thus, aggregate income (price times quantity) will tend to be less volatile than either price or yield considered separately. For individual producers, however, income might be highly volatile since their yields may be down at the same time that those for others may be up, thus having both a low yield and a low price. Obviously, the income volatility problem depends to some degree on whether the crop is grown regionally (and all producers may be victimized more or less by the same environmental factors that affect yield) or nationally (with growers in some regions suffering yield reductions and growers in other regions having increases.) The broader the geographic base of production, the less volatility in incomes will be observed.

Price and yield volatility are not the only sources of instability. Another is the asset-fixity problem (Tweeten 1989, 145). When economic conditions are good, farmers find it profitable to invest in land, machinery, and capital improvements, which are highly specific to farming. But when times are bad, production may continue unabated at high levels as farmers attempt to maintain their incomes by using land and the fixed capital tied up in machinery and equipment. Because they are specific to the industry, these inputs have low or zero value elsewhere in the economy and will continue to be used as long as expected output prices cover the variable input costs. This phenomenon helps to explain why agricultural output remains at high levels in periods of recession when other sectors of the economy reduce output to match reduced demand.[15] The resulting low prices are a financial hardship to farmers who are making high interest and principal payments relative to earnings. Hence, protection from volatile price swings is desirable, and government price supports at least partially accomplish this.

However, the volatility problem is complicated by a number of factors that must be evaluated before it is clear that price supports are an effective solution.

Reducing Market Noise

A common perception is that short-run price changes in commodity markets are larger and more frequent than necessary to guide resources efficiently to their highest-valued uses (Houck 1990, 176). Put another way, the unfettered market contains random price "noise" that causes resources to be allocated away from efficient long-run employments. The volatility in the basic farming sector might then spread to industries that serve agriculture (for example, transport, finance, chemicals, labor markets) and to consumers who must purchase agricultural commodities with incomes that do not move in sync with volatile food prices. This can be a serious problem for poor people, especially those in low-income countries where the inability to purchase basic food requirements can jeopardize life itself. Therefore, the argument is that if prices are stabilized to reduce these random influences, more efficient allocations of resources will occur and humanitarian purposes will be served.

Despite the surface appeal of this argument, it probably is not valid. Eliminating market noise may not be efficient. Noise is alleged to be random, but markets are not. What may appear to an outside observer as noise may be genuine shifts or signals that expectations have changed about either costs on the supply side or valuations on the demand side. Efficient allocation requires that resources be reallocated as long as the net value of the new employment exceeds any costs of adjustment. But only the resource owners can evaluate these values correctly. No outside observer has the requisite information to do so. Therefore, to stabilize a price so that it cannot respond to the real shifts that occur in the economy is to forfeit the efficiency gains that could have been captured by the resource reallocation.

Reducing Risk

Reducing risk is another efficiency argument for price stabilization. If farmers are to avoid or reduce risk on their own, they must take actions that are costly—for example, diversifying crops. But this is costly unless enterprises are perfect substitutes for each other in efficiently using resources. Resources must be diverted away from alternatives that produce the greatest net average returns. Hence, diversification is a trade-off—increased production costs versus a reduction in risk. If risk didn't exist or could be reduced by government policy, costs could be lowered (Houck 1990, 178). Hence, price support programs reduce risk by stabilizing prices and incomes, ensure an abundance of food and fiber at reasonable prices, and at the same time produce a stable industry.[16]

A time may have existed when these stabilization arguments had more validity than they do now. Obviously, if prices are supported at fixed levels for a given production period and are known in advance by producers, an important element of risk is removed from production decisions. But the other side of the coin is that government schemes to stabilize incomes in agriculture have also been major sources of uncertainty. Although the types of policies governing agriculture have remained essentially unchanged for a half century, the details for many commodities change with every five-year farm act if not more often.

It is easy to demonstrate that farm programs are a significant source of uncertainty. When prices were high in the early and mid-1970s, farm programs eliminated production restrictions, and farmers were encouraged to plant fencerow to fencerow. Exports to the former USSR (and other places) were subsidized as they are now. Later, when prices fell, a new farm bill was passed with severe acreage reductions and President Carter imposed an embargo on exports to the former USSR as a protest against the Soviet invasion of Afghanistan. In other words, farmers' incomes were hostage to U.S. foreign policy. The overall merits of such a complex policy are not being questioned here, only the impact on U.S. agriculture. An interventionist government that imposes embargoes is itself an important source of uncertainty and instability in the economy. And a government accustomed to intervention will probably be less reluctant to intervene again and again.

Besides, because of the way the political system works, those who benefit from price supports are not content simply to stabilize prices and incomes. Government action is almost invariably used to *increase* incomes and thus draws excessive resources into the sector.

Market and Farmer Strategies to Cope with Instability

The ultimate case against government intervention producing stability in agriculture, however, is found in the fact that the market itself could and to some extent does provide opportunities for making profits if prices are volatile. For storable commodities, volatility in production and prices provides opportunities for arbitrageurs to profit from holding stocks that are accumulated during periods of large supplies and low prices and then placed on the market when current production is low and prices are high. It must be obvious that the activities of these "speculators" will reduce the volatility of market supplies and prices and provide more stability in the market. As long as the government does not compete with private arbitrageurs by holding stocks and thus increasing the risks of this arbitrage, the quantity of private stocks held for these purposes might well be socially optimal and efficient.

Contracting between individual producers and processors provides opportunity for sharing and redistributing risk. Excellent examples are found in broiler- and hog-feeding contracts.[17] More than 90 percent of broilers are now raised under contracts for which growers are paid entirely on the basis of their conversion of feed into meat. Shifts in the market prices of feed and broilers do not affect their returns. These price risks are borne entirely by the large integrated processing and marketing firms like Tyson and Perdue, which contract with growers. These publicly held firms are presumably more willing to bear price risk and can efficiently employ risk-reducing techniques such as hedging on futures markets. The implication is that they can be expected to behave in a much less risk-averse manner than do individual farmers.

In addition, the farmer-producer may employ various strategies and utilize available financial instruments to reduce risk. Some examples of the former are diversification, flexibility, and liquidity (see Tweeten 1989a, 141); of the latter, futures and options markets. Following a "flexible" strategy means that a farmer can move among production alternatives in a cost-effective manner. For example, renting farm equipment makes possible a shift among enterprises in response to changes in prices that would not be profitable if costly crop-specific machinery were owned. "Liquidity" is holding sufficient cash reserves to cover any contingencies that might put the farmer in financial jeopardy. While these practices might reduce risk, they also may increase costs. Thus, in principle, the problem is to find the optimal quantity of each strategy.

But a liquidity strategy may have inefficient as well as risk-reducing aspects (Tweeten 1989a, 144). Large farms on average operate with a lower ratio of equity to assets than do small farms because they take on more debt. They also function with a higher ratio of production costs to gross farm receipts. Thus, on average, risk of financial collapse is greater for large farms than for small ones. But large farms generally yield higher rates of return on scarce labor and capital resources than do small farms because of economies of size. Hence, if large farms are forced out of business because of instability in the sector, the result could be that production is shifted to small farms and the aggregate costs of the sector could increase.

A financial squeeze might also arise for capable young farmers who might be highly leveraged with debt. Efficiency would be served if unfavorable economic conditions eliminate the high-cost producers, but these highly leveraged young farmers may have less staying power than higher-cost but lower-leveraged older ones.

Futures and Options Markets

Perhaps the most compelling argument against government attempts to stabilize agriculture with price supports is that farmers and those handling agricultural products who might be affected by price fluctuations now have other vehicles to mitigate, if not eliminate, the risk of fluctuating yields and prices. And more private tools would undoubtedly be available if the government abdicated price support, crop insurance, and disaster programs.

Futures and options markets can be utilized to hedge against price risk. Futures markets enable a commodity producer to shift the risk of price change by selling a futures contract to a speculator who is willing to bear the risk in exchange for the prospect of making a profit. A farmer with a crop to sell at some time in the future can sell it before harvest at the going futures price. Later, at or near the expiration date of the futures contract, the farmer will sell the crop through normal market channels and buy back the futures contract. The purchase or sale of a futures contract always offsets the opposite position in the cash market. Ideally, the loss in one market will be offset by a gain in the other, thus producing the hedge that eliminates the price risk (Powers 1973, 109).

Futures markets have not been very popular with most agricultural producers, however. The reasons are quite unclear and probably complex. Some believe that futures are unwieldy for farmers to use since contracts are stated in large and lumpy quantities (such as 5,000 bushel blocks), and the farmer's production may not coincide with the contracted amounts. Others argue that commissions are too high to warrant the risk protection provided. Some even believe that futures markets are rigged against farmers because of information asymmetries and problems with the "basis."[18] Still other observers believe that farmers do not hedge because they are not really risk averse and, therefore, are willing to take their chances in the regular or spot market when the time to sell arrives. Everyone agrees that government support prices have somewhat obviated the need for price hedging for those crops that are supported.

Options markets provide an even simpler way of hedging against price risk.[19] Options are bought and sold on futures contracts for agricultural commodities such as corn, wheat, soybeans, soybean meal, oil, oats, and pork bellies in regulated, competitive exchanges such as the Chicago Board of Trade and the Chicago Mercantile Exchange.[20] Options give the purchaser of a call (or put) the right, but not the obligation, to buy (or sell) the underlying futures contract at a specified price (Neal 1992, 21). A farmer could hedge against downward price risk by buying a put option at the going premium price. For example, at planting time a farmer could buy a

November 750 put option that would establish a minimum selling price of $7.50 a bushel for soybeans, known as the strike price. If, by harvest, soybean prices have declined, the option to sell a futures contract at the option strike price can be exercised for a short futures position or the option can be sold to someone else. Either way, the resulting profit should roughly offset the decline in the price of soybeans. If the November futures price at harvest declined to $6.50, a profit of $1.00 per bushel could be realized by exercising the option to sell a November futures contract at the higher option strike price of $7.50 (Chicago Board of Trade 1986).

If the market price falls below the strike price before the expiration date, the farmer could "put" the specified amount of his crop to the writer of the option and collect the strike price. For the option of exercising this privilege he must bear the cost of the premium up front as well as a commission to the broker who negotiates the transaction. If the market price remains above the strike price, the farmer will simply not exercise the option and will be out the premium and the commission for the privilege of hedging against price risk. Some observers believe that options are more flexible instruments than futures contracts for hedging against price risk (B. L. Gardner 1977, 989).

In one sense, put options are remarkably similar to nonrecourse CCC loans now in vogue with commodities such as wheat, the feed grains, soybeans, cotton, and rice. If the market price is below the loan rate (strike price), the farmer simply turns the crop over to the government (the writer of the put). The difference is that the farmer does not pay the CCC anything for price protection.

If price support programs were eliminated, and if volatility of prices were indeed a problem in free markets, there is little doubt that options markets would arise to solve the risk problem.[21] With the tools available to insure against both production (crop insurance to be discussed shortly) and price risk, there is little justification for government programs to undertake these tasks.

It is encouraging that a new agricultural options pilot program, introduced by Sen. Rudy Boschwitz (R-MN) and Sen. Wyche Fowler, Jr. (D-GA) was included as an amendment to the Senate version of the 1990 farm bill.[22] If farmers are skeptical about private-market alternatives to avoid risk, this pilot program should provide the experience needed to reassure them that such programs will indeed work. Then private institutions can mount a significant program industry-wide.[23]

Once the risk-reducing features of the program have been demonstrated, however, the government should turn over all risk management to private institutions. To get recruits for the pilot program, it probably will be necessary to guarantee strike prices equivalent to target prices in the government programs. But since these target prices are above costs of production for most farmers, subsidizing the protection against risk at this high level will draw excess resources into the sector. This is inefficient. Of course, if farmers wished to pay premiums in the options market for strike prices equivalent to target prices or even higher, they could always do so. But they, not the government, should pay for it if the program is to be efficient.

Marketing Orders as Devices to Provide Stability

Marketing orders are organized under the supervision of the USDA and provide a mechanism for groups of producers to control supply and, therefore, increase price. However, the rationale commonly given for these orders is to provide a stable marketing environment for domestic producers of perishable commodities such as milk, eggs, nuts, fruits, and vegetables. Such stability would reduce risk and conduce to economic efficiency. Since perishable commodities cannot be stored for long periods of time, it is either impossible or very costly to support producer prices by simply targeting prices and managing stocks of commodities such as is done by the CCC for storable crops like wheat, the feed grains, cotton, rice, and the oilseeds.

However, federal marketing orders for agricultural commodities are coming under increasing scrutiny both by consumers, who pay higher prices, and by some producers, who would like to be free from order regulations that prevent them from competing at the level they would prefer.

Eliminating the orders would impose some wealth losses on producers who benefit from them, but the gains to consumers would more than offset these losses, and thus society as a whole would be better off. Like most other policies to protect agricultural producers, marketing orders are anachronisms that survive from a time when farmers were poorer than their urban cousins, which is no longer the case. And the protection of growers from the rigors of full competition has produced industries that are bloated and inefficient to the detriment of consumers and efficient producers.

Actually, marketing orders are little more than government- sponsored cartels controlled by committees of growers. Only a majority vote of producers is required to form an order in a given commodity market. The minority, which are opposed, must comply with the regulations or they cannot market their output. In fact, if they fail to comply with the regulations of the order, they are subject to fines and even imprisonment.

Orders tend to exist in those agricultural sectors dominated by large cooperatives that have enormous political power and are important contributors to political campaigns through their political action committees (discussed in Chapter 9). A consequence of this political power is that orders do not receive critical examination and supervision from either executive or legislative branches of the federal government, and corruption is widespread.

Marketing orders increase prices and producer incomes in two fundamental ways: via marketing quotas that reduce the quantities of the product that get to market, and by the collection of mandatory fees from checkoff producers, which are used for generic advertising to increase demand for the commodity. Economic theory provides some insights for understanding the rationale for these forms of collective action.

The Effects of Imposing Quotas

The law of demand postulates that if the supply reaching the market is reduced by quotas, the product will be sold at a higher price. Whether this action results in higher producer incomes, however, depends on how much the price responds to the reduction in supply. Income is the product of the quantity sold and its price. For example, if a 10 percent reduction in the quantity supplied results in a 15 percent increase in the market price, then withholding supplies from the market will increase producer revenues. (As discussed in note 13, economists refer to demand curves where the change in price is proportionately greater than the change in the quantity demanded as *inelastic*.) Since many agricultural commodities have inelastic demand curves, artificially restricting the supply by a device such as a marketing quota is an effective way of increasing producer revenues.

A characteristic of all cartelized efforts to control supply is a powerful incentive to cheat on the supply-reducing regulations. In the case of many marketing orders, this pressure on the cartel agreement is provided by existing producers and potential entrants who want to cash in on the higher prices without being subjected to the quantitative restrictions. Potential entrants will often couch their arguments against the regulations in terms of restrictions on their personal freedom to produce what consumers are willing to buy. This phenomenon is highly visible in controversies that have surfaced in California, where new and smaller producers are threatening the stability of marketing orders in citrus and almond production.[24] Established producers, particularly large cooperatives like Sunkist in citrus and Blue Diamond Growers in almonds, who have the most to lose from the breakup of cartelized agreements, respond to these pressures by gaining control of committees organized to limit supply and often resort to questionable means of regulating producers who threaten the status quo.

Generally the rules of an order require a pro rata reduction in marketings of *all* members of the order. But sometimes these reductions are facilitated by size and quality specifications that exclude small and extra-large fruits and those that may be immature and have cosmetic defects. The very large and established growers can afford to invest in technologies and management practices affecting quality that may not be available to small and independent producers and hence the quality specifications discriminate against the latter vis-à-vis the former.

Of course, these squabbles among different classes of producers, while important, are not the main issue. It must be remembered that consumers always lose more from cartelized limitations in supply than producers gain, and hence the cartel will reduce aggregate welfare unless a very compelling case can be made for protecting producers. Such might be the case, for example, if the producers were poor as compared with consumers. However, in the majority of cases with marketing orders it is the large-scale and wealthier producers who benefit most from the orders at the expense of much poorer consumers.[25]

The reasons for efficiency loss are not difficult to establish. Suppose that the marketing quota is two-thirds of production. The quotas on supply produce a higher market price than would exist in free markets. This artificially high price stimulates production beyond that which would exist without the marketing order. But one-third of this production must be shunted off to lower-valued uses, such as animal feeding, or it is completely wasted. At the margin, the supply costs are higher than the value of this production. In other words, resources are utilized to produce the restricted commodity that have higher-valued alternative uses elsewhere in the economy. Further, to this deadweight loss must be added the personnel costs represented by the orders committee that inspects individual growers for compliance.

The Economics of the Checkoff Promotion of Commodities

The other activity associated with marketing orders is mandatory fees imposed on all marketed output to promote generic advertising. Every gallon of milk or box of oranges marketed under an order would be so taxed. A strong rationale exists for this collective activity. To the extent that it is effective, generic advertising increases the demand for the commodity and benefits all producers under the order. Collective activity is necessary because the benefits of generic advertising are a collective good that cannot be withheld from individual producers, whether or not they participate in the promotion effort. This "free-rider" problem exists with all collective goods (discussed in detail in Chapter 7). Since all producers have similar incentives to shirk on voluntary contributions, the inevitable result is underinvestment in the activity unless individuals are compelled to participate. Producers may not like the compulsory nature of the marketing-order checkoff system, but it effectively solves the free-rider problem.

Whether the investment in generic advertising has a positive payoff is quite another matter, a question that, interestingly, is seldom asked. Empirical studies suggesting an answer are scarce. Can you imagine a private firm investing millions of dollars in advertising that would not have at least an expectation of producing more benefits than costs? In the case of generic advertising marketing orders, the free-rider problem is stood on its head. Who cares if the investment has a positive payoff if the bulk of the resources are in fact provided by others? The clear implication is that much of the generic advertising may be wasteful, and some of the larger brand-name growers argue that their resources would give them larger payoffs if used to promote their own brands.

The conclusion is that marketing orders have outlived their usefulness, if indeed they ever had any. Standards of living and economic efficiency would be enhanced if these government-protected cartels were abolished. Consumers would get products at lower prices; cost-increasing shackles would be removed from existing producers; new and efficient entrants to the market would put competitive pressures on existing producers, and resources would be freed up for higher valued alternatives.

Crop Insurance, Disaster Assistance, and Economic Efficiency

In countries like the United States with advanced financial institutions, economic actors can protect themselves against many types of risk by buying insurance. In agriculture, the federal government subsidizes crop insurance and strongly encourages farmers to participate. The government has also mitigated production risks to farmers by providing disaster payments for natural hazards such as killing frost, floods, and drought. Two questions are addressed in this section: How effective have these programs been in reducing risk, and what has been the effect of crop insurance and disaster payment programs on efficiency in the agricultural sector?

Crop Insurance

The 1938 Federal Crop Insurance Act authorized the establishment of the Federal Crop Insurance Corporation (FCIC) after private attempts to provide all-risk crop insurance failed. Programs were expanded by a similar act in 1980, which legislated that the federal government pay up to 30 percent of premiums to private insurance companies who served as agents for the FCIC (Halcrow 1984, 243). Insurance is available for a variety of commodities, including most of the price-supported crops. Farmers may choose to insure 50, 65, or 75 percent of their normal yields.[26] They may also choose the market price at which they wish to insure. Given that premiums are subsidized, it was expected that up to 50 percent of farmers would participate in the insurance program, but by 1988 only 25 percent of the eligible crop acres was insured (Barnaby and Skees 1990, 9).

Crop insurance that is not actuarially fair, that is, subsidized, is expected a priori to have a number of impacts that might reduce economic efficiency. If producers are protected against natural hazards, they will be more likely to locate in risky environments where losses from floods, drought, and hail are more prevalent. Another source of inefficiency is in the choice of cropping patterns. If incomes are protected by subsidized insurance, crops that have highly variable income streams due either to yield or price variability will be produced in greater quantities because the protected individual making the decision does not bear the full costs of choices that turn out to be unprofitable. Moreover, why should farmers even invest in information that reveals the risks of alternative crops if they do not bear the cost of such risk? Consequently, there is "underinvestment" in information relevant to prudent decisions.

The potential for these efficiency losses was increased recently when the government broadened the crop base that could be covered by insurance. The government provides farmers with a complete list of more than 200 crops that are insurable in their county (see, for example, National Crop Insurance Service 1990). Obviously, insurable crops are less risky than those that are not. In 1990, North Dakota farmers were allowed to insure dry beans against loss, even though this area is not well suited to growing beans. Predictably, crops failed, and insurance was paid.[27]

Outright fraud is also sometimes alleged to exist with crop insurance programs. Crops are harvested; then it is claimed that the crop failed and insurance payments are collected. Or farmers plant and insure crops they have no intention of harvesting. Very few additional inputs are committed. The crop is then reported as failed and the farmer collects the insurance. Obviously, monitoring the farmer is costly, and the government has insufficient resources to do an adequate job of preventing abuses. No systematic evidence is available, however, to indicate the extent of such fraud.

Disaster Assistance

Because of subsidized premiums, crop insurance should be financially attractive to farmers, but the low enrollment of eligible acreage shows otherwise. One reason is the realization by farmers that federal disaster payments will cover at least part of their losses due to natural hazards that could be covered by crop insurance.[28] Although some natural risks are local and even farm specific (hail being a good example), most are regional and can therefore generate the political support for disaster assistance. Ad hoc disaster assistance has been made available to farmers somewhere in the United States practically every year. In 1988 and 1989, for example, Congress passed legislation mandating disaster payments for farmers who suffered losses because of a variety of weather conditions, primarily drought. These payments were based on a percentage of what farmers normally would have produced but were subject to a ceiling of $100,000 annually per person. These payments were generally available to most farmers in an affected region despite occasional warnings from the USDA that those farmers who could but did not purchase crop insurance would not be provided with disaster assistance. Obviously the warnings lacked credibility.

Crop Insurance versus Disaster Programs

A continuing and lively controversy has existed at least since the early 1970s over whether farmers should be protected with subsidized crop insurance or direct disaster assistance. It has always been recognized that disaster programs may encourage farmers to produce in hazardous locations and situations. Why not, if the federal government will bail out producers at taxpayer expense? (see Horwich 1990). In addition, some producers are kept in business that would likely have left the sector had disaster programs not been available. Thus, what is often presented as a humanitarian program to help people victimized by natural forces beyond their control is also socially wasteful because without the availability of disaster assistance farmers would not have chosen to commit resources in risky environments.

A similar problem arises with crop insurance. In a world of imperfect and costly information, where premiums are established at average risk levels over all producers, farmers who have information not available to others that their own production situations are either more risky or more inefficient may buy insurance in disproportionate amounts. The result is producers are kept in business who otherwise would have been unable to compete had the premiums been based on perfect information.[29] The insurance business in general has always been plagued by this "adverse selection" problem.

It probably was the observed abuses of crop insurance that motivated the opposition of the USDA in the hearings held on the 1990 FACTA. Otherwise, it is difficult to understand why an administration that said it was dedicated to free market principles would prefer disaster assistance to crop insurance. With crop insurance, farmers at least pay premiums up front and must weigh the benefits and costs of enrolling. No such discipline exists with disaster programs. The real problem for resource use efficiency is the incompatibility of the two systems. It is difficult to see how insurance programs can succeed if disaster programs serve as a substitute by taking much of the risk out of farming.

Nevertheless, in hearings for the 1990 FACTA, USDA Secretary Yeutter maintained that federal crop insurance had not achieved the objectives intended and that the administration would recommend its discontinuance. The secretary pointed out that only 25 percent of eligible acres were insured under the federal program, even though premiums were heavily subsidized, and that insurance programs had cost an average of $600 million annually since 1981, even though they had been primarily ad hoc.[30]

If the secretary was recommending that the government should stop subsidizing crop insurance so that private insurers could provide protection that is actuarially sound and unsubsidized, a positive step has been taken on efficiency grounds. But with the disaster programs strengthened, is it reasonable to expect that private insurers could succeed? Given the liberality of the terms of both government FmHA credit and disaster programs, farmers have not wished to pay a premium to enroll in insurance programs, subsidized or not.

In any case, the 1990 FACTA did not give the secretary his wish for an end to government crop insurance. The act does mandate a number of changes designed to improve the actuarial soundness of the existing crop insurance program.[31] And, indeed, the FACTA strengthens disaster programs.[32] The act authorizes a comprehensive disaster assistance program for 1990 crop losses similar to the programs enacted in 1988 and 1989, thus perpetuating the efficiency losses.

Subsidies, Trade Barriers, and Efficiency of World Agriculture

In a complex modern international economy, average living standards are affected by forces that extend far beyond domestic political boundaries. It is not only the efficiency of the agricultural sector relative to other sectors in the U.S. economy that is important. In a trading world it is the relative efficiencies of the different sectors among trading countries that also matters. Just as national regulations affect the mobility of resources among various sectors of the domestic economy, so do barriers to free trade distort prices and costs internationally.

Almost since the settlement of the American colonies, agriculture has been a major part of foreign trade. Tobacco was a major export crop even before independence of the colonies from the British Crown. The exportation of American cotton to the mills of Lancashire in England and elsewhere was of paramount importance in the politics of the Civil War. Vicissitudes in foreign trade of agricultural commodities, perhaps more than any other factor, have produced the sharp cycles in U.S. net farm income. Agricultural exports have been the dominant influence, producing both the sustained rise in land values from 1936 to 1980 and the precipitous decline in the early 1980s (Phipps 1982). Hence, barriers to free international trade are of major significance to the prosperity of the domestic agricultural sector[33] and the question of efficiency of resource allocation worldwide.

Consumers obviously benefit from free trade whenever comparative advantage (meaning that commodities are produced at the least cost relative to other commodities in the economy) guides production decisions in the various trading countries.[34] However, owners of immobile resources (such as land) that are used to produce goods that lack comparative advantage often benefit from protective devices to insulate them from international competition. In fact, agricultural protectionism "can be seen as an effort to resist and delay the adjustments required of the agricultural sector to remain competitive with other countries and with other sectors in a rapidly changing economic environment" (Sanderson 1990, 6). Unfortunately, unless protection is expressly prohibited by constitutional mandates, democratic political systems will almost always deliver protection to politically potent interest groups of producers. Trade barriers in agriculture are among the highest and most persistent in the world.

Protectionism, however, does not in practice deliver its supposed promises even to those producers who desire it. Fred Sanderson (1990, 6) has written:

> *The massive costs of agricultural support have not brought commensurate benefits to farmers. Less than half of the costs end up as increased income in their hands. Further, most of the benefits go to large commercial farmers who do not need assistance. Even on the large farms, incomes benefit only in the short run. In the long run, high support prices are capitalized in the price of land, driving up production costs for new entrants and for farmers who rent their land.*

Sanderson's conclusion is borne out for the European Community by Blandford and Dewbre (1994). They show that under reasonable assumptions for the elasticity of supply of farm-supplied resources and the elasticity of demand for agricultural exports, subsidized farmers in the European Economic Community receive in higher incomes only 20 percent of the costs consumers bear because of higher prices resulting from the subsidies. The relevant elasticities may be slightly different in the United States, but the probability is very high that the final result is similar.

Levels of Protection in the Advanced Countries

Distortions in worldwide agricultural production brought about by internal governmental intervention and external trade barriers are very large. It is a well-known fact, and something of a puzzle at first glance, that nearly all economically advanced countries subsidize their agricultural producers and that nearly all less-developed countries (LDCs) tax theirs.[35] As a consequence, poor countries as a whole underproduce their consumption needs and most advanced countries overproduce theirs. To dispose of costly surpluses, the advanced countries then dump large quantities on world markets at subsidized prices or concede them under favorable terms to poor countries through programs such as "Food for Peace." The result is often catastrophic for the farmers of poor countries. They become less capable of providing their own food requirements to say nothing of producing for foreign markets where they might have comparative advantage under free trade.[36] Resources are wasted and living standards are reduced worldwide as a consequence.

An Australian study by Anderson and Tyers finds that the average cost of farm protection to consumers and taxpayers in the developed countries amounted to about $1,400 a year for each nonfarming household in 1990, and that it would increase to about $1,800 a year by 2000 (*Economist* 1992, 7). Significantly, the study also found that for every dollar reaching producers, 37 cents is wasted, which amounts to $60 billion of waste for the developed countries.

The Organization for Economic Cooperation and Development (OECD) estimates that farm programs cost American taxpayers and consumers roughly $24 billion a year. OECD uses an inclusive definition of support to agriculture and suggests that annual consumer and taxpayer costs almost doubled between the period 1979–81 and the period 1984–86. These costs declined in 1988, but in the absence of significant changes in protectionist policies in the advanced countries, the decline is likely to be temporary (Bovard 1990a).

In the advanced world, Switzerland, Japan, Sweden, Austria, and the European Community (EC) are the most protective of their agricultural sectors. Even though Japan has been a net importer of agricultural commodities, protectionist measures have produced very high prices for Japanese consumers. For example, in 1987 the Japanese producer price for rice was supported at seven times the world market price (Bolling et al. 1990, 160–176), and they are no lower now. The EC countries have produced large surpluses of subsidized crops and have disposed of them through heavy export subsidies to the disadvantage of competitors in the advanced countries such as Australia, Argentina, Canada, and the United States, as well as many LDCs who might have otherwise supplied these markets. The EC spends twenty times as much on export subsidies as does the United States, even though the export subsidy is not inconsequential here (*Wall Street Journal* 1990e). The bulk of these costs are borne by Europe's urban taxpayers.

Economists have developed tools for showing levels of producer and consumer subsidies to a given sector. These are called producer and consumer subsidy equivalents (PSEs and CSEs) and are discussed in Webb et al. (1990). They provide detailed, quantitative information on the effects of domestic and trade policies that governments use to transfer income support to producers and consumers of agricultural products.

PSEs are defined as the net assistance provided through market price supports and other government programs that benefit the agricultural sector, expressed as a percentage of total farm receipts.[37] A PSE can be computed for an individual product or a group of products and it can be either positive (a subsidy) or negative (a tax) (Ballenger 1988, 36).

These income transfers may be measured in two ways. The first traces the flow of both direct and indirect government expenditures to producers and consumers. A dollar of government expenditures is assumed to count as a dollar of transfers. The burden from budgetary expenditures is assumed to fall upon taxpayers. The second way gauges the effects of policies by calculating the difference between actual domestic prices and what they would have been in the absence of impediments to trade. The burden of these price distortions is assumed to fall upon consumers when government policies cause the domestic price to be higher than the free-trade price.[38]

For the OECD countries (essentially Western Europe, the United States, Canada, and Japan), the average level of agricultural protection in terms of PSEs soared from 28 percent in 1980 to 47 percent in 1986 (Sanderson 1990, 6). The level of protection is highest in Japan and the EC, but the sharpest increases in the past few years have occurred in the United States and Canada. Most PSEs in the United States, however, declined somewhat after 1986, not because of changes in policy, but because of the recovery in world prices that began in 1987. These higher prices reduced the difference between market and target prices and hence the deficiency payments to farmers. For the United States in 1987,[39] the weighted average PSE was 33 percent compared with 39 percent for Canada, 52 percent for the EC, and 79 percent for Japan.[40]

Many farm products that are not directly subsidized are protected by high tariffs in the United States and other advanced nations. The U.S. tariff on orange juice is 40 percent; on yogurt and ice cream, 20 percent; dried egg yolks, 22.3 percent; fresh cabbage, asparagus, and broccoli, 25 percent; carrots, 17.5 percent; cantaloupes, 35 percent; soybean and cottonseed oil, 22 percent; and apricots and apricot jam, 35 percent. Import quotas are an even more inefficient and mischievous form of protection than tariffs since they are largely hidden from consumers. The U.S. International Trade Commission (ITC) recently studied U.S. farm import quotas to estimate what the tariff equivalents of the current quotas would be. ITC's conclusions were that the sugar quota was equivalent to a 233 percent tariff; butter, a 190 percent tariff; cheddar cheese, a 132 percent tariff; American-type processed cheese, a 172 percent tariff; and non-fat dry milk, a 142 percent tariff;[41] the peanut quota has the same effect as a tariff of up to 90 percent on peanut imports.[42] Thus, it is obvious that quotas protecting domestic producers are a very serious obstacle to trade and impose large costs on American consumers.

Given the widely different levels of protection that countries use to distort prices and production, resource misallocation among nations must be significant. The available econometric models, however, suggest that free trade would increase only modestly the total volume of agricultural trade. It would, however, redistribute production and trade in favor of efficient exporters. It would also tend to raise the international trading prices of many commodities now being dumped on world markets.

Fred Sanderson argues that it would be wrong to conclude that trade liberalization would serve the interests of only a few traditional agricultural exporting countries, with the EC and Japan bearing most of the cost. This would not be the case even if attention were focused narrowly on the farm sectors. Because of the present high levels of protection, North American producers would have to accept short-run losses. However, if consumer and taxpayer interests are taken into account, all countries would gain, with the EC and Japan receiving most of the benefits:

> *Although estimates of the size of this social dividend vary, it probably would have amounted to U.S. $30 to 40 billion in 1986 for the OECD countries as a whole. If gains to the non-agricultural sectors are also counted, the total welfare benefits could be over $70 billion. To this should be added the unquantified but probably even more important social dividend that could be expected to accrue from the "dynamic" effects of liberalization, in terms of more rapid economic growth. In the long run, per capita farm incomes would tend to recover everywhere because increased competition would accelerate the process of farm consolidation and modernization. (Sanderson 1990, 7)*

The system of deficiency payments used to support incomes for many U.S. crops may distort trade less than do market price support programs, such as those used for dairy, wool, honey, tobacco and peanuts. At least deficiency payments to producers per se do not increase market prices and depress domestic consumption. In fact, to the extent that deficiency payments increase supply, consumers benefit due to lower market prices. However,

> *heavily subsidized stabilization and disaster relief programs, large income payments (even if decoupled from current production), lavish adjustment assistance without a firm phase-out schedule, producer cartels, and two-price systems (even if they limit price supports to quantities consumed domestically) are all open to challenge because they cause substantially more resources to be retained in agriculture than would otherwise be the case. Furthermore, any program that raises domestic market prices will not be workable without import barriers. (Sanderson 1990, 8)*

A reform in the U.S. deficiency payments programs would remove the income payments from production decisions, so-called decoupling. The idea is to pay farmers a certain level of income support irrespective of their level of production. If payments are unrelated to production or sales, at the margin the payments would neither affect production decisions, increase output, nor misallocate resources. This may be true for the short-run decisions of existing farmers. However, almost any farm subsidy, even if decoupled from a farm's current production, will cause more resources to be retained in agriculture in a given country than would be justified by pure comparative advantage. This would be particularly true of farm labor, since, presumably, the decoupled income payments would be paid only to bona fide farmers who remain in the sector.

The proposal to decouple payments from output or sales has been stoutly resisted by most farm organizations, which are generally opposed to payment schemes that give any hint of "welfare" payments. In countries such as the United States, where budget deficits are perceived to be a problem, however, subsidy schemes that increase budgetary outlays appear to be more politically objectionable than trade barriers, which impose costs on consumers rather than taxpayers, even though trade barriers may be more inefficient.

Failure to Reform the GATT

The United States and other traditional agricultural exporting countries believe that they have comparative advantage in producing agricultural products and naturally favor the elimination of the exemptions provided for agriculture in the General Agreement of Tariffs and Trade (GATT).[43] GATT reforms proposed by these countries would prohibit export subsidies, import quotas, variable levies, and voluntary export restraint agreements, which would be replaced by fixed tariffs that would be reduced simultaneously with reductions in domestic support of the agricultural sectors (Sanderson 1990, 9).

Specifically, as far back as 1991 the U.S. proposed a 90 percent cut in export subsidies for primary agricultural products over a ten-year period and a six-year period for phasing out export subsidies on processed agricultural products. The United States also proposed that commitments be given for quantitative reductions of exports that receive such support and, further, that limits be placed on governmental outlays for subsidies on exports that are involved in our own Export Enhancement Program (EEP). In addition, to increase market access for agricultural exporters, the United States proposed that all nontariff barriers to imports, such as quotas, be converted to tariffs, which would then be reduced an average of 75 percent over ten years. The final tariff levels could not exceed 50 percent of the value of the products. Internal supports, widely used to subsidize farmers, also should be cut 75 percent over ten years. Supports that do not distort trade so much would be reduced 30 percent over the same period.

The USDA estimates that U.S. farm export sales by the mid-1990s would be $6 to $8 billion higher than expected if a GATT agreement were not achieved—about 16 to 22 percent higher than in 1992.[44] U.S. cash farm income would be at least $1 to $2 billion higher, perhaps even more.[45]

But the European Community and Japan strongly resisted the proposal. On December 6, 1990, at a crucial meeting on farm trade in Brussels, Japan joined with the EC to block a compromise that would have cut back the role that subsidies play in international trade of farm commodities. Progress of a sort, however, occurred at a Brussels meeting of EC farm ministers on May 21, 1992. A reform plan was agreed to that would replace many trade-distorting subsidies with direct payments to farmers. The plan would guarantee stable income to the 10 million farmers in the EC in exchange for an agreement by farmers to remove 15 percent of their cropland from production. As in the U.S. experience, however, the reduction in output would be much less than 15 percent because of farmer responses to add other inputs and remove the least productive land. Still, production was estimated to decline from 4 to 10 percent (Du Bois and Wolf 1992).

In late 1992, the flap between the United States and the EC over GATT reform reached new heights. Oilseed crops were the center of attention. The United States wanted assurance from the EC that the degree of subsidization of the oilseed crops would be reduced and that a quantitative restriction would be placed on the tonnage of oilseed crops that would be produced.

The United States threatened a huge increase in tariffs on certain EC imports, with French white wine specifically targeted, if the EC did not cooperate. The Europeans agreed, not to curtail production but to reduce acreage in the oilseed crops, which is not the same thing for reasons already discussed. However, the EC also agreed to gradually cut the volume of subsidized exports by 21 percent. An estimate by economists is that total U.S. soybean exports could rise by about 60 million bushels, or roughly 7 percent, if these measures are adopted (Kilman 1992).

After sometimes fierce bargaining throughout 1993 and before, a GATT agreement for agriculture was announced on December 14, 1993, just before the December 15 deadline for completing the Uruguay Round. Of course, each country must individually approve the agreement for it to become law, and it is far from clear that the critical actors in the agreement—the EC, Japan, and even the United States—will do so. As of September 1994 there is still uncertainty over whether the U.S. Congress will debate the GATT treaty in 1994 or will postpone it until 1995. There is even some doubt about whether the treaty will be approved at all. As with the North American Free Trade Agreement with Canada and Mexico, opposition seems to be centered in labor and environmental interests that see U.S. producers disadvantaged by higher labor costs and more severe environmental regulations than those faced by their competitors in world markets. In addition, the political climate in Washington is extremely confrontational, and other issues are dissipating attention and energies that might have been devoted to approving this important GATT agreement.

The agreement calls for the volume of subsidized exports to be reduced by 21 percent over six years (*Wall Street Journal* 1993). Bans on rice exports in Japan and South Korea will be lifted for the first time in recent history. Japan agreed to allow the share of imported rice to increase to 4 percent of total consumption in 1995 and to 8 percent over six years. Exports of subsidized European wheat are proposed to fall to 13.5 million from about 25.5 million tons, while other grains face smaller reductions (Davis and Ingrassia 1993, A1). Quotas for imports of sugar, dairy, and peanuts to the United States will be phased out and replaced by tariffs. The largest tariff cuts are for cut flowers; the smallest for dairy products (A1).

Even though reaching an agreement was itself historic, the magnitude of the changes in existing policies are quite small. The developing countries, particularly, are disappointed in GATT results. They hoped that the major Western nations would totally drop subsidies for their producers, lower tariffs sharply, and open markets by easing quotas. Some progress was made along these lines but much less than hoped for (Ingrassia 1993).

The U.S. Export Enhancement Program

The Export Enhancement Program (EEP) was initiated by the U.S. government in 1985 to counter the loss of markets to the EC due to its heavy export subsidies. EEP initiatives target virtually every market where U.S. producers face what are perceived to be unfair EC subsidies in sales of certain agricultural products. Since the program's inception, EEP-assisted sales have annually accounted for up to 65 percent of U.S. wheat exports, 63 percent of flour exports, 12 percent of semolina exports, 10 percent of rice exports, 98 percent of barley exports, 26 percent of vegetable oil exports, 29 percent of frozen poultry exports, and 5 percent of table egg exports.[46]

The 1990 FACTA includes reauthorization of the EEP through 1995. It continues the USDA policy of not issuing new EEP initiatives that would adversely impact the agricultural exports of nonsubsidizing competitors.

The Budget Reconciliation Act of 1990 contains some major adjustments in the event there is no GATT agreement. Specifically, $1 billion was appropriated for export promotion,[47] a marketing-loan program for wheat and feed grains was mandated, and acreage reduction minimum requirements may be waived. All these programs were designed to bring pressure on subsidizing competitor nations. Since the GATT agreement was not concluded by July 1993, the secretary had to consider waiving the spending reductions in the bill, increasing funding for export promotion, and instituting a marketing loan for wheat and the feedgrains.[48] These are very strong requirements indicating how politically sensitive these foreign trade matters are. But given the GATT agreement, which has yet to be approved by individual nations, it is highly probable that many of these measures will be put on hold until final disposition of the treaty is known.

Under the EEP, government subsidies are offered to domestic exporters who sell certain commodities to specified approved countries.[49] Most EEP initiatives have subsidized exports of wheat and wheat flour, the commodities with which the EC competes most aggressively with the United States.[50] Under the EEP, exporters sell U.S. wheat and other commodities at the world price and collect bonuses in the form of surplus, government-owned commodities. The bonus makes up the difference between higher U.S. prices and world market prices.

An Evaluation of the EEP Efficiency

Notions known as "diversion" and "additionality" come into play when gauging the resource allocation effects of the EEP. Diversion occurs when EEP subsidized sales to one country simply diverts EC sales of the commodity to other countries to which the United States might have exported. Likewise, if the EEP subsidizes sales that would have taken place even without the EEP, the program does not result in "additional" exports of U.S. products but simply causes a loss of export revenue.

Including the years 1985 through 1990, the EEP financed the movement of more than $2.6 billion worth of surplus commodities out of government storage and into export channels.[51] How effective the program has been to increase U.S. exports, however, is far from clear? It is true that both the volume and the value of U.S. farm exports have increased over the years of EEP operation. In fact, farm exports increased more than 50 percent in value from fiscal year 1986 to 1990 (Paarlberg 1990, 14).

But is the EEP responsible? According to a USDA study, the EEP accounted for less than a third of the rapid expansion in U.S. wheat sales that took place between 1985 and 1987. The study estimates that only 20 percent of all expansion in wheat exports between 1987 and 1990 resulted from the EEP. It has been further estimated that in 1987–88 only about 10 percent of all EEP wheat shipments were in addition to shipments that would have been made anyway (and at higher prices) (Paarlberg 1990, 15).

Robert Paarlberg argues that the EEP may have actually constrained rather than stimulated exports. A costly layer of company bids and CCC bonus-bushel authorizations have been placed between normally efficient private-sector exporters and their customers overseas and may have prevented transactions that might have otherwise occurred. In addition, the EEP slows sales by encouraging a hesitant attitude on the part of eligible importers; these importers do not want to buy from the United States until they know exactly how many bonus bushels the CCC will make available. And finally, the program discriminates against a few good customers that have not been made eligible for EEP subsidies—Japan and Korea, and until 1986, the former Soviet Union (Paarlberg 1990, 15).

In the final analysis, an important concern about the EEP is its "cost-effectiveness." The problem is to estimate correctly the cost of disposing of a subsidized commodity in foreign markets. One way would be to look at the budgetary implications: the sum of the acquisition cost to the government (probably the loan rate), the storage costs borne until disposition occurs, and the value of the commodities paid out as a bonus to the exporters. It costs the government $4.08 for every bushel of added wheat exports achieved under the EEP, according to estimates by Coughlin and Carraro of the St. Louis Federal Reserve Bank. The average export price out of U.S. ports for wheat during this period was only $3.16 a bushel.

> *In other words, if the purpose of the CCC during this period was to dispose of surplus wheat, it would have been almost a dollar a bushel cheaper simply to buy surplus wheat on the free market and then destroy*

it, rather than to give it away under EEP in the vain hope of producing additional foreign sales. (Paarlberg 1990, 16)

But if the good will of recipient nations is worth something, then subsidizing exports may have value to the nation not captured in a comparison of government costs and returns. But, by the same token, ill-will toward the United States is produced by the program in those countries that compete with us for export sales.[52]

Another question is whether the EEP really puts pressure on the EC, especially since the EEP costs the EC much less than it costs the United States. However, the EC does not appear to be as worried about budget deficits as is the United States (Paarlberg 1990, 16). And if Americans think that the EEP would cause the EC to modify its opposition to the reform of GATT as proposed by the United States, it obviously has not worked since at this writing the EC has not modified its opposition although there are encouraging signs.

An important empirical question that has never been definitively answered is who really benefits from the EEP? The foreign customers who receive commodities below world market prices would appear to gain, although agricultural producers in those countries obviously lose. In addition, the agribusiness firms that export under the EEP appear to be direct beneficiaries unless they dissipate the net value of the bonuses by making payoffs to those politicians and bureaucrats who provide the right to export.[53] All surplus disposal programs in the end appear to benefit farmers if the surplus stocks would otherwise have been put back into the market where they would depress prices. It is apparent that much empirical work is needed to answer these questions more definitively.

Conclusion

Perhaps the best conclusion of the economic effects of trade protection was written by D. Gale Johnson of the University of Chicago over twenty years ago:

The income transfers associated with protection of agriculture in the industrial countries appear to go on more or less indefinitely, largely without analysis of what groups are adversely affected or of what net social gains, if any, are achieved. It would appear, that after such protection has been maintained for a period of time, the main argument for continuation is that the substantial losses would be imposed upon resource-owners in the protected sector. In the case of agricultural protection, there would be large losses in the capital value of land and other relatively long-life assets and the readjustment in the labor supply would be painful and serious. It is difficult for governments who have misled a significant and vocal fraction of their citizens to admit that the policies they have been following have been of relatively modest benefit, that most of the net benefits go to relatively high-income groups and that the continuation of the present high transfer costs, or even higher costs, is necessary merely to maintain the status quo with respect to real product prices. (1973, 247)

Notes

1. For a good discussion of agricultural efficiency, see Kilmer and Armbruster (1987).
2. The important effects of redistributive policies on efficient production and on economic growth have nowhere been argued more forcefully than in Olson (1982).
3. The Pareto criterion was named after an Italian sociologist-economist, Wilfredo Pareto, who did much of the work on these issues in the early part of the twentieth century.
4. The Hicks-Kaldor criterion for efficiency does not require that compensation to losers *actually* be paid, only that it could be paid. It must be squarely recognized, however, that the Hicks–Kaldor criterion itself does not successfully account for the "equity" problem as postulated in the Pareto criterion, since there are admitted losers who are not compensated and thus the Pareto criterion is violated. But the Hicks–Kaldor criterion is consistent with economic efficiency as already defined because all changes that pass the Hicks–Kaldor compensation test, if implemented, will maximize the net aggregate output of the community.
5. There may be good reasons for believing that taking more than $1 from one group to give $1 to another group is not in the public interest. "This is because the losers could, in principle, pay cash to the gainers and make both groups better off without the policy. While this approach cannot be guaranteed to be practicable and while it is not always a suitable policy guide, there is usually good reason for being suspicious of a policy that takes away more from one individual than it gives to another." See B. L. Gardner (1981, p. 64).
6. This activity is known as rent-seeking by public choice theorists.
7. Loan rates are prices established by the government for the purpose of determining loans made to farmers when they enroll in government programs. For example, a wheat loan rate of $3.50 per bushel means that farmers growing wheat under the program can receive a loan from the government of $3.50 for every bushel that qualifies. The wheat crop is used as collateral for the loan.
8. This prerogative of the secretary is known as the Findley Amendment. See Kennedy and Visser (1990, p. 30).
9. A deficiency payment is a direct government payment made to producers of program crops when the average price received by farmers falls below the target (support) price. If the market price is below the target level, then eligible producers may apply to the government for deficiency payments equal to

the lesser of the differences between the target price and either the average market price or the nonrecourse price-support loan.

10. For wheat and the feed grains, the loan rate for 1991 through 1995 marketing years will be 85 percent of the average of market prices for the previous five years, excluding high and low years, but cannot drop more than 5 percent from the previous year. The secretary, however, may reduce the loan rate by up to 10 percent based on the projected end stocks-to-use (S/U) ratio for the marketing year. U.S. Senate (1990a), *Food, Agriculture, Conservation, and Trade Act*, Report 101-357 (Washington DC: July 6), Title III—Wheat, Section 301, and Title IV—Feed Grains, Section 401.

    For cotton, the loan rate will be the lower of 85 percent of the weighted average spot price for the previous five years, dropping the high and low years, or 90 percent of the current adjusted Northern Europe price. The secretary must permit loans to be repaid at the lower of the loan rate or (1) the adjusted world market price or (2) a fixed loan repayment rate, which was added by the FACTA. The loan repayment rate, however, cannot be less than 70 percent of the loan rate. U.S. Senate (1990a), Title V—Cotton, Section 501, amended Sec. 103B(a)(5)(A). As with the FSA, if the adjusted world market price falls below the loan repayment rate, the secretary shall make certificate payments to cotton buyers in the amount of the difference. The certificates, which are claims on surplus commodities in government hands, can then be redeemed for a specified quantity of cotton.

    For rice, the formula for establishing the price support loan and purchase rate is unchanged from prior legislation: The minimum loan rate is $6.50 per hundredweight, and annual reductions are limited to 5 percent. Price support loans may be repaid at the lesser of the loan rate or the higher of the world market price or 70 percent of the loan rate. However, a significant change is that authority for loan deficiency payments is no longer discretionary but mandatory. Such payments will be available on loan-eligible production rather than payment-yield production on producers who forgo loans and purchase agreements.

11. The oilseed crops affected are soybeans, sunflowerseed, canola, rapeseed, safflowerseed, flaxseed, mustard seed, and other oilseeds the secretary may designate. Loan rates in each year from 1991 through 1995 are not to be less than $5.02 per bushel for soybeans and not less than $0.089 per pound for most of the other oilseed crops. Rates for the others designated by the secretary shall be set in a "fair and reasonable" relationship to the soybean rate.

12. These payments will be calculated as the loan deficiency payment rate times the quantity the producer would otherwise have been eligible to place under loan. In turn, the loan payment rate is the amount by which the loan rate exceeds the loan repayment rate. As with cotton and rice, the secretary may make such payments in the form of generic certificates. U.S. Senate (1990a),

Title XI—General Commodity Provisions, Subtitle C—Provisions Related to Agricultural Act of 1949, Section 1121, amended Sec 107C(a)(2)(B).

13. U.S. Department of Agriculture (n.d.), *Budget Reconciliation Provisions Related to Agriculture.*

14. Elasticity is a device used to measure what happens to quantity demanded or supplied as the price shifts. Consider elasticity of demand. If, as a consequence of a price increase of, say, 10 percent, the quantity demanded decreases by 20 percent (or more than proportionate to the price change), the elasticity of demand is -2 or relatively elastic. If the change in the quantity demanded is less than proportionate, say, 5 percent, in response to a price change of 10 percent, the demand curve is inelastic. It follows that price volatility will be greater the more inelastic the demand curve.

15. It has been shown that asset-fixity may be a serious problem in the agricultural sector in that both capital and agricultural labor adjust slowly to their long-run equilibrium levels. See Yir-Hueih Luh and Spiro E. Stefanou, "Productivity Growth in U.S. Agricultural Under Dynamic Adjustment," *American Journal of Agricultural Economics, 73*(4), (November 1991), pp. 1117–1124.

16. U.S. Senate, *FACTA.*

17. These examples were pointed out to me by Professor Wally Thurman of North Carolina State University.

18. The basis is the difference between two prices representing different locations, different qualities of the commodity, different markets, or different times. Often these factors are captured in the difference between a trader's local cash price and the futures price at any given time.

19. An option is an agreement between two parties that gives one party the right, but not the obligation, either to buy whatever it is that the option allows to be bought, or to sell whatever it is that the option allows to be sold. An option that conveys the right to sell something at a specified price prior to a specified date is known as a "put" option. One that conveys the right to buy something at a specified price prior to a specified date is a "call" option.

    A commodity put option would be useful to farmers seeking protection against declining prices. Likewise, a call option would be used to protect a livestock feeder against rises in grain prices. The price hedge provided by the option is valuable, and for this service the purchaser must pay a price, called the premium. The person who receives the premium is said to "write" or create the option. The purchaser of a call option profits if the market price rises above the specified strike price loan rate by an amount greater than the premium plus the commission costs. The writer of a call option pockets the premium if the market price does not rise above the strike price and thus the call is not exercised. Of course, the opposite holds for put options.

20. Hence, a specific futures contract (such as a November soybean futures contract) that can be bought in the case of a call or sold in the case of a put is the underlying option contract. For example, a soybean option designated as a "Nov. 750 put" would give the buyer of the option the right to sell a November soybean futures contract (5,000 bushels) at a price of $7.50 a bushel at any time prior to expiration—regardless of what the futures price is at the time.

21. The farmer could even choose the strike price to be insured for; the higher the strike, of course, the higher the premium he must pay.

22. Chicago Board of Trade (1990, pp. 3–4). The program will be conducted for the crop years 1991–1995 in various counties that produce significant quantities of corn and for 1993–1995 in areas that produce wheat and soybeans. The program will be conducted through the CCC. Participation in the program is voluntary, and requirements are minimal. Enrollees must attend at least one options pilot program educational seminar conducted by the Cooperative Extension Service. Participants also will be required to maintain a separate brokerage account for the purpose of trading options contracts covered by the program. Strike prices would be equivalent to existing target prices.

    Producers who participated in the 1991 corn program were reimbursed for the cost of premiums for options with a strike price equivalent to the target price. The eligible bushels covered by the option payments are determined from the enrolled farm's corn base acreage and program yield. Production from the farm's corn base acreage greater than program production will be covered by loan rate equivalent options. Participants will also receive a payment of not more than 15 cents per bushel to cover miscellaneous costs associated with the pilot program such as transaction fees and interest cost. Since options hedging is designed to be a substitute for government programs, producers enrolled in the pilot program will not be eligible for price support loans or deficiency payments on the acreage in the pilot program.

23. The program's goals include: (1) providing farmers with a reasonable measure of protection from crop price fluctuations; (2) evaluating the viability of the use of put options as an alternative to government price support programs; (3) transferring commodity price risk from the government to the marketplace; (4) reducing market distortions caused by current price support programs; and (5) achieving possible budgetary savings for the federal government.

24. In 1991, the USDA decreed that as part of a program of marketing orders to artificially inflate prices, California farmers were prohibited from selling 42 percent of the navel oranges produced, over 50 percent of their lemons, and roughly 20 percent of their almonds and filberts. These restrictions added hundreds of millions of dollars to the cost of fresh fruit and nuts.

25. This and other equity questions are discussed in Chapter 5.

26. See Kennedy and Visser (1990, pp. 27–46). Yield losses are not covered under

the 1980 act if such losses were due to farmer neglect, poor farming practices, or crop theft. Penalties are also imposed if crops are planted after the FCIC's final planting date; coverage is reduced 10 percent for every five days past the deadline.

27. Private correspondence with an insurer in North Dakota.

28. At the end of 1991, President Bush signed into law a measure providing $995 million for payments to producers who had crop losses due to natural disasters in either 1990 or 1991. Producers with qualifying gross revenues of less than $2 million per year could file claims for losses on both program and non-program crops. Producers with crop insurance must have had losses greater than 35 percent, and those without crop insurance must have had losses greater than 40 percent. Producers could request benefits for 1990 on one farm and for 1991 on another farm. U.S. Department of Agriculture, Office of Public Affairs, *Selected Speeches and News Releases*, (Washington, DC: January 2–8, 1991), p. 1.

29. This problem is discussed in greater detail in Chapter 5.

30. The possibilities for disaster assistance were addressed by Secretary Yeutter:

    Once a county is declared eligible, individual farmers would receive assistance on the difference between the producer's harvested yield and 60 percent of the normal harvested yield for the county. The payment rate on eligible losses would be 65 percent of a 3-year average market price. . . . Producers of 200 crops currently covered by Federal Crop Insurance, plus hay and forage, would be eligible. These crops account for over 93 percent of total U.S. cropland.

    Private insurers may develop companion policies that provide protection not covered by this disaster assistance program. By providing protection on catastrophic losses, private insurers are better able to cover types of agricultural risks that are effectively insurable. Further, hail and fire insurance would continue to be available. . . . Moreover, the disaster assistance program would provide protection to those producers who have not participated in the crop insurance program in the past because they felt it failed to address their risk management needs.

    Statement by Clayton Yeutter, Secretary of Agriculture, before the Senate Committee on Agriculture, Nutrition, and Forestry, February 7, 1990. *Selected Speeches and News Releases*, February 1–8, 1990, p. 14.

31. Most notable of these changes are premium rate increases of up to 20 percent per year and opportunities for the development of more innovative policy coverage, such as insurance based on area loss rather than individual farm loss. This feature could be a start in eliminating incentives for fraud. And there is talk of requiring farmers who receive disaster assistance to have crop insurance. However, this idea has been promoted before, but when "push

came to shove" in a real disaster, the USDA has always caved in to congressional pressure to waive the requirement.

32. The 1989 Disaster Assistance Act was amended in the FACTA to grant mandatory payment provisions for sugar cane and valencia orange losses, and additional assistance is provided, subject to appropriations for losses in timber, sugarcane, and double-cropped commodities due to 1989 weather conditions. The commodity titles of the act contain standing authority for disaster assistance identical to those of the 1985 FSA.

33. It was estimated that U.S. agricultural subsidies cost $10 billion in budget outlays in 1993 and another $30 billion in consumer costs, the latter resulting mainly from trade restrictions. "The failure to find cooperative solutions to production and trade problems within this world system costs taxpayers and consumers in the OECD countries alone $300 billion a year. And those who can afford it least—the farmers in developing countries—lose $26 billion in income each year because of export subsidies, protectionism, and other trade distorting measures." U.S. Department of Agriculture, Office of Public Affairs, *Selected Speeches and News Releases,* (Washington, DC: November 7–13, 1991), p. 2.

34. The USDA estimated fiscal 1992 agricultural exports at $41 billion; the second highest export value ever, surpassed only by the fiscal 1981 figure of $43.8 billion. See U.S. Department of Agriculture, Office of Public Affairs, *Selected Speeches and News Releases,* (Washington, DC, May 28–June 3, 1992), p. 3.

35. Farm subsidies cost the industrial world an estimated $250 billion a year, with the bulk of that being spent by the European Community (EC) under its Common Agricultural Policy. See Sanderson (1990, p. 7).

36. A study from the International Fool Policy Research Institute in Washington, DC concluded that worldwide liberalization would lead to $7.5 billion in extra exports from low- and middle-income developing countries. Reported in *Economist* (1992).

37. For example, the PSE percentage is total transfers divided by value to producers. The formula is

$$\text{Percentage PSE} = \frac{Q^*(P_d - P_w{}^* X) + D + I}{Q^* P_d + D}$$

where: Q^* is the quantity produced
P_d is the producer price in domestic currency units
$P_w{}^*$ is the world price in world currency units
X is an exchange rate conversion factor
D is direct government payments
I is indirect transfers through policies such as input subsidies, marketing assistance, or exchange rate distortions.

38. In practice, it is not always possible to separate the contribution of every trade impediment or domestic policy to an aggregate PSE or CSE. The principal reason is that policies are interlinked. Where elements cannot be individually measured, their combined effect is calculated from the difference between the domestic price and a world trade price (adjusted if necessary for marketing processing costs and for quality differences). For example, an OECD study shows the following percents above the 1991 world price consumers in various countries paid for sugar: Japan, 354%; EC, 156%; Switzerland, 132%; Sweden, 108%; United States, 92%; Australia, 81%; Canada, 10%; and New Zealand, 0%. See *Economist* (1992, p. 6).

39. There is some variation in PSEs and CSEs from year to year. For example, total policy transfers for the twelve commodities covered in the U.S. estimates decreased slightly from 1986 to 1987. The composite twelve-commodity PSE ratio declined from 36 to 33 percent as the aggregate value of gross receipts increased 7 percent. The PSE percentage for most commodities showed modest declines as a result of strengthening world prices, although the wheat PSE increased modestly as the value of production plus direct payments decreased. Rice and sugar PSEs fell sharply from 1986 to 1987. Increased world prices reduced the amount of net government support for these commodities, and the value of production for both increased. Dairy transfers were reduced from 1986 to 1987, because U.S.–world price differences declined, and cheese and nonfat dry milk production decreased. Total milk production was lower in 1987 than in 1986 because of the Dairy Termination Program.

40. These data were updated in 1991 as reported in the *Economist* (1992): Switzerland, 80%; Japan, 66%; Sweden, 59%; Austria, 52%; EC, 49%; Canada, 45%; United States, 30%; Australia, 15%; and New Zealand, 4%.

    In the United States the PSEs for various crops in 1987 were: barley, 72%; corn, 46%; oats, 11%; rice, 49%; sorghum, 43%; wheat, 63%; soybeans, 8%; milk, 58%; and sugar, 60%. Comparable CSEs for the United States were: -52% for barley, -2% for rice, -23% for wheat, -29% for milk, and -43% for sugar. The weighted average was -12%. See Webb et al. (1990, pp. 4–5).

41. New Zealand farmers can produce dairy products for half the price of the average U.S. dairyman; yet strict quotas effectively ban New Zealand from the U.S. market. See Bovard (1991a).

42. U.S. International Trade Commission (1990), *Estimated Tariff Equivalents of U.S. Quotas on Agricultural Imports and Analysis of Competitive Conditions in U.S. and Foreign Markets for Sugar, Meat, Peanuts, Cotton and Dairy Products*, Publication no. 2276 (Washington, DC: April).

43. This would be especially true of the so-called Cairnes Group (Argentina, Australia, Brazil, Canada, Chile, Colombia, Hungary, Indonesia, Malaysia, New Zealand, Philippines, Thailand, and Uruguay).

44. EC farm subsidies have grown sixfold since 1975. In 1992 they were expected to reach $44 billion in budget outlays, and another $85 billion was paid by consumers as higher food prices. Comparing Paris, France, and Washington, DC, shoppers in the former pay 20 percent more for milk than those in the latter, twice as much for sugar, and two-and-a-half times as much for butter, largely because of EC farm policy. (Davis 1992a).

45. U.S. Department of Agriculture, Office of Public Affairs, *Selected Speeches and News Releases* (Washington, DC: May 2–8, 1991), p. 12.

46. U.S. Department of Agriculture, Office of Public Affairs, *Backgrounder* (Washington, DC: November 8–15, 1990), p. 9.

47. The Market Promotion Program is spending about $200 million a year to boost U.S. food, alcohol, and tobacco exports. See Bovard (1991b).

48. U.S. Department of Agriculture, Office of Public Affairs, "USDA Updates Status of Export Enhancement Program Commitments for Fiscal 1991," *Selected Speeches and News Releases* (Washington, DC: March 6–14, 1991), pp. 8–9.

49. Kennedy and Visser (1990). EEP proposals to provide commodities to a certain country are approved by an interagency review group. The recipient country then solicits offers from U.S. exporters. Once the exporter and the purchasing country agree on the price and terms of the sale, the exporter submits its contract to the USDA for approval together with a request for the specific amount of subsidy (bonus) needed to make the sale. Bonus payments are made in the form of commodity certificates redeemable for CCC-owned commodities. In sales to the former USSR, the department has provided exporters with the flat amount per ton that it was willing to offer as a subsidy rather than allowing exporters to request their own levels.

50. Wheat sales account for over 80 percent of sales of EEP commodities, and EEP wheat sales accounted for 50 percent of total U.S. wheat exports from 1985 to 1989. See USDA, *Backgrounder*, pp. 10–11.

51. In mid-1990, the so-called export bonuses under the EEP exceeded $50 a ton. The USDA subsidized the sale of more than 500,000 tons of wheat in a single week. Export bonuses on a 100,000-ton sale of hard red winter wheat sent to Tunisia averaged $49.23 a ton, while bonuses on a 12,000-ton wheat sale to West African nations averaged a record $54.01 a ton. See Ingersoll (1990).

52. For example, in 1990 the U.S. government paid dairy farmers about 98 cents a pound for butter but sold it abroad for roughly 55 cents. Also, the USDA spent over $50 million to dump 140,000 tons of dry milk on world markets at rock-bottom prices. "The USDA expected to buy over 8 billion pounds of surplus milk in 1990. Though the dairy export subsidies, like the wheat export subsidies, are intended to teach the Europeans a lesson, the main victims are the world's most efficient dairy farmers—New Zealanders, who receive less

than half the price for their dairy products that American farmers receive for theirs." Bovard (1991b, p. 10).

53. This point will receive major attention in several upcoming chapters.

3

Evidence for Wasted Resources in U.S. Agriculture

The previous chapter presented mostly theoretical arguments that agricultural policy wastes resources and reduces standards of living. But this makes only a partially convincing case for the need of reform; complementing theory should be empirical evidence that resources are wasted.

This chapter first focuses on the utilization of inputs—land, labor, and capital—and ascertains if the empirical evidence supports inefficiency because of government policies. (Government credit resources available to the agricultural sector are regulated by a separate set of policies, which are treated in Chapter 4 as a case study.) The effects of tax policy on investment in agriculture are also discussed briefly, and the chapter closes with a review of studies on the impact of agricultural policies on important macroeconomic variables such as saving, trade balances, and budget deficits.

Land

The influences of agricultural policy on land use are complex. Still, some rather clear effects emerge:

- ✦ Government payments and subsidies have driven up land prices and increased agricultural acreage, particularly in program crops.
- ✦ Because agricultural land is an inflation hedge in investment portfolios, inflationary conditions result in more land being held in the sector, especially because a surprisingly large fraction of it is owned by nonfarmers.
- ✦ Higher land prices resulting from government policies constitute a barrier to entry of new farmers.
- ✦ Because supply control programs have required land set-

asides, such as the Acreage Reduction Program, land is inefficiently utilized and production costs are higher.

- Land rents are forfeited by idling acreage through the Acreage Reduction Program, although the added flexibility for planting nonprogram crops provided by the 1990 Food, Agriculture, Conservation and Trade Act (FACTA) have reduced these losses in the years since 1990.[1]

Data on Land Use

Land is unique among productive inputs since it is impossible to change the size of the earth. But only part of the earth's land surface at any one time is utilized for any agricultural purpose.

Farmland is utilized for growing crops and grazing livestock. Since colonial times, a gradual shift from rangeland and forestland to cropland has occurred as the demand for food increased. The area in cropland in the forty-eight contiguous states was approximately 319 million acres in 1900 (Wooten 1950, 1953, and later years). By 1920, cropland had increased to 402 million acres and by 1930 reached a peak of 413 million acres. Cropland acres have remained near that level in the years since.[2]

Grazing land amounted to 831 million acres in 1900, but decreased steadily to 750 million acres in 1920. Rangeland had further decreased to 708 million acres by 1930 and to only 659 million acres in 1982. Over most of the period, rangeland was converted to cropland, although since World War II, the conversion of rangeland to urban and transportation uses has been most important.[3] Of course, these conversion trends imply nothing about what might have been socially optimal, which is the matter under investigation here.

Federal land disposal via direct sales or grants to settlers, such as occurred under the Homestead Act of 1862 and the National Reclamation Act of 1902, was the primary means of expanding the cropland base. Population expansion, from both natural growth and immigration, increased the demand for farms well into the current century. However, land settlement by farmers had pretty much run its course by the 1930s, when extensive government policies were introduced in Roosevelt's New Deal. Now it is government income support policies and the accompanying land control and conservation regulations that are the major determinants of cropland acreage.

Two land use margins are of special interest here: the margin between cropland and other land uses, and the margin between land actually growing crops and cropland that is idled by government programs.[4] The cropland base is likely larger than it would have been without federal income support programs. Price supports have increased the profitability of growing crops and have brought land under cultivation that would have remained as range or forests, especially in semiarid and arid regions in the Great Plains and Rocky Mountains.

Moreover, price support programs have influenced cropping patterns by increasing the land area devoted to program crops vis-à-vis nonprogram crops. The total deficiency payments made to farmers growing wheat, the feed grains, cotton, and rice are approximately proportional to the acreages in these crops on each farm. Farmers receive payments only for "eligible" production, defined as a farm's *program acreage* multiplied by its program yield (see Kennedy and Visser, 1990, p. 28). The program acreage base is the average area planted or considered planted to the program crop during the past five years.[5] Under the 1985 Food Security Act (FSA), farmers who exceeded their allowed program acreage were ineligible to receive government support payments on any of their program crops, so the incentives were powerful to use the whole base but not exceed it.[6] These policies have kept land in the cropland base that would have had higher value in alternative uses were it not for the regulations. Thus, the policies have produced inefficient land use.

Agricultural land is not always owned by farmers and is used by nonfarmers as well as farmers as an inflation hedge. The price of land usually follows inflationary trends in the economy. Therefore, land prices are higher than if they had been based on demand from profits generated in agricultural production alone. Thus, more land is held in the agricultural sector than would have been the case if the inflation hedge did not exist.

The Acreage Reduction Program

Wasteful land use results from the stringent acreage set-asides required of enrollees in government programs. The Acreage Reduction Program (ARP) requires that farmers leave a certain percentage of their base acreage idle or severely restricts its use. In thirty of the thirty-four years before 1990 (the mid-1970s were an exception), the government mandated an ARP in hopes of reducing the costs of agricultural programs.

The quantity of idled cropland fluctuated sharply over the period 1965–1988, however, with large annual set-asides in the 1960s and until 1972, when world food shortages and very high market prices began to emerge (see Table 3-1). From 1974 to 1983, annual set-asides were insignificant. Since market prices were near or even exceeded target support prices, deficiency payments were zero or very low; thus, there were few budgetary pressures to idle acreage to reduce supply. By 1983, however, grain surpluses had again reached costly levels, and the Reagan administration initiated the

TABLE 3-1 U.S. Cropland Acreage Idled, 1965 to 1988 (in millions of acres)

	Annual reduction	*0/92, 50/92 programs*	*Long-term reduction*	*All idled*
1965	41.9	0.0	14.4	56.3
1966	47.5	0.0	15.7	63.2
1967	25.2	0.0	15.6	40.8
1968	35.7	0.0	13.7	49.4
1969	50.2	0.0	7.8	58.0
1970	53.1	0.0	3.9	57.0
1971	33.8	0.0	3.4	37.2
1972	58.7	0.0	2.8	61.5
1973	16.3	0.0	2.8	19.1
1974	0.0	0.0	2.7	2.7
1975	0.0	0.0	2.4	2.4
1976	0.0	0.0	2.1	2.1
1977	0.0	0.0	1.0	1.0
1978	18.2	0.0	0.0	18.2
1979	13.0	0.0	0.0	13.0
1980	0.0	0.0	0.0	0.0
1981	0.0	0.0	0.0	0.0
1982	11.1	0.0	0.0	11.1
1983	77.9	0.0	0.0	77.9
1984	27.0	0.0	0.0	27.0
1985	30.7	0.0	0.0	30.7
1986	42.6	3.5	2.0	48.1
1987	53.2	7.0	15.7	75.9
1988	44.3	8.8	24.5	77.6

Source: Robert Green and Harry Baumes (1989), "Supply Control Programs for Agriculture," in *Agricultural-Food Policy Review: U.S. Agricultural Policies in a Changing World*, Agricultural Economic Report no. 620, Economic Research Service, U.S. Department of Agriculture, November.

payment-in-kind (PIK) program. The PIK program paid large deficiency payments to farmers enrolled in government programs in the form of CCC stocks of surplus commodities. Eligibility was achieved by complying with a large acreage set-aside, which in aggregate reached over 83 million acres, about a quarter of the cropland base and an all-time high. Annual set-asides have been large since 1983, although they have fallen since 1991 as surplus stocks have decreased.[7] In fact, announcements from the USDA indicate that ARPs for 1993 crops were to be near or at zero, and they have been at low levels since.[8] The acreage set-asides in the 0/92 and 50/92 programs for 1986–1992 have been a fairly small fraction of the total.

Cropland is also removed from production through long-term conservation programs. These reductions were sizable in the Soil Bank Program in the early 1960s and in the Conservation Reserve Program (CRP) after 1985 (long-term reduction). These long-term set-asides were a larger fraction of the total in the years 1988–1992, however, since CRP acreage is normally tied up in ten-year contracts and is increasing while short-term ARP set-asides fluctuate from year to year and recently have been declining.

Since 1981 the budgetary costs of existing federal farm programs have been a deterrent to increases in government expenditures because of the enlarging budget deficit. Thus, probably the most important determinant of acreage set-aside programs is the budgetary costs of the price support programs and stocks in storage. The bulk of these costs is deficiency payments, of course.

Efficiency Effects of the Acreage Reduction Programs

What are the economic efficiency effects of retiring land from the production of those crops that would have been grown in the absence of government programs? The primary objective of the set-asides is to reduce the supply of program commodities produced as a consequence of "high" support prices. Reducing commodity supplies is deemed necessary because excess supply exerts downward pressure on market prices and, therefore, increases both deficiency payments and government storage costs.

Convincing evidence shows, however, that acreage control programs have not been very effective in reducing supplies or surpluses. A USDA study found that excess supply is highest for commodities that have traditionally been given the most subsidies and subjected to the most stringent acreage controls (Bovard 1990b). Subsidized crops have four times as much excess supply as unsubsidized crops. A clear implication is that the acreage set-asides have not offset the output-increasing effects of subsidized production. One reason is that farmers minimize their costs of complying with the ARP by setting aside their least productive land. Another is that farmers may compensate for a reduction of land inputs by increasing other substitute inputs, such as water, fertilizers, and pesticides (discussed further in Chapter 11).[9]

This is not to argue that set-asides are innocuous in affecting the efficiency of land use and costs of production. James Bovard, a journalist with the Cato Institute, states:

> *The Agricultural Policy Working Group, a private research institute in Washington, estimates that set-asides, by forcing farmers to leave good land unplanted, increase the average cost of production for a bushel of corn by 33 cents. Since the variable cost of production in the most efficient corn-growing areas is only $1.25, this has a big impact on American competitiveness. A recent USDA study concluded that acreage reduction programs alone have added about 7 percent to farmland values. But Government cannot drive up land values without increasing farmers' costs, and thus decreasing competitiveness. The EEC has boosted its wheat exports by 40 percent since 1985 while the U.S. has had almost no gain.*
>
> *Set-asides are intended to drive crop prices higher than they would be otherwise. Yet, at the same time farms have been shut down to drive up crop prices, the U.S. has also spent billions of dollars since 1985 on export subsidies to make American crops cheaper overseas. Export subsidies are the antidote to set-asides and other Federal programs making American crops uncompetitive on world markets. (1990b, p. 11)*

The net costs to the farmer of removing land from supported crops through the ARP depend on the regulations that govern what use can be made of the land. The 1985 FSA generally prohibited haying or grazing of idled land, but gave the secretary of agriculture some discretion to modify this requirement.[10] The 1990 FACTA and the Budget Reconciliation Act further liberalized the use of set-aside acres under the ARP.[11]

The 1990 FACTA specified that, for determining deficiency payments, the acreage shall be the lesser of (1) the number of acres planted to the program within the farm's permitted acreage or (2) 100 percent of the crop acreage base on the farm less any "reduced acreage," defined as acreage idled under the ARP or under any paid land diversion program. However, under the Budget Reconciliation Act the acreage on which payments can be made is limited to 85 percent rather than 100 percent. The act does not specify rules for use of the 15 percent idled land, so farmers will consider market prices in determining which alternative crops offer the most promising net returns.[12]

So what is the efficiency cost of the ARP? One estimate is that the ARP under the FSA and the FACTA withheld an annual average of 63.5 million acres over the period 1986–1992, approximately 15 percent of the acreage planted to the principal program crops in the high production year of 1981 (Baumes and Spitze 1990). One estimate of the "true" efficiency cost of the ARP, therefore, would be the lost economic rent that would have been earned on the idled land; that is, the difference in net rents (total revenue minus all nonland costs) between what the land would have earned under a free market regimen and what it earned under ARP restrictions. Estimating these costs is difficult, however, because the prices that would have existed in the absence of government programs and trade restrictions are not observable. A safe bet is that these costs are very substantial. Other factors of production such as labor and capital are comparatively mobile, especially in the long run, and have alternative uses that are nearly as valuable as those in agriculture. To not use them in agriculture means that most will be employed alternatively, and the net social loss will likely be small. However, the same argument cannot be made for agricultural land. Since agriculture is generally the marginal user of land, were land not used for growing crops it is likely that the full land rent earned in farming would be lost.

What is a reasonable estimate of this loss? In 1987, the net rents paid to nonoperator U.S. landlords was $6,964 million.[13] The acreage rented by farm operators was approximately 15 percent of total cropland or about 154 million acres.[14] Thus, the average per acre rent was $45 across the entire country. Over the period 1982 to 1992, the accumulated loss in land rents due to the ARP set-asides is about $20 billion. This estimate is conservative, however, because the per acre rents in corn and wheat producing areas, where so much of the acreage set-aside is located, would likely be higher than the national average.

If government payments are paid per unit of output, such as is done for wool and honey, then variable inputs, such as labor and operating expenses, which vary directly with output, will be overused. If the entitlement to payments is based on acreage rather than output, which is the case for crops that have acreage bases, but payment yields are fixed, then more land will be used to produce supported crops than would have been the case otherwise. If the income support were paid to all bona fide farmers as a lump-sum payment, then it is the number of farmers in the agricultural sector that would be in excess of the efficient number.

The fact that agriculture is the lowest-valued user of land does not necessarily mean that investment in land is less profitable than investing in other assets. However, it is commonly believed that owners of real agricultural assets like land earn less monetary returns than they do in alternative investments such as common stocks, bonds, and government securities. The alleged reason for this is that farming is considered by some as a hobby or as a consumption good and that part of the returns are nonmonetary consumption benefits. This question will be discussed next.

Land as an Inflation Hedge

Total annual returns from owning farm assets have been compared with those from owning other assets typical of an investment portfolio.[15] Peter J. Barry, an agricultural finance expert, assessed the risk and return from farm real estate compared with other investments. He found that investment in farm real estate contributes little additional risk to a well-diversified portfolio of other assets and that farm real estate offers higher rates of return than does the capital market as a whole (Barry 1980).

Barry's analysis was extended by others to compare returns from farm real estate with those from widely held alternative investments over the period 1940–1988, and the same findings were confirmed (Irwin et al. 1988). In a later report, total returns were defined as the sum of net income and capital appreciation. Investors were assumed to consider both average returns and risk in choosing among alternative investments (Irwin and Hanson 1989). Risk is defined as the variability of the returns stream from year to year, so that, for example, a farmer who has wide swings in annual income would face greater risk. It follows that risk-averse investors prefer stable annual income flows to highly variable ones and must be induced to hold riskier assets by receiving a higher return on their investment.

Farm assets were compared with common stocks, small stocks, long-term corporate bonds, long-term government bonds, intermediate-term government bonds, Treasury bills, and inflation with respect to risk and average returns. Inflation is added to the list because it alone causes the market value of many assets to rise through time, although at different rates, and any comparison of yields should consider the market yield relative to the rate of inflation.

Farm assets yielded the third highest average return and the third lowest risk (see Table 3-2). Only common stocks and small stocks had higher average returns, but these were earned at the cost of substantially higher risk than that of agricultural assets. In the case of small stocks, risk was nearly four times higher than for farm assets. Moreover, farm assets had both higher average returns and lower risk than did both corporate and government bonds. Intermediate-term government bonds had lower average returns but also less risk than did farm assets.

One way to reduce risk is to diversify a portfolio's assets, and the performance of farm assets should be analyzed in a portfolio context (Irwin and Hanson 1989, p. 22). This may be done by correlating asset classes to

TABLE 3-2 Annual Asset Total Returns Comparison, 1941 to 1988

Investment	*Average return*	*Risk**	*Correlation*
Farm assets	8.1	8.1	
Common stocks	13.2	16.4	-.13
Small stocks	20.0	29.3	.11
Long-term corp. bonds	5.0	9.5	-.39
Long-term govt. bonds	4.5	9.4	-.42
Int.-term govt. bonds	5.1	6.1	-.47
Treasury bills	4.3	3.5	-.37
Inflation	4.6	4.1	.41

*Risk is the standard deviation of returns.

Source: As quoted in Irwin and Hanson (1989, p. 22).

determine if they move together through time or opposite one another.[16] The final column of Table 3-2 correlates whether yields from a given asset move with yields of farm assets through time, revealing how much an asset combination will reduce or increase the risk of the portfolio. Except for small stocks, the correlation of farm assets with the other asset classes is negative, suggesting that adding farm assets will reduce the risk of the portfolio. The positive correlation with inflation indicates that the returns to farm assets move in the same direction as general price levels and hence that holding farm assets provides an inflation hedge.

Of course, none of these findings implies that farmland is always a sound investment. Reversing a general trend of increasing land values that began in the 1930s (Gardner and Nuckton 1979, p. 4), land values dropped sharply in the 1980s. The USDA estimates that 200,000 to 300,000 farmers were foreclosed, had their debt restructured, or quit farming due to financial problems encountered in the early 1980s (Irwin and Hanson 1989, p. 23). Obviously, the expectations of American farmers for continuing profitable production were shattered in the 1980s after the good times of the 1970s. Given expected prices and costs, the sector would have to give up resources before land prices could resume their upward path. Therefore, no stronger evidence can be found to support the hypothesis of excessive resources in the sector than the sharp decline in land prices of the early 1980s.

Labor

U.S. agriculture is probably the most productive in the world in its use of labor. The productivity of farmworkers over time has increased significantly, each farmer feeding himself and thirty-seven others in 1965, fifty-eight others in 1975, and seventy-five others in 1985.[17] This increase in productivity is in part due to the specialization of farmers and farmworkers. Services previously performed on the farm, such as processing, transporting, and retailing farm products, have shifted to nonfarm firms. An estimated five to six nonfarmworkers are employed for every one farmworker. A very productive and extensive land base, favorable climate, abundant and technologically advanced capital, and perhaps most important, large investments in human capital have driven the productivity of labor in agriculture to levels unsurpassed in history. And it is significant that as farm size has expanded, farm labor productivity has continued to outpace that of the nonfarm sector by at least a factor of two (Baumes and Spitze 1990).

One of the reasons that labor is so productive in the agricultural sector in the U.S. is that the ratio of capital and land to labor is high compared with that of most other countries. A contributor to this high ratio is the mobility of labor in search of higher incomes. The movement of workers from the agricultural sector to other employment is one of the most pervasive and important economic phenomena of modern times in almost all developed countries. In fact, many experts regard the substitution of capital for labor in agriculture as the sine qua non of economic development. Meeting the basic needs of food and fiber with less labor has been conducive to higher employment in other sectors that contribute to the general standard of living.

In the United States the absolute quantity of labor employed in production agriculture has been falling since the Great Depression. It was over 9 million in 1940 and fell to just over 7 million in 1950 (see Barkley 1990). The slide continued to about 5.5 million in 1960 and to about 3.5 million in 1970. The *rate* of decline slowed in the 1970s, and by 1980 the number of farmers was about 3.4 million. By 1990, there were only 2.89 million farmers, and this decline occurred despite a population increase in the nation as a whole over the entire period (U.S. Department of Commerce 1993, Table 1092).

The question of interest here, however, is whether the rate of migration of the sector has been economically efficient. Further, what is the impact of agricultural policies, especially price supports, on labor mobility? Historically, the per capita average incomes of farm families were below those of their urban counterparts. Since other determinants of the standard of living and quality of life in rural and urban areas, such as education, medical care, community services, and safety, are not the same, it is not adequate to look at relative incomes alone to infer which direction labor will move. However, even with this caveat, as long as rural incomes were substantially below urban incomes, it should not have been surprising to observe income-equalizing migration from farm to city. However, now that per capita farm incomes have caught up with urban incomes and even surpassed them in some recent years, further rural-to-urban migration is not expected with the same strength and regularity as occurred previously.

Some of these questions have been addressed by Andrew Barkley (1990), who concludes:

> *Farm labor is found to be mobile. Mobility is measured by the relatively high elasticities of annual changes in farm employment to changes in the relative returns to farm labor. Given a high degree of mobility, policies that attempt to raise farm income through price supports or direct payments are likely to result in lower levels of migration out of agriculture. While government payments did not influence changes in agricultural employment directly, an indirect impact may have occurred through increased land values. (p. 573)*

Barkley's finding is consistent with part of the past section's argument concerning the mobility of labor and capital. However, Barkley finds that the impact of agricultural policies on labor migration is more complex than appears at first blush. On the one hand, income assistance in the form of price supports and target prices slows the rate of migration out of agriculture; but on the other, acreage set-asides reduce the demand for complementary labor, increasing exit from the sector. These effects approximately cancel each other. However, the capitalization of program benefits into land values has produced a larger number of farmers. This conclusion rests on the assumption that landowners must be farm operators if they are to capture the wealth gains from farm programs. But this conclusion is not so strong as it might be since many landowners are not farm operators. In 1974, for example, 37.3 percent of the farmed acres in the United States were operated by renters.[19]

It is not only the aggregative effect of subsidies on labor employed in the sector that is important but also whether that labor is being efficiently combined with land and capital. A clear implication of Barkley's results is that if the wealth effects of increased land values resulting from subsidies have induced labor to remain in the sector, that labor must be less productively utilized than it would have been without the programs producing the appreciated land values.[20]

Strong confirmation that agricultural policies have kept labor in farming that would otherwise have left is provided by Rucker and Alston. They examined how different policies affected farm failures in the 1930s. Policy responses included: the commodity programs of the Agricultural Adjustment Administration of the New Deal (price support programs that were very similar to those now in vogue); the expanded role of the federal government in the agricultural credit market (there is a much greater role today); and legislation passed by twenty-five states in the early 1930s that placed a moratorium on farm foreclosures (such action was also taken by many states during the agricultural crises of the 1980s). It was found that each program was significant in reducing farm failures and that, in aggregate, about 200,000 farms (about 4 percent of all farms) were prevented from failing (Rucker and Alston 1987).

Farm failures imply a reduction in the number of farmers but not necessarily a proportionate decline in farm output. Land and capital inputs do not normally leave the sector when a farm fails since, to some degree, these inputs substitute for labor. If farm failures result in an increase in average farm size, then the capital-land/labor ratio will likely increase. If resources are then more productively used by new farmers, a safe presumption if it is the least efficient farmers who fail, a gain in efficiency for the sector as a whole is implied as some farmers fail.

Failures of individual businesses are not necessarily a signal of failure in the economic system as a whole. A hallmark of capitalism is that firms are free to succeed or fail, and shocks due to rapid technological change, for example, may produce business failures in a healthy overall environment. The market rewards those first to adopt technical change since they normally reduce their costs before supply increases reduce output price. Competition drives slow innovators and inefficient producers out of the sector and makes way for the more efficient. Consumers ultimately capture most of the efficiency gains in lower real prices. But this conclusion should not be interpreted to imply that the more failures, the better. A large number of failures also implies economic hard times and the need for extensive resource adjustments. These adjustments may be socially costly in a sharply fluctuating economy. If "efficient" firms that would have survived had economic circumstances been normal fail under duress, then consumers may benefit from measures to keep these firms in business when times are bad so they have "another day" when times are good. However, if government subsidies perpetuate inefficient firms that otherwise would have failed, then subsidies contribute to inefficiency. What this discussion seems to imply is that a certain number of business failures is "optimal," and this conclusion applies to farms as well as to other businesses.

Much of the public rhetoric surrounding farm failures is focused on saving family farmers and has been used to justify farm income support more than any other reason. Behind this goal is an assumption that some people would rather live and work on farms than anywhere else and that these preferences cannot be satisfied without government support. It is claimed that those who are forced to leave the sector bear high "psychic" costs from the move itself as well as from acclimating themselves to a new and unfamiliar environment. A corollary is that farmers have been "pushed" off the farm against their wills by unfavorable market forces rather than "pulled" off by life-improving alternatives elsewhere.

Both push and pull factors have undoubtedly contributed to the reduction in the number of American farmers. Many who leave the farm might have preferred to remain in agriculture as long as income could be kept at near competitive levels. However, evidence suggests that, in general, farmers who leave the agricultural sector consider themselves to be better off after they have made the adjustment to alternative jobs and residences (Perry et al. 1991). Those who left farming in midcareer in particular indicated that their lives were actually better off the farm, both from their subjective beliefs and on several objective criteria, including higher incomes and better housing, community services, and other quality-of-life indicators.

Capital

Chapter 4 discusses the Farmers Home Administration and provides evidence that excessive labor and capital are held in the agricultural sector because of subsidized credit and other lending policies of the federal government. However, government credit is only one facet of capital use in agriculture. The policy vehicle that provides entitlement to government subsidies is a very important capital asset to farmers who gain such subsidies. When the entitlement vehicle is landownership, as is true for target prices and loan rates, economic rents (per acre revenues minus all nonland costs) get capitalized into land values. Potential beneficiaries of these rents must acquire this higher-priced land. Therefore, higher land values become part of the avoidable costs that determine whether entry of new farmers will occur. Existing producers, in contrast, have already made the investment in land, and thus these costs are fixed rather than avoidable or variable. In the short run, therefore, existing producers (even though they may be less efficient) have a variable-cost advantage over potential new entrants. This means that the distribution of total output among producers cannot be efficient and resources are misallocated.

Other entitlement vehicles are production and marketing quotas in the dairy, peanut, and tobacco programs and permits to take subsidized grazing on the public lands. The capital requirements needed to acquire these entitlement assets constitute another barrier to entry of efficient producers in the agricultural sector. Peanut and tobacco quotas, sugar contracts, and grazing permits will be discussed as examples of how these entitlements to government subsidies impinge on capital markets.

Peanut and Tobacco Quotas

The peanut program. The peanut subsidy is channeled to growers through a marketing quota. The program requires that peanuts produced on the farm be identified as "quota" and "additional" peanuts. Quota peanuts are those eligible for domestic edible use, which include food peanuts, seed, and peanuts used on the farm. Sales of quota peanuts from a given farm may not exceed a poundage quota that the farmer has been given by the government or has leased from another farmer. Peanuts not grown under quota are "additional." These are designated for crushing to make oil, for export, and occasionally, when there is a domestic shortage, for additions to the quota pool.

Both categories receive price protection, but the support price for quota peanuts is much higher than that for additional peanuts. For example, the USDA announced that the national average support level for 1992 crop quota peanuts was $674.93 per short ton, compared with $642.79 for the 1991 crop. The support level for additional peanuts was only $131.09 per short ton in 1992 compared with $149.75 for the 1991 crop.[21]

The 1949 Agricultural Act, as amended, requires that the national average support level for quota peanuts reflect any increase in the national average cost of peanut production for the preceding year, excluding any change in the cost of land. Hence, the government guarantees that quota owners will recoup their production costs each year, thus insulating domestic producers against foreign competitors. One study estimates that the minimum selling price for quota peanuts was about 50 percent higher than the world market price, a sizable subsidy (Ingersoll 1990a). The act also provides that the support price for the quota crop may not exceed the support price for the preceding year by more than 5 percent. The price support level for additional peanuts, however, must be set at a level that ensures no loss to the CCC when it disposes of the peanuts acquired under a nonrecourse loan program. The secretary of agriculture determines the annual quota but may not set it below 1.1 million tons. This national quota is then apportioned among farms based on historical production. However, farmers may sell or lease quota to other farmers located in the same county (Kennedy and Visser 1990, p. 36). This requirement guarantees that the quota never leaves the county and therefore concentrates peanut production geographically. Local businesses linked to peanut production benefit because local peanut production is insulated from competition that might have occurred in other counties that do not have quota. Moreover, the policy would appear to reduce the total value of quota, since peanuts are not necessarily produced where costs are lowest and rents are maximized.[22] In any case, the law has entrenched Georgia, Alabama, and Texas as the dominant peanut-producing states. In fact, about 15,000 Georgia farmers control 1.3 billion pounds of quota, or 41 percent of the national allotment (Ingersoll 1990a).

An important provision of the peanut program is the "buy back," which allows for repurchasing nonquota peanuts into the domestic edible market at the quota support price. In other words, peanut producers may buy back from the government additional peanuts that then become available for the same uses as quota peanuts. The buy-back mechanism ensures that the peanut program will operate at low cost to the U.S. Treasury.

More importantly for economic efficiency, the domestic support price on quota peanuts is maintained by placing severe restrictions on imported peanuts. Assuming that some additional peanuts are produced and exported, the relevant marginal price for producer decisions is the export price. That is, the export price determines the acreage in peanuts and the production per acre at the margin because farmers will produce to the point where marginal costs equal the export price. Unlike many other commodity programs, therefore, this feature of the peanut program produces an efficient level of U.S. peanut production vis-à-vis other countries.[23] Of course, the high price support on quota peanuts guarantees high economic rents to quota production and is ultimately reflected in the quota price.

Table 3-3 contains data on average lease and quota prices for the period 1978–1987 for important peanut-growing states. The lease and quota prices are simple averages for a sample taken from each state. Total lease and quota values are computed by taking the average lease and quota prices and multiplying them by the average poundage of peanut quota for the same years.

The total quota value is almost $1 billion. To provide some context for this number, an estimate of total annual receipts (including the government support payment) from producing peanuts is $1.132 billion.[24]

Political uncertainty surrounds all government programs since any congress can change the rules. A quantitative estimate of program uncertainty in the case of the peanut program is provided by the implied discount rates in Table 3-3. In a perfect lease market for quota, that is, one without uncertainty, the annual lease value should reflect the economic profits arising from holding quota. The quota value should be the capitalized value of the annual lease price, calculated by dividing the annual lease value by the opportunity cost of capital, generally taken to be the risk-free interest

TABLE 3-3 Lease Prices, Quota Values, and Implied Discount Rates for Peanut Producing States, 1978 through 1987

States	*Average lease price per pound ($)*	*Average quota value per pound ($)*	*Implied discount rate (%)*	*Total lease value ($ mil)*	*Total quota value ($ mil)*
Alabama	0.066	0.275	0.240	30.92	128.84
Florida	0.094	0.314	0.299	17.99	60.10
Georgia	0.071	0.339	0.209	116.83	557.82
N. Carolina	0.049	0.228	0.228	20.38	94.85
Oklahoma	0.052	0.135	0.385	9.98	25.91
Texas	0.042	0.194	0.216	16.64	76.88
Virginia	0.043	0.185	0.232	11.06	47.58
Weighted average	0.063	0.286	0.239		
Total				**223.80**	**991.98**

Sources: Raymond Fabre and Randal R. Rucker (1978, pp. 17–18).

rate. For example, if the lease price were .075 dollars per pound of quota and the interest rate were 10 percent, the quota would have an expected value of .75 dollars per pound if there were no uncertainty. If the quota does not have this expected value, there must be uncertainty about the prospects of future profits from holding quota.

The implied discount rates in Table 3-3 are calculated by dividing the average annual lease price by the average quota value. They vary from 20.9 percent in Georgia to 38.5 percent in Oklahoma. The aggregate weighted average is 22.6 percent. Since these are much higher than any estimate of risk-free rates of interest in capital markets, farmers must believe that the peanut program is fraught with uncertainty.

There are two significant implications of the preceding analysis. First, peanut farmers have large amounts of wealth tied up in quota. Primarily for this reason, they vote to keep the quota system and poundage limits, as well as lobby Congress to maintain the peanut program.[25] Second, the capital costs of entering the business of growing quota peanuts are high compared with costs that would exist without the subsidized government quota program. These costs constitute an important barrier to entry for prospective new peanut farmers.

The program costs to the federal Treasury are about $4 million a year, a small sum compared with that of other subsidy programs. However, the program is very costly for consumers. Estimates vary widely depending on the time they were made and world peanut prices. One processor estimate shows consumers paying an extra $369 million a year for edible peanuts—a hidden subsidy to quota holders (Ingersoll 1990a). The USDA, using different assumptions, came up with $190 million a year. Rucker and Thurman (1990, p. 503) estimate the annual cost to consumers at $401 million in 1987. A more recent estimate puts the figure at $553 million, reflecting the drought conditions affecting the 1990 crop (Pattison 1991).

Politicians are inclined to argue the effectiveness of government programs in terms of Treasury outlays even when costs to consumers are very high. Writing for Scripps Howard News Service, Rep. Charles Hatcher (D-GA), a member of the House Agriculture Subcommittee on Tobacco and Peanuts, argued: "Because of the 1990 drought, peanut supplies are tight, but there is no shortage. We have demonstrated conclusively that, in spite of the drought, American farmers produced fully adequate supplies of peanuts to meet all domestic needs" (Hatcher 1991). What economic nonsense is this? If markets clear, there will always be some price that will equate domestic demand and supply, regardless of how low the supply is. Because peanuts have substitutes in consumption, however, the quantity demanded will be choked off by high prices to equal the amount that government policy dictates will be supplied. But consumers will transfer huge amounts of wealth to domestic producers of quota peanuts and foreign suppliers lucky enough to control the import quotas. Yet the politicians maintain that the program is not causing shortages and thus justify conveying large benefits to their producer constituents.

The tobacco program. The tobacco and peanut programs are both structured around marketing quotas. Also like peanuts, tobacco legislation is permanent and, therefore, does not come up for renewal every five years as is the case with most other subsidized commodities.[26] And, like peanuts, land to which tobacco quotas are attached is fixed, and if new farmers wish to produce and market tobacco they must purchase or rent land with a quota allocation from an existing quota holder in their own county.

The national marketing quota for the 1991 flue-cured tobacco crop was set at 877.7 million pounds, unchanged from 1990.[27] For burley, the national marketing quota for the 1991 crop was 726 million pounds, up from the 1990 quota of 602.3 million pounds.[28]

What is the market value of quota? A 1978 estimate was $1.20 per pound (B. L. Gardner 1981, pp. 77–78). Assuming this value is applied to poundage of both flue-cured and burley tobaccos, the 1991 quota established by USDA would be worth nearly $2 billion, roughly twice the estimate for the peanut quota. Interestingly, the 1988 farm value of tobacco produced by the U.S. was $2.198 billion.

Therefore, for both tobacco and peanuts, the estimated value of quota is about equivalent to the total annual value of production.[29]

The conclusions reached concerning the value of peanut quota and barriers to entry for new growers of peanuts are equally applicable to tobacco. Income transfers from consumers to producers of tobacco are not so obvious as was the case with peanuts, however, since the United States is a very significant exporter of tobacco products and world tobacco prices are not as far below domestic prices, as was the case for peanuts.

Sugar Contracts

Only about 11,000 growers produce sugar beets and cane in the United States. Sugar production is subsidized through a complex system of price supports, tariffs, and import quotas. The cost of this subsidy is roughly $3 billion per year and falls primarily on consumers, although producers of other competitive crops also bear some costs as will be discussed (Kennedy and Visser, 1990, p. 35).

The 1985 Food Security Act required the secretary of agriculture to support the price of raw cane sugar at a minimum of 18 cents per pound, and the support price of beet sugar is set at a level that is deemed to be fair and reasonable in relation to that of cane. For the 1993 crop, the average price support loan rates were 18 cents per pound for raw cane sugar and 23.63 cents per pound for refined beet sugar.[30] These support prices are offered as nonrecourse loans to sugar refiners who process raw sugar.[31] The loan rates offered to refiners are adjusted depending on the location of production. Michigan and Ohio refiners get the highest rates for beets, and Louisiana, Puerto Rice, and Texas refiners get the most for cane.[32]

The price support for growers is the minimum amount that must be paid to them by the processors participating in the price support loan program. Based on established regional loan rates, the minimum price support levels for sugar beets and sugarcane vary by region; in 1993 for beets they were $33.94 to $39.75 per ton, and for cane, $17.50 to $26.23 per ton.[33]

The feature of the sugar program of most interest here is who receives the benefits from the support price and how high are they? The acreage in sugar crops is not controlled by the government, as is true for peanuts and tobacco. Therefore, historic acreage in sugar crops is not the entitlement for receiving the subsidy. No farmer can sell beets or cane without a contract with a processor. Thus, it is the sugar refiners who distribute the subsidy through the support price that must be paid each cane and beet producer with a contract. Each refiner has a limited capacity to produce sugar and therefore can handle only so many tons of beets and cane.[34] Sometimes the processor that draws up the contract with the growers is a cooperative owned by the beet and cane growers. Since the economic rents in producing sugar are substantial because of the "high" support price and the protection from foreign suppliers, these contracts, like peanut and tobacco quota, take on value of their own. In principle, these contract values represent the capitalized rents (the difference between support price and cost) obtained from the sugar program over the expected life of the contract.

Those who have contracts can produce on their own land or they can rent land from others. If the latter, the landowner may participate in the benefits of the sugar subsidies, since growers with a contract will usually outbid the growers of other less profitable crops for rented land. Naturally, if the land rents are bid up in a region the landowners renting land gain while the producers of other crops who must compete in the land rental market are hurt by the sugar subsidy.

In one area of southern Minnesota in the spring of 1991, soybean growers complained that the sugar growers were paying 35 percent more for rented land than could be afforded by farmers without sugar contracts. Some of the soybean growers responded by utilizing chemicals toxic to sugar beets on their rented land, thus hoping to keep rented land out of the hands of the subsidized beet growers and thereby reduce the land rent (Sands 1991). One must wonder how long landowners would put up with this practice before preventing it by contractual arrangements.

Of course, farmers who do not now grow sugar beets could do so for a price by buying up contracts from those who hold them. The price of a single contract share to grow beets on one acre was from $900 to $1,000 in one area of Minnesota in 1991 (Sands 1991). As with other government programs, the price would be higher but for the fact that the future of the sugar program is so uncertain.

The contract with the refiner is the vehicle for controlling entry into the business of growing beets and cane. Even though the contract is a different type of asset than the peanut and tobacco quotas, its value may be determined in the same way—capitalizing economic rents over the expected life of the contract. The investment required to obtain a contract deprives the sector of other forms of productive capital, such as chemicals, machinery, and veterinary services. The result has to be a sugar growing industry inefficient in its use of capital.

Grazing Permits

Subsidized livestock grazing on the public lands of the West provides another example of the inefficient use of capital in the agricultural sector. The quantity of allowable grazing is controlled by the regulatory agencies, the Forest Service in the USDA and the Bureau of Land Management (BLM) in the Department of Interior, ostensibly to prevent overgrazing and depletion of the range vegetation and despoliation of the soil resources. The allowable grazing is then rationed to eligible livestock producers through a permit system, and a grazing fee is charged that is lower than the value of the grazing.[35] The permit normally has a ten-year life, is renewable, and specifies the location of the grazing allotment, the class of grazing livestock, the quantity of allowable grazing, and the season of use.

In most areas, the government allows the grazing permits to be transferred among eligible ranchers, although sometimes the permit must be transferred with either the ranch property to which it is attached or with the designated livestock.[36] A serious source of uncertainty arises when the amount of permitted grazing is reduced when transferred to a new permittee if the public range managers believe that the ranges are overgrazed or if they want to use the range for other purposes (B. D. Gardner 1989). This threat obviously reduces the likelihood that an existing permittee will transfer the permit, even though the grazing might go to a more efficient grazier, thus contributing to inefficient allocation of the forage.

The pricing of federal grazing below its value to the permittee creates economic rents that get capitalized into the value of the grazing permit, the entitlement asset. Ranchers who wish to avail themselves of the low-priced grazing and can otherwise become eligible must purchase a permit from an existing permittee. In most areas, an active market for permits exists.

This is an appropriate juncture to discuss an important and commonly misunderstood point about the "subsidy" that is alleged to exist in the case of peanut, tobacco, sugar, and forage entitlements. It is true that the government programs confer rents on each unit of output in the sense that direct costs are below the value of output. However, if these rents get fully capitalized into the value of the entitlement asset, owners subsequent to the initial asset holders must pay the going market price to obtain it. The cost of the entitlement asset thus becomes part of production costs for new entrants. There is really no continuing subsidy to the purchaser of a grazing permit (quota, contract) if the permit market is efficient. For example, a grazing transferee must pay the transferor for the expected value of future economic rents derived from the subsidized fee. The rancher's permit and other additional costs of using the public lands aggregate to a sum that is approximately equal to the costs of grazing comparable private pastures. These public grazing systems are now at least fifty years old. The original recipients of subsidized grazing captured a wealth windfall when their permits were issued and then transferred to others, but these original permittees have nearly all passed from the scene. Clearly, subsequent permittees who purchased permits did not receive comparable windfalls unless unexpected new rents were created by government fees failing to keep up with the value of the forage.

An interesting aspect of the contemporary grazing scene is that the environmental community has strongly pressed for elimination of the grazing subsidy by insisting that the government raise the grazing fee to "fair market" value. To environmentalists this means the rental value of comparable private range. Following this course would eliminate any economic rents in public grazing and reduce the permit values on average to zero.[37] This is why raising grazing fees is so controversial politically. Rancher permittees have already paid for their permits, and they do not believe that it would be either efficient or equitable to wipe out permit values by raising fees. Hence, as would be expected, the ranching community is a vigorous lobbyist for maintaining the subsidized grazing fee.

The consequence of subsidizing grazing on public lands through the permit system is similar to subsidizing peanut and tobacco production through the quota system. The capital costs of gaining access to the subsidized forage are higher than they would be without the low fee because of the capital tied up in permit value.

In 1986, the Forest Service allocated 8.6 million animal-unit-months[38] (AUMs) of forage to permittees and the BLM 10.5 million AUMs. Applying the 1989 permit value of $590 per head (assuming a grazing season of three and one-half months, 8.6 million AUMs translates into 2.46 million head) an estimate of rancher wealth tied up in forest permits would be $1.450 billion. The BLM permits would be worth $2.226 billion. The sum is $3.676 billion of wealth tied up in federal permits.[39] Thus, the capital structure in ranching is distorted by the permit system, and higher production costs exist than if public grazing was not subsidized and was simply auctioned off to the highest bidder.[40]

Deadweight efficiency losses associated with these entitlement programs also result from the expenditures of capital to maintain them. Since large amounts of wealth are tied up in quotas, contracts, and permits, farmers will expend large amounts of capital to make sure that the subsidies that give rise to the value of the entitlements are continued. On the other side of the political spectrum are interests who want the entitlements eliminated, and they too engage in similar political activity. These are called rent-seeking costs by public choice economists, and they are very substantial, as will be demonstrated in Chapter 9.

Tax Policy and Excessive Investment in Agriculture

Many sectors of the U.S. economy have received preferences in the form of tax shelters and various write-offs, and agriculture is no exception.[41] James Long points out:

> *American agriculture has enjoyed a variety of general and specific income tax preferences since 1915. . . . The most important tax advantages included (a) the option to use cash accounting, which requires no inventory records and allows input expenses to be deducted in the year actually paid even if they [farmers] produce no income in that year; (b) tax regulations that permit farm assets such as livestock, real estate, and timber to qualify for long-term capital gains taxation; (c) accelerated depreciation of animals held for breeding purposes, single-purpose livestock structures, plants and trees, and certain other items; and (d) the ability to deduct the cost of developing certain capital assets, including the cost of raising dairy or breeding livestock and the cost of developing orchards and vineyards. (1990, pp. 1–2)*

The major efficiency effect of these provisions is to increase the after-tax yield on capital in the agricultural sector and hence to increase its use beyond the efficient level. During much of the period since World War II when these tax policies have been in effect, agriculture has been a notorious tax haven for high-income persons, including those in the medical, legal, entertainment, and dental professions.

Particularly before the Tax Reform Act of 1986, provision (d) just cited was significant in inducing investors to convert ordinary income into long-term capital gains, which were taxed at a lower rate than ordinary income. One of the consequences of this investment in agricultural assets was to drive up the price of those assets, particularly land, making it more difficult and costly for bona fide farmers to enter the sector.

Perhaps not as significant as the direct effects produced by the tax code, but important nevertheless, is the "psychic" or nonpecuniary income provided by farming that is not taxed. This would include farm recreation like "playing" with livestock, or cultivating gardens, or breeding and racing horses. Investors manipulate their asset portfolios such that returns (monetary and psychic) from alternative investments are equal, net of taxes. If psychic income is not taxed, more investment will be generated in activities that produce it, and more labor and capital will be attracted to the sector as a result. Scholars have argued that many Americans, especially among the wealthy, consume nontaxable benefits derived from the agricultural sector and the "rural way of life" (Pope 1987). In sum, the tax code induced individuals "to farm the tax code in order to shelter income from taxation"

(Long 1990, p. 10). This tax-loss farming has made it more difficult for bona fide farm operators to compete and earn competitive returns.

Moreover, data show that a very large fraction of farmers do not pay income taxes. From 1980 through 1986, net farm income of all farmers derived from the actual marketing of agricultural products was negative, reaching a loss in 1984 of $13.095 billion (Long 1990, p. 2). Apparently, farmers had effective ways of taking advantage of tax loopholes to avoid paying taxes. In each year from 1974 through 1986, the number of farmer tax returns with a reported farm income loss exceeded the number with a farm income gain, and the difference grew steadily through 1984. However, the aggregated amount of farm losses exceeded the aggregated amount of farm profits only from 1980 until 1986, a period of recession in the agricultural sector. A clear inference drawn from these data is that, in the late 1970s, smaller farms were proportionately more likely to report negative farm incomes than were larger farms, partially because a greater fraction of them were "hobby" and "part-time" farms, but by the 1980s large farms were also reporting net income losses.

The 1986 Tax Reform Act produced a sharp change in tax regulations affecting agriculture. Nearly everyone concedes that, in the long run, this act will reduce tax shelter investments across the economy and thus will increase the efficiency of capital allocation. The act requires farmers to produce a profit in at least three of the preceding five years to satisfy the "farming-for-profit" test that allows them to offset other income gains with farm "losses." Also under the Tax Reform Act, long-term capital gains will be fully taxed in the year when they are realized, and the length of time over which capital assets must be depreciated was increased (Long 1990, p. 3). The 1986 act also repealed the investment tax credit, and preproduction expenses must now be capitalized rather than deducted in the year expended if the development period exceeds two years. This tightening of income tax provisions affecting agriculture should reduce the excessive capitalization of the sector over time, but how rapidly these adjustments will occur is conjectural.[42] Another inevitable consequence of eliminating the loopholes is to reduce the price of agricultural assets, and this may have contributed to the financial squeeze suffered by many farmers in the 1980s.

Different marginal income tax rates can also distort investment. Investors with the highest rates have incentives to search for shelters that are most attractive. Since the highest rates are normally paid by those with the highest incomes, the wealthy will invest disproportionately in tax shelters. The sharp supply-side reduction in marginal tax rates that was implemented in the first Reagan administration can therefore be expected to increase the efficiency of capital allocation.

Macroeconomic Inefficiency and Agricultural Subsidies

For more than half a century, economists have argued that macroeconomic variables such as employment, the quantity of money, interest rates, inflation, and foreign exchange rates have had significant impacts on the agricultural sector.[43] It is quite possible, in fact, that these external policies have had more influence on the prosperity (or lack of it) of the agricultural sector than have internal policies such as price supports, water and credit subsidies, and scientific research. It is also important to note that these variables and the policies that affect them are largely beyond the control of farmers and those working on congressional agricultural committees.

Of the numerous economic problems confronting the nation, none has received more attention in recent years than the federal budget deficit. Economists disagree as to how serious the deficit problem is, but most would agree that large government spending programs, especially those that do not generate significant revenues, will be scrutinized very carefully especially by the Office of Management and Budget.

The direct government payments to farmers in 1986, about $26 billion, represented approximately 12 percent of the federal budget deficit of $220 billion in that year. These direct transfers to farmers were made through the various deficiency payments, conservation program payments, and the Export Enhancement Program (EEP). In addition, more than $20 billion was spent on food assistance programs in 1986, mostly for food stamps. This sum is an implicit payment to "qualified" consumers to finance their consumption of food at below-market prices (Feltenstein 1989). These subsidies have increased the quantity of food demanded. The impact on producer incomes is problematic, however, since the effect would depend on what the government might have done with surplus stocks in the absence of these programs.

A few studies have attempted to establish linkages between agricultural policy and the national economy. Modeling ten basic industry groups, agriculture being one, Feltenstein estimated that if agricultural price subsidies had been eliminated, the budget deficit would have declined by 1 percent of Gross Domestic Product (GDP) in 1985 and by 0.8 percent in 1986. A reduction of agricultural subsidies of $58 billion over the two years would have saved $74 billion in accumulated budget deficits. The trade balance would have improved by 0.8 percent of GDP in 1986 as compared with the base situation (Feltenstein 1989, p. 213). These are not inconsequential numbers.

Budget deficits represent government dissaving and diminish the pool of domestic saving that is available for investment. However, saving can be, and generally is, acquired from foreign as well as domestic sources as long as the United States has a trade deficit, which provides dollar reserves to foreigners. The implication is that reduced federal budget deficits would decrease the nation's dependence on foreign savings to make up the deficiency between domestic investment and domestic saving.

Robinson et al. also have analyzed the prospective impact on the macroeconomy from removing U.S. agricultural subsidies. Results are similar to those reported by Feltenstein. Policy reform eliminating subsidies leads to a reduction in both trade and government budget deficits (Robinson et al. 1989, p. 222). Getting rid of subsidies also changes the functional distribution of income and leads to the migration of labor out of the agricultural sector (p. 223). The clear implication is that agricultural subsidies have immobilized excess labor in the sector. Perhaps the most important, although hardly surprising, finding of the study is that liberalization of trade along with elimination of subsidies produces more gains to the economy than losses (p. 223). This is strong corroborative evidence that government programs in agriculture have produced an inefficient sector that contains excessive capital and labor resources. There is also 5.2 percent more savings and investment resulting from the net improvement in the government budget deficit (p. 223). Without the EEP's export subsidies, the level of domestic supply would be increased, and the export volume of grains would fall to 52 percent of the level achieved in 1986 and would be 57 percent lower than the base projection to 1991 with programs intact.[44]

In another experimental model, Robinson et al. postulate the effects from the unilateral removal of all trade barriers in addition to elimination of all subsidies:

> *With neither the constraints nor the subsidies, land use in agriculture increases by 4.7 percent overall (1.1 percent in grains, 17.0 percent in other agriculture). Even more capital and labor leave the farm sector as land is substituted for the other factors. The use value of land also falls 25.6 percent against the 1991 base rate of return. Output and exports of grains nevertheless increase marginally. Complete unilateral dismantling of U.S. farm programs, even without assuming an impact on world import prices, results in a $9.6 billion increase in GNP. (1989, p. 249)*

These macroeconomic studies strongly confirm the conclusions reached earlier in this and the preceding chapters that agricultural subsidies are misallocating resources in the economy, that the sector contains excessive quantities of capital and labor, and that land is inefficiently used.[45] Proposals to reform these policies and achieve greater efficiency are presented in Chapter 13.

Notes

1. Paul C. Westcott (1991) shows various options farmers have for handling the idled acreage under the provisions of the 1990 FACTA.

2. This includes cropland idled by government programs and fallowed.

3. A review of agricultural land uses is found in B. D. Gardner (1991).

4. In Chapter 10, dealing with environmental issues, some of the connections between agricultural policy and the quantity and quality of land growing crops and how soil erosion is affected will be discussed.

5. "There are many cases where land left idle or planted to other crops is considered planted to the program crop for the purpose of maintaining the crop acreage base in future years. Considered planted acreage includes land idled under Acreage Reduction Programs (ARP), land left unplanted under the 0/92 or 50/92 provisions, and in certain cases, land devoted to other crops (Kennedy and Visser, 1990, p. 29).

   The 50/92 provision was introduced into the 1985 FSA and 0/92 was added some time later. They refer to legislated programs that permit farmers to receive deficiency payments on acreage not planted for harvest. In the case of the 50/92 provision, if farmers plant crops for harvest on at least 50 percent but less than 92 percent of their established base acreage, and if the remaining base acreage is placed in a conservation use or in a nonprogram crop, then the farm program acreage on which deficiency payments are made equals 92 percent of permitted acreage. The 0/92 provision allows no acreage to be planted to a program crop and yet 92 percent of base acreage may receive a deficiency payment. Growers of cotton and rice, however, can avail themselves only of the 50/92 provision. Farmers are also eligible for deficiency payments if their crops fail after planting.

6. Some major changes in how the acreage base may be used were made in the 1990 FACTA. These changes will be reviewed in the next section.

7. In fact, on September 29, 1991, Secretary of Agriculture Madigan announced that the ARP required acreage reductions for the 1992 crops of corn, grain sorghum, and barley would be 5 percent, down from 7.5 percent for 1991. The ARP set-aside for oats was zero as was the case in 1991. For the 1992 rice crop the ARP set-aside was zero, while for cotton it was 10 percent. U.S. Department of Agriculture, Office of Public Affairs, "USDA Announces 1992 Feed Grain Acreage Reduction," *Selected Speeches and News Releases,* (Washington, DC: September 26–October 4), 1991, p. 11. In the case of wheat, the required acreage reduction was reduced to zero in 1993 and was maintained at zero for 1994 (USDA Office of Public Affairs [1993a], "USDA Announces 1994 Wheat Program Provisions," *News Releases and Other News Material,* no. 5493 [Washington, DC" May 24–28], p. 15). In the case of grain sorghum, barley,

and oats, the announced required acreage reduction was also 0 percent and was unchanged from 1993 for barley and oats, but down from 5 percent for grain sorghum. For corn the announced 1994 required acreage reduction was 5 percent, down from 10 percent in 1993. (USDA Office of Public Affairs [1993c], "USDA Announces 1994 Feed Grains Acreage Reduction Program Percentages," *News Releases and Other News Material,* no. 9493 [Washington, DC: September 27–October 1], p. 11).

8. U.S. Department of Agriculture, Office of Public Affairs, *Selected Speeches and News Releases,* (Washington, DC: May 28–June 3, 1992), p. 4.

9. An extended discussion of these issues is found in Chapter 10. My colleague Rulon D. Pope pointed out that, for southern cotton production, water is the limiting productive factor. Spacing the cotton plants can increase yield by almost the same proportion as the reduction in acreage, another reason why set-asides do not decrease production.

10. For example, producers who sought authorization to plant soybeans on program permitted acreage under the 1990 commodity price support and production adjustment programs were allowed to do so without jeopardizing their acreage bases. U.S. Department of Agriculture, Office of Public Affairs, "Soybean Plantings to Be Allowed on Program Permitted Acreage," *Selected Speeches and News Releases* (Washington DC: March 1–8, 1990), p. 2.

11. For example, for wheat, the 1991 ARP set-aside cannot be less than 15 percent and for 1992–95 will be based on a ratio that considers stocks on hand relative to utilization. The secretary may also permit the planting of designated crops on up to 50 percent of the reduced acres in return for a specified reduction in deficiency payment acres. The secretary may also increase or decrease the ARP set-aside in exchange for an increase or decease in the target price. If a producer elects to plant permanent cover crops on ARP acres, the government will participate in cost sharing. Similar changes were made for the feed grains.

12. The efficiency gains of this flexibility have been pointed out by Westcott (1991).

13. U.S. Department of Agriculture, Economic Research Service (1990a), *Agricultural Outlook* (Washington, DC: November), p. 60.

14. USDA, Economic Research Service (1990c), "Cash Rents for Farms, Cropland, and Pasture, 1960–89," *Statistical Bulletin, No. 813* (Rockville, MD), p. 5.

15. For example, the *Wall Street Journal* reports a study from the southwest part of Minnesota suggesting that, between 1960 and 1988, income and land value increases in agriculture yielded 10.7 percent compared with 10.4 percent for common stocks and 10.5 percent for mutual funds. See Kilman (1991).

16. For example, when one asset's returns move upward through time, if the

other always moved up, the correlation coefficient would be +1. If they moved perfectly in opposite directions, the coefficient would be -1.

17. U.S. Department of Agriculture, National Economics Division, Economic Research Service (1987b), *Economic Indicators of the Farm Sector: Production and Efficiency Statistics, 1985* (Washington, DC: April).
    During a trip to Kansas in 1992, I observed numerous signs along the freeways claiming that the average Kansas farmer now feeds ninety-two others.

18. This point is elaborated in Chapter 5.

19. U.S. Department of Commerce, Bureau of the Census (1978), *Census of Agriculture, 1974: Tenure, Type of Organization, Contracts, Operator Characteristics, Principal Occupation* (Washington, DC: September).

20. Technology is a crucial element in determining the demand for labor. Labor-saving technological change reduces the demand for agricultural labor: Either fewer workers will be demanded in agriculture or workers who remain in the sector will earn lower returns than they otherwise would.

21. U.S. Department of Agriculture, Office of Public Affairs (1992), "USDA Announces Support Level, by Type, for 1992 Peanuts," *Selected Speeches and News Releases* (Washington, DC: May 7–13), p. 12.
    The 1990 Omnibus Budget Reconciliation Act required a marketing assessment on peanuts of 16.06975 cents per pound for quota peanuts and 03.744375 cents per pound for additional peanuts on both growers and buyers.

22. A study in North Carolina, however, found that restricting transfers of quota to a given county had no effects on lease rates or the location of peanut production within the state. See Rucker et al. (1991).

23. An excellent analysis of the broad welfare impacts of the peanut program is found in Rucker and Thurman (1990).

24. This number was estimated by multiplying the 1988 acreage in peanut production of 1,617,850 acres by $700 receipts per acre. See U.S. Department of Agriculture, National Economics Division, Economic Research Service (1989), *World Agricultural Trends and Indicators, 1970-88*, Statistical Bulletin, no. 781 (Washington, DC: June), p. 62; and U.S. Senate (1990a), *Food, Agriculture, Conservation, and Trade Act of 1990*, Report no. 101-357 (Washington, DC: July 6), p. 116.

25. Peanut producers approved poundage quotas for the 1991 through 1995 crops as a result of a mail referendum held December 10–13, 1990. Of the 12,302 votes cast, 98.2 percent favored peanut poundage quotas for the next five crop years. Two-thirds of the farmers voting must favor continuing peanut poundage quotas for the quotas to remain in effect. U.S. Department of Agriculture, Office of Public Affairs, "Peanut Growers Approve Poundage

Quotas," *Selected Speeches and News Releases* (Washington, DC: January 31–February 6), p. 7.

26. The enabling legislation is the 1938 Agricultural Adjustment Act, which requires cigarette manufacturers to report annually to the USDA their intended purchases of tobacco from U.S. auction markets and producers. These data are then used along with anticipated export demand and reserve adjustments to determine the USDA's annual tobacco marketing quota. For flue-cured and burley tobacco, the act further provides for the conversion of the national marketing quota into a national acreage allotment which is then prorated to farms. Individual farmers cannot opt to participate in the government program. If they grow tobacco, participation is mandatory. Kennedy and Visser (1990, p. 36).

27. U.S. Department of Agriculture, Office of Public Affairs, "USDA Announces 1991-Crop Flue-Cured Tobacco Program," *Selected Speeches and News Releases* (Washington, DC: December 13–20, 1990), p. 4.

    The support level for the 1991 crop was $1.528 per pound, up 4 cents from 1990. The national acreage allotment for the 1991 crop was 420,354 acres, the same as in 1990. The effective quota was about 892 million pounds, or 44 million below the 1990 level. The marketing assessment under the Omnibus Budget Reconciliation Act of 1990, was 0.764 cents per pound levied on both growers and buyers.

28. U.S. Department of Agriculture, Office of Public Affairs, "USDA Announces 1991 Burley Tobacco Quota," *Selected Speeches and News Releases* (Washington, DC: January 24–30, 1991), p. 20.

    The support level for the 1991 crop was $1.584 per pound, up 2.6 cents from the 1990 level. The marketing assessment under the Omnibus Budget Reconciliation Act of 1990 was .792 cents per pound on both growers and buyers.

29. U.S. Department of Commerce, Bureau of the Census (1990), *Statistical Abstract of the United States* (Washington, DC), p. 663.

30. U.S. Department of Agriculture, Office of Public Affairs, "USDA Announces 1993-Crop Sugar Price Support Loan Rates," *News Releases and Other News Materials* (Washington, DC: June 28–July 2), p. 4.

31. The 1990 FACTA continues the loan rate at 18 cents per pound. However, for any fiscal year that imports of sugar for U.S. consumption are estimated to be less than 1.25 million short tons, the secretary of agriculture shall establish marketing allotments on processors of sugar at a level that will result in imports of not less than 1.25 million short tons for that year. When sugar allotments are in effect, crystalline fructose marketing allotments not to exceed the equivalent of 200,000 short tons of sugar will be established.

32. USDA, "USDA Announces 1993-Crop Sugar Price Support Loan Rates."

33. The 1985 act also requires the secretary to operate the program so that the U.S. government bears no net cost. The secretary must maintain the domestic price of sugar at a level high enough to prevent refiners from forfeiting their loans to the government, which has required the use of import quotas to limit supplies from abroad. Quotas are given to foreign nations who wish to export to the United States. In addition, U.S. trade law currently imposes a tariff of 2.5 cents per pound of sugar imported.

34. A discussion with representatives of the Southern Minnesota Beet Sugar Cooperative near Renville, Minnesota, indicated that it picks only bona fide farmers as contractees. Its contracts range from 25 to 1,200 acres.

35. Only bona fide ranchers are eligible for permits and they must own ranch property that can support their livestock when not grazing the public lands. This is known as the "commensurability" requirement. B. D. Gardner (1962).

36. This policy seems to be in flux now. Some government officials are more rigid in limiting transfers than others, but in all areas some restrictions are imposed.

37. In fact, were federal fees raised to the level of most private pastures, there would be no demand for federal grazing since the nonfee costs of grazing public lands are considerably higher than those for grazing private pastures. This is probably what the environmental community really wants. See B. D. Gardner (1989).

38. An animal-unit-month is the quantity of forage required to maintain a mature cow on the range for one month.

39. Even though there is an active market for grazing permits, little systematic study of permit values region-wide has been undertaken. No doubt these values vary widely throughout the West depending on the quality of the forage in the allotment. A recent study from New Mexico has estimated values for both Forest Service and BLM permits. BLM permits had a value of $947 in 1980 and reached a decade-long peak of $1,218 per head for the 1984 grazing year. The 1989 value was only $742. For Forest Service permits, the comparable values were $1,629 in 1980 and only $590 in 1989. Permit values were declining during the 1980s, reflecting the more and more tenuous government grazing policy. The lower recent Forest Service permit values reflect the more uncertainty of continued forest grazing since these are the lands most hotly contested by environmental groups. See Torell and Doll (1991).

40. The grazing season tends to be longer than three and one-half months for many BLM permittees. If so, there would be fewer livestock numbers than assumed here, and total value of permits would be lower than here indicated.

41. Writing of 1972, Galper and Zimmerman (1977) demonstrated that oil and gas extraction and real estate received the most favorable tax treatment, but

livestock feeding and breeding, forestry, and fruit, tree, nut, and vegetable farming were also among the most favored.

42. In the recent presidential campaign and since the election there has been much discussion about reviving the investment tax credit to stimulate investment. This seems to be a high priority of the Clinton administration.

43. This has been a significant theme in the work of Nobel-prize-winning agricultural economist Professor Theodore W. Schultz of the University of Chicago. His book *Agriculture in an Unstable Economy* (1945) is one of the most influential books ever written in agricultural economics. Also see Tweeten (1980).

44. Imports of grains increased because of the 60 percent increase in the relative price of domestic to imported grains. Imports of dairy and meat products tripled with the relaxation of the quota constraints, and dairy and meat exports fell 16.1 percent relative to the 1991 level. Robinson et al. (1989, p. 248).

45. A very interesting analytical point has been made by Alston and Hurd (1990, p. 149). They show how policy studies of U.S. farm programs suppose that the economic welfare consequences are estimated by assuming that the social opportunity cost of $1 of government spending is exactly $1, and that the net social cost of government spending is measured entirely as the indirect cost of the changes in consumer and producer surpluses. These assumptions are probably too heroic. Such an approach does not consider the welfare costs of distortions caused by the collection of taxes elsewhere in the economy to finance government spending in farm programs.

    The marginal social welfare cost of a dollar of government spending is estimated to be between $1.20 and $1.50, which means that efficiency costs of making welfare transfers are larger than usually estimated.

4

A Lender Of Last Resort and Wasted Capital Resources–The Farmers Home Administration

The USDA's Farmers Home Administration (FmHA) is a prominent example of a government agency burdened with highly inefficient policies established by Congress. These policies immobilize resources to the detriment of consumers, taxpayers, and even in the long run, most farmers. The FmHA is the principal governmental vehicle for subsidized financial assistance to rural Americans and communities who "cannot obtain commercial credit elsewhere at affordable terms."[1] However, by mandating such terms Congress has made it impossible for inefficient farmers who want to stay in business to fail. The consequence is that more and more farmers are sinking into a quagmire of debt, subsidized by taxpayers to remain in an increasingly inefficient sector of the economy.

The American public is not accustomed to looking at these types of problems in terms of the effect on the standard of living. Rather, it has been bombarded with information about the horrors of the federal budget deficit and, therefore, tends to visualize this and other government programs mostly in terms of what they cost the government in budgetary expenditures. The inefficiency costs of FmHA credit programs, however, are quite independent from any considerations of governmental expenditures, although these are not inconsequential. The more important real costs borne by taxpayers and consumers are found in the misallocation of capital resources to uses that create lower levels of output than would have been produced if the resources had been market directed without subsidy (Pasour 1989, p. 184).

Under the New Deal, the FmHA was known as the Resettlement Administration and was established to help "destitute or low-income families become self-supporting" (Luttrell 1989, p. 71). The agency was renamed the Farm Security Administration in 1937 and in 1946 became part of today's FmHA. Regardless of the name, the early focus of the organization's lending enabled people to own and operate farms and to finance water projects in the seventeen western states. From 1949 to the present, however, lending activities have been greatly broadened to provide subsidized credit for a wide variety of purposes, some of them beyond the farm: senior citizen housing, low-income farmworker housing, emergency loans, disaster loans, rural renewal, and nonfarm rural recreation projects (Luttrell 1989, p. 71).

A number of federal statutes passed since 1947 have defined FmHA purposes and administrative responsibilities. The Rural Development Service was merged into the FmHA in 1977, and the agency was charged with implementing the Small Community and Rural Development Policy Act of 1980.[2] "These programs have helped to provide safe, modest housing; modern, sanitary water and sewer systems; essential community facilities; and job- and economy-boosting business and industry in rural areas."[3] These claims of broad social benefits are made in the absence of evidence that they were produced in a cost-effective manner. This chapter demonstrates that misallocation of credit resources in agriculture is serious and that it is becoming more so over time.

The FmHA maintains offices in forty-six states, 250 districts, and about 1,950 counties scattered throughout the country,[4] so its tentacles reach into nearly every agricultural county in the nation. This point is critical to understanding why the agency has such broad political support and why credit policies are so resistant to change and meaningful reform.

FmHA Loans and their Administration

For an agency that began by making loans to farmers, the range of loans now available from the FmHA is quite remarkable: Loans are made for farm ownership, farm operation, soil and water conservation, to limited resource farmers, youth projects, rural housing, rural rental housing, housing repair, and mutual self-help housing loans, as well as rental assistance payments, water and waste disposal loans and grants, "other" community facilities loans, and business and industry loan guarantees.[5] It is difficult to imagine any investment project that a farmer, or any other rural resident for that matter, may want to undertake that would not be covered by at least one of these loan and grant programs.

By far the most important classes of loans for the farm sector are the farm ownership and farm operating loans. The FmHA makes direct loans to individual farmers in amounts up to $200,000 for these purposes. The agency also guarantees loans made by commercial banks to borrowers with a 10 percent debt service margin.[6]

In addition, the FmHA administers emergency loans for climatic and physical emergencies such as drought and floods, as well as economic emergencies. Economic emergencies occur when costs and prices are so unfavorable that farming becomes unprofitable and there is a high risk of loan default. Explicit instructions have been prepared for designating events and geographic areas qualifying as "disasters" or "emergencies." Emergency decisions are coordinated with local county officials and often are recommended at the state and national levels in presidential and secretary of agriculture designations. Usually before an area is designated, however, expected net income must be less than 70 percent of that in a normal year.

Loans for farms and single-family housing are supervised by FmHA county offices, while those for community facilities, multifamily housing, and business and industrial development are normally controlled by the FmHA district and state offices.[7] FmHA loans are financed out of the repayment of old loans, from sales of existing loans to the U.S. Treasury's Federal Financing Bank (Farmer Macs), by direct Treasury borrowing, and from budget funds appropriated by Congress.[8]

A Lender of Last Resort to the Agricultural Sector

A very large fraction of the economic misallocation of resources created by FmHA policy arises from the requirement that borrowers must be unable to obtain credit from conventional sources, such as commercial banks, insurance companies, and the USDA's Farm Credit Administration (FCA). Thus, the FmHA becomes a "lender of last resort" for a farmer whose financial status or collateral base are inadequate to qualify for conventional credit.[9] For this reason alone, it is quite predictable that FmHA defaults would exceed those of other lenders to the agricultural sector, an expectation fully confirmed and extensively discussed in coming sections of this chapter.

A stated goal of FmHA policy is to help farmers attain financial self-sufficiency and therefore to "graduate" to commercial credit. Ironically, however, graduation means giving up a subsidized interest rate and a host of other benefits if the loan gets into trouble—benefits not available to commercial borrowers. The effect is that "farmers nearing a financial position which would allow (require) graduation have little incentive to maximize income or reduce expenses, including family living expenses, when all, or a major part, of the income improvement would be paid to the commercial lender to cover the higher interest payment" (LaDue 1990, p. 775). Therefore, despite intentions, the FmHA is seldom successful in graduating farmers to commercial credit loans.

Loans may be made by the agency directly to borrowers, or the FmHA may guarantee the loans made to borrowers by conventional commercial lenders. If the loan is guaranteed, the usual practice is for the agency to contract to reimburse the conventional lender for a certain percent of principal and interest in case the loan is defaulted.[10] Thus, loan risk is largely shifted to the taxpayers. These loans may also be "subordinated," which means that the commercial lender may have first access to any machinery, livestock, or real estate used as collateral for the loan. As a consequence, when times are tough for the agricultural sector, conventional lenders avoid risk due to the higher probability of loan default. Either more loans are shifted to the FmHA as the lender of last resort, or the commercial lenders ask the FmHA to guarantee loans to reduce their risk. In neither case is the mobility of capital to more productive uses encouraged.

This result is powerfully reinforced by the "limited resource" farm loans that are available on more liberal terms than are ordinary FmHA loans. These loans are available to farmers who are deemed unable to pay the regular FmHA rate of interest because of low incomes.[11] When the loan is made initially, limited-resource farmers pay a reduced interest rate (normally 3 percent below the "regular rate" for operating loans, and 5 percent below in the case of farm ownership loans). The regular rate is usually what it costs the government to borrow money,[12] but administrative and default costs are ignored (Bosworth et al. 1987, p. 116). However, if repayment difficulties arise after the loan is made, the interest rate may be reduced and is then based on the farmer's "repayment ability" within circumscribed limits.[13]

The 1990 FACTA liberalizes limited-resource loans even more. It authorizes these loans for water conservation and protection and provides for limited-resource farm ownership and farm operating loans to be made at the same interest rates. Limited-resource loans may also be used to finance nonfarm enterprises that will help farmers supplement their farm incomes. Hence, an increasing fraction of future FmHA loans can be expected to qualify for the heavily subsidized limited-resource loans, compounding the capital misallocation problem.

Some Recent Data on the Extent of FmHA Lending Activities

FmHA data suggest that nearly 2 million families acquired homes through rural housing loans from the agency.[14] These loans are made only to qualified low-income families. The interest rate on home ownership loans ranged from 1 to 8.75 percent in late 1991, much below market rates.[15] Thus, these loans were also heavily subsidized. Rural rental housing projects financed by the FmHA are also subsidized.[16] In 1984, the average subsidy across all types of FmHA loans was calculated to be 30 percent (Bosworth et al. 1987, p. 119). In addition, the FmHA has financed some 20,000 water and waste disposal systems by providing loans to small rural communities. Their interest rates are also less than conventional rates.[17] For a USDA lending agency to be involved in these types of subsidized loans must come as a surprise to many American citizens.

The FmHA claimed to be the federal government's largest direct lender, holding a portfolio of loans amounting to about $63 billion in 1988.[18] However, primarily because the FmHA is a lender of last resort, its 1988 loans were only about 15 percent of the total farm debt outstanding in the nation, including both operating and real estate debt.

Significantly, though, FmHA debt has been growing very rapidly, both in absolute amounts and as a fraction of total farm debt. The number of FmHA loans was 241,790 in 1965, 470,267 in 1970, and well over a million in the mid-1970s. It is obvious that the rate of increase vastly exceeded the rate of rural population growth. The rise continued unabated during the 1980s. Whereas only 7.2 percent of the nation's farmers in 1965 received FmHA loans, by 1983 over half (52.8 percent) received them (Luttrell 1989, p. 75).

The percentage increases in the total outstanding principal have been similar to the percentage increase in the number of loans. In 1940, FmHA loans totaled about $600 million, or 6 percent of the total farm debt issued by all lenders. By 1960, FmHA loans had risen to $1.1 billion. Then they really spiraled upward, by 1965 to $2.2 billion, by 1975 to $5.2 billion, and by 1980 to $19.5 billion. In 1985, these loans exceeded $27 billion. By September 1989, the total principal outstanding in the FmHA's portfolio had skyrocketed to over $54 billion (Luttrell 1989, p. 71), a staggering absolute and percentage increase between 1960 and 1989.[19]

In contrast to this huge increase in FmHA debt in the 1980s, commercial bank lending to the farm sector in the 1980s actually slowed compared with that of the 1970s. The annual rate of loan growth in the rural United States ranged from 2.7 percent in farm counties to 8.8 percent in retirement counties, again indicating the slower growth in the farm sector in the 1980s (Brabenstott and Morris 1989, p. 1315). The FmHA accounted for 9.9 percent of all real estate farm debt outstanding in 1985 and 20.8 percent of all non-real-estate farm debt. Therefore, over the decade of the 1980s the rapid increase in FmHA debt was counter to the experience of other lenders to the sector and no doubt was a direct consequence of the very favorable terms offered by the agency.

TABLE 4-1 Outstanding FmHA Portfolio Loans, September 1989 (in billions of dollars)

Direct Farm Loans	
Farm ownership	$7.003
Farm operating	5.226
Emergency (physical disasters)	7.683
Economic emergency (unfavorable economic climate)	3.065
Other farm program	0.596
Total direct farm	*23.573*
Direct Rural Housing and Development Loans	
Insured-principal single-family	18.667
Rural rental housing	8.996
Water and waste disposal	2.852
Community facilities	0.856
Insured business and industrial	0.020
Total direct housing development	*31.391*
Total all direct	***54.964***
Guaranteed Loans	
Farm ownership	0.772
Farm operating	2.371
Economic emergency	0.095
Emergency livestock	0.005
Total guaranteed farm	*3.243*
Housing	1.436
Business and industrial	1.417
Total guaranteed nonfarm	*2.853*
Total all guaranteed	***6.096***
Grand Total	**59.643**

Source: Data obtained from Farmers Home Administration.

Table 4-1 contains a detailed breakdown of total FmHA debt among the different loan categories. Direct loans greatly exceeded guaranteed loans in FmHA's portfolio in late 1989; nearly $55 billion to just over $6 billion, respectively. Of the direct loans, farm loans were about 43 percent, whereas housing and development loans were about 57 percent. By far the largest class of loans among housing and development loans was single family insured-principal housing.

Farmers in Trouble with Loan Repayment

The FmHA's primary mission is to assist family farmers and especially those who cannot obtain credit from commercial credit channels, as already pointed out.[20] Almost all loans are subsidized to some degree, and loans to limited-resource farmers are heavily subsidized. Moreover, strong measures have been taken by the agency to keep farmers with FmHA loans in business.

Special programs have been devised to help farmers who have problems repaying FmHA loans.[21] The agency has a set of instructions for borrowers who might be in danger of default on their loans,[22] including how the borrower might get more information, how to apply for help, and how to appeal if applications are denied. The instructions are to "assist in identifying, combining, and documenting the loan service programs that will keep the farmer on the farm and provide the best net recovery to the Government."[23] It is explained that:

> *Borrowers' accounts must be managed with an overall objective of keeping the farmer in business and at the same time, minimizing loan costs and losses.*[24]

It is truly remarkable the degree to which the regulations go to keep farmers in business. To qualify for the service programs, borrowers must be unable to repay the FmHA loan for any one of a host of reasons, such as "natural disaster, weather, or insect problems; family illness or injury; loss or reduction of off-farm income; disease in livestock herds; low commodity prices and high operating expenses; or other circumstances beyond the control of the borrower."[25]

The following options are permitted to service delinquent accounts and are generally applied by agency officials in the order listed: loan consolidation, loan rescheduling, loan reamortization, interest rate reduction, loan deferral, and debt write-down.[26] These measures are all designed to prevent the borrower from going broke and leaving the sector.

Another set of options exists when these measures cannot save the farmer. They permit borrowers to purchase or lease their own farm, home, and outbuildings plus a limited amount of land from the government on very favorable terms.[27] If the government must take a borrower's land in a foreclosure, the farmer has 180 days to apply to purchase or lease the property back from the government.[28]

This discussion pertains to direct FmHA loans made to farmers. What about loans by commercial lenders that the FmHA guarantees? Presumably these are made at market rates of interest, although the banks must agree that interest rates are not above prime rates. However, in addition, the commercial lender is asked to meet two conditions to qualify for FmHA guarantees. First, the lender must agree to an interest rate reduction if the loan runs into trouble. A 2 percent reduction by the bank is matched by a 2 percent reduction paid for by the FmHA.[29] Second, the lender must commit to employing the whole package of options described before troubled borrowers can be foreclosed on.

This review of the regulations utilized by FmHA shows how far the government will go to keep farmers in business. Two conclusions are obvious: These regulations have kept many farmers in the agricultural sector who otherwise would have gone broke and exited, and the regulations waste capital resources by immobilizing them in the agricultural sector when they would have been more productive elsewhere in the economy. Empirical support for these conclusions is presented next.

The Extent of the Current FmHA Debt Problem

The FmHA pointed out in 1983 that in its forty-seven years of existence, less than 1 percent of the principal advanced had been written off in loan losses, on the surface not a bad record.[30] However, as indicated, much of the lending has occurred since 1983, and it is too early to ascertain precisely what proportion of loans will be eventually defaulted. Signs and trends are not encouraging. Even as early as 1982, 16 percent of farm ownership loans, 29 percent of farm operating loans, 2 percent of water and waste loans, and 24 percent of individual housing loans were considered to be delinquent.[31] This deteriorating situation should have been seriously heeded at the time as a sign of even worse things to come.

Karl Zinsmeister claims that two-thirds of the FmHA's $93 billion in outstanding loans in 1990 were owed by delinquent borrowers (1990, p. 34). Loans are defined as delinquent if the contractual payment is not made within thirty days after the due date. Delinquency is certainly not equivalent to loan default, however. In fact, FmHA procedures call for an annual review of problem cases to determine the specific reasons for delinquency, to decide on corrective actions, and to initiate and carry out these actions.[32] Thus, loan delinquency merely begins the involved evaluation and remedial process described, which may or may not result in foreclosure.

Table 4-2 contains FmHA data regarding the number of delinquent loans that were serviced over the period between the time the 1987 Agricultural Credit Act was passed and November 1989. Accounts are classified as resolved or unresolved.[33] Several inferences can be drawn from these data. The number of unresolved cases (56.81 percent) is larger than those resolved (43.19 percent). However, the act was in effect for only a short time, between 1987 and November 1989, and it is difficult to know if the period was long enough for the act to make an impact on clearing up delinquent loans. Still, it is obvious that the FmHA had an enormous task ahead in dealing with the large number of troubled loans, and 75,352 notices were mailed to borrowers.

Of those accounts that became delinquent, less than 2 percent of the total loans and less than 5 percent of the resolved accounts had been fully paid by November 1989. Caution must be used, however, in inferring that these low percentages reveal a highly troubled sector since it is not clear when the loans were made and, therefore, what a reasonable schedule for discharge of the debt would be. It is significant, however, that of those loans that became delinquent, only about 6 percent of the total and 14 percent of those resolved were brought into the nondelinquent category. It is troublesome that the majority (59.1 percent) of the resolved loans had to receive primary servicing with the host of preferential and subsidized programs such as debt rescheduling and payment deferment, write-downs and write-offs. These data, therefore, clearly support the conclusion that the sector contains tens of thousands of farmers who would have failed under less generous commercial loan terms.

It is striking that over three-fourths of the unresolved accounts appeared to have been in a state of suspended animation. That is, they were in the process of foreclosure or appeal, were being litigated, or were unresolved. This suggests that the FmHA was heavily burdened with loans in trouble that had yet to be disposed of in any definitive way. The FmHA monitors borrower graduation from their loan programs, wherein borrowers become creditworthy for commercial loans. One conjecture would be that graduation would be affected both by the prosperity of the local rural economy and by the diligence and attitudes of FmHA supervisory staff. These officials have enough discretionary authority to put pressure on borrowers to cease feeding at the government-subsidy trough, either by getting out of the business or by becoming worthy borrowers at commercial institutions. However, officials may see it as their mandated function to keep as many farmers in business as possible, regardless of the merits of their

TABLE 4-2 FmHA Loan-Servicing Activity through November 30, 1989 (1987 Agricultural Credit Act)

	Number of notices mailed	*% total notices*	*% resolved or unresolved*	
Resolved Accounts[1]	**32,548**	**43.19**		
Paid in full	1,424	1.89	4.38	
Paid in current	4,593	6.10	14.11	
				% servicing granted
Primary servicing granted	19,236	25.53	59.10	
rescheduled/deferred	9,599	12.74	29.49	49.90
write-downs	4,608	6.12	14.16	23.96
write-offs[2]	5,029	6.67	15.45	26.14
	(19,236)	(25.53)	(59.10)	
Debt settlement	6,341	8.42	19.48	
				% liquidations completed
Liquidations completed	920	1.22	2.83	
FmHA foreclosure	254	.34	.78	27.61
sale/assumption	389	.51	1.20	42.28
volume conveyance	104	.14	.32	11.30
foreclosure by prior/jr. lien	173	.23	.53	18.81
	(920)	(1.22)	(2.83)	
Department of Justice Prosecution	34	.05	.10	
Unresolved Accounts[1]	**42,804**	**56.81**		
Acceleration notice mailed; liquidation not complete	3,297	4.38	7.70	
Preservation servicing	2,452	2.25	5.73	
Mediation pending or unresolved	4,774	6.34	11.15	
Other[3]	32,281	42.84	75.42	

Note: [1] Includes borrowers who failed to respond. [2] Write-offs are net recovery buyouts. [3] Appeals, bankruptcy, servicing actions not complete, litigation, lack of good faith of civil action unresolved.

Source: Data obtained from Farmers Home Administration, USDA.

fundamental economic situation. In any case, the data in Table 4-2 suggest a seriously deteriorating situation with the number of delinquent loans.

Cole Gustafson believes that more liberal attitudes toward credit and debt repayment generally have contributed to the growth of agricultural debt:

Farmers' use of credit rose from $7.6 billion in 1945 to a peak of $206.5 billion in 1983. Between 1972 and 1983 alone, farm debt more than tripled. . . . The rapid growth in farm borrowing was not caused by physical expansion or real capital formation in the sector. From 1945 to 1983 total input use including land, labor, machinery, and operating inputs actually declined, although capital inputs continued to substitute for labor, leading to a greater share of inputs being purchased. In reality, liberal attitudes toward credit, expansionary monetary policies, mounting inflationary pressures, and expectations of rising worldwide demand for food became capitalized in asset values and motivated farmers to increase credit usage. (1989, p. 1145)

A Provisional Assessment

It is significant that the average FmHA farm borrower in 1985 had a debt-to-asset ratio of 83 percent, compared with that of 26 percent for all farmers (Bovard 1989, p. 138). A debt-to-asset ratio of over 40 percent is often considered to be a sign of danger of insolvency. In 1986, even new FmHA borrowers had a debt-to-asset ratio of 70.6 percent. These data also appear to confirm the conclusion that it is predominantly farmers in debt trouble whom the FmHA is supporting with subsidized credit. In fact, in late 1990 the FmHA anticipated a $10 billion write-off due to uncollectible and unsecured loans made to the farming sector.[34]

Perhaps these dismal signs are simply a reflection of widespread trouble in the agricultural sector as a whole (carrying over from the early 1980s) that are no longer applicable. After all, when economic forces affecting agriculture abruptly changed in the 1980s and the farm economy began to deteriorate, many farmers had difficulty servicing their high levels of debt built during the prosperous 1970s. Some of this debt had been used to purchase high-priced land that in the early 1980s plummeted in value. From 1980 to 1985, the average income of farm proprietors fell 40 percent from the levels of the 1970s (Bosworth et al. 1987, p. 112). Real land values declined an estimated 37 percent over the period 1980–1984 and in some states fell as much as 50 percent.[35] These developments pushed many farmers into financial insolvency. Bosworth et al. argue:

Because the government chose to combat inflation in the 1980s with an economic policy of extreme monetary restraint combined with fiscal expansion, agriculture bore the brunt of the adjustment costs. Sharply higher interest rates were costly to a capital-intensive industry, and the rise in the foreign exchange rate limited the export market. Both of these problems can be traced to government policy decision. (1987, p. 112)

However, through debt restructuring, debt forgiveness, and more conservative use of credit, total farm debt in the sector declined an unparalleled 26 percent between 1985 and 1990. In the early 1990s, the overall farming industry was in a more prosperous condition than it had been for many years. Net farm income was at record levels in 1990, although a large fraction of it came directly from government program payments. In 1990, Zinsmeister reported that "a painful farm shakeout has worked itself through—only 7 percent of all operations are today classified as under severe financial strain. Experts say 85 percent to 90 percent of the individual-debt problem that dogged farmers for most of the last decade has finally been digested" (1990, p. 34). If this was true for most farmers, it apparently was not true for those with debt held by the FmHA. But, of course, helping farmers in financial trouble was exactly what the agency was supposed to be doing, even in prosperous times. It is this very fact that is so ominous in its implications for efficient resource allocation.

The 1990 FACTA contains provisions that may make FmHA loan repayment even more unlikely in the future. The act proposes that if the secretary of agriculture acquires easements for conservation, recreational, and wildlife purposes, a part of a qualified borrower's debt may be canceled.[36] It will be very interesting to see how many FmHA debt-ridden farmers will take advantage of this new opportunity to renege on debt obligations.

It is striking that almost at every turn and in every detail, the rules of loan restructuring within the FmHA operate to benefit the borrower at the expense of the government lender and ultimately the taxpayer. This is true of combining loans, increasing the length of the loan period, reducing the interest rate, writing off loans, and delaying or abandoning the various foreclosure proceedings. It is inconceivable that a private lender could accommodate borrowers in this way and survive as a business in competitive capital markets.

How bad would financial conditions have to be in agriculture, or how inefficient would FmHA farmer-borrowers have to be to fail if they really wanted to remain in the sector? It is no surprise that more and more farmers are participating in FmHA programs and borrowing ever larger amounts. When this type of government support is available, the surprise is that any rational farmer would assume the risks of commercial borrowing, where default on a loan could mean almost certain foreclosure and perhaps bankruptcy.

There are at least two reasons, however, why some farmers continue to resist the lure of FmHA loans. First, because of subsidies and favorable treatment not available to everyone in the industry, involvement with the FmHA must carry a stigma that some farmers wish to avoid. Given the importance of financial success in Western culture, it is uncomfortable, if not demeaning, for farmers to show that they are not worthy of credit at a commercial lender. And it would be equally demeaning personally, in associating with peers and neighbors, to submit to the various stages of loan restructuring to stay in business required by FmHA procedures.

Second, the costs of complying with government-imposed regulations and the haggling over whether this or that can or should be done, must be substantial. With all the rules comes a serious encroachment on personal freedom of action in management that involves explicit and implicit costs. James Bovard provides an example of what too often must occur:

> *One Mississippi farmer was almost debt-free when he accepted a low-interest disaster loan for $41,300. This made him automatically eligible for subsidized disaster loans in the following four years. By 1983, the farmer owed the FmHA $661,000 and had a negative net worth of more than half a million dollars. So the FmHA gave him another $204,000 to put in another crop and stay on the land for one more year.* (1989, p. 135)

The Efficiency Impacts of the Debt Problem on FmHA Borrowers

Even though it is hazardous to generalize from anecdotal evidence alone, individual cases such as Bovard's Mississippi farmer strongly suggest that something is seriously amiss. But these cases may be just the "tip of the iceberg." From the viewpoint of overall economic efficiency, there is a more worrisome aspect to these programs. Given the regulations under which the FmHA must operate, how could anyone seriously question that these policies induce the most marginal farmers to remain in business in the agricultural sector and thereby reduce its efficiency?[37] The ultimate consequence inevitably must be a reduction in the average standard of living for all Americans.

The impact of these credit policies on agricultural output itself is not obvious, however. Belongia and Gilbert postulate that "farm credit will be diverted to its highest-valued opportunities and [if] these are not in farm production, the existence of the federal credit agencies may have little impact on farm output" (1990, p. 770). In other words, farmers will find a way to divert subsidized credit to it highest-valued use. This conclusion is doubtful. It is true that capital is fungible, and were it not for the regulations governing use, subsidized credit may be used elsewhere. However, in fact, the FmHA carefully monitors subsidized credit to ensure that it is used by the farmer who borrowed it.

The effect on output and on consumer prices is still not clear, however. If excessive resources are held in the sector, then output may well be larger than would have been the case in a purely market-directed economy. But if those resources are inefficiently employed, that output will be produced at higher cost.

The important implication is that competitive markets for capital and labor resources, markets that reward efficiency and penalize inefficiency, cannot work under the current set of rules used by the FmHA, despite the efforts of agency personnel who might be trying to operate an efficient program. Even those farmers who could be efficient enough to compete in fair and open capital markets are provided with powerful incentives to be less efficient than they might otherwise be so they can qualify for the favorable treatment provided by FmHA policies. The program of subsidized loans increases the returns of belonging to that genre known as "a family farmer in trouble." Some farmers who might be on the margin will choose to reduce their incomes and efficiency sufficiently to become eligible for the subsidies (Wagner 1989, p. 61). According to the FmHA's own records, by far the most frequent cause of bankruptcy among its borrowers is poor farming practices, such as inadequate care of livestock or crops.[38] FmHA personnel indicate that borrowers who perceive their probability of financial success as low do not maintain their collateral. Animals or machines are frequently not replaced. It is unclear whether this reflects explicit operator recognition that the returns to such maintenance are low or zero or an inability to purchase replacements because of cash flow limitations (LaDue 1990, p. 777).

Moral Hazard and Adverse Selection

Because the FmHA is a "lender of last resort" and assists financially troubled producers, two phenomena known as "moral hazard" and "adverse selection" arise. They account for much of the sector's inefficiency created by FmHA policies.

Moral hazard is a legal term describing a situation where individuals are able to escape full accountability for their actions. For example, if participants in FmHA farm credit or disaster programs know that the government will bail them out from almost any financial difficulty, whether of their own making or not, they will not take the same careful measures to prevent or avoid such costly situations (moral hazard). These borrowers may even actively take steps to ensure that their economic performance is bad enough to disqualify them from receiving credit from commercial lenders. In either case, they transfer much of the costs of their imprudent behavior to others.

Adverse selection occurs when the regulations of a program or institution attract participants whose productive performance is lower or more risky on average than that of competitors not subject to such regulations. If sufficiently favorable subsidized credit is available only to those to whom commercial credit is unavailable, whether because of poor economic circumstances or an unfavorable business environment, then the program will attract the least creditworthy borrowers (adverse selection). In the FmHA case, it would appear that the worse their financial plight, the better are farmers' chances for the most favorable FmHA loan terms. And the more misfortune that occurs during the period of the loan, the greater the probability that the government will ease the terms of the loan. Thus, on the face of it, opportunities for economic waste in the sector arising from FmHA programs would appear to be substantial.

Evidence for moral hazard and adverse selection is found in data presented earlier that the average FmHA farm borrower in 1985 had a debt-to-asset ratio of 83 percent, compared with that of 26 percent for all farmers. And in 1986, even new FmHA borrowers had a debt-to-asset ratio of 70.6 percent, proving adverse selection. It is obvious, therefore, that moral hazard and adverse selection destroy the incentives for making prudent decisions that would conduce to more effective management, more responsible behavior, and more efficient production in the sector.

The USDA itself recognizes moral hazard problems:

> *The USDA Office of the Inspector General and the General Accounting Office have reported the type of problems with FmHA guaranteed loans that moral hazard would be expected to generate. On the loan-making side, they found incomplete assessment of repayment ability, inadequate verification of income and debt, and imperfect documentation of collateral. Documented loan-servicing deficiencies include not obtaining periodic financial statements, not performing required collateral inspections, and making unauthorized loan advances under the guarantee. (LaDue 1990, p. 777)*

One of the most serious consequences of farm debt problems, such as those encountered in the 1930s and again in the 1980s, is that state legislatures have interfered with existing debt contracts by passing debt moratorium laws. Lee Alston (1984) has studied the situation in the 1930s in some detail and found that farm foreclosure moratorium laws were enacted in twenty-five states. Even when the debtor defaulted on a loan, these laws essentially prevented creditors from obtaining title to the debtor's land for a specified or court-determined period of time. Alston's analysis shows that moratorium laws were more likely to be enacted in states suffering relatively high levels of farm distress. It is clear that some farmers avoided foreclosure because of these laws, but it is far from obvious that the net impact was in the public interest. Naturally, lenders responded to the legislation by rationing loans or raising interest rates to cover the increased risk of debts that could not be collected. This made it more costly to get credit and probably precluded new farmers from entering the industry by purchasing a farm (Alston 1984, p. 456). There can be little question that these very same consequences followed similar laws enacted in the 1980s.

Federal fiscal policy has also burdened many federal lending agencies such as the FmHA. To meet the expenditure reduction requirements of the Gramm–Rudman–Hollings Act, FmHA was required to turn over the "cream" of its housing loans to commercial lenders, primarily commercial banks, for something like 52 cents on the dollar. County FmHA officials report that some accounts were paid in full shortly thereafter, giving a good profit to the bank, but depriving the FmHA of some of its best prospects for managing healthy loans and graduating borrowers to commercial lenders.[39]

Other Efficiency Effects of FmHA Loan Programs

What about those farmers who try to survive and prosper on loans from "regular" credit channels and who must pay higher rates of interest over much shorter time horizons than do FmHA borrowers? Consider the situation where two farmers each have $500,000 in debt, one farmer paying 10 percent interest on a loan from a commercial lender and the other only 5 percent for an FmHA loan. The latter will have $25,000 less costs annually. The FmHA program thus could provide less efficient farmers a sufficient net-income advantage in many instances to more than offset any lack of managerial skill.

It is quite possible that the indirect effects of FmHA policies on the agricultural sector may be even more important than the direct effects. "Subsidized credit actually reduces the well-being of non-subsidized farmers through its impact on farm production costs and product prices" (Luttrell 1989, p. 84). If the subsidized loan programs keep farmers in business who otherwise would fail, and in the process immobilize resources in the sector, then those who would have survived if the competitive game had been allowed to be played out are worse off. They receive lower prices for what they produce and pay higher prices for productive inputs. Because of the family-farm bias of most government programs, and the FmHA's in particular, farmers who are kept afloat by credit subsidies are smaller and less efficient than the average in the sector.[40]

The mix of inputs (land, labor, machinery, chemicals, veterinary services, and so forth) used in agricultural production is also affected by FmHA credit policies. So is the production technology. If interest rates on operating loans are subsidized, then capital used for operating inputs will be overused compared with long-term capital such as land. This has the effect of artificially raising production costs.

But since, under FmHA rules, subsidized production loans are made to people who must be farmers, the credit subsidy induces farmers to remain in the sector that would not otherwise be there. Even if an effort is made to limit total production by output-control devices such as acreage set-asides, the overall effect will be to induce inefficient resource combinations. In fact, land-control measures simply induce inefficiencies of their own by idling a large fraction of the nation's productive land, as demonstrated in the preceding chapter.

Even credit users outside the agricultural sector may be negatively affected. Assuming that the quantity of credit available for investment is limited to the savings generated in the economy, as credit in agriculture is subsidized and more is demanded as a result, fewer capital resources are available to other sectors of the economy.[41] Interest rates in those sectors will be higher than if the agricultural credit were not subsidized (Pasour 1989, p. 329).

Of course, FmHA and conventional credit may not compete for savers at the local level. Since FmHA notes are sold to investors nation-wide in secondary financial markets, FmHA loans may give a net boost to the local economy. In fact, Bosworth et al. argue: "Borrowers may lack access to national credit markets. . . . Borrowers dependent on their local bank may find that funds available for loans are contracting at the time they are most in need. Agricultural credit programs are commonly justified on this ground." (1987, p. 7)

But from the national perspective and the economy as a whole, loans in one sector must be a substitute for loans in other sectors. If loans are subsidized, allocating them to less efficient users in the subsidized sector must retard economic growth and impede efficient resource allocation in the economy as a whole. Also, the secondary market securities, the so-called Farmer Macs, created by the 1987 Agricultural Credit Act, are sold nationwide, if not worldwide, and must substitute for other credit devices in those broad markets.[42]

Finally, the bureaucratic costs of administering the FmHA's complex programs must be very high. Real human and capital resources are squandered in creating loans, monitoring the performance of borrowers, and in the endless procedures utilized to keep farmers in business. Many of these human resources are of high quality, and their waste must be costly for the economy as a whole.[43]

What Lies Ahead for Farm Credit?

In February 1990, the secretary of agriculture appeared before the Senate Agriculture, Nutrition, and Forestry Committee to discuss the administration's plans for introducing a new farm bill. On the subject of farm credit, he stated:

> *The time has come to reform our farm credit programs by emphasizing that they should be consistent with a commercial, market-oriented industry. In other words, they should fill a carefully defined credit niche; they should not be disguised welfare programs. Our Farmers Home Administration (FmHA) should provide targeted assistance to beginning farmers with demonstrated management capabilities. Greater emphasis should be placed on improved loan application and reporting procedures, and on financial disciplines that are required of commercial borrowers.*
>
> *FmHA credit programs will continue the shift toward the use of loan guarantees initiated in the 1985 act. Under our proposal existing FmHA borrowers and beginning farmers, who receive direct operating loans would face tighter loan eligibility and application requirements, limits on the period of eligibility for FmHA loans, requirements for demonstrated farming abilities and a needs test for limited resource loans.*[44]

The secretary also argued that loans should be increasingly shifted toward guaranteed commercial sources of credit, that the farm ownership loan program be targeted to disadvantaged applicants, and that loan eligibility procedures be strengthened to reflect the farmer's equity and experience.[45]

The general thrust of the secretary's statement must be applauded. He correctly identified the major problems: the need for a market-oriented industry rather than a welfare program, the need for better loan application and reporting procedures, the need of stronger tests for determining eligibility for limited-resource loans, and a need for much stronger financial discipline in administering loans.

As has occurred so many times in the past, however, the Congress was not responsive to the reforms suggested. Members of Congress want power to redistribute income and will resist every effort to eliminate this power. In the 1990 FACTA, the secretary got his trivial recommendation that allows

Farmer Mac to pool FmHA guaranteed loans for marketing without having to meet the usual underwriting requirements. But as for the more important and substantive matters, the administration came away from the legislative process in 1990 pretty much empty-handed. And yet President Bush signed the 1990 FACTA bill, which raises questions about how serious the executive branch was in its budget reform proposal.

Presumably, however, the budget reconciliation agreement reached late in 1990 was to be the final word on government expenditures. After months of bitter haggling and negotiation, congressional leaders and representatives of the Bush administration agreed to a package that was alleged to reduce the deficit. This act directs agencies of government, including the USDA, to cut expenditures. Agricultural credit was among the victims.

The act requires substantial reductions in direct farm loans made by the FmHA, resulting in savings in outlays estimated at $465 million in 1991 and $1,556 million through 1995.[46] It is not clear, however, whether these savings are reductions in direct loans that may or may not be paid back or are the estimated value of loan writeoffs. The act also modifies the existing interest rate reductions program by eliminating the matching requirement for private lenders in hopes that this will facilitate guaranteed loans as an offset to reductions in direct loans. To ensure the reductions in direct loans, the act requires that at least 30 percent of those served by the interest rate reduction program be former FmHA borrowers. The legislation also mandated a $482 million reduction in direct loans to farmers in 1991 and required that farm ownership and operating loans be reduced to under $300 million by 1995. However, the act provided for increases in guaranteed loans to about $3.7 billion by 1995. Given the terrible condition the FmHA finds itself in with delinquent loans, it will be most interesting to see if these goals can be accomplished or if the provisions enacted will be watered down as their political impacts become manifest.

Notes

1. U.S. Department of Agriculture, Office of Information (1988), *A Brief History of Farmers Home Administration* (Washington, DC: November).
2. U.S. Department of Agriculture, Farmers Home Administration (1983), *A Brief History of Farmers Home Administration* (Washington, DC: February).
3. U.S. Senate (1990a), *Food, Agriculture, Conservation, and Trade Act of 1990,* Report no. 101-357 (Washington, DC: July 6).
4. USDA, *Farmers Home Administration.*
5. Ibid.
6. U.S. Senate, *FACTA,* p. 237.
7. The FmHA county supervisor is the key decision maker and is responsible for making all determinations of individual loan eligibility at the local level, but elaborate appeal procedures are provided in case the county supervisor rules against any applicant. A special staff exists to handle appeals. A review is first made at the initial decision level, then at the state level, and finally at the national level if needed.
8. USDA, *Farmers Home Administration,* p. 11.
9. The 1990 FACTA provides for outreach efforts within the USDA to make sure that "socially disadvantaged" farmers receive a fair share of USDA programs and extends requirements for allocating FmHA farm operating and real estate loans to socially disadvantaged farmers.
10. USDA housing loan guarantees enable private lenders to offer housing loans with no down payment to moderate-income rural residents. A local lender makes the loan, and the FmHA provides a guarantee that protects the lender against 100 percent of a loss up to 35 percent of the loan amount, and 85 percent of a loss on the remaining 65 percent of the loan. See U.S. Department of Agriculture, Office of Public Affairs, "USDA Accelerates Availability of 1992 Housing Loans," *Selected Speeches and News Releases* (Washington, DC: January 9–15, 1992), p. 15.
11. See USDA, *Farmers Home Administration,* p. 15.
12. Ibid., p. 8.
13. These limits are some "minimum" rate for limited-resource farmers on the low side and the full rate ordinarily charged for FmHA farm loans on the high side.
14. USDA, *Farmers Home Administration,* p. 1.
15. A scale of rates was obtained in private correspondence from an FmHA

county supervisor in 1991. What interest rate a family pays on this scale is determined by its payment ability. A family is expected to contribute 20 percent of its adjusted gross income to payment of principal and interest, real estate taxes, and house insurance, while the government pays off the promissory note. Eligibility for this program is reviewed annually. Sometimes employers are asked to cooperate in keeping monthly payments in the "affordable" range, and a verification of employment is usually required.

16. If a loan gets into trouble, foreclosure proceedings are subject to the law of the state where the project is located. Prior to a foreclosure action, however, the FmHA follows a strict loan delinquency servicing plan, which can include partial payment until the account becomes current, a moratorium on payments if circumstances creating the delinquency are beyond the family's control (for example, medical bills due to emergencies), and voluntary conveyance instead of foreclosure if the family has acted in good faith.

17. Interest rates charged are usually determined by the distribution of family incomes within the community. If a high fraction of families live below the poverty line, the interest rate is highly subsidized compared with a market rate.

18. USDA, *Farmers Home Administration,* p. 1.

19. These data are in nominal dollars not constant-value or real dollars. Even though there was considerable inflation over the period considered, even the percentage increase in real dollars would be very large.

20. Family farms are defined by the FmHA as those that a family can operate and manage itself with a reasonable amount of hired labor.

21. These are known as Primary Loan Service Programs and Preservation Loan Service Programs. These programs are described in United States Department of Agriculture, Farmers Home Administration (1988), *FmHA Instruction 1951-S with Attachments* (Washington, DC).

22. Essentially, FmHA Instruction 1951-S spells out a set of conditions that the FmHA will meet to (1) prevent default by its borrowers, and (2) direct what actions are to be taken if default cannot be avoided. the purpose of 1951-S is "to help you [the borrower] repay the loan and keep your property." FmHA Instruction 1951-S is accompanied by a detailed set of guidelines to County Supervisors on how to apply the rules of these programs. See U.S. Department of Agriculture, Farmers Home Administration (1988), *FmHA Instruction 1951-S with Attachments* (Washington, DC).

23. Ibid., p. 8.

24. Ibid., p. 2.

25. Ibid., p. 4.

26. Loan consolidation provides opportunities for farmers to combine loans that

would otherwise not be repayable. Loan rescheduling allows a lengthening of the repayment schedule or period to reduce the periodic payment. Up to fifteen years can be allowed on loans of much shorter initial duration. Loan reamortization revises the terms for loans secured by real estate. The repayment period may be extended and the interest rate may be reduced (ibid., p. 2).

Loans may be changed from either operating loans or farm ownership loans to limited-resource loans, which carry a lower interest rate. In one county office visited in early 1990, the county supervisor indicated that he had the discretion of deciding what interest rate was to be charged on farm operating loans if the borrower could not pay the government cost of borrowing. He had a range of from 5.5 percent to 8.5 percent that was being charged on loans that were originally designated as farm operating loans.

The loan deferral provision allows the payments of principal and interest on loans to be delayed for up to five years. Those requesting deferral must be able to show that they *cannot* pay essential living expenses or maintain their property and pay their debts. They must also be able to show, however, that they *can* pay at the end of the delayed period; otherwise, foreclosure procedures are initiated. In this case also the interest rate can be adjusted if the current rate is lower than the original rate on the loan.

Debt write-down, the most extreme measure of all, gives the FmHA the power to reduce both the principal and the interest payments of the debt. When a mortgage loan is made, property covering the loan is required as collateral. If the collateral falls in value, debt write-down allows the debt to be reduced to the recovery value of the collateral property. If there are other prior liens against the collateral property, they may be subtracted from the repayable debt as well. This provision is permitted only after the previous five provisions have been shown to be insufficient for the borrower to show that he or she has a "feasible" plan. The 1990 FACTA imposes a lifetime cap of $300,000 on write-downs and write-offs per borrower and limits them to a single write-down on loans made after January 6, 1988. This addition to the law should reduce the loss to the taxpayers from previously frequent and large write-downs and write-offs.

27. The lease time is for up to five years, and the lease will include an option to buy back the property leased. Ibid., p. 5.

28. Buy-back or lease-back rights apply not only to farmers, but also to their spouses and children if they have also been active in farming. The 1990 FACTA limits eligibility for loan lease-backs and buy-outs to borrowers who have acted in good faith. The 1990 act also adds beginning farmers to those who may receive sale preferences and provides sales at appraised market value rather than at capitalization value. Ibid., p. 5.

29. These regulations were obtained from a county supervisor.

30. USDA, *Farmers Home Administration,* p. 10.

31. Ibid., p. 33.

32. U.S. Department of Agriculture, Farmers Home Administration (1982), *Information for Farmers Home Administration County Committees* (Washington, DC: May).

33. The loans are considered resolved if the delinquent loans have been fully paid off and there is no debt outstanding with the FmHA, if the delinquency has been removed by bringing payments up to date (if primary servicing has begun), or if debt settlements and liquidations have been completed. The unresolved accounts include those in which negotiations of various kinds have been undertaken, including notification of delinquency, preservation servicing, pending or still unresolved loan mediation, or an in-progress appeal.

34. Received in private correspondence with an FmHA county supervisor, February 1990.

35. U.S. Department of Agriculture, *Agricultural Resources* (July 1987), p. 7.

36. U.S. Senate, *FACTA*, p. 244.

37. Rucker and Alston (1987) have estimated that federal credit programs in the 1930s were a significant factor in preventing farm failures. This reinforces the point made here that the sector is larger than it would be were it not for subsidized credit.

38. U.S. General Accounting Office (1986), *Farmers Home Administration Financial and General Characteristics of Farmer Loan Program Borrowers* (Washington DC: January), p. 2.

39. These observations were provided in private correspondence with an FmHA county supervisor.

40. In 1990 FmHA policies placed a maximum size on various loans as follows: insured operating loans, $200,000; guaranteed operating loans, $400,000; insured farm ownership loans, $200,000; and guaranteed farm ownership loans, $300,000. Emergency loans tended not to be so limited, and some FmHA loans are in trouble because of past "emergency loan" designations. Received in private correspondence with a county supervisor, February 1990.

41. Based on their regression results, Belongia and Gilbert (1990, p. 769) conclude that when growth in total credit slows, the share of farm credit originating from federal agencies rises.

42. The 1990 FACTA allows Farmer Mac to pool FmHA guaranteed real estate and operating loans for marketing without having to meet the usual underwriting requirements.

43. Some plausible explanations for why credit policies have developed as they have are presented in Chapter 7.

44. U.S. Department of Agriculture, Office of Public Affairs (1990a), "Statement by Clayton Yeutter, Secretary of Agriculture, Before the Senate Committee on Agriculture, Nutrition, and Forestry, Feb. 7," *Selected Speeches and News Releases* (Washington, DC: February 1–8), p. 13.

45. Ibid.

46. U.S. House of Representatives (1990), *Omnibus Budget Reconciliation Act of 1990,* Report no. 101-964 (Washington, DC), Attachment B.

5

Making Wealthy Farmers Richer at the Expense of Taxpayers

Despite general public approval of governmental income transfers to American farmers, especially family farmers, a shrill outcry of indignation occurred when it became known that a single California producer of cotton and wheat received over $20 million of government payments in a single year under the programs of the 1985 Food Security Act (G. S. Becker 1986, p. 13). As never before, the "equity" of farm programs came into sharp focus.

Economic justice or equity deals with how the economic pie is sliced, how the national income is divided. Income is viewed here in a "broad" sense including returns from ownership of resources obtained from market sales and from transfers from other parties, private and public. For over a half century, transfer payments from government have been an important source of income for many citizens, including farmers.

Using governmental action to redistribute income and wealth has long been accepted in Western democracies, despite vigorous protestations by some of our most brilliant scholars and philosophers, who have pointed out the impact on incentives and productivity.[1] A complex trade-off between efficiency and equity almost always occurs. The problem is how to redistribute income to satisfy basic human needs without destroying incentives to increase productivity and efficiency. Indeed, it has been argued that efficiency and equity are incommensurable and that no moral code exists in society to arbitrate conflict between them. For this reason, any allocation of resources requiring a weighing of these values appears unprincipled, unpredictable, and arbitrary (Gray 1990, p. xvii).

One view of equity is simply the distribution of income among households; for example, the fraction of total income captured by the various deciles of the population of households ranked by income. If each decile of households received approximately 10 percent of the total income, the distribution would be regarded as highly egalitarian or equitable in the prevailing vernacular. However, if the top 10 percent of households received 50 percent of the national income, and the bottom 10 percent only 2 percent, the distribution would be skewed, or inequitable.

Several aspects of the equity problem are relevant to a study of the political economy of the agricultural sector. The first is that in the 1920s and 1930s when government farm programs were first introduced, equity provided one of the most compelling rationales for government action. On average, rural households lagged behind urban households in income and wealth, and pressure for equality was generated to alleviate poverty and human suffering. It is therefore germane to ask whether that rationale is still valid given the distribution of income and wealth that exists today. The simple answer is that although cyclical factors in both farming and the general economy cause the relative incomes to vary, in recent years average incomes of farmers have exceeded those of the urban sector.[2]

A second issue is the distribution of income within the agricultural sector. Despite declared intentions to equalize incomes, in fact do government policies produce a more egalitarian distribution of income within the sector than would exist without those policies? The answer here is unequivocal. Farm programs primarily benefit wealthy commercial farmers who are enrolled and thus exacerbate income and wealth inequality in the sector.

A third equity issue, also confined to the sector, is who are the principal beneficiaries of income support subsidies: landowners, laborers, or owners of capital?[3] The answer is that those who own land and who first receive supply-reducing vehicles such as dairy, peanut, and tobacco quotas and grazing permits capture the bulk of the benefits from government programs.

Urban and Rural Differences in Income and Wealth

Until the 1960s, a safe generalization had been that farm families have had lower incomes on average than urban families.[4] This has been the case in almost all countries, especially today in the less developed countries. Rural-to-urban migration, so pervasive across the world, has been one consequence of such perceived income disparities as rural people have sought opportunities for more lucrative employment and the possibilities of a more satisfying life because of better services provided by both the public and private sectors in urban areas.

The fact that the generalization appears no longer to be true in the

United States, however, will come as a surprise to many, if not most, Americans, who commonly perceive that farm incomes are lower. The question is whether data that show farm household incomes ahead of urban incomes are an aberration or are likely to persist into the future.

The relevant data are found in Table 5-1. Although there have been some changes concerning what is counted as income for farm-operator households over the period, it is unlikely that the comparisons with urban incomes have been seriously biased.[5]

Before the sharp increase in agricultural prices in the early 1970s, average incomes of farm households were near parity with the U.S. average of all households. (The income ratios in the final column of Table 5-1 indicate comparisons between 1967 and 1992.) However, before 1960 all the way back to the 1920s and 1930s, as a general rule, average incomes of urban Americans exceeded those of farmers. But because of the instability of farm prices, incomes of farm households have been much more volatile year to year than incomes of urban Americans. It is worth observing that average incomes of U.S. households have been increasing monotonically over the entire period. Since World War II, the off-farm component of farm family incomes has been increasing relative to the income obtained from farm sales, and the latter has been much more unstable than the former.

The relationship between farm and nonfarm incomes was altered in the 1970s as farm prices surged, primarily through the impetus of export demand. Then, as exports fell in the 1980s, the agricultural sector experienced a major recession; land values fell precipitously in most regions of the country, and farm-operator incomes fell below the U.S. average again. The 1981 and 1985 farm acts kicked in large government payments, and farm-operator incomes moved back toward equality in the mid-1980s and have exceeded the U.S. average since 1986.

It is important to recognize, however, that these comparisons are for farm and nonfarm households and include all sources of income. This is quite appropriate because the goal here is to use income as a surrogate for standard of living. Because of the way the United States Census defines a farm (essentially those who produce $1,000 worth of farm commodities), however, income and wealth comparisons between the farm and nonfarm sectors would be seriously misleading if only farm incomes were used to represent the standard of living of farm households. Even the majority of those considered by the census to be farmers do not receive the bulk of their incomes from farming.

On the other hand, average farm operator income may not be representative at all of those farmers who receive most of their incomes from farming. If only "commercial" farmers who produce a high fraction of

TABLE 5-1 Comparison of USDA Average Income of Farm Operator Households and Average U.S. Income, 1967 to 1992

Year	*USDA average income of farm-operator households*[1]	*Average U.S. income*[2]	*Income ratio of farm to U.S. population*
	(dollars)	*(dollars)*	*(ratio)*
1967	8,486	7,989	1.06
1968	9,049	8,760	1.03
1969	10,302	9,544	1.08
1970	10,845	10,001	1.08
1971	11,758	10,383	1.13
1972	14,238	11,286	1.26
1973	20,925	12,157	1.72
1974	19,822	13,094	1.51
1975	19,614	13,779	1.42
1976	18,765	14,922	1.26
1977	18,370	16,100	1.14
1978	22,538	17,730	1.27
1979	25,207	19,554	1.29
1980	20,891	21,063	0.99
1981	25,751	22,787	1.13
1982	24,965	24,309	1.03
1983	20,968	25,401	0.83
1984	30,561	27,464	1.11
1985	32,920	29,066	1.13
1986	37,133	30,759	1.21
1987	42,754	32,144	1.33
1988	42,379	34,017	1.25
1989	42,951	36,520	1.18
1990	45,511	37,403	1.22
1991	42,287	37,422	1.12
1992	40,068	39,020	1.03

Notes: [1] USDA average income equals to average of total net farm income plus off-farm income. [2] From U.S. Department of Commerce, Bureau of the Census, *Current Population Reports*, various years.

Source: U.S. Department of Agriculture, Agriculture and Rural Economy Division, Economic Research Service (1989), *Economic Indicators of the Farm Sector: Farm Sector Review, 1987* (Washington, DC: April).

agricultural sales were counted as farmers, the income and wealth comparisons of farmers and nonfarmers might look quite different. One estimate is that the top 20 percent of U.S. farmers in terms of the value of sales (numbering fewer than half a million) produce about 85 percent of the nation's agricultural output. These are predominantly family farmers who own, manage, and furnish the bulk of the labor for their farms. Most of the rest included in the census definition are really part-time farming families who have found agriculture a good complement to a day job, an off-farm business, or a spouse's salary (Zinsmeister 1990).

In commenting on James Bovard's *The Farm Fiasco* (1989), the editors of the *Atlanta Journal* remark:

> *The entire farm bill [the 1990 FACTA] is built on myth. In truth, Mr. Bovard notes, the average full-time farmer is a millionaire with a net worth of $1,016,000—13 times greater than the average American family. His 1988 income was $168,000. What's more, the number of farmers with sales over $100,000—a class that collects 80-90 percent of all farm income—is not declining. From 1980 to 1988, the class increased by 20 percent, from about 270,000 farmers to 323,000. (1990, p. A10)*

It must be apparent that income comparisons are heavily influenced by the way income data are collected and tabulated. Guy Gugliotta (1990b) reports the results of a USDA study showing that per capita income in counties designated as farm counties in 1988 was only 75.9 percent of the national average and that in the first three months of 1990, rural unemployment and underemployment stood at 10 percent of the population, 2.6 points higher than that in urban areas. No doubt these data could be and were used by apologists for farm subsidies.

But these data do not provide a comparison between farm and nonfarm people; it is between those who live in so-called farm counties and those who live in urban counties. As pointed out in Chapter 1, some farm operators live in urban areas although probably not a large fraction of the total. But more seriously in producing bias, many nonfarmers live in designated farm counties. Moreover, costs of living may be quite different in farm than in urban counties. Hence, it is dubious whether any reliable conclusions can be drawn from these data as to relative farmer and nonfarmer incomes and the income and wealth effects of farm programs.

Perhaps the conclusion of most relevance for this study is that average farm-operator incomes, even with the definition of a farm used by the census, are not now below those of the average urban family and are not expected to be so in the future unless the agricultural sector is victimized by another serious recession.

TABLE 5-2 Average Net Farm Income and Average Direct Government Payments, by Value of Sales Class, 1975 to 1988

	Value of Sales Class							
Year	*$500,000 and over*	*$250,000 to $499,999*[1]	*$100,000 to $249,999*[2]	*$40,000 to $99,999*	*$20,000 to $39,999*	*$10,000 to $19,999*	*$5,000 to $9,999*	*Less than $5,000*
				Average Net Farm Income (dollars)[3]				
1975	599,545	99,000	41,802	17,146	6,508	2,621	539	-608
1976	559,846	87,955	37,514	15,148	5,487	2,091	277	-711
1977	540,077	75,711	32,459	12,762	4,159	1,317	-101	-865
1978	536,291	72,321	31,778	12,846	4,012	1,439	414	-676
1979	505,873	70,623	29,158	9,737	2,061	17	-494	-1,148
1980	452,883	67,776	28,286	8,564	1,394	-664	-938	-1,530
1981	439,922	64,433	22,229	3,694	-1,1501	-1,986	-1,408	-1,576
1982	463,648	76,522	24,895	5,712	34	-981	-691	-1,273
1983	520,825	87,533	27,003	5,324	-380	-1,083	-1,190	-1,614
1984	501,371	77,043	24,024	2,912	-1,409	-1,589	-969	-1,443
1985	604,778	105,489	36,816	10,023	2,213	-259	-442	-1,502
1986	665,121	113,668	41,985	13,463	4,165	796	1	-1,323
1987	710,884	122,569	47,653	17,283	5,956	2,187	1,320	-999
1988	712,414	129,844	49,957	17,420	6,570	2,634	1,135	-906

Average Direct Government Payments (dollars)								
1975	5,182	1,684	1,094	731	444	261	174	68
1976	3,692	1,568	1,047	713	380	194	138	49
1977	7,923	4,089	2,798	1,913	924	416	312	103
1978	10,028	6,308	4,437	3,055	1,359	538	430	131
1979	4,323	2,709	1,909	1,313	585	232	185	57
1980	3,838	2,405	1,695	1,166	519	206	164	51
1981	5,495	3,444	2,427	1,669	743	295	235	73
1982	9,805	6,144	4,330	2,978	1,236	526	419	130
1983	49,012	27,724	13,312	5,793	2,305	1,097	298	149
1984	33,331	20,506	12,970	5,296	2,194	863	342	76
1985	30,488	19,115	10,915	5,579	2,858	804	364	82
1986	33,838	24,818	17,196	9,764	5,224	1,882	756	198
1987	42,896	35,716	24,366	13,885	6,805	3,199	1,587	347
1988	40,238	31,978	21,118	11,283	5,730	2,331	1,010	374

Notes: [1] For the years 1975–1981, data are for sales class $200,000 to $499,999. [2] For the years 1975–1981, data are for sales class $100,000 to $199,999. This means that the large increases from 1981 to 1982 in average net farm income and in average direct government payments in these classes were at least partially attributable to changes in the classification that occurred in 1981. [3] Net income includes direct government payments.

Source: U.S. Department of Agriculture, Agriculture and Rural Economy Division, Economic Research Service (1988), *Economic Indicators of the Farm Sector: National Financial Summary, 1988* (Washington, DC: September), pp. 43, 48.

High- and Low-Income Farmers and Government Payments

Evidence from the Census

The Census of Agriculture divides farmers into sales classes (see Table 5-2), with the top group selling over $500,000 of farm products and the bottom group less than $5,000. It is important to note at the outset of this analysis that the population of farmers includes both those who receive government payments and those who do not.

One way of discovering the distribution of agricultural program benefits is to analyze how farmers in various gross sales classes are affected by direct benefits paid out by the government. Direct payments include deficiency, conservation reserve, and disaster payments, but do not include Commodity Credit Corporation loans (which normally will be paid back or will be discharged by the CCC collecting the collateral crop) or defaults on other government direct or guaranteed loans. Unfortunately, minor changes in the classification system occurred in 1981 that make comparisons between the years before 1982 and after 1981 a little hazardous (see Table 5-2, note). Still, changes in the middle of the period in only two of the eight classes do not appear to have had a significant impact on the general trends occurring over the complete period from 1975 to 1987.

The data in Table 5-2 have some striking features. First, comparing years 1975 and 1988, the first and last years in the series, average net farm income in the three top sales classes rose over the period (the increases were 19, 31, and 20 percent, respectively). For the remaining classes, however, changes in average net farm income were small.[6] Second, in the lower sales classes, average net farm income was often negative, especially for the smallest sales class (net income less than $5,000). This is probably an indication that the census-defined farmers in this class were really only part-timers, retirees, or those who farm as a hobby. Third, for all sales classes, the increases in average direct payments from the government were substantial, especially in the later years of the period. Both falling market prices and more generous government programs were responsible for the increasing payments. Fourth, for any given year, the average direct government payments were invariably larger the higher the sales class, reflecting the fact that payments are based primarily on sales. Fifth and significant, however, as a *percentage* of average net farm income, direct government payments were much smaller for the higher sales classes than for those in the middle sales classes. Consider 1987 as an example. For the sales class of $500,000 and over, payments represented only 6 percent of average net farm income. For the $250,000 to $499,999 class, payments were 29 percent of average net farm income; for the $100,000 to $249,999 class, 51 percent; for the $40,000 to

$99,999 class, 80 percent; and for the $20,000 to $39,999 class and lower sales classes, payments actually exceeded net farm income. Since it is commonly alleged that large farms receive the bulk of benefits from government programs, this finding requires the following rather extended analysis.

Table 5-3 contains data that permit additional inferences about the distribution of government payments. These data are percent distributions of annual cash receipts and direct government payments among the various sales classes. The time trend in percentage of cash receipts received was generally positive for the three largest sales classes, but was down for all of the classes below $100,000 of sales. Growth in the percentage of cash receipts was especially high for the largest class of farms selling over $500,000 per year, no doubt reflecting the period trend that farms were getting larger and more farms were moving into this class. The percentage of direct government payments going to the largest sales class did not increase as much over the period as it did for the next two largest classes, but they were all up sharply. The percentage increased mildly for farmers in the $40,000 to $100,000 range. For those classes below $40,000 of sales, however, the trend of the percentage of government payments was down sharply. The implication must be that the bulk of the government direct payments was going increasingly to those farms that produce from $40,000 to $500,000 of sales, not the largest farms nor the smallest as classified by sales. This result casts serious doubt on the widely held perception that farm programs systematically discriminate against middle-sized "family" farms.

Several possible explanations compete for the finding that farms with the largest sales did not share proportionately in direct government payments. The following are most likely. First, farms with the most sales were producing crops and livestock not covered by programs that yield government direct payments. Many very large farms across the country produce fruits and vegetables, poultry and eggs, and livestock products that do not have direct price support programs and thus would have been outside the direct payment pipeline.[7] The other side of the coin is that farms in the lower sales classes were enrolled in government programs to a much greater degree *because* they produce supported crops.

Second, even if producing government-supported crops, farmers in the largest sales class may have opted to remain outside government programs because of special marketing arrangements that are associated with size, or they were unwilling to bear the costs of enrolling in government programs such as meeting the acreage set-aside requirements. Examples of the former are very large cotton farms in California that have special marketing arrangements with foreigners and have opted not to be in government programs. On the latter point, if farms have high quality and homogeneous

TABLE 5-3 Cash Receipts and Direct Government Payments, by Value of Sales Class, 1975 to 1988

Year	*$500,000 and over*	*$250,000 to $499,999*[1]	*$100,000 to $249,999*[2]	*$40,000 to $99,999*	*$20,000 to $39,999*	*$10,000 to $19,999*	*$5,000 to $9,999*	*Less than $5,000*
			Cash Receipts (percentage distribution)					
1975	22.3	14.1	16.6	24.8	11.3	5.6	2.8	2.5
1976	23.9	15.0	17.1	23.7	10.3	5.1	2.6	2.3
1977	24.5	15.3	17.2	23.4	9.9	5.0	2.5	2.2
1978	27.3	17.0	18.1	21.4	8.2	4.1	2.2	1.8
1979	28.9	18.6	18.6	19.7	7.2	3.6	1.9	1.5
1980	28.8	20.1	19.4	18.7	6.6	3.3	1.7	1.3
1981	30.0	20.1	19.4	18.7	6.6	2.9	1.5	1.2
1982	32.4	15.2	25.1	16.5	5.4	2.8	1.5	1.1
1983	27.7	16.6	27.2	17.1	6.0	2.8	1.5	1.2
1984	34.2	17.8	23.3	15.1	4.6	2.5	1.5	1.0
1985	30.3	19.4	24.2	15.8	5.0	2.8	1.4	1.1
1986	34.4	18.4	23.0	14.3	4.7	2.7	1.4	1.0
1987	37.2	17.6	21.8	14.0	4.5	2.6	1.4	1.1
1988	36.6	18.0	22.0	13.6	4.7	2.6	1.4	1.0

			Direct Government Payments (percentage distribution)					
1975	7.0	7.9	13.0	28.6	17.3	10.1	6.7	9.4
1976	7.0	7.9	13.0	31.5	16.0	8.2	5.8	7.3
1977	5.7	10.1	16.8	34.0	15.3	6.9	5.3	5.9
1978	5.6	12.5	19.8	35.0	13.1	5.2	4.5	4.2
1979	6.4	13.9	20.9	33.5	12.2	4.9	4.2	3.9
1980	7.1	15.2	21.9	32.2	11.4	4.6	4.0	3.7
1981	7.7	15.2	21.9	32.2	11.4	4.6	4.0	3.7
1982	8.4	11.1	28.8	30.5	10.2	4.2	3.6	3.3
1983	11.8	19.2	34.3	22.2	7.1	3.1	0.9	1.4
1984	12.4	18.8	35.3	22.2	6.4	2.8	1.3	0.7
1985	10.4	19.5	31.3	24.7	9.0	3.0	1.4	0.9
1986	8.1	15.6	31.2	26.5	10.9	4.5	1.8	1.3
1987	7.7	15.6	30.7	26.9	9.6	5.1	2.7	1.6
1988	8.4	16.9	31.5	24.9	9.9	4.4	1.9	1.9

Notes: [1] For the years 1975–1981, data are for sales class $200,000 to $499,999. [2] For the years 1975–1981, data are for the sales class $100,000 to $199,999.

Source: U.S. Department of Agriculture, Agricultural and Rural Economy Division, Economic Research Service (1989), *Economic Indicators of the Farm Sector: National Financial Summary* (Washington, DC: September), pp. 42, 43.

land, it is more costly to reduce acreage under the required set-asides than if the land is more heterogeneous (Gardner and Howitt 1986).

Third, statutory limitations on payments that a farmer may receive from the government may have been binding on the largest farms to a greater extent than on farms that sold less. This would have induced more of the large farms to stay out of the program, and even if they were in it would have kept them from receiving a proportionate share of the government payments. (This issue will be discussed later in the chapter.)

All of these explanations would appear to have some validity a priori, and only further research can ferret out their importance.

Evidence from the Farm Costs and Returns Survey

The USDA Farm Costs and Returns Survey contains information for 1987 and 1988 not previously available on the distribution of direct government payments to those who *were enrolled* in price support programs.[8] The survey also reports on the amount of nonfarm income earned by different economic classes of enrolled farm operators.

These data have been analyzed by Shaffer and Whittaker who indicate that many of the nation's largest farms were indeed outside the government programs in 1987 and 1988. They show that it was the high-income farmers *enrolled* in government programs who received the bulk of the direct payments resulting from price supports (Shaffer and Whittaker 1990a). These data are not inconsistent with the census data already analyzed that indicated that small farmers received a much greater fraction of their incomes in direct government payments. Recall that Tables 5-2 and 5-3 show the distributions of average net income and direct payments received for *all* farmers, not just those enrolled in government programs. Therefore, if the complete population of the largest farmers did not receive a proportionate share of government payments going to all farmers, but large-scale farmers enrolled received a greater than proportionate share of payments made to all enrolled farmers, then it must be true that many of the large-scale farmers must not have been eligible for payments, either because they produced nonprogram crops or livestock, because they were not enrolled, or because the payment limit must have been binding.

In 1988, the USDA paid out about $14.5 billion in direct payments under the farm commodity programs (Shaffer and Whittaker 1990a, p. 30). Not included in this total are benefits captured by farmers from trade restrictions of various kinds that limit supply (such as the quota on sugar and peanut imports), domestic supply restrictions (such as the dairy, peanut, and tobacco quotas), and surplus disposal programs (such as Public Law 480, foreign food aid, and domestic food stamps). Thus, it is clear that direct payments significantly understate the total income transfers from taxpayers and consumers to farm operators and those who own farmland. However, Shaffer and Whittaker believe that the total transfers may not be distributed very differently from the direct payments, although a larger number of farmers receive benefits than receive direct payments since a farmer does not have to enroll in a program to capture benefits from trade barriers and demand enhancement programs (Shaffer and Whittaker 1990a, p. 30).

The USDA survey reported that "farm" businesses (defined as farm operators and partners) received about $9 billion in 1987. Thus, over one-third of the payments (about $5.5 billion) went to other individuals, presumably farmland owners who are not themselves farmers but who lease or rent land to farm operators.[9] Very little is known about the economic characteristics of these landowners who are not themselves farmers—what their precise ties are to agriculture, what their professions are, or what their incomes are (Shaffer and Whittaker 1990a, p. 30). What is clear is that they are not farmers, and therefore, a sizable fraction of farm subsidies cannot be justified in the name of income support for farm families since farm families do not receive it.

Table 5-4 contains economic characteristics of those farm operators in the survey who received the largest government payments.[10] Several striking conclusions emerge. The approximately 60,000 farm operators receiving the highest direct payments collected 42 percent of the total payments even though they were only 3.6 percent of the farmers enrolled. The top 18 percent of farmers received about 90 percent of all payments. Hence, payments were highly skewed toward a relative few but high-income enrolled farmers, suggesting a highly inequitable distribution. To operators in the top group, the average payment was over $75,000, or about 78 percent of their average net cash farm income of nearly $97,000. These farmers averaged nearly $20,000 of nonfarm income and had an average net worth of over $745,000 each. The conclusion is that a large fraction of government payments are going to high-income and wealthy farm operators enrolled in government programs.

The average income and wealth figures drop off in every category for farmers in the top 18 percent class compared with those in the top 3.6 percent class, but those figures are still large compared with the income and the wealth of average Americans living in either rural or urban areas.

An even more complete picture of the inequity of farm programs is provided by the data in Table 5-5 for 1988. Only about 36 percent of the farms included in the survey received any direct payments at all. Consistent with the data presented in Tables 5-2 and 5-3, most of those not receiving

TABLE 5-4 Economic Characteristics of Farm Operators Receiving the Largest Government Payments, 1987

	Top 3.6%	*Top 18%*
Percentage of direct payments	42%	90%
Average direct payments	$75,586	$32,367
Average net cash farm income	$96,942	$49,293
Average nonfarm income	$19,705	$16,536
Average net worth per farmer	$745,814	$466,817
Approximate number of farm operators	60,000	300,000

Source: Shaffer and Whittaker (1990a), "Average Farm Incomes: They're Highest among Farmers Receiving the Largest Direct Government Payments," p. 30.

TABLE 5-5 Distribution of Direct U.S. Government Payments to Farm Operators, 1988

Percentage of farmers receiving payments	*Average payments to farm operators ranked by level of direct payments*[1]	*Percent share of total direct payments*	*Average net cash farm income*	*Average net worth per farmer*
3.6%	$61,623	42.9%	$96,000	$804,000
3.6	28,034	19.8	41,000	514,000
3.6	17,831	12.5	34,000	383,000
3.6	12,584	8.9	25,000	380,000
3.6	8,932	6.3	19,000	316,000
3.6	6,112	4.0	21,000	320,000
3.6	4,014	2.9	12,000	233,000
3.6	2,331	1.7	11,000	244,000
3.6	1,230	0.9	6,000	218,000
3.6	432	0.3	7,000	222,000
64.0	—	—	12,000	283,000
All	14,257	100.0	27,000	362,000

Note: [1] Direct payments include deficiency, conservation reserve, and disaster transfers to farmers.

Source: Data are from the USDA Farm Cost and Returns Survey of more than 13,000 farm operators. James D. Shaffer and Gerald W. Whittaker (1990b), "The Distribution of Direct Payments to Farm Operators in 1987 and 1988: Some Questions about Policy Objectives," Discussion paper no. FAP90-08 (Washington, DC: National Center for Food and Agricultural Policy, Resources for the Future, May).

payments consist of farmers who for one reason or another elected not to participate in government programs. This point has important equity implications not widely understood by the public: Direct subsidies do not reach the majority of American farmers.[11] Further, of those enrolled, payments were made disproportionately to operators with the highest average farm income. For example, the 3.6 percent of the farms with the highest average payments of $61,623 each had average net cash farm income exceeding $96,000. Payments to this 3.6 percent of enrolled farm operators accounted for almost 43 percent of the total amount of direct payments disbursed. No doubt it is the inequity of the payments distribution that has prompted congressional imposition of statutory payment limitations.

What are the major implications of the foregoing analysis for economic efficiency and equity? Because the percentage of total farm operator incomes consisting of direct government payments is much larger for low-income than for high-income farmers, the income support programs have decidedly negative effects on efficiency. At the margin, the payment system encourages resources to remain in agricultural production on small inefficient farms—resources that would be more productive outside the sector. At the same time, of those farmers enrolled in government programs, the bulk of the income support payments goes to the highest-income and wealthiest farm operators. Thus, income support programs have no redeeming value on either efficiency or equity grounds.

The Ineffectiveness of Payment Limits

For many years the government has placed a ceiling on the amount of direct payments that an eligible agricultural "person" may legally receive through government programs. As stated by Congress, these payment limits have two goals: to reduce farm program costs, and to improve equity between family farms and large commercial operations.[12]

In the 1981 Agriculture and Food Act and in the 1985 Food Security Act (FSA), the sum of conventional deficiency and land diversion payments was limited to $50,000 annually per eligible person, while disaster payments were restricted to $100,000 each. Other agricultural program payments authorized in the 1985 FSA, such as marketing-loan deficiency and inventory-reduction payments, were not initially included in these limits. However, the marketing loans for cotton and rice in particular came under sharp public criticism on equity grounds when it was revealed that many large-scale cotton and rice producers received large amounts in deficiency payments in 1986 (Becker 1986, p. 13). Congress responded to strong public pressure by passing the 1987 Continuing Appropriations Act, which placed a $250,000 per person per year limit on all program payments except those for the long-term Conservation Reserve Program.[13]

Payment policy under the 1985 act provided for another exception to the payment ceiling known as the "Findley Amendment." The USDA could exercise its authority to reduce loan rates more than 5 percent annually to make U.S. commodities more competitive in world markets. The USDA, in fact, did apply the amendment in 1986 by lowering wheat and feed grain loan rates by an additional 20 percent. The effect was to increase the gap between target prices and the effective loan rate, thus boosting the amount of the deficiency payment. The large producers argued successfully that deficiency payments so created should not be restricted by the payment limit. The result was an even more severe skewing in the distribution of payments. For example, even though only 6 percent of corn producers received more than the $50,000 limit, 24 percent of the total corn payments went to those same producers (Becker 1986, p. 14). Because of the marketing-loan provision in the 1985 act for rice and cotton, the skew was even greater for these crops. The 12 percent of cotton farmers receiving over the $50,000 limit got about 55 percent of the cotton payments. The 20 percent of the rice farmers receiving over the limit got 61 percent of the rice payments.

The 1990 Food, Agriculture, Conservation, and Trade Act (FACTA) continues the $50,000 limit for deficiency payments but imposes a $75,000 limit on marketing-loan deficiency payments. The total of all payments is still subject to the $250,000 limit enacted in 1987.[14]

In 1988, when the Gramm–Rudman–Hollings deficit-reduction legislation threatened across-the-board sequestration cuts, lawmakers recognized the potential inequity between farming operations of different sizes. It was estimated that an 8.7 percent sequester in fiscal year 1988 would result in an 8.8 percent cut in net income for farms in the bottom 25 percent ranked by size, a 31 percent cut in the 26–50 percent category, a 10 percent cut in the 51–75 percent category, and only a 4 percent cut in the 75–100 percent category.[15] The heavier burdens of the sequesters on the medium-sized farms simply added to the public perception that payment programs favor operators of large farms.

Across-the-board reductions in payments to farmers were mandated by the 1990 Omnibus Budget Reconciliation Act, which had the grand design of reducing the federal budget deficit. This act contained governmental cost-saving provisions that include, a 15 percent reduction on acreage for which deficiency payments may be earned, loan origination fees or assessments on nonprogram crops, deficiency payments based on a twelve-month-average price instead of the five-month-average that had been used historically,[16] and other changes to either increase receipts or decrease outlays.[17]

An interesting equity problem strictly within the agricultural sector has arisen because of the way market price is treated in the calculation of deficiency payments for wheat, cotton, rice, and the feed grains.[18] The USDA calculates an average *national* market price that applies to all wheat producers in the country and then uses this national price for determining deficiency payments. Suppose the market price is higher than the loan rate so the difference between market price and the target price becomes the basis for computing the deficiency payment. This means that the per bushel deficiency payment is identical for all wheat producers. However, wheat is not a homogeneous commodity and different types command different market prices. For example, producers of durum and white wheat get a higher price in the market but also receive the same deficiency payment as all other wheat producers. In fact, it may be possible for durum and white wheat to have higher market prices than even the target price, but their producers still receive the deficiency payment. It seems far-fetched that Congress intended to treat producers of different types of wheat in this inequitable way or that taxpayers should pay deficiency payments to producers who receive market prices higher than those targeted for income support.

A question has always existed about how efficacious payment limits are because of ambiguities in the regulations, high enforcement costs, and loopholes that allow circumvention of the limits that Congress imposes. For example, it is not always clear who a "person" is for purposes of determining eligibility. The regulations require that a program payment recipient be "actively engaged" in either farm labor or management, representing an effort to include both farm owners and farm operators who might be renting farms. But it is sometimes difficult and costly to prove that a party does not have an active engagement in farming. Consequently, "entities" have been created fictitiously that qualify as persons to receive up to the payment limit, even though several entities may be affiliated with a single farm unit. Obviously, the goal of creating these entities is to circumvent the payment limitation regulations.

Illustrative of what is going on, Burton reports a case in which a farmer divided his farm holdings into many smaller pieces and used seventeen relatives, ten employees, thirteen corporations, three partnerships, and six trusts, each of which collected payments at or under the limitation. The government sent checks to these separate entities, who would then turn over the funds to the partnership representing the farm owner. In this way, the real farm owner received millions of dollars in government payments. The

USDA challenged this arrangement as an abuse of the regulations, but in court the partnership claimed that the USDA knew what was happening and gave its approval. This view seems to be corroborated by the fact that the agency's records show that it routinely approved many of the steps the partnership took before the final challenge (Burton 1990).

But since abuses of the payment-limit provisions have become so notorious, the USDA has begun to prosecute blatant violators. In a CBS telecast of "60-Minutes" on December 8, 1991, Secretary of Agriculture Edward Madigan reported that the USDA had initiated over 3,100 lawsuits against farmers who are alleged to have created unlawful entities to receive government payments.

The payment limitation was changed by the 1990 FACTA, which gives the secretary discretion to count spouses of farm operators as eligible persons who may receive the payment limit. Secretary Yeutter announced in early January 1991 that the USDA would allow spouses to be considered separate persons for the 1991 through 1995 crop years. Secretary Yeutter said:

> *During the past several years, many farm organizations have brought to my attention the manner in which payment limitations have adversely affected family farms. I believe my decision today will provide for a much more reasonable and equitable treatment of spouses . . . they will be treated exactly as two siblings who are farming together.*[19]

There has always been public dissatisfaction with large government payments going to wealthy farmers. In the congressional deliberations on all recent farm bills, attempts have been made to tighten up on payment limits. It has often been proposed that farmers exceeding some income limit would receive no payments at all. In other words, payments would be "targeted" to farmers who really needed them to reach some modicum level of income. However, so far all such efforts have been beaten back either in the agricultural committees when new legislation was considered or by defeating targeting amendments when the bills were voted on by members of Congress.

The underlying reasons for the failure of targeting to be adopted are somewhat complex. One is that the equity case for targeting is incomplete, since information on precisely who gets the payments has been lacking. It is not known, for example, what the incomes are of landowners who receive payments but who are not farm operators. However, this argument cannot be stretched very far since the survey data already discussed indicate that a large fraction of payments goes to wealthy enrolled farmers. A more likely explanation for the rejection of targeting is that members of Congress, and particularly those on the agriculture committees, are simply defending turf, which includes making income transfers to important constituents and political supporters. The reasons officially given by the agricultural committees for rejecting targeting, however, are that economic efficiency will be thereby enhanced. How can this be?

Some Tradeoffs between Equity and Efficiency

Payment Limits and Economic Efficiency

Placing a ceiling on incomes beyond which farmers would be ineligible to receive price support payments has implications for resource-use efficiency. Two impacts work at cross-purposes. Given that a payment program exists, one impact will be to reduce the average size of farm below the level that would exist if all farmers received the same payment per unit of output. For incomes above the limit, there will be no government payment. Even the average payment per unit of output will be lower the larger the output as long as the limit is in effect. Therefore, the first effect is to discriminate against larger farms and cause economies of size to be sacrificed. The sector will produce at higher costs and will not be as efficient as would be the case if all farmers were treated the same per unit of output.

It was argued in Chapter 2, however, that the payment programs induce resources to remain in the sector that otherwise would have more productive employments outside. Therefore, any policy, such as payment limits, that reduces the marginal returns to resources will induce the movement of some of them out of the sector. Therefore, resource-use efficiency between sectors will be improved. Empirical studies are needed to sort out the net effect of these two efficiency impacts of payment limits.

Furthermore, and very important politically, government programs may not accomplish their stated purposes if targeting induces farmers to remain out of government programs. Any farmer facing a payment limitation must face a tradeoff—bear the costs of the program restrictions and receive the benefits associated with enrollment, or opt out of the program altogether. If the forgone profits resulting from a payment limit become too high, farmers simply will not enroll. In this regard, it is not only the payment limitation costs that are relevant. Perhaps even more significant are the costs of complying with the acreage set-asides described in Chapter 3. If farmers elect not to enroll in the government programs for either of these reasons, and they are free to produce all they wish, production can be expected to increase. Market prices would fall and benefits would be conferred on consumers.

It does not necessarily follow, however, that aggregate government program payments would decline. Since deficiency payments on many commodities are the difference between target price and the higher of the loan rate and the market price, if loan rates are kept low to keep American farmers competitive in world markets, then the market price would determine the level of deficiency payments. If farmers are out of government programs and not restricted by acreage set-asides, then market prices might well be lower and deficiency payments higher than if more farmers were enrolled. Thus, it is not clear whether more severe payment limits, tighter targeting of payments to small-scale farmers, or more stringent acreage set-asides will increase or decrease the cost of government programs. These questions need to be explored empirically with simulation models that estimate the production and price effects of targeting payments.

The environmental impacts are less ambiguous and, in fact, came up in deliberations over the 1990 FACTA. An amendment was proposed by strange cooperators, conservative Rep. Armey (R-TX) and liberal Rep. Schumer (D-NY), to target program payments to small-scale family farmers. The amendment produced an idiosyncratic coalition of opponents to targeting consisting of the Agriculture Committee in the House and the environmental community, normally antagonists in the political arena (Gugliotta 1990). In exchange for keeping the provisions in the bill that environmentalists wanted (water quality, penalties for draining and planting wetlands, and wetland easements) and for including environmental measures still outstanding before the committee (pesticide record keeping, compliance with conservation regulations, pesticide use to improve appearance of produce, labeling organic foods, and prohibitions on overseas sale of banned pesticides), the committee wanted the support of environmentalists to kill the amendment. In fact, the Armey–Schumer amendment was defeated, 263 to 159.

Strange irony that environmentalists ended up supporting subsidies to rich farmers, a policy normally anathema to them:

> *"These farmers are people who are very, very rich," Representative Schumer said in defense of the amendment. "If they need a subsidy, everybody needs a subsidy." . . . Schumer and other supporters emphasized that the measure affected only 21,000 of the nation's 2.2 million farmers and could save the government up to $700 million per year in program payments. (Gugliotta 1990, p. A6)*

But given the highly skewed distribution of program payments among farmers, the question is why the House as a whole voted to defeat the amendment. It is true that many representatives have farm and environmental constituencies that they depend on for political support, but the explanation is probably more complex. Many members of Congress were persuaded that the commodity programs have goals other than those of maintaining or increasing farm incomes and ensuring environmental quality.[20] If the wealthy farmers opted out of farm programs because payments were withdrawn, the government's ability to ensure a stable food supply and low food prices and to realize many of the environmental benefits now linked to program participation could be much more limited.

The 160-acre Limitation in Irrigation Policy

This efficiency–equity trade-off has its counterpart in irrigation water policy, which should be discussed here although the environmental aspects are treated more completely in Chapter 10. The 1902 Reclamation Act authorized the federal government to build and manage water projects in the West. Farmers can receive subsidized water from a federal project as long as they reside on irrigated farms within the confines of the project and own no more than 160 acres each to which the federal water would be applied. This acreage limit is called the 160-acre limitation.

The act's objective was essentially to widely distribute subsidized water to "family" farmers who lived on the land. Any farmer owning more than 160 acres of irrigated land (later amended to be 160 each for farmer and spouse) called "excess land," had ten years to sell it at a price reflecting the value of the land before the project was built. This price was fixed at the raw land value to prevent the farmer from capturing the benefits of subsidized water through capitalization of the created economic rents into land values as soon as the distribution of water was announced.

In every farm community that received subsidized water, these policies shifted thousands of dollars of wealth among farmers. A farmer with excess land had strong incentives to circumvent the rules, and as with deficiency payment limits, the same strategies were employed. Additional farm entities were created by giving land to other family members or employees, each of whom could qualify for subsidized water, but the land would remain under the operating control of the farmer. Another loophole was an interpretation of the rules that permitted farmers to lease land receiving subsidized water. This enabled farmers to meet the ownership rule and yet achieve a total operating acreage that could efficiently utilize economies of size such as heavy machinery. Of course, the distribution of benefits from subsidized water on the leased acreage depended on the local land lease market, but in most cases the benefits were divided by the landowner and the lessee (see Huffaker and Gardner 1986a). In any case, opponents of subsidies to wealthy farmers claim this practice thwarts the purposes of reclamation subsidies to aid family farmers.

The Bureau of Reclamation has long been criticized for lax enforcement of the acreage limitation rules (Taylor 1975). Especially in California's Central Valley, where farms are very large by almost every standard and where the federal Central Valley Project allocates millions of acre-feet of water annually, enforcing the acreage limitation has been very controversial.

The upshot of the controversy was that, in 1982, the Reclamation Reform Act (RRA) was passed and the acreage limitation rules were changed (see Huffaker and Gardner 1986b). The RRA increased the acreage limitation but redefined it to include leased as well as owned land.[21] The residency requirement was eliminated.

Farmers who exceed the relevant acreage limitation must pay the "full cost" of the water, rather than the subsidized price. In many areas of the West, the full taxpayer cost of project water may exceed the subsidized price by ten times or more.[22] Thus, it is clear that the RRA will produce a shift in the size of farms, unless the regulations can be circumvented.[23] The costs of leasing land to achieve economies of scale beyond the 960-acre limit for an individual farmer will be very high if the full cost of water exceeds the subsidized price by a substantial amount. Thus, there will be strong economic pressures to increase farm size up to but no more than 960 acres unless powerful economies of size can more than offset the increased water costs. It seems to be clear that operating costs will be higher, and the consumers will pay higher prices for food than if the acreage limitation did not exist.

Notes

1. One of the most persuasive is Bertrand de Jouvenel (1952).
2. This would be even more true if the number of people who are unemployed in the nonfarm sector were included in the divisor to calculate average income. Official rates of unemployment are higher in the nonfarm than in the farm sector.
3. This approach to equity has a long history in economics going back to the founding fathers, Adam Smith, David Ricardo, and Thomas Malthus. They were interested in understanding why landowners were getting an increasing fraction of the national income as time passed whereas wages going to labor appeared to be fixed near the subsistence level.
4. However, one must be careful about making such facile generalizations. Alston and Hatton show, for example, that real earnings differences between agricultural and manufacturing laborers in the United States were much smaller (only 10 to 15 percent lower in agriculture) between the two world wars than is commonly believed. The principal reason for the exaggerated difference is that payment-in-kind income available to farm workers, and not included in their incomes, was not available to urban workers. See Alston and Hatton (1991, p. 96).
5. Average income figures represent *families* before 1966 and *households* thereafter. No apparent reasons suggest that this change in the accounting unit has biased the results, however.
6. These net income data are in nominal terms. In real terms, with the nominal amounts corrected for inflation, the increases for the top classes would be substantially less, and for the lower classes, there would be even higher net income losses than are indicated in Table 5-2.
7. This is not to say that these large farms were not benefited by other government programs that do not provide direct payments such as marketing orders, tariff protection, and production and trade quotas.
8. Approximately 13,000 farm operators were sampled in the survey. By criteria utilized to define the population of farms from which the sample was drawn, there were 1,671,786 farms in 1987 and 1,764,088 in 1988.
9. In 1982, for example, only 59 percent of all U.S. farms were operated by farmers who owned all the land they operated, and only 35 percent of total farm acreage was cultivated by farmers who owned all their land. U.S. Department of Agriculture (1986), *Agricultural Statistics* (Washington, DC), Tables 536 and 537.
10. Some further clarification is needed if the data in Table 5-4 are to be clearly

understood. Farm operators are ranked by the amount of direct payments they received from government programs in 1987. The top 3.6 percent of these farmers are then identified and several characteristics are measured for this group as given in the table. The same measurements were also made for the top 18 percent similarly identified.

11. Of course, this does not argue that farmers outside government programs are not affected by them in any way. Those not participating in government programs may be affected if market prices are altered by programs, which they most assuredly are, but the effect is indirect rather than direct. Farmers outside of government programs had an average of only $12,000 of net cash farm income, which was less than half the average of $27,000 for all farmers included in the survey. Still, the average net worth of the farmers of this group was $283,000, a sizable sum.

12. For a brief history of payment limits, see U.S. Senate (1988), *The Administration and Enforcement of the $50,000 Per Person Payment Limitation for Farm Programs,* Senate Hearing 101-595 (Washington, DC) Appendix 1.

13. See United States Statutes at Large Public Law 97–98.

14. U.S. Senate (1990b), *Food, Agriculture, Conservation, and Trade Act of 1990,* Report no. 101-357 (Washington, DC: July 6), Title 11—General Commodity Provisions, Subtitle B—Payment Limitations, Section 1111.

    It is interesting that the FACTA for the first time imposed payment limits on wool and mohair producers. In 1991, payments for each program were limited to $200,000 per eligible person.

15. U.S. House of Representatives (1987), Amending the Food Security Act of 1985, and For Other Purposes, Report no. 100-497 (Washington, DC: December 21), p. 6.

16. Recall that the deficiency payment is based on the difference between the target price and the market price, as long as the market price is greater than the loan rate. Since the twelve-month-average price is usually higher than the five-month-average price just after harvest, using the former would produce a lower deficiency payment. Because the 1990 legislation was enacted after much of the winter wheat crop was planted, however, Congress permitted two options for calculating deficiency payments for wheat. The winter wheat option may use the twelve-month-average market price for calculating the deficiency payment, but is not subject to the removal of 15 percent of the acreage base as required by the Budget Reconciliation Act. Under this option, the deficiency payment was expected to be $1.40 per bushel of eligible production. Under the standard option, which automatically applies from 1992 to 1995, deficiency payments will be paid only on 70 percent of the base acreage (the base acreage minus both the 15 percent budget act reduction and the 15 percent normal acreage reduction), and the average market price is figured

on the five-month basis. The deficiency payment under the standard option is expected to be $1.47 per bushel of eligible production.

17. U.S. House of Representatives (1990), *Omnibus Budget Reconciliation Act of 1990,* Report no. 101-964 (Washington, DC).

18. Nuckton and Gardner (1992).

19. U.S. Department of Agriculture, Office of Public Affairs (1991), "Spouses Considered Separate 'Persons' for Payment Limitation Purposes in 1991," *Selected Speeches and News Releases* (Washington, DC: January 3–9), p. 15.

20. U.S. Senate, *FACTA.*

21. The RRA categorizes recipients of project water into "qualified recipients" and "limited recipients." The former are entities benefiting twenty-five individuals or less, and they are entitled to irrigate up to 960 acres with subsidized water. The latter group are entities, such as corporations, which benefit more than twenty-five individuals, and they may operate only up to 640 acres with subsidized water.

22. See U.S. Department of the Interior (1980), *Acreage Limitation,* Draft Environmental Impact Statement, Westwide Report (Washington, DC), Appendix G—Full Cost Pricing Option.

23. This may well prove to be the case. A 1990 report by the General Accounting Office noted that the J. G. Boswell agricultural company had evaded the new limits by placing its 23,000-acre Boston Ranch in California into 326 employee "trusts," thus remaining eligible to receive subsidized water while retaining management control. Davis (1992a, p. 530).

PART 2

The U.S. Congress and Agricultural Support Programs

6

Why Do We Have Farm Programs?

Given that farm price support programs are both wasteful and inequitable, why do these policies exist and, perhaps even more of a puzzle, why do they persist?[1] If they reduce average standards of living and benefit mostly rich landowners, why don't American voters, through their elected representatives, get rid of them? Is it simply a matter of public ignorance about what is occurring or is there something more fundamental in our political structure that systematically causes farm support to be created and then endured? Robert Paarlberg (1989) has provided the most complete discussion of these questions, and his work will serve as a point of departure for the discussion that follows.

Paarlberg examines three possible explanations for farm programs. The first has its historical and philosophical roots in the value systems of most Americans, who regard farming as deserving of public support. Running a family farm is considered to be a morally superior way of life that would probably not persist in its present form without governmental subsidy.[2] Paarlberg (1989, p. 1157) calls this the "ethnocentric" explanation of why farm income support exists.

The second is known as the implicit or social contract explanation. In this framework, agricultural policy represents a rational and efficient agreement or contract between the agricultural sector of the economy and the remainder of the body politic. The elements of policy are the terms of trade of an implicit transaction from which both sides gain. In other words, the broader society protects and subsidizes the agricultural sector as a quid pro quo for certain benefits received, such as dependable, low-priced food and fiber, viable rural communities, and exemplary citizens. It is obvious that the first and second explanations are related, except that, in the social contract view, the community anticipates getting something in return for its support of the agricultural sector.

The third explanation is known as public choice, which postulates that special interests in the body politic, especially in the agricultural sector, successfully manipulate the political system and thereby capture wealth transfers from taxpayers and consumers. An important argument in this explanation is that political markets that allocate subsidies to various sectors of the economy (including agriculture) are inefficient and have substantially reduced living standards for the average American.

The question of which explanations are valid, if any, has important and far-reaching implications for the set of policies under review here. If political markets produce a social contract with specific policies that rationally and efficiently respond to perceived national needs and from which all gain, then it is unlikely that these policies should be reformed or changed. This would suggest that the ostensibly inefficient and inequitable consequences of subsidies discussed in previous chapters must be an incomplete depiction of the real world. Indeed, if they exist, these costs must be more than offset by largely noneconomic and unmeasurable, and thus unconsidered, social benefits. But if policies are inefficient and inequitable as alleged and the public is ignorant of the real costs, then an educational effort as well as policy reform might produce salutary results.

In principle, of course, these explanations need not necessarily be competing and mutually exclusive and, in fact, may be complementary. For example, one explanation may be more valid in accounting for the origins of certain policies whereas another may be more compelling in explaining why they persist. In any event, a further exploration of these issues and their implications is warranted and is the topic of this chapter.

Support for Farm Programs as a Belief System

The ethnocentric rationale for policy support to agriculture incorporates the Jeffersonian notion of the moral merit of the yeoman farmer as exemplary citizen and efficient producer. Agricultural scholars Browne and Bonnen (1989) refer to this vision as a set of prescriptive beliefs that constitute the fundamentalist agrarian vision. And even though Browne and Bonnen themselves believe the vision to be largely a myth, they agree it is pervasive enough in the American psyche to be significant as a causal explanation for farm programs. Browne and Bonnen explain:

> *An agrarian myth developed in the United States in the early years of the Republic and continues to communicate a very simple image of farming throughout society. Agricultural scholars have criticized its lack of realism for over 50 years. Selective belief systems evolved and served to sustain segments of a geographically isolated and economically vulnerable society by developing unifying, utopian images of contemporary*

> *social issues and interests. . . . Today, with a farm-based political majority long gone, this agrarian myth persists. It persists precisely because most people have limited experience with agriculture and its economic issues, and because those in agriculture have an important stake in romanticizing its social role and seeking widespread public support. . . . Features of modern communication make it possible for an active minority to proselytize and keep an agrarian myth vital and supportable even when its basic tenets are disputable and under consistent intellectual attack. ((1989, p. 9–10)*

The agrarian myth does not persist only because those who gain from it successfully promote it, however. The message seems to fall on willing ears. Every state has many farmers, and nearly all Americans have a rural ancestry, many of them only one or two generations removed. Many immigrants came to the United States with the intention of becoming farmers and assuming ownership of "cheap" land. And those of us reared in rural areas tend to romanticize about our childhoods and naturally identify with those still attempting to maintain that lifestyle.

Evidence of this romanticism abounds in the printed media, movies, and popular songs. Some of this nostalgia is captured in the lyrics of this contemporary folk song, *Georgia Mules and Country Boys*:

I know the world goes on; we can't keep living in the past.
Still, there's a thing or two I sure do wish could last.
I've got a crazy case of blue nostalgia,
Rememberin' mules and corn fields out of my past.

CHORUS:
Well, you don't see many mules these days.
You don't see many mules.
And you don't see many old boys baling hay.
I ain't knockin' progress,
but it hurts me some to say
that Georgia mules and country boys
are fadin' fast away.

I see lots of kids these days in jeans of faded blue.
They never saw a mule, but they're nostalgic too.
They're tryin' hard to capture what is missing,
although they know deep down those days are through.

CHORUS

How many girls do you know that have ever milked a cow?
How many boys that ever walked behind a plow?
And who have you seen lately churnin' butter?
Who do you even know that might know how?

CHORUS[3]

Part of the mystique goes beyond the social and political merit achieved by people who tend the land. It was, and still is, widely believed that farmers are disadvantaged economically compared with their city cousins and thus deserve governmental intervention designed to even things up. It is widely perceived that farmers have lower incomes on average and face great volatility in prices and yields. They have little or no control over the prices of the output they sell or the inputs they purchase, and farmers often are victimized by ruthless monopolistic businessmen who trade with them. Moreover, farmers must daily contend with the vicissitudes of nature and have fewer of life's amenities and comforts than their urban counterparts. If all this were true, and many believe it is, it is small wonder that farmers seem to draw sympathy and can find willing allies in the political arena where farm policy is fashioned (Browne and Bonnen 1989, p. 13).

Besides, every person has contact with farming, direct and indirect. All consume food and therefore should have a vital concern about what happens on the farm. In 1980, 20 percent of American workers were involved in farm production or food distribution service (Browne 1988, p. 4). Further, 17.9 percent of the 1984 GDP was in some way related to the agricultural sector, broadly defined.

This close identification of the average American with farms and farmers shows itself in polls indicating broad support for farm programs. Jordan and Tweeten (1987) find that a majority of citizens across a broad spectrum of incomes, races, and social classes believe in "agricultural fundamentalism" and support programs they believe will help farmers, especially family farmers. Interestingly, the degree of support is significantly greater among women than men, whites than blacks, the aged than the young, the married than the never married, the less educated than college graduates, families with low incomes than those with high incomes, conservatives than liberals, voters than nonvoters, those who attend religious services than those who do not, members of labor unions than nonmembers, those who have taken no course in economics than those who have, and those who are close to agriculture compared with those who are more removed. It would be interesting to attempt to account for these distinctions, but this would take us far afield. Besides, public opinion surveys are notoriously unreliable since respondents are not required to make trades or give anything up. Words of support or opposition come easy when they are free. And there is no way of knowing the intensity of stated preferences. Hence, it is not surprising that a majority of those surveyed in the Jordan–Tweeten study said that while they support farm programs, they would be unwilling to pay higher food prices to do so. Apparently they believe that farm programs do not really cost them anything.

These results were corroborated by another study, which used data from a national survey of public attitudes toward agriculture to estimate the structure of citizens' preferences for policies to preserve the family farm and support agriculture (Variyam et al. 1990). While the distribution of responses to particular survey questions indicated considerable support for agricultural policies, the support quickly eroded when the questions were asked in a context that revealed the true distribution of benefits and costs of these policies. This finding also casts doubt on the arguments sometimes heard suggesting citizens' altruistic motives in support of redistributive agricultural policies.

Robert Paarlberg explores some of the key elements of the ethnocentric thesis:

> *U.S. policy is said to protect agriculture because of something distinctive in our nation's ideology, a Jeffersonian belief in the unique virtue of small yeomen farmers. Alternatively, it is because of something distinctive in U.S. history, such as the original need to win support from southern agricultural states for the United States Constitution. Alternatively, it is because of something distinctive in our national political institutions, such as the separation of powers between the executive and Congress, which gives farm lobby groups multiple access to the policy process. (1989, p. 1157)*

Since all of these points have a plausible ring to them, it is not difficult to conjure up support for at least some of them. The problem is to know how potent they are as scientific explanations when evidence, from surveys like those reported, is largely judgmental and anecdotal. To admit the existence of ethnocentrism does not in any way indicate its explanatory power.

Indeed, Paarlberg raises the pivotal question for appraising the validity of the ethnocentric approach versus the alternatives. This explanation for farm programs might be more credible if farm subsidies were as distinctly American as are the attitudes and institutions incorporated into the American ethnocracy. What is observed, however, is that nearly all economically advanced countries have similar support programs that purport to aid farmers and farm families: Western Europe, Japan, Canada, Australia, and until recently, New Zealand. The levels of agricultural support in some of these countries even exceeds those in the United States, as explained in Chapter 2. But these countries have different histories and institutions and cannot be considered even remotely or prototypically American. There was only one Thomas Jefferson. Paarlberg says:

> *It does not seem to matter if they [countries] are culturally Protestant or Catholic, Christian or non-Christian, European or Asian. It does not seem to matter if their governmental form is a strong presidential system (as in France), a congressional–presidential separation of power system (as in the U.S.), or a parliamentary system without any separation of powers (as in Canada). Neither does it seem to matter if the industrial state is a one-party democracy (such as Japan), or a two-party democracy (Great Britain), or a multiparty democracy (Germany and Italy). Given the recent tendency for some states with authoritarian regimes (such as South Korea and Taiwan) to begin protecting farmers, the state in question may not even have to be democratic. (1989, pp. 1157–1158)*

This reasoning is compelling. Given the cultural and institutional diversity of countries where farm support programs exist, as well as the vacuity of explanatory power in the ethnocentric approach, other explanations must be sought if scientific understanding is to be acquired. Besides, the ethnocentric approach in the United States seems to contain contradictions. In its rhetoric at least, low-income disadvantaged farmers are entitled to special assistance. But how is it that nearly all price support and conservation programs confer the bulk of their benefits on wealthy farmers who sign up? If farm programs are a deliberate attempt to favor family farmers, why has society bungled the effort and produced programs that have conferred their largest gains on rich landowners? Congress has time and again refused to target policy benefits exclusively to low-income farmers. Why? There must be some other explanation for public subsidization of rich farmers.

The Public Choice Explanation for Farm Programs

An important point to understand is that agricultural policy is a complex web of quite distinct policies for individual and grouped commodities. Separate programs exist for wheat, feed grains, cotton, rice, soy beans, tobacco, dairy products, sugar, wool, honey, and peanuts. Other government support can be found in supply controls, such as marketing orders that regulate dairy and some fruit and nut producers. Why do separate programs exist? Public choice theory postulates that it was not simply the fortuitous and haphazard evolution of unrelated policies or the result of a deliberate social contract between society and agricultural producers.[4] Rather, separate programs derived predictably from the manipulation of the political system by special interest groups.

"Public choice" is an effort to apply economic reasoning to politics (Gwartney and Wagner 1988, p. 17). Political as well as economic decisions and processes are assumed to be dominated by rational and self-interested agents who interact and negotiate with each other. The preeminent founders of the public choice school, James Buchanan and Gordon Tullock state:

> *The voter who selects among political alternatives is the same person who selects among market alternatives. . . . The men and women working in government as politicians and bureaucrats are pretty much the same as their counterparts in the private sector. The self-interest postulate in public choice theory uproots the common belief that government creates new policy with the good of the whole always in mind. We see, rather, that political as well as market decisions are made based on individual interest. (1965, p. 38)*

"The point of departure for the literature on public choice is that policy outcomes result from people's pursuing their interests within a particular institutional or constitutional setting that constrains and shapes the specific expression of those interests" (Wagner 1989, p. 14). Thus, if interest groups have the constitutional option of using their available resources to buy political favors and if doing so is expected to yield higher returns to these resources than will alternative uses, they will engage in purposeful collective political action.[5] However, it isn't quite as easy as it sounds because of several problems inherent in joint or collective action in the political arena.

The Costs of Collective Action

First, the benefits of collective action are likely to fall unevenly on group members, benefiting some more than others. For example, assume that farmers are able to get governmental deficiency payments that are proportional to the marketable quantity of the crop, obviously favoring high-income farmers much more than low-income farmers. This may discourage the willing support of all group members. As Buchanan and Tullock (1965, p. 72) point out, only a decision process that requires unanimous agreement of all the participants can absolutely assure that all expect to gain from collective action in the political marketplace. If all beneficiaries of public action were required to pay for a pro rata share of the costs of such action, then unanimous agreement would guarantee that all expect to benefit. This principle was set forth by the Swedish economist Knut Wicksell (1986) as explained by Wagner:

> *Wicksell's suggestions were intended to prevent some people from undertaking projects only because they were being paid for through costs*

> *imposed upon others. . . . If people did not think that they were getting good value for their contributions, government would shrink in size. In other words, government would become subject to the same rules of economical conduct as private citizens. . . . In that order rights of ownership are well defined and protected, and resources get shifted from one use to another by agreement among the owners of those resources rather than through the use of the state by one subset of owners to abridge the rights of other owners. (1989, p. 211)*

So why don't we commonly observe unanimity in collective decisions? "The sheer weight of the costs involved in reaching decisions unanimously dictates some departure from the 'ideal rule'" (Buchanan and Tullock 1965, p. 96). If only a very few individuals had to negotiate differences and conflicts so that all could be better off, the bargaining costs of reaching a joint decision would likely be small. However, if many people have to reach agreement, the costs could be prohibitive. In fact, some individuals might choose not to participate in the collective decision at all,[6] producing the commonly observed result that small interest groups dictate the majority of all public policy (Wagner 1989, p. 126).

Concentrated Benefits and Diffused Costs

Probably the most potent of all public choice principles that contribute to explaining farm programs is "concentrated benefits and diffused costs." This principle contends that the political apparatus that creates and changes policy can be more effectively manipulated to redistribute income and wealth on behalf of an interest group if the beneficiaries are relatively small in number and individually have a large stake in the outcome, while those who pay for it are very numerous and individually have a small stake. For example, import quotas for sugar may have a very large impact on the income of a relatively few protected producers, while its costs are spread over many millions of consumers.

Soliciting political influence to transfer income is called rent-seeking by economists and is defined as "actions taken by individuals and groups to alter public policy in order to gain personal advantage at the expense of others" (Gwartney and Wagner 1988a, p. 22). Capturing a transfer in the public sector, however, may not be inexpensive, especially if there is strong competition for government favors. In principle, each competing interest group should be willing to pay an amount just less than or equal to the expected size of the transfer to obtain it. So the size of the transfer and the probability of obtaining it are significant factors in accounting for rent-seeking expenditures by interest groups (see Chapter 7).

Resources spent in the pursuit of these transfers, however, while beneficial from the viewpoint of the rent-seeker, could have been utilized to add to the total economic product of the community. Thus, rent-seeking expenditures that result only in the redistribution of income and wealth are largely wasted when it comes to increasing the average standard of living. The potential aggregate losses from resource expenditures by competing groups to capture rents from government favors are probably quite large in a constitutional environment that allows such favors.

The political process does not stop this kind of waste because those who pay for the transfers are generally the very numerous taxpayers and consumers who each have a relatively small individual stake. These individuals will allow their wealth to be confiscated as long as the individual costs of changing such political outcomes are greater than the amount of wealth taken. Suppose an interest group makes up 10 percent of the population. To provide a subsidy of $900 to each group member, it will cost the remaining 90 percent of the population just $100. In contrast, if the interest group is only 1 percent of the population, it will cost each of the remaining people just $9 to provide the same subsidy. Thus, the smaller the interest group, the less it costs the other population members to provide a subsidy. And the lower the cost of the subsidy, the less the likelihood that voters, taxpayers, and consumers will band together to oppose it. Despite the huge transfers via price supports to a relatively few farmers (approximately $26,000 in direct payments per farm in 1986), the costs per taxpayer for these subsidies (approximately $250) was much smaller. Individual taxpayers, therefore, had much less incentive to expend resources to block the transfers by political means than individual farmers had in promoting them.[7] "When the benefits are concentrated and the cost diffused, politicians will be led as if by an invisible hand to serve the purposes of the well-organized, concentrated beneficiaries. . . . While each such program individually imposes only a small drag on our economy, in the aggregate they drain our resources, threaten our standard of living, and impair our liberty" (Gwartney and Wagner 1988b, p. 21).

The same basic structure of agricultural policy has existed in the United States since the 1930s. Its staying power in the face of dramatic changes in the economy is quite remarkable. It is commonly argued by economists that over time the inefficiencies of subsidy and regulatory policies will rise as relative prices are increasingly distorted. The principle of concentrated benefits and diffuse costs answers why policies don't change. Ironically, "the greater the waste and inefficiency induced by a government program, the more difficult it is to modify or repeal the program" (Lee and Orr 1980, p. 115). Once subsidies are in place, repeal would involve concentrated losses and produce widely diffused gains. Therefore, those who stand to lose marshal resources to keep programs in place, while those who would gain a small amount do not consider it worthwhile to invest in program elimination. It is therefore not surprising that repeal of inefficient programs is so seldom successful.

The vote-seeking politicians are the intermediaries between competing interest groups, and between interest groups and taxpayers and consumers, in the market for income transfers. They receive higher gains from supporting the concentrated interests of an influential minority than from supporting the interests of a largely apathetic majority, especially in the form of campaign contributions and personal perquisites. This relationship between politician and clientele is of critical importance in the public choice paradigm. The assumption is that rival politicians seek to maximize their chances of remaining in office. But they must compete in a "political marketplace" and will succeed in their election aspirations only if they produce sufficient favors to satisfy their constituents.

How do special interest groups and politicians package government programs? Naturally, they make the benefits as highly visible and attractive and the costs as invisible as they can. For example, import quotas for sugar that create high prices for consumers are quite invisible because they do not involve government outlays like deficiency payments for wheat and rice do. Consequently, taxpayers and consumers fuss much less about quotas than they do about deficiency payments that deliver the same benefits to producers.

In fact, sugar import restrictions provide an excellent example of concentrated benefits and diffused costs. The U.S. Department of Commerce reported that in 1988 U.S. sugar quotas enriched 12,600 U.S. sugar beet and cane farms by $260,000 each (or roughly $76,000 for each farm operator producing beets and cane) (*Wall Street Journal* 1990b).

Rational Ignorance

It is clear that one of the challenges laid on public choice theory is to explain how it is possible that the concentrated interests of a small group can dominate those of a much larger group in the political arena. The reason is "rational ignorance" (Downs 1957). The assumption is that decision makers weigh the benefits and costs of becoming informed about a particular issue, and if their knowledge cannot be translated into more benefits than the costs of acquiring such knowledge, they will remain ignorant about the issue. Their ignorance is quite rational. This explains why so many voters are notoriously ignorant about candidates and issues, even at election time. They rationally calculate that the probability of their votes or their voices making any difference in an election and in the formation of policy is minuscule. Thus, the perceived benefits of becoming informed are small compared with the costs. They remain rationally ignorant and may not even vote.

On the other side of the political spectrum, politicians in democracies bear extremely high information costs. To be effective representatives, they should know something about a wide variety of issues. They don't lack information; their offices are inundated with information from a variety of sources, most of it slanted toward the interests of those who submitted it. Lobbyists arise to fill any information vacuum and may even economize on information retrieval for the politician. The significant point is that by heeding the information provided by interest groups, politicians increase their chances of being elected and reelected because the majority of their campaign support comes from these groups.

This is not to argue that the number of voters does not matter to the politicians. Obviously they must win elections to remain in office. But what counts in winning elections is acquiring resources from concentrated interests that may be utilized to influence voters, many of whom are largely ignorant about important issues confronting the body politic as a whole and are, therefore, easily led. This is accomplished generally by increasing the exposure of the politicians, particularly through television and radio spots.

As a scientific proposition, the great distinction between ethnocentric and public choice approaches is that the latter is capable of generating scientific hypotheses. Thus, public choice implications can be empirically tested. It is difficult to see how the ethnocentric approach could be similarly tested because of the absence of any theoretical underpinnings.

Empirical Support for Public Choice

Anderson and Hayami (1986) maintain that the public choice explanation has empirical support not evident with the other explanations. Consider the phenomenon of advanced countries protecting their farmers. Anderson and Hayami examined the variation in the rate of nominal protection given to the agricultural sector in fifteen industrial and industrializing countries from 1955 to 1980. The nominal rate of protection is defined as the internal-to-border price ratio. A full 70 percent of the variation in the nominal protection of agriculture among countries is explained by variables representing an industrializing economy. As industrialization increases, the production cost of industrial products declines relative to those produced in agriculture. But when this occurs, public policy increases the nominal rate of protection of agriculture. And this happens quite independently of a country's unique history, culture, and institutions and therefore does not support the ethnocentric explanation.

Paarlberg agrees that the Anderson–Hayami conclusion is compelling.

> *The explanatory power of this less parochial approach is impressive. This approach not only predicts that U.S. farmers will receive protection; it also predicts with some precision the average level of that protection, which crops will be protected the most, and the structural and demographic circumstances under which that protection will be extended. (Paarlberg 1989, p. 1158)*

Anderson and Hayami find that efficiently produced and exported crops will be protected less than those that compete with imports. U.S. wheat and feed grains are protected less than sugar and dairy products. When American farmers produced agricultural products relatively efficiently in the nineteenth century, it was industrial products that were more heavily protected. With the industrial revolution virtually complete in the mid-twentieth century, the nation then turned to subsidizing the rapidly declining agricultural sector more heavily than industry.[8]

It is significant, moreover, that the same phenomenon is occurring in nearly all advanced countries. But why? Obviously, pointing out the existence of the phenomenon is not the same as providing an explanation for it. Public choice principles, discussed earlier, provide an explanation, but they are not presented in a systematic and convincing way in Anderson and Hayami (1986).[9]

Farm Programs as a Social Contract

None of the Anderson–Hayami findings appears to support the social contract explanation. Why should the public at large necessarily be disposed to make a social contract with a declining economic sector? Perhaps one can reach for an explanation, but it is a long stretch. If a sector produces an "indispensable" commodity not available from any other source, then the nearer the sector approaches extinction, the greater the political favors will be needed to keep it alive. This rationale is used to explain why public policy protects endangered species of plants and animals. But why should it hold for a nation's farmers when alternative supplies of food and fiber are available from so many other countries? Japan defends its subsidies at least partially on grounds of national security, but we don't often hear this defense in the United States.

Still, of the three explanations accounting for the existence of farm programs, Paarlberg argues that the social contract approach is free from at least some of the difficulties he associates with the ethnocentric and public choice approaches. For example, he argues that the origins of most costly farm programs are not found in political maneuvering and pressure brought by farm interest groups but from federal initiatives to do something about "bad" economic conditions in the sector. In the case of the United States, it is said that it was Roosevelt's "brain trust," consisting chiefly of Ivy League professors, that played the critical role in creating the most important initial price supports through the 1933 Agricultural Adjustment Act (Paarlberg 1989, p. 1160). While this may have been true initially, surely it cannot be validly argued that Ivy League professors have played a prominent role in sustaining and extending these programs to the point where they are today.

In fact, "by the middle of Roosevelt's second term . . . newly dependent and increasingly well-organized farm lobby groups were beginning to transform what began as an improvised, emergency farm benefit program into a more permanent set of quasi-contractual farm protection entitlements" (Paarlberg 1989, p. 1160). But this is precisely the kind of policy evolution that the public choice paradigm predicts—one centered on the power of special interest lobbying and rent-seeking. Therefore, the strongest argument that can be made in support of the implicit contract explanation is that others besides farm pressure groups were instrumental in *originating* the subsidy programs. But, while granting this point, it is relevant to ask if there may not have been important political pressures that helped motivate the professors who were in powerful decision-making positions? President Roosevelt and most advisers around him were nothing if they were not political.

It is possible, of course, that Roosevelt's team envisaged some kind of a quid pro quo from the farming community that is the basis of the social contract approach. The country was in a desperate economic plight it is true, and there was a belief that something drastic was required to get it out of the morass into which it had fallen. However, it was not only agriculture that received special help from subsidy and relief programs that originated in the Depression era. What was the quid pro quo expected from those other sectors? A productive and prosperous economy from which all benefit, perhaps? Such a general and nondescript goal could be sought from any policy proposal and shifts the nature of the scientific test of a hypothesis derived from theory to a trivial tautology.

It is also asserted that the level of protection granted to U.S. farmers after the 1930s continued to depend on various macro-shocks and problems beyond their control: war, inflation, and recession (Paarlberg 1989, p. 1161). But even if true, does this evidence support the social contract thesis, which postulates a quid pro quo? What was agriculture contributing to the national welfare in return for special consideration during these periods of national stress? A much more plausible explanation for aid to farmers in war and depression is the contention by Robert Higgs (1987) that governmental power sharply expands during periods of national crisis. Higgs shows that major expansions in government programs occurred during the Civil War, World War I, the Great Depression, and World War II. It would have been surprising indeed had federal power and influence not extended to agriculture. However, the exact responses of government to problems in the agricultural sector during national crises have not been carefully documented.

More to the point of this inquiry, what is the mechanism by which any crisis gets translated into favorable government policy for certain groups? A trading of favors as postulated by the social contract explanation? This, it is argued, would minimize the opposition of competing groups that may not be so disadvantaged. But if there is a quid pro quo in governmental support, the social contract devotees should be explicit about what it is that society expects to gain from granting subsidies to agriculture. If it is virtuous farmer-citizens, then this explanation merges into the ethnocentric thesis. Is it public goods such as open space and environmental amenities that economic markets alone would fail to produce and that are acquired in exchange for support prices? But markets in fact do produce open space and environmental amenities, although perhaps in suboptimal quantities.[10] Even so, society is not getting much of a bargain if it is trading amenities and the perpetuation of family farms for the huge subsidies granted to the sector. In Chapters 3 and 5 it is shown that the principal beneficiaries of subsidies are landowners, not necessarily operators of family farms. And equally as important, subsidies actually have produced some very negative environmental consequences in toxic chemical contamination and soil loss. Either American citizens and politicians are badly informed as to the real results of agriculture support, or the social contract explanation does not account for much.

After World War II and the Korean War, price supports for many commodities were reduced from 90 percent of parity to levels as low as 60 percent, and this has been claimed to bolster the social contract explanation. Price support was reduced during this period because to achieve food security and other agricultural policy goals society didn't need to encourage agriculture so much (Paarlberg 1989, p. 1161). But there were other factors at the time, such as rapid technological advance, that increased the net income position of farmers. Much of the new technology was produced through subsidized research by the USDA and the state experiment stations with both state and federal funds. The index of productivity of the primary factors of production utilized in agricultural production rose from 73 in 1950 (1967 = 100) to 102 in 1970, probably indicating a sharp reduction in average real production costs.[11] Thus, it is possible that the falling unit costs produced by more efficient technology more than compensated for the reduction in price supports, leaving farmers just as well off as they were under the higher levels of support.

Further empirical support for the proposition that real subsidy levels (price supports and new technology) may not have declined during this period is found in a time series of land prices, corrected for inflation. Land prices tend to move directly with changes in expected returns to land. These returns are roughly the difference in expected per acre revenues and variable costs. Of course, revenues consist of income from private market sales and from government payments. A definitive test of declining government support levels during this period would require a breakdown of revenues into their two component parts. It is significant that throughout the 1950s and 1960s, real agricultural land prices were rising. In fact, from 1930 to 1980, only twice, in 1960–61 and 1969–70, did real land prices decline on a year-to-year basis.[12] It is unlikely that land prices, corrected for inflation, would have continued to rise yearly had not expected profits (including government payments) from land use been increasing.

Another hypothesis Paarlberg connects to the social contract explanation is that farm protection increases when the macroeconomic cycle is in the recovery and boom stages and does not decline proportionately if at all during the declining and recessionary phases of the cycle. When economic activity is brisk and incomes are increasing, the taxpayer transfers to farmers are not noticed so much and therefore are not resisted. And when the business cycle turns down and taxpayers are more pressed, farmers tend to be in even greater financial stress, which engenders sympathy in the form of more transfers. "The government, having assumed a quasi-contractual obligation to protect the welfare of farmers, will thus be inhibited on the downside from asking farmers to give away all that they earlier gained on the upside. In unstable macroeconomic times, protection levels will ratchet upward" (Paarlberg 1989, pp. 1162–1163).

There appear to be empirical problems with this thesis. What is the evidence that farm programs pay off more when times are good, that is, that they are procyclical? In fact, the deficiency payment rules in vogue work in precisely the opposite direction. Deficiency payments are the difference between target prices and the higher of market prices and loan rates for wheat, rice, cotton, and the feed grains. These target prices and loan rates tend to be established in the farm bills, which are passed roughly every five years. Therefore, during prosperous periods when agricultural market prices are rising, with target prices and loan rates more or less fixed, deficiency payments are automatically reduced rather than increased, and vice versa in periods of stagnation and recession. There appears to be no yearly ratcheting up of income support in these procedures. In the prosperous period of the mid-1970s, for example, most farmers received no deficiency payments at all because market prices were so high.

Another Paarlberg argument for the social contract explanation is the well-known fact that program price support and conservation payments are not targeted at low-income farmers (Gardner 1985). The beneficiaries of most government payments are farmers who are least affected by the pressures of the competitive market. Many of those enrolled in government programs are the most modern, most highly capitalized, and wealthiest commercial farmers who produce the bulk of marketed farm commodities:[13]

> *Three quarters of all U.S. commodity program budget outlays go to the wealthy minority of farmers (22 percent) who are in the $100,000 sales class and above. The average government payment to each of these farmers in 1986 was $42,000, well above the $27,735 median family income of U.S. taxpayers. Meanwhile, nearly one-half of all financially stressed U.S. farmers in 1986 received no program outlays at all. (Paarlberg 1989, p. 1161)*

But why should these equity data be construed to support the social contract theory rather than the public choice theory? Paarlberg explains:

> *When the original social contract to support U.S. farmers was first forged, during the Great Depression more than fifty years ago, farm size and farm structure were far more homogeneous. It seemed both equitable and just, at that time, to allocate farm program benefits through price guarantees on a per unit of production basis. In the intervening years, through a process of uneven consolidation, U.S. farm structure became increasingly skewed, and a wealthy minority of large-sized farmers eventually came to produce the majority of all supported farm products, thus capturing the majority of all support benefits. This was not what either the government or the larger society originally intended. By then, however, farm program price guarantees had long since been capitalized into asset values, thus taking on the character not of a program benefit but a property right. (1989, pp. 1162–1163)*

It is not clear that this line of argument favors the social contract explanation vis-à-vis public choice. It may well be true that farm structure was more homogeneous in the 1930s than it is today. But does this imply that nonfarmers were more anxious to support farmers then than is the case now? It is not obvious that the distribution of payments was equitable even then, since the proportion of farmers who did not produce for the market and, therefore, did not receive program payments was probably just as great then as now.

Further, it is not clear that basing program payments on marketed output is more supportive of social contract than public choice explanations.

The power of the farm bloc and its lobbyists was strong in the 1930s, when the programs were initiated. It may be difficult to know now what the government intended then, but it is far from clear that there is widespread disaffection with price support programs now. During the agricultural "depression" of the 1980s, a surprising amount of very visible public support was given to agriculture in a variety of media events.

It is true, of course, that if price supports were removed, landowners would lose. It is difficult to believe, however, that if the political process were entirely rational and efficient, that subsidies underpinning land values would persist as they have to benefit less than 1 million rich landowners. These stylized facts point more to the political power of agricultural interest groups than to the social contract explanation.

Finally, there is an additional argument for the social contract thesis that must be dealt with. The policy of idling land is uniquely American, since it has not been imitated as yet by other advanced nations.[14] This policy renders some parts of U.S. agriculture less competitive by removing tens of millions of acres of good cropland every year and, in the process, confers gains on overseas competitors (Paarlberg 1989, p. 1162). It is argued that part of the social contract quid pro quo is for farmers to be subsidized in exchange for putting this land into conservation uses through the Conservation Reserve and Acreage Reduction programs.

However, these land retirement programs have clearly misallocated resources as Chapter 3 demonstrates. Moreover, there are even reasons to doubt their effectiveness in producing a higher quality environment, as will be pointed out in Chapters 10 and 11 on the environment. This is a critical point, since if inefficient price support programs are not producing environmental (or some other) amenities, then what are U.S. citizens getting from the social contract to support farmer incomes? To argue that land retirement programs are the least costly way to support commodity prices is no argument against the public choice hypothesis. In fact, as is argued in Chapter 3, land retirement may be one of the most costly ways to support agricultural prices. It is true that idling land may reduce supplies by partially, if not wholly, hiding the subsidy from consumers and taxpayers. This may have the effect of improving the image of farmers since they appear not to be receiving welfare handouts, but why does this result support the social contract explanation for farm programs?

Informal institutional characteristics, such as the post-1974 weakening of the seniority system within Congress, the concomitant proliferation of subcommittees, and the weakness of the national two-party system, all reduce the discipline and accountability of government in response to farm lobby demands (Paarlberg 1989, p. 1157). However, these are not social contract variables, but precisely the type of factors that lead to political market failure as postulated by public choice theories.

Conclusions

In closing this chapter it is good to remind ourselves again about the complementary relationship between the various explanations for farm policy. There is really no need to disparage either the ethnocentric or the social contract approaches. If the agrarian myth continues in contemporary America, the public choice variables explaining farm policy may be even more potent because special interest groups within agriculture are less effectively resisted by others. It is beyond dispute that many Americans hold a special place in their minds and hearts for farmers, their lives, and their land. The same point is valid for the social contract theory. The American people may feel that they receive some benefits from supporting farm programs, although it is not always clear just what they are. If so, taxpayers and consumers may be more easily taken in by manipulation of the political marketplace by narrow interests. Still, it is public choice theory that provides the most fruitful theories and insights as to why farm programs exist and why they are so persistent in a rapidly changing economy. Testable hypotheses that derive from this theory will constitute most of the empirical work reported in later chapters. Something of importance will be demonstrated if it can be shown that agricultural subsidies produced by political markets and driven by public choice theories have given us an inefficient sector that imposes costs on consumers, taxpayers, and even farmworkers; that the damages to the natural environment have been significant; and that only landowners have benefited very much. Chapter 7 will develop a conceptual public choice and political market model that will then be used in the empirical tests.

Notes

1. My colleague Rulon Pope (1986)was one of the first agricultural economists to systematically discuss this set of issues.

2. This idea goes back in history a very long way. Adam Smith, the father of economics, says, "How much the lower ranks of people in the country are really superior to those of the town, is well known to every man whom either business or curiosity has led to converse much with both" (1937, p. 127).

3. "Georgia Mules and Country Boys" by Boudleaux Bryant and Felice Bryant, ©1977 by House of Bryant Publications. Permission to reprint granted by House of Bryant Publications, Gatlinburg, TN.

4. Rausser and Zusman (1992) have convincingly argued against the idea that government is nothing more than an arbiter or a clearinghouse for special interests or that the public sector is a benign pursuer of the public interest.

5. The classic work on collective action is Olson (1965).

6. The free-rider problem will be discussed at length in Chapter 7.

7. Buchanan and Tullock (1965, p. 38).

   It may well be that the concentrated benefits and diffused costs principle is a significant reason why farmers are subsidized in nearly all advanced countries where the number of farmers is relatively few, and are taxed in the less-developed countries where the number of farmers is relatively large.

8. There is something paradoxical about this conclusion. It is true that the agricultural sector has been declining in terms of employment and income as a fraction of the entire economy. The question is: What factors produced this decline? In the case of the United States, it clearly was not the relative decline in productivity of the agricultural sector. Output per unit of input has been much higher in agriculture than in the industrial sectors of the economy. In fact, it is this increasing productivity that has put downward pressure on prices and incomes and has produced the demand for political intervention in behalf of the sector.

9. Anderson and Hayami do make an additional point about the political feasibility of protecting farmers in different ways in highly industrialized countries. They note that added costs to taxpayers for farm programs, appearing as subsidies in the federal budget, are very visible and are more likely to be opposed than are increased costs to consumers, which get hidden in market prices. The latter type of protection is characteristic of import controls and tariffs. This insight predicts that net-food-importing countries will be able to offer their farmers more protection than will net exporting countries. Net importers can throw the burden of protection entirely onto consumers through

border restrictions, which do not have to carry any budgetary costs. The empirical evidence generally supports this prediction, but many exceptions exist.

10. For many examples, see Anderson and Leal (1991).

11. United States Department of Agriculture (1972), *Agricultural Statistics* (Washington, DC).

12. United States Department of Agriculture, National Economic Analysis Division, *Farm Real Estate Market Development* (Washington, DC: various years).

13. Chapter 5 deals with this and other equity issues.

14. However, the EEC meetings in Brussels, referred to in Chapter 3, indicate that the Europeans have agreed to land removal policies as a measure to reduce surpluses.

7

A Model of the Political Market

Why is it that each producer of sugar beets garners tens of thousands of dollars of government income support annually while poultry or carrot producers get little at all, if any? Or why is it that growers of crops like wheat and rice receive direct deficiency payments while others producing oranges and apples are controlled by marketing orders? This chapter reviews and further develops some theoretical principles that explain which interest groups are most successful in the political arena in collecting subsidies and other favors. Chapter 8 describes the U.S. legal framework for bringing political pressure: election campaign contributions, speaking honoraria, and lobbying. Then, in Chapter 9 these theories and principles are applied to the political environment in which agriculture operates and some empirical tests are made of hypotheses developed earlier.

Gary S. Becker, Nobel laureate economist at the University of Chicago, argues:

> *The economic approach to political behavior assumes that actual political choices are determined by the efforts of individuals and groups to further their own interests. Competition among these pressure groups for political influence determines the equilibrium structure of taxes, subsidies, and other political favors. (1983, p. 372)*

Thus, a useful way to look at political influence is as a market in which pressure groups demand political favors and politicians, who make the laws that regulate income transfers through taxes and subsidies, supply such favors (see Peltzman 1976, p. 212).

Factors Affecting the Demand for and Supply of Political Favors

Both demanders and suppliers of political favors have scarce resources to allocate to the political process. It is valuable alternative uses of these resources that make them scarce and create the need for economizing.

Political markets are where trades are negotiated and where the terms of trade (the prices) are established. Pressure groups and politicians are assumed to be rational and to maximize the net benefits to themselves from trades. Maximizing net benefits requires that both demanders and suppliers allocate resources among alternatives such that the marginal net gains from each activity chosen are equal. Naturally, if interest groups become more efficient in bringing pressure, that is, reduce their costs, or if politicians improve their ability to benefit from pressure, the equilibrium quantity of political pressure will rise.

Of course, as in all markets, each participant has some commodity to trade and something wanted in return, and a transaction will occur when that commodity has more net value (in terms of what it is traded for) to someone else than it has to its owner. At least two tangible products are desired by typical politicians as they trade with pressure groups: votes needed to acquire and remain in political office and, after successful elections, the perquisites that come with the job. Interest groups can provide direct votes at the polling booth or can make election campaign contributions in cash or services. The latter become the means of informing and persuading voters and getting them to the polls, including those outside the particular interest group. Other commodities of value transferred to politicians from pressure groups generally include personal perquisites (traveling junkets, living and recreational facilities, food and drink, preferences of various kinds for family members, friends, and political supporters) and honoraria for appearances that have economic as well as political value to interest groups. And it is not unknown for politicians to be bribed. Some valuable by-products of holding political office may last long after leaving office if a stock of accumulated knowledge and contacts has been built up that can be tapped later. After leaving public office, many, perhaps most, politicians remain on the scene in Washington in jobs that capitalize on contacts and expertise gained while in office.

Legislators or other politicians favor interest groups with programs such as legislated subsidies, tax reductions, and regulations such as protection against imports, all of which are expected to enhance demander profits and wealth. In addition, political favors might be the absence of harm caused by government action if a transaction had not occurred. Legislators who have the power to raise taxes, reduce subsidies, or invoke unfavorable regulations, for example, may desist in such actions for a price. In any case, the effect is expected, ex ante, to leave pressure groups better off than if the transaction had not occurred. Of course, whether or not interest groups are always better off, ex post, is another matter, since actions in political markets, like those in all markets, often produce unanticipated inimical effects.

What is the "price" of political favors exchanged for votes and job perquisites? Let's frame the problem in terms of the variables of supply and demand analysis utilized in conventional economic theory.

Obviously the price will depend on the expected intrinsic values of the products transferred and the costs of making transfers. Some political favors will be worth more than others to the interest groups.[1] Of course, on the other side of the market, valuable favors may cost politicians more to provide, implying a "high" equilibrium price. If the price is not flexible enough to reach an equilibrium level where suppliers and demanders are simultaneously satisfied, no favor will be transacted.

Costs to politicians are generally of two kinds: political and economic. Legislators know that the monetary costs of subsidies will be borne by either taxpayers or consumers, not by themselves. Direct income subsidies are transferred from the U.S. Treasury and are borne by taxpayers. Other income enhancing policies, such as import quotas, do not involve Treasury outlays but raise prices to consumers. Unless these costs are hidden from those who pay, there will be political costs to legislators in the form of lost support from taxpayers and consumers. In addition, the subsidies may cause misallocation of resources or deadweight efficiency losses, which fall on the economy as a whole (B. L. Gardner 1987a, p. 291). Of course, deadweight losses may also produce political repercussions to the extent that they are known to the general public and are associated with a specific politician or party. (Both classes of costs are discussed later in the chapter).

The upshot is that the returns and costs to both parties in the transaction will determine exactly what is traded and on what terms. Of course, efficient political markets, like efficient economic markets transferring goods and services, will transfer the most valuable favors to interest groups net of costs or at the lowest possible cost to politicians. By the same token, interest groups will provide politicians with the combination of votes and perquisites of most value to the latter, net of the costs of supplying them. For example, in a very tight election race an interest group might get more "bang for the buck" by providing votes rather than the perquisites of political office, and vice versa in a safe election. Thus, it is assumed that among alternative transaction "currencies," those with the highest net value to each party will be the ones exchanged. It is possible that an equilibrium will contain various currencies where the marginal net values of all are equal.

The competitive structure of the political favors market will also influence the price that will be paid. That is, the degree of competition both among politicians and among interest groups will also influence the price.[2] Consider the supply side of the market. Those demanding favors from elected officials hope to pay as little as possible. They will seek out and utilize those politicians who can give them what they desire for the least possible cost. However, if a legislator has exceptional leadership abilities, sits on a particular congressional committee or subcommittee, or oversees a regulatory body that influences the flow of economic rents to the demanders, he or she may respond to pressure groups at lower costs and with greater benefits than could other members of Congress. This is why certain congressional positions are coveted and often vigorously contested by legislators. Essentially, an influential position or a special ability may give a member of Congress an opportunity to extract "monopoly" rents from the favors market.

But this power is never unlimited. Thus, much as they might like higher payoffs for services rendered, individual legislators have limits to their bargaining power. Therefore, on the one hand, a small payment in the form of a campaign contribution may indicate that the possibilities for political influence are widespread, that suppliers are very competitive with each other, and that opportunities to take rents are very limited. As a consequence, interest groups may not have to pay much to get what they desire. On the other hand, a small payment may mean that the political favor has a small value regardless of whether the political system is competitive or highly monopolistic. To understand the magnitude and distribution of benefits derived from the political influence market, both the value of the political favor and the competitive structure of the market must be known, which may be very difficult to establish empirically.

Elasticity of demand for a group's subsidized agricultural products will influence the benefits to be captured in the political arena.[3] If demand is relatively inelastic, a small output is worth more than a larger output—decidedly an advantage to producers, but a disadvantage to consumers.[4] Of course, if demand is elastic the reverse is true: A larger output brings larger revenues than a smaller output.

Elasticity of demand thus can have important implications for both the amount of political pressure brought by any group and the type of policy desired. In a competitive industry with many producers, if demand is inelastic, incentives will exist for the producers as a group to pressure the government for policies that will reduce the total supply available in the market and thereby increase total revenues. Such a policy might be marketing allotments, import quotas, or acreage reductions. But if demand is relatively elastic, it will pay for the producers themselves to expand output, and government policies that increase output will be favored. Examples might be policies that increase productivity, such as funds for plant breeding, soil conservation payments, or subsidized water. Thus, the more elastic the demand, the less the pressure for public policies to support incomes directly. If the interest group still finds it profitable to bring pressure, the less will be the equilibrium pressure for output-reducing policies (de Gorter and Zilberman 1990, p. 131–137).

Consider next the distribution of the economic rents from the vantage point of the legislator. Assume initially no legal limits to payments by pressure groups. A legislator's payoff will be affected by how much the favor is worth and by how competitive the groups are who seek political favors. A legislator's ability to deliver favors may be constrained by available budgetary resources and the extent and nature of his or her political position and influence. And one interest group's gain may be another's loss (a zero-sum game)—for example, if time and financial resources are severely constrained. If pressure groups are highly organized and very competitive, they may be forced to bid up the payoffs to legislators to a level just above the full value of the second-highest-valued favor. However, if favors are virtually unrestricted and the resources available to the legislator are large, all benefited groups may have to make "high" payoffs to the supplier. Clearly, if demanders are competitive and the supplier can play one group off against another as a monopolist, payoffs could be great. But if pressure groups are not competitive, they might be able to capture much of the value of the favors for themselves. Again, obviously the payoff will depend both on the value of the favors and on how competitive interest groups are for those favors.

In short, while a high level of competition among the politicians will lower their own level of individual payoffs, competition among favor seekers will raise the payoffs to the politicians. Therefore, as long as opposition to specific interests is either poor or disorganized, payoffs to legislators will be lower than if competition is more vigorous.

The fact that legislators must periodically stand for election complicates the rent distribution picture significantly. If legislators were limited to one term, they would have incentives to maximize the payoffs to themselves vis-à-vis the value bestowed on their constituents, a case of "get while the getting is good." This phenomenon is pervasive in some Third World governments, which pillage their countries during the short time they are in office. But if legislators want to be reelected, they will maximize their chances by looking after the interests of their constituents as well as their own during the first term. The more public largesse they can transfer to those seeking political favors, the better their election chances are the next time around. This explains why political pork barrel expenditures often rise in election years. The longer a politician is expected to be in office, however, the more it will pay an interest group to invest heavily in his or her election and political decisions. A long incumbency gives favor seekers more opportunity to capture the returns from their investments. Judging from the number of term-limit acts passed and bills currently proposed in a number of states, the public must be convinced that this point is important.

Of course, catering to special interest groups has political costs as well as benefits. A legislator accused of favoring "narrow" interests, vis-à-vis the "collective" interest, may be more likely to lose an election contest. Thus, a secure legislator with no strong challengers is likely to have a freer hand to pursue private gain than one who faces a close reelection contest. But those who face a close contest will need a large war chest to fight off opponents, and this may require the credible promise of many political favors (see Ackerman 1989). Legislators therefore face the delicate balancing act of transferring benefits to their constituents to ensure their support, of appearing to support the "general" interest as well, and of taking as many "rents" from the political process for themselves as is feasible (Jackson 1990b).

This framework of political markets is not dissimilar to the well-known "iron triangle" model of political decision making, where the benefited group combines with its elected representatives and the government bureaucracy to extract valuable favors and regulations from government action, mainly at the expense of the taxpayer (see Fort and Baden 1981). The third leg of this triangle, not yet considered in this discussion is the bureaucrat or regulator who may receive benefits from both the elected representatives (higher budgets, salaries, perquisites) and pressure groups (favorable publicity, pleasant living and working conditions, and sometimes bribes). One thing is reasonably clear. Placing the "transaction" in the political market at the center of the analytical model will show what each leg of the triangle contributes and receives from the transaction.

Other models of the political market have been constructed. Rausser and Foster (1990), for example, argue that government is involved in two classes of policies: PESTS, which are essentially redistributive in character and are thus negative sum in their aggregative effects; and PERTS, which are designed to reduce transactions costs in the private sector by correcting market failure or by supplying public goods.[5] PERTS are generally considered to be positive-sum policies because they improve the efficiency of the economy. Thus, if compensation were paid to any losers, all could be made better off. In this model of political action, government policy is a rational vehicle for combining PESTS and PERTS in proportions that are politically viable if not economically efficient.

Suppose a public action (such as productivity-enhancing research) produces an increase in output in a sector where demand is inelastic, such as in the agricultural sector. Consumers benefit by having a larger output available at a much lower price, obviously a PERT. But producers of the output reap lower revenues due to the government action and, unless their costs fall more than their revenues, are losers. Thus, the government may introduce a PEST, say a subsidy, to compensate producers for the loss of revenue resulting from the PERT. Because PESTS are combined with PERTS in this way, it is possible that both producers and consumers could be better off.

In this model, government policies can be produced by rational decision makers involved in maximizing some "political preference function." This model thus has attractive scientific and predictive qualities, but public choice theory casts severe doubt on whether the real political world can operate in this mutually improving and rational way. The question of how efficient political markets are is debatable, and an appendix to Chapter 7 focuses on this issue.

Some Demand-Side Issues in the Market for Political Favors

Each pressure group can be viewed as having a production function in which output is political influence and inputs are resources spent on maintaining a lobby, attracting favorable votes for a target legislator, issuing pamphlets, contributing to campaign expenditures, paying honoraria, and cultivating bureaucrats and politicians in any number of ways (Becker 1983, p. 372). Political influence can be expanded by expenditures of time and money on these inputs. Of course, time and money so spent involve opportunity costs since they have other potential uses in the economy. Importantly, expenditures on inputs generate diminishing returns at the margin. If a group becomes more efficient in procuring inputs or in producing outputs from these inputs, the costs of supplying pressure fall, and the optimal quantity brought by the group would rise.

The efficiency of the production function for political pressure is determined by: the costs of controlling free riding, the size of the group bringing pressure, and the deadweight costs of the programs resulting from the pressure (Becker 1983, p. 375).

Free Riding

One of the most severe constraints on organizing collective action is the "free-rider" problem (Olson 1965). When any joint activity takes place where a number of individuals contribute as members of a group toward some objective, free riding is likely to occur. It is common for each group member to agree to certain performance standards. But if an individual shirks on his or her performance, all the benefits derived from the shirking are captured by the individual, whereas costs in reduced group effectiveness due to the shirking are shared by all members of the group. Therefore, there are tremendous incentives for individuals to shirk (free ride) unless the group can prevent such behavior by imposing sanctions. This phenomenon is well known to all large organizations, especially those in the public sector, and is a significant cost to all organizations (Alchian and Demsetz 1972).

Partial control of free riding can be achieved "by policing behavior, punishing deviant members, intimidation and fines, and by implementing rules for sharing benefits and costs that reduce the incentives to shirk" (Becker 1983, p. 377). But coercion or regulation is costly. Therefore, coping with the free-rider problem raises the costs of producing group political pressure, and "the total cost of bringing pressure is the sum of the costs of direct political activity and the costs of controlling free riding" (p. 377). The more successful a pressure group is in overcoming the free-rider problem, the greater will be the pressure brought by that group on the political decision maker.

Three factors largely determine the magnitude of free riding: (1) the homogeneity of the group undertaking collective action, (2) the joint nature of the collective effort itself, including the way benefits are distributed, and (3) the size of the group engaged in collective action.

Group homogeneity. The most politically effective groups tend to be composed of homogeneous members, particularly with respect to their interests. Factors that reduce consensus will make collective action more costly, less likely, and less effective. Compromise is costly since each member cannot be certain that the benefits received will be sufficient to cover the individual costs of supporting collective action. Bickering among members is a signal that collective action will be difficult and costly.

Benefit structure of group effort. If all group members receive benefits equally regardless of their individual efforts, free riding is most likely to occur. However, when certain kinds of restrictions are placed on receipt of benefits from the group effort, free riding is less likely to present a significant problem.

Group size. The free-rider problem can be expected to increase with the size of the group bringing pressure. The fewer the individuals, the more efficient the group is likely to be in its internal organization and in seeking political influence (Becker 1983). In addition, increasing costs characterize political pressure as group size gets larger, and these diseconomies will limit the size of the group that will be successful in the political arena (Peltzman 1976, p. 213). In fact, as the size of a group increases, the costs of organizing the group increase even faster because of the free-rider problem; and the larger the group that seeks the transfer, the narrower the base of the expected opposition and the greater the per capita stakes that determine the strength of the opposition. Thus, lobbying and political campaign costs will eventually limit the size of the group bringing political pressure.

If every American household were taxed to make a transfer to a small group of farmers, say honey producers, only a few dollars from each household would amount to a huge transfer to the beneficiaries. The honey producers could be expected to mount a vigorous political campaign in support of such a transfer. But if the recipient group was the entire population, then no motivation for the transfer would exist since it would simply be taxing itself. This principle has been advanced to explain why the political power of the elderly might be expected to decline as the proportion of the elderly in the population increases (McKenzie 1991).

This theory of group size hypothesizes that smaller and more focused commodity groups (such as sugar producers) will be more effective in lobbying for transfers than will large multipurpose organizations (such as the American Farm Bureau Federation, which represents hundreds of thousands of farmers producing diverse commodities). Thus, commodity groups will succeed in acquiring protection in part because of the shrinking numbers of their membership. Thus, while farmer collectives are motivated to find the resources for group action and demand protection, urban consumers and taxpayers are losing the motivation to resist those demands.

Besides the shrinking membership of farm groups, primarily because of increases in farm size, one of the reasons that agricultural interest groups have been so successful in the political marketplace is that mechanisms have been found to mitigate the free-rider problem, usually with the aid of government action of some kind. In many cases, government programs mandate participation of all enrolled farmers producing a certain commodity. Examples are acreage reduction, which is required to receive deficiency payments, and "check-off" payments, which are collected from all producers in a marketing order and are then used to promote marketing. In other words, to be eligible for benefits from the program, producers must comply with the regulations and cannot opt out and ride free.

Two conclusions emerge from this theory. First, given a group's success in overcoming the free-rider problem, the degree of pressure brought by any group to receive a government subsidy will be inversely correlated with the size of the group.[6] Second, to minimize the free-rider problem, very large producer groups may organize into cooperatives or other institutions and bring pressure for government regulations to control free riding. This theoretical reasoning notwithstanding, Gary Becker reminds us:

> *A group may be highly subsidized, even though it cannot control free riding very well because it has much better control than other groups. Therefore, the emphasis on free riding in many discussions of the effectiveness of pressure groups is a little excessive because political success is determined by relative, not absolute, degree of control over free riding. (1983, p. 380)*

Moreover, Peltzman points out that politically successful groups tend to attract additional members, which in turn dilutes the gains of established members (1976, p. 213). Therefore, established members try to limit entry by lobbying for subsidies that are less vulnerable to entry. Peltzman's example is acreage restrictions that prop up prices and encourage fewer new farmers versus output subsidies in the form of higher support prices. Bruce Gardner's (1983) empirical study confirms Peltzman's predictions.

The Impacts of Other Interest Groups

Political action to redistribute income seldom affects just one group. Consider, for example, the quotas on foreign sugar imports to subsidize sugarcane and beet growers. Domestic growers can be expected to pressure politicians to implement the quotas. But other domestic groups, such as domestic sugar processors and producers of corn sweetener, may also be affected by the subsidy, some favorably, others unfavorably. If the import quota results in an expansion in the domestic sugar-producing industry, then input suppliers and output handlers will also benefit from the quota policy and will be expected to lobby for the quota.[7] The reverse is true for those who are hurt by higher-priced sugar. But a subsidy is not provided out of thin air. The resources must be provided either by the taxpayers, in the event of a cash or in-kind subsidy, or by consumers, who stand to lose if the policy forces the domestic price above the world price. Of course, if foreign producers and consumers are affected by the subsidy, then a complete reckoning of the costs and benefits would include the effects on them. They also might bring pressure against the legislators proposing the subsidy.[8] Therefore, lawmakers may get pressure both for and against a subsidy.

Deadweight Costs

Government transfers, such as taxes and subsidies, distort relative prices and cause misallocation of resources that ultimately reduce both output and living standards. The deadweight costs of having a market in political favors make up a significant part of the real costs borne by citizens (Becker 1983, p. 373). Much of this theory and its supporting empirical evidence was presented in Chapters 2 and 3. Also of importance are the real resources expended in the political arena to acquire a subsidy: the process of rent-seeking. The value of these resources in alternative uses must be added to deadweight costs to arrive at the total costs of a subsidy (Tullock 1967). If the subsidy were simply a "pure" transfer and there were no deadweight costs, then losses to taxpayers and consumers would be exactly offset by gains to producers receiving the subsidy. Hence, "equity" criteria would be sufficient to determine whether the subsidy was justified. If farmers were "poor" and consumers and taxpayers were richer, then such transfers would result in a more equal distribution of income. Many would judge this outcome socially superior to the distribution of income that would exist without the transfer.[9]

The existence of deadweight losses, however, suggests that efficiency criteria are also highly relevant. As a matter of fact, deadweight and rent-seeking costs associated with any subsidy imply that losses to taxpayers and consumers always exceed gains captured by beneficiaries. One study estimates that, in 1986–87, U.S. farm programs cost taxpayers $30.3 billion, while farmers gained only $26.3 billion (Roningen and Dixit 1988). In addition, consumers lost $6 billion because of higher prices caused by program subsidies. Another study estimated that consumers and taxpayers paid $1.38 for every $1.00 transferred to farmers (Alston and Carter 1989, p. 1). As a consequence, it is obvious that farm subsidies qualify as a negative-sum game.

Gary Becker reaches three important conclusions relative to deadweight costs:

> *(1) Deadweight costs generally rise at an increasing rate as taxes and subsidies increase.*
>
> *(2) Since deadweight costs to taxpayers fall as the tax per person falls, the opposition of taxpayers to subsidies decreases as the number of taxpayers increase.*
>
> *(3) All groups favor and lobby for efficient taxes (taxes with lower deadweight costs) because these improve the welfare of subsidized as well as taxed groups. (1983, p. 391)*

The first point has two clear implications: an economy with high levels of income transfers resulting from distortive taxes and subsidies will be less efficient than one with lower levels, and those industries that are heavily taxed or subsidized will be more inefficient than those that are not.

The second point is closely related to the theory discussed earlier that the effectiveness of a pressure group will be greater the smaller its size. The reverse is true for taxpayers. If the burden imposed on the individual taxpayers to subsidize an interest group is small, taxpayer opposition to the subsidy will likely be small.

Since some taxes and subsidies are more efficient than others, the third point says that, given the option, taxpayers and subsidy recipients will favor the more efficient, since the deadweight losses will be lower. So-called lump-sum taxes and subsidies that do not distort relative prices (such as payments to farmers that are unrelated to output, or "decoupling") will be preferred over those that distort prices (such as support prices paid per unit of output).

Who wins the contest for political pressure in competitive political markets? Gary Becker concludes:

> *Pressure tends to be greater by more efficient groups, by subsidized groups with smaller deadweight costs, by taxed groups with larger deadweight costs, by groups with intrinsically more influence, and by subsidized groups whose benefits are financed by a small tax and many persons. (1963, pp. 390–391)*

It has been argued by Wittman (1989) that political markets are efficient in generating electoral outcomes and, in fact, function much like economic markets. Whether or not this is true is the topic discussed in the appendix of this chapter. An excellent example of these theoretical principles operating in the agricultural sector is provided by the credit problem discussed in Chapter 4.

A Plausible Explanation for the Credit Disaster

Given the conclusion that taxpayers and most farmers other than FmHA borrowers lose from credit subsidy programs, the intriguing question is why do they exist and how do they persist? The most plausible answer consists of two parts.

The first is that the distribution of program costs and benefits are not well known nor understood by the voting public or taxpayers, so there is no substantial public pressure for reform. In other words, an education problem exists, primarily because of rational ignorance. The second and probably more important explanation is that these programs result in a large transfer of net benefits from poorly organized and politically impotent groups, such as taxpayers and consumers, to highly visible and politically strong groups, such as farmers with overhanging debts. What American has not been exposed to the spate of movies, popular songs, and rallies designed to generate sympathy and support for troubled farmers, especially so-called family farmers? The reality is that most farmers are not financially troubled and many are quite wealthy. In other words, the public choice principle of concentrated benefits and diffused costs is clearly at work.

There can be little question that subsidized credit is an income redistribution tool loved by politicians. It is yet another case where the politics of what Wagner has called "majoritarian democracy" yields transfer benefits to special interests, and there is not enough political counterweight to either stop or reduce such transfers (1989, p. 151). As Wagner explains:

> *The demanders are the clients of the suppliers who are the legislators. Regardless of reasons or motivation, all of them will be engaged in satisfying or supplying the demands of their clients. Legislators get elected because a sufficient number of people in their geographical territories think they will best serve their interests. (1989, p. 151)*

As with other federal programs, the government is organized to deliver subsidized credit through FmHA loans to every nook and cranny of the nation. This organization is no accident. Politicians serve their *own* interests by delivering a share of the federal bounty to their constituents, but with insufficient regard to the efficiency impacts on the economy as a whole. But, of course, it is taxpayer money the politicians are moving around. This is clearly predicted by the public choice model.

A prominent agricultural credit scholar, Peter J. Barry of the University of Illinois, has written:

> *Credit programs are popular, expedient instruments for policy makers to use, often on concessionary terms. They are relatively easy to administer; the administrative and risk-bearing costs are difficult to measure and are effectively hidden from taxpayers; they can be quickly developed in crisis situations; they are highly visible to constituents; they do not directly influence commodity and resource markets; and they imply financial soundness from intended loan repayment, although delinquency rates are typically high. These politically attractive features along with various subsidy elements give these programs highly sensitive socioeconomic effects, with the balance sometimes swinging in a negative direction. (1985, p. 342)*

Clearly, the efficiency problems of the FmHA are not due to the quality of its bureaucrats. They are probably at least as high-principled and capable as the population at large. Many of them are conscientious about their work, and some agree that the system needs to be reformed. This was clearly demonstrated when the FmHA itself proposed avoiding loans to borrowers who had defaulted on previous loans. But legislators simply would not sanction this step. In fact, the Senate Agricultural Committee condemned the FmHA for proposing the "disenfranchisement" of eligible borrowers (Bovard 1989, p. 141).

Even the courts have played a role in preventing the FmHA from reducing inefficiency. In a lawsuit (*Coleman v. Block*) brought in North Dakota by a delinquent borrower against Secretary of Agriculture John

Block (and later against his successor Richard Lyng), the court enjoined FmHA from foreclosing on insolvent borrowers until the lawsuit was finally settled.[10] This moratorium on FmHA foreclosures was a strong disincentive for farmers to repay FmHA loans. Farmers who could not make all debt payments received a clear signal that the FmHA should go to the end of the queue (LaDue 1990, p. 775).

Bovard succinctly argues the critical political issue:

Politicians want the FmHA to keep farmers in business at any cost. . . . Congressman Byron Dorgan reacted strongly to reports that the FmHA had advised some farmers to quit farming: "What kind of government is it that counsels agriculture's future to get out of agriculture? That says to young farmers, 'you ought to quit'? That is not a government that has its priorities right." (1989, pp. 142–143)

It is not only politicians at the national level who desire to protect farmers in financial trouble. During the squeeze on farm profits in the 1980s, Iowa legislators passed a law that placed a moratorium on farm foreclosures, and several other states have at least considered if not passed such laws (see Rucker 1990, p. 24). While such action is useful in keeping farmers in business who otherwise might fail, the long-term consequences will be to dry up the supply of loans from private lenders. During the Great Depression, there was much farm relief legislation enacted at the state level. Rucker has shown that while this legislation may have reduced farm failure rates, it significantly reduced the supply of loans from certain types of private lenders (1990, pp. 24–32). Even though the industry may be different now—the Farm Credit System relatively larger and the FmHA a major player—it is virtually certain that foreclosure moratorium laws would cause private lenders to place their money elsewhere in the economy to the detriment of the agricultural sector.

Bovard does not overstate the case when he says:

Federal credit programs are a farce because congressmen disguise a huge welfare program in the trappings of banking respectability. It is much easier politically to defend a million-dollar loan than a million-dollar handout. . . . Whenever subsidies are being distributed on the basis of vague or illogical criteria, political pull will soon determine who gets the hand-outs. Local and state FmHA offices receive numerous calls from congressmen's offices, pressuring them to lend to campaign contributors and other politically preferred borrowers. (1989, p. 147)

Conclusions

Some hypotheses can be deduced from the foregoing analytical framework and discussion concerning the relative ability of various agricultural groups to garner and perpetuate subsidies and other political favors.

- The smaller the membership of an interest group, the larger will be the degree of its subsidy. Defining the size of the relevant group, however, is a problem. Is it numbers of producers that count or does it include their surrogate organizations that speak and lobby for them in the political arena?
- The more successful the interest group is in controlling the free-rider problem, the larger will be the degree of subsidy. Very large groups have pressured the government to provide "check-off" systems that raise funds for political activities and for market promotion of the group's product. In this way they have attempted to at least partially solve the free-rider problem.
- The greater the competition on the demand side of the political market, the more interest groups will bid up the shadow price of political favors, but the smaller will be the share of the net yield captured by them and the greater will be the share of the net yield captured by politicians.
- The greater the degree of competition on the supply side of the political market, the greater will be the value of the favors bestowed, but the smaller will be the share of the net yield captured by politicians and the larger will be the share of the net yield captured by interest groups. Later tests of these factors must involve an analysis of political contributions by political action committees to relevant committee members and other leaders.
- The greater the value of the subsidy, the greater the level of pressure for political favors.
- The lower the deadweight costs of the favor bestowed, the larger will be the magnitude of the favor.
- The more elastic the demand for a pressure group's commodity, the less will be the pressure for public policies to support incomes; and if the pressure group finds it profitable to bring pressure, the smaller will be the pressure for output-reducing policies.

A career could be spent in conducting definitive empirical tests of these hypotheses. A modest and limited attempt in this direction will be made in Chapter 9.

APPENDIX
Are Political Markets Efficient?

The theoretical reasoning employed in this chapter has implied that political markets do not allocate scarce resources efficiently. The reasons are (1) imperfect competition, on both the demand and the supply sides of the market for political favors, (2) the free-rider problem, and (3) deadweight and rent-seeking costs. Of course, theorizing why inefficiency should obtain proves nothing. The proof must ultimately be empirical.

The case for efficient political markets has been made by economist Donald Wittman (1989). He writes: "Democratic political markets are organized to promote wealth-maximizing outcomes, these markets are highly competitive, and political entrepreneurs are rewarded for efficient behavior" (p. 1395). Are these claims valid? Do political markets achieve efficiency in the same sense that economic markets do?

It is not enough to show that political markets "promote" wealth-maximizing outcomes. Promoting is not maximizing or even necessarily achieving efficiency. In light of this chapter's framework, a critical question is whose wealth is being maximized? In the evaluation of efficiency, the relevant entity over which wealth is maximized must be the aggregate economy. If the political market is concerned largely with making wealth transfers, then gains and losses of affected groups must be estimated to determine if wealth gains occur in the aggregate and, if so, by how much. This obviously would include losses incurred by taxpayers and consumers who must bear the costs of rent-seeking inefficiency created by special interest groups. Efficiency is achieved only if political action produces the maximum difference between aggregate benefits and aggregate costs, and this result is highly unlikely in political markets.

Wagner has pointed out one of the essential problems with political markets:

> *The legislative creation and the bureaucratic implementation of public policies can be understood within the framework of economic analysis. The legislature is not bound by the rules of property and contract in relating to the other members of society. If the legislature wants to gain control of someone's property or just wants to restrict its use, it does not have to buy that property or purchase some form of easement; it can simply take the property or restrict its use through zoning, announcing some public purpose in the process. (1989, p. 155)*

Nothing in the process described by Wagner, which is repeated in political markets ad infinitum, produces confidence that these markets can be efficient in the same sense that economic markets are. The necessary property rights framework simply does not exist.

Political entrepreneurs can be and are rewarded for efficient behavior under some conditions, but generally they are not so rewarded. Inefficient behavior is more likely if knowledge is not symmetrically shared among those affected by political action. As indicated earlier, one of the most powerful principles of public choice theory is that those who stand to gain by a political transfer will be knowledgeable, while voters and taxpayers who each have a much smaller individual stake in the action remain "rationally ignorant" about the issues and political candidates over which they believe they have little say or control.

Wittman (1989, p. 1399) believes that arguments concerning voter ignorance implicitly assume that the major cost of information falls on voters. A politician gains from providing information to voters that he or she wishes them to have. Quite true. But is the type or reliability of this information what citizens need to provide input promoting the wealth of the community? Who is providing an alternative view that would produce balanced knowledge? Only at election times do challengers enter the information game, and they hardly have equal access to potential voters. Besides, because of the very nature of political campaigns and the exaggerated claims that are made, voters heavily discount much of the information that is received. For this and other reasons, polls on what voters do and do not know seem to contradict the assertion that they are well informed.

The tremendous political advantages captured by incumbents is widely recognized and empirically supported by the number who are reelected (in the House of Representatives, for example, over 90 percent of those running in the last several elections). Economists have argued that free entry to and exit from economic markets are vital to achieving efficiency (see Baumol 1982). How will resources find their highest-valued employments if they are not free to move there? The same could be argued for political markets. Since incumbents indisputably have intrinsic advantages over challengers, then political markets hardly have relatively free entry. Incumbents have access to constituencies and financial resources that either are unavailable to challengers or would be very costly to duplicate. Probably most important is access to subsidized information conveyance via the free mailing privilege. This places incumbents in a near-monopoly position inimical to the operation of efficient political markets.

Campaign contributions are quite restricted by regulations, although many loopholes exist for circumventing the regulations. (These issues will be discussed in Chapter 8.)

The political process can usefully be modeled as a principal–agent relationship, where elected officials act as agents for the voters. As with all principal–agent relations, there is in theory the potential for opportunistic behavior by the agents (politicians) in the form of shirking, accepting bribes, or taking positions contrary to what voters would adopt if fully informed. Wittman believes that competition among politicians, knowledge of their reputations, and monitoring by the voters reduce this opportunistic behavior. This might be true up to a point. But given the structure of Congress, especially how committee leadership positions are organized, which may be crucial to developing a legislator's power base, how can there be effective competition among politicians? They do not have equal access to political power.

If the political process consisted simply of voters and elected officials, the argument that political markets are efficient might be more persuasive. But as pointed out, the political process is far more complex when pressure groups are added to the picture. In fact, it is probably more realistic to model politics as interest groups and politicians mutually serving each others' interests at taxpayers' and consumers' expense—politicians, of course, being constrained by the need to get elected and reelected by the voters.

It is also alleged by Wittman that political parties in the political arena are analogous to franchises in an economic market and that parties monitor shirking by members of Congress. There may be a small grain of truth to this point. The party gains if all members are loyal and exemplary. But U.S. political parties are notoriously weak and are probably growing weaker as they lose power to congressional committees and subcommittees.[11] As a strictly empirical proposition, can anyone seriously contend that U.S. political parties are effective monitors of members' performances and voting records? If this were the case, how can the notorious absenteeism and poor voting records of many members of Congress and the well-known "mavericks" in both parties be explained? With the weakening of political parties in campaigning, there seems to be scarcely any effective party control over members of Congress. In fact, in several recent instances, members have been of great embarrassment to their parties and to the congressional bodies in which they serve. Some, though convicted of criminal acts, have even been returned to their seats by the voters. The case for party discipline and effectiveness would probably be stronger in a parliamentary system, where the parties control both the executive and the legislative branches.

Competition among candidates for political office does provide some control over shirking (Wittman 1989, p. 1398). Political opponents can gain advantage by providing evidence of a competitor's malfeasance in office or in life generally. But shirking is often difficult to detect in the political arena, and how important do voters think it is anyway? The issue seems to surface mostly during election campaigns and is largely ignored at other times.

Wittman argues that an election can be viewed as a relatively low-transaction-cost method of exercising political takeovers, but this tenet is also questionable. Elections for political office, particularly at the national level, are characteristically expensive affairs and are becoming increasingly so through time. Moreover, an election is not quite like a takeover in an economic market, which can occur at any time. The tremendous advantages of incumbency in an election make real competition for political office doubtful.

It has been suggested that the committee and subcommittee framework allocating assignments to those who are most interested in the issues at hand is efficient (Wittman 1989, p. 1403). For example, the negative externalities imposed on urban areas by the Agriculture Committee are alleged to be slight since, if that were not so, urban legislators would be observed on the committee. This argument is inconsistent with the evidence. Environmental externalities of agricultural production may indeed be significant in urban areas (discussed in Chapter 11), but primarily legislators from agricultural states serve on agricultural committees. All that one can safely say is that membership on the agriculture committees is more valuable to those with a rural than an urban constituency, probably because the political system encourages the creation of favors that make appointment to a certain committee most attractive to a rural legislator with a given constituency. It says little about the impacts on urban residents being unimportant. In upcoming chapters, it will be demonstrated that the congressional committee system is one of the primary sources of inefficiency in political markets and that the system shifts tremendous costs to people outside the agricultural sector.

Those who believe in efficient political markets must come to grips with the rent-seeking phenomenon discussed earlier. The efficient political market thesis contends that to the extent that rent-seeking exists, it will involve minimal social costs and rents will be shifted efficiently (Wittman 1989, p. 1404). The reason for this contention is that politicians have designed a number of devices to shift rents efficiently. Wittman demonstrates his point with an example from agricultural policy. Farm price supports with acreage restrictions may be a reasonable approximation to an efficient rent redistribution (p. 1403). Higher support prices inefficiently increase supply, so they must be constrained by acreage controls. Both the logic and empirical validity of this proposition are questionable. Acreage restrictions (or quantitative restrictions on any factor of production, for that matter) must be one of the most inefficient ways to achieve redistribution. Idling agricultural land to support prices has a very high opportunity cost since agricultural land has no valuable alternative use. The entire rent is forfeited by idling land. It is difficult to imagine any alternative policy that could distort resource allocation so much.[12]

Finally, Wittman argues that there are limits to political domination by those few who have concentrated interests over those many who have only a slight interest. He questions the tenet of public choice theory that it does not pay those who are slightly affected to get involved politically when only small stakes are involved. "This argument confuses individual motivation on one issue with overall political effect. In fact, quite plausible arguments can be made that concentrated interests are at a great disadvantage in majority rule systems" (Wittman 1989, p. 1407). However, if "rational ignorance" and "concentrated benefits and diffused costs" are invalid, how do you explain the fact that a few hundred sugar producers politically dominate 200 million consumers? Can it be true that taxpayers and consumers really want to subsidize wealthy sugar producers? It stretches credulity to believe so.

Notes

1. Of course, the intrinsic value will also depend on the recipient's wealth, which will be determined by the distribution of property rights, which may partially be a constitutional question.
2. This idea was developed in a different context by Susan Ackerman (1989).
3. A negatively sloped demand curve means that the larger the output to be sold, the smaller the price that can be charged to clear the market. Total revenue for the producers (or total cost to consumers) is the price of the commodity times the quantity exchanged.
4. If the demand is inelastic, the price reduction required to sell increases in output is proportionately larger than the increase in quantity, so lower revenue results from a larger output.
5. Rauser and Foster's terms PESTS and PERTS are not acronyms indicating some other compound words.
6. These ideas are thoroughly discussed in Olson (1982, p. 29).
7. A good discussion of the complexities of agricultural lobbying can be found in Alston and Carter (1989).
8. Who can forget the lobbying activities of Mr. Tongsun Park of South Korea over a decade ago in pressuring members of Congress for favorable terms on U.S. rice exports to South Korea? Interestingly, the *Wall Street Journal* recently ran a story revealing that Mr. Park has surfaced in Zaire, where he is aiding President Mobutu to acquire American foreign aid.
9. These issues were discussed in Chapter 5.
10. *Coleman v. Lyng* (663 F. Supp. 1315 D., North Dakota 1987). Primarily these lawsuits brought by Coleman maintained that the FmHA was not giving due process in servicing FmHA delinquent accounts. The FmHA argued that it was attempting to service accounts in a manner that would provide minimal loss to the government. After an appeal to the original decision, the FmHA was finally upheld in being able to service delinquent accounts, but the court ordered a revision of forms and procedures used to provide this service.
11. It has been argued by Kiewiet and McCubbins that political parties and congressional committees are interconnected in subtle as well as formal ways. The parties maintain control over the assignment of members to various committees. The majority party names a majority of members to each committee. "The jurisdictions of some committees, however, are dominated by issues of policy that do not directly impinge on what voters (or even party activists) perceive to be the major differences between the parties" (1989, p. 681).

12. In general, quantitative restrictions such as acreage limitations have high deadweight costs in markets where supply, demand, or both are inelastic. For price restrictions (taxes, price ceilings) the opposite is true: A given price distortion has less deadweight cost when demand, supply, or both are inelastic.

8

Congressional Structure and the Influence of Special Interests

Chapter 7 identified the federal legislators who supply agricultural policy and the special interest groups who demand benefits from government action. Key legislative players are congressional committee and subcommittee members who are primarily responsible for creating the farm legislation that affects interest group wealth. All students of markets understand, however, that *both* demanders and suppliers expect to benefit from exchanges, and political markets are no exception.

Given that institutions determine the rules under which trades are made and that stakes for both sides in the political market are so large, the expectation is that institutions would evolve to more easily facilitate political exchanges, by reducing costs.[1] This implies that demanders will organize and minimize the costs of favor seeking. Similar incentives motivate legislators to modify political institutions, permitting them to receive and respond to rent-seeking efforts more economically.

This chapter will briefly describe both the legal framework within which influence seeking occurs in government and the relevant structural characteristics of Congress that facilitate the market for political favors. Then the discussion will turn to the political action committees (PACs), one of the most significant vehicles for influence peddling in Washington. A few other related mechanisms that facilitate political transactions will then be briefly discussed. The chapter is not directed specifically at the agricultural sector, but applies broadly to all political influence seeking. Agricultural pressure and its impact on political decisions are the concerns of Chapter 9.

Recent Congressional Reforms and the Committee Structure

Several structural characteristics of the policy process facilitate rent-seeking activity by those who expect to gain from political action. The congressional committee structure and other recent "reforms" head the list of these characteristics.

Over the past two decades, the changing structure of Congress has diminished the role of political parties, weakened the influence of party leadership, eroded the seniority system, and at the same time, strengthened and expanded the number of relatively autonomous committees, subcommittees, and caucuses. At the same time, interest groups have become more numerous and specialized, and more importantly, have learned how to exploit the changed structure more effectively. They have become more efficient in lobbying for special favors and influencing elections, primarily through the contributions of their PACs.

In addition, campaign-finance reforms have made members of Congress more dependent on PACs for campaign contributions and increased the incentives for piecemeal, special interest legislation. Highly specialized subcommittees have replaced broad-based committees as prime initiators of special interest legislation. A former secretary of agriculture, Clifford Hardin, has written: "Through a process of self-selection, subcommittees are composed of legislators who represent constituencies with the highest stakes in a given policy area. Furthermore, each subcommittee has a nearly complete monopoly . . . over some set of policies and programs" (1986, p. 8).

Thus, subcommittee members would appear to be prime targets of political pressure by interest groups. The latter do not have to expend resources to cajole or persuade the entire Congress, or even a broad committee in each branch of the Congress. Inducing the smaller subcommittees to produce favorable legislation for the interest group works just fine. However, giving more power to congressional subcommittees has concentrated power and reduced the influence of traditional checks and balances, including those provided by the "encompassing" political institutions like political parties and the separate branches of government. These institutions tended to view policy from a longer term perspective than do individual politicians and pressure groups (Tweeten 1986b, p. 1107).

These structural changes have decreased the costs of rent-seeking and increased the productivity of resources utilized to acquire political favors. And because of the lower cost (price), the quantity demanded has increased sharply. Over one decade alone, the number of registered federal lobbyists increased from 3,420 in 1976 to 8,800 in 1986. Since the primary interest of this study is the agricultural sector, it is relevant to note that approximately 25 percent of these lobbyists represent some type of farm, food, fiber, or related trade group (Browne 1988, p. 7). Fully one-third of the most active lobbying organizations attempting to influence the 1981 and 1985 farm bills originated between 1969 and 1979, demonstrating that interest groups will emerge to fill newly created policy niches if established organizations do not do so (p. 21). The *Wall Street Journal* (1990a) reported that 3,200 trade associations alone operate in Washington. They employ 100,000 people, or 187 per member of Congress. Gwartney and Wagner point out:

> *As recently as 1979 New York City had twice as many national trade associations as Washington, D.C. By 1983 the number of Washington trade associations exceeded New York's by nearly 20 percent. A recent study found that 65 percent of the chief executive officers of the top 200 Fortune firms are in Washington on business at least once every two weeks, up from 15 percent a decade ago. (1988, p. 20)*

The old seniority leadership system in Congress rested on the premise that committees would be chaired by long-time incumbents who were not likely to be seriously threatened by challengers in elections and, therefore, by the possibility of removal from office (Bonnen 1984, p. 65). This security of tenure allowed chairpersons to look at issues over a longer term than could new members struggling to establish their positions by rewarding their constituencies and guarantee reelection (Rieselbach 1986, p. 136).

Congress also sought to increase its power vis-à-vis the executive branch by enlarging its data resources, increasing its staff, and augmenting its own ability to block executive action. Total congressional staff increased from about 6,000 in 1950 to over 40,000 in 1980 (Bonnen 1984, p. 69). Most are involved in serving constituents, which is what produces big payoffs for members of Congress at election time.

Journalist Brooks Jackson reports an aid of the powerful former Congressman Sisk (D-CA) having estimated that more than 10,000 people a year from Sisk's district received some sort of direct benefits, mainly through the work of the congressman's staff (Jackson 1988, p. 37). These are specific and direct favors, not the indirect sort that may have come via agricultural and irrigation water subsidies or other federal income transfers affecting virtually all constituents.

These larger congressional staffs have also produced what is known as "staff-dependent" lobbying, meaning that lobbyists filter information through staff members, who have the time to study the information, evaluate it, and pass on their conclusions to members of Congress (Browne 1988, p. 69). There can be little doubt that these staffing developments have significantly increased the power of congressional subcommittees (Smith and Deering 1984, p. 131).

Also, in recent years disciplining of congressional members by political parties has been significantly weakened. This was demonstrated convincingly by the haggling over the federal budget at the end of 1990, when party leaders simply did not have sufficient influence to induce party members to follow the leadership in supporting the plan. Virtually all candidates up for reelection in 1990 opposed the plan. This party weakening is partly because the parties are no longer the most important financiers of political campaigns. Few incentives exist for legislators to rigidly adhere to party agendas and vote the party line; they can more effectively serve the needs of special interests. Thus, so-called reform has actually facilitated interest group access to members of Congress and has produced legislative results favorable to special interests (Browne 1988, p. 47).

Over the same period that these reforms have made legislators more accessible to interest groups, so-called sunshine laws attempted to make the system more responsive to what are perceived to be "public" needs. These laws required that meetings be public, that votes be recorded and published, and that campaign contributions and debts for each congressperson be made a matter of public record (Rieselbach 1986, p. 138). However, little evidence has been brought forward that these reforms have made any difference in increasing public accountability (Bonnen 1984, p. 68).

Political Action Committees

Congress has enacted legislation that allows the organization of political action committees (PACs), which are used by interest groups to funnel campaign contributions to candidates who might produce political favors.

The Growing Importance of PACs

There can be little doubt that PACs have been utilized effectively by campaign committees of both parties in both houses of Congress. Brooks Jackson has written a fascinating account of how these committees have virtually guaranteed the reelection of incumbents and influenced policies to benefit contributors—policies including the federal government's vast array of subsidies, entitlements, tax breaks, and commercial regulations (1988, p. 7). Jackson describes the process graphically:

> *The campaign-money reforms of the 1970s, far from ending the days when lobbyists furtively passed around sacks of cash, have only brought the traffic in campaign money into the open, given it legal sanction, and turned lobbyists and commercial interests into regular collection agents for lawmakers. (p. 9)*

It is clear that lawmakers have become more and more dependent on PACs. For example, House members elected in 1976 got an average of 25.6 percent of their campaign funds from PACs, while those elected in 1986 got 42 percent. In 1976, senators got less than 15 percent of their election funds from PACs, while in 1986 they got 27 percent (Jackson 1988, p. 89). And these higher percentages occurred despite the fact that the costs of an election campaign have risen sharply. As members of Congress have received increasingly greater contributions, they are more and more beholden to PAC constituent groups.

It is significant that PAC donations to incumbents exceed those to challengers by more than five to one (Ladd 1986), an important factor in explaining why over 95 percent of incumbent House members were reelected in the past few elections (H. Carter 1990). In the 1990 election, for example, despite an alleged anti-incumbent mood in the country, 96 percent of House incumbents were reelected. Only one senator, Boschwitz (R-MN), was defeated. As journalist Hodding Carter puts it, "As usual, money is the root of evil, the evil in this being a Congress that can't be beat because their incumbency opens checkbooks while closing them to potential challengers all over the country" (1990, p. A21). Agricultural economist James T. Bonnen notes, "They [PACs] put money on the 'right side' in campaigns. Many interest groups systematically contribute to both sides (e.g., the dairy lobby), but usually give more to incumbents than challengers" (1984, p. 64). In other words, contributors cover their bets just in case an incumbent is defeated, even though the probability of such a defeat is exceedingly small. PAC funds have been instrumental in employing modern technology such as polling, television advertising, and computer-driven mail, all to the benefit of incumbents relative to challengers (Jackson 1988, p. 8).

The *Wall Street Journal* reported the results of a Common Cause study showing that of the 405 House members seeking reelection in the 1990 campaign, 382 had either no major-party opponent or, if they had one, the challenger had raised less than $25,000 of campaign funds. Only 23 House incumbents faced challengers who had raised even half as much money as they had. The study points out that incumbents went into the campaign with more than $177 million—including $58 million left over from 1988 races—while challengers had less than $15 million (Jaroslavsky 1990). Even though more incumbents were defeated in 1992 than in recent previous elections, there is little indication that the financial advantages of incumbency were any less.

In another indication of the growing importance of PACs, Jackson reports that at the end of 1974, only 608 PACs existed, including 201 sponsored by unions and 89 by corporations. The remaining majority represented a variety of trade groups, professional associations, agricultural cooperatives, and free-standing political groups. By 1975, however, the number of corporate PACs alone had increased to 433. The number nearly doubled again in the next two years and by 1988 had exceeded 1,700 (1988, p. 72).

Data provided by the Federal Election Commission (FEC), suggested that PACs increased their contributions to candidates, political parties, and other political committees to $68.7 million in 1988, up 24 percent from the previous nonelection year of 1987. Abramson and Jackson believe that

> *the chief beneficiaries were House members, particularly Democrats, who hold the majority and thus control the all-important committee and subcommittee chairmanships. . . . The average Democratic House incumbent received $81,380 from PACs while the average Republican took in $61,122. . . . The increase in PAC receipts was less dramatic in the Senate. Sitting senators took in a total of $17.7 million from PACs last year, up just $2 million from the total two years earlier. Democrats got $10.5 million from PACs, representing 28 percent of their net receipts. Republicans got $7.2 million, making up 23 percent of net receipts. . . . Political-party committees consumed PAC money last year in amounts roughly double what they took in four years earlier, at a comparable point in the presidential-election cycle. (1990, p. A20)*

One might think that PACs would be ideologically oriented, that is, that labor union PACs would be supporters of the Democratic party, their long-term political ally, while corporate PACs would favor the Republicans, who are generally more friendly to the business sector. This proposition turns out to be false. Most PACs, in fact, support incumbents who are in key legislative positions to affect policy. The reason that business and professional PACs support Democrats is that the donors care more about particular bills than about any broad philosophy (Jackson 1988, p. 87). "When Republicans talked about being pro-business, they were speaking of freedom from government regulation. When Democrats said they were pro-business, they more often were touting federal subsidies or tax loopholes" (p. 87).

According to a study by Common Cause, U.S. senators collectively received $96.3 million in campaign contributions from corporation and labor union PACs in a recent six-year period. Forty-four Senators received more than $1 million each from 1983 to 1988. Financial-services industry PACs, including those sponsored by savings and loan associations, were the biggest corporate contributors, giving senators more than $8.5 million. PACs representing oil and gas companies, utilities, and other energy interests gave senators more than $7 million. Labor union PACs gave more than $14 million (Abramson 1990a).

The Teamsters Union operates by far the largest PAC, which took in nearly $5.4 million in 1989. Its nearest competitor, the American Medical Association's PAC, had $2.9 million in 1989 receipts. As shall be seen in Chapter 9, some of the large agricultural PACs did not lag far behind.

These numbers suggest the growing importance of PACs in the election process. Some understanding of the rules and regulations that govern them, and how these rules can be circumvented, will be useful later in understanding the influence of agricultural PACs.

Rules Regulating the PACs

The relationship between a PAC and a member of Congress may be complex and take years to develop. PACs collect funds and make expenditures to influence the outcome of an election, the voting behavior of members of Congress, and the legislation generated in Congress by lobbying efforts. The legislation need not be favorable to the interest group to get its attention. Threatened unfavorable action may also be of vital concern.

PACs are regulated by the FEC, which has the mandated responsibility of "protecting" the public from abuses that can arise from the election process. As evidenced by the work of economists, notably the late Nobel laureate George J. Stigler of the University of Chicago, regulating in the public interest is very difficult and is seldom done. Interest groups have strong incentives to try to influence regulators to initiate and administer rules favorable to interest groups instead of the public (Stigler 1971). All of the major regulatory agencies have been "captured" to a greater or lesser degree by pressure groups, and the FEC is no exception. FEC personnel have been described as "election law enforcers who serve the politicians, not the public" (Jackson 1988, p. 4).

PACs are classified as "party" committees if they are established by one of the major political parties and as "candidate" committees if they are set up by supporters of a given political candidate. All that is legally required to establish a PAC is a statement filed with the FEC that includes some organizational and fiduciary stipulations.[2]

PACs are further classified as being "multicandidate" committees[3] or as having "separate segregated funds."[4] If a PAC is not a multicandidate committee, it is considered to be an "individual" committee and must abide by specific regulations.

Separate segregated funds are discussed in a section of the U.S. Code that deals with the illegality of contributions made directly by corporations, labor unions, and trade associations. In fact, corporate, labor, and trade association PACs emerged as a consequence of these restrictions on their parent organizations. These PACs are permitted to make contributions from these organizations, but only under carefully defined stipulations.

Corporate PACs are established under the condition that "contributions to such separate funds must be voluntary and held apart from the regular treasuries of the founding organization; their political purposes must be clearly and publicly stated" (Sorauf 1984, p. 31). Assets of a corporation must also be segregated from its PAC's funds, and it is illegal for a company directly to fund its own PAC. In raising money, however, a PAC may solicit the company's stockholders and its executive and administrative personnel (Sorauf 1988, p. 76). In addition, it may solicit the corporation's nonexecutive employees twice annually via mail to the employees' homes. Other legitimate methods of fund-raising include group seminars, telephoning, payroll deduction, and earmarking (which permits the contributor to designate the recipient of the donation) (Sabato 1984, p. 53–60). Another stipulation states that a PAC cannot accept a contribution from a U.S. government contractor (Oldaker 1982, p. xx).

Contributions are limited *from* PACs as well as *to* PACs. If a PAC is a multicandidate committee, the limit from the PAC is $5,000 per candidate per election (primary and general elections being separate). "Earmarked" contributions are counted as "individual" gifts—not to exceed $1,000 per candidate per election per individual contributor—but are not counted in the PAC's limit. Thus, in addition to earmarked individual contributions, a PAC can still give its maximum of $5,000 per candidate per election (Oldaker 1982, p. xx). In other words, an individual can make his or her contribution *through* but not *by* a PAC, which is not affected in any way, except for any credit it might receive by identifying the donor as one of its members (Sabato 1984, p. 64).

No *aggregate* spending limit exists for multicandidate PACs. However, only $15,000 or less can be given by a multicandidate PAC to a national committee or a political party, which may then distribute this amount as it pleases. Also, a multicandidate PAC cannot contribute more than $5,000 to any other PAC in any one calendar year.[5]

While individual committees have a $1,000 limit per candidate per election, only contributions over $200 must be itemized on federal disclosure forms by the candidate receiving the contribution (Abramson 1990c). Moreover, a $25,000 aggregate limit exists per calendar year for any contributing individual. When it comes to contributions *to* PACs, however, no PAC may accept more than $5,000 per year from any contributor. Also, PACs cannot accept *cash* contributions that exceed $100 (toward their $5,000 limit) from any person for use in federal elections.[6] An important qualification is that "contribution" limitations do not apply to transfers between PACs of the same political party.[7] As shall be seen later, this is a significant loophole in the law that permits "soft money" to be almost unbounded.

The U.S. Code specifies how "excess" contributions to a political candidate by a PAC can be lawfully utilized:

Amounts received by a candidate as contributions that are in excess of

> *any amount necessary to defray his expenditures, and any other amounts contributed to an individual for the purpose of supporting his or her activities as a holder of Federal office, may be used by such candidate or individual, as the case may be, to defray any ordinary and necessary expenses incurred in connection with his or her duties as a holder of Federal office, may be contributed to any organization described in section 170(c) of title 26, or may be used for any other lawful purpose, including transfers without limitation to any national, State, or local committee of any political party; except that, with respect to any individual who is not a Senator or Representative in, or Delegate or Resident Commissioner to, the Congress on January 8, 1980, no such amounts may be converted by any person to any personal use, other than to defray any ordinary and necessary expenses incurred in connection with his or her duties as a holder of Federal office.*[8]

The code also contains a section defining "charitable contribution," which allows the use of PAC contributions for public, religious, charitable, scientific, literary, or educational purposes or for the prevention of cruelty to children or animals, but not for any part of the net earnings that inure to the benefit of any private business shareholder or individual.[9] In a nutshell, a candidate can transfer his or her excess contributions to help any candidate, campaign, or charity.

It is this charitable contribution feature of the law that has been the subject of controversy. Internal Revenue Service regulations allow the use of tax-deductible money to sign up voters, as long as canvassers don't ask in advance which party or candidate the potential voter favors. Thus, many large contributors to PACs have written their contributions off as deductions on their federal income-tax returns. The effect is that tax-exempt "charities" have been created that register voters, and these are especially important in the case of poor and minority voters, who are mostly Democrats (Jackson 1990c). On the one hand, this vehicle of the law has been defended as a laudable effort in getting people to the polls. But on the other hand, the discovery during 1990 that savings-and-loan magnate Charles Keating, Jr. had given $850,000 to three voter registration groups in which Senator Alan Cranston (D-CA) was involved has been sharply criticized and certainly helped bring the "Keating affair" into public focus,[10] finally resulting in a reprimand for Senator Cranston by the Senate Ethics Committee.

There is a significant exception to these uses of excess PAC contributions, however. While it is illegal for most members of Congress to convert their campaign funds to personal use, those who were already in the House when the law took effect in 1980 were exempted from the requirement. Under a "grandfather" clause, these more senior members could keep their political funds when they retire from political office (Jackson 1988, p. 66). However, changes adopted by Congress in 1989 require that members seeking reelection in 1992 would automatically lose the right to convert these funds to personal use (Rothenberg 1990). Since there were twenty-nine such members of the House who had over $400,000 in campaign kitties and seventy-nine who had more than $200,000, it was once believed that many would take the opportunity to retire. However, given the scrutiny of Congress by such public interest organizations as Common Cause, and by the public at large, members of Congress were reluctant to leave under any suspicions that they took advantage of rules to aggrandize themselves. Instead, many have and will serve beyond 1992 and then move into other jobs where they can profit from the contacts made while in Congress (Calmes 1991). But the check-kiting scandal in the House and other perceived congressional misdeeds caused a huge public outcry, and an unprecedented number of senators and representatives did opt out of 1992 reelection races.

Loopholes in PAC Requirements

The foregoing discussion makes it quite apparent that the regulations governing PACs are very complex, and it should not be surprising that the rules are often violated and abused. Whenever stakes are high, clever and opportunistic people will usually manage to find loopholes in the rules, no matter how tightly drawn. This is certainly true for rules governing PACs.

One loophole concerns "in-kind" gifts of goods and services, which are not restricted by law. Another concerns "independent expenditures" in which a PAC makes the "final allocation" of the resources in the campaign. Final allocation means that a PAC can make any kind of expenditure either for or against a candidate as long as it "is made without consultation with, or the cooperation of, any candidate or campaign" (Sabato 1984, p. 96). There is no limitation to independent spending for any committee or individual (Sorauf 1988, p. 63). A PAC may allocate the resources in the campaign in any way it pleases as long as the consultation stipulation is met.

This regulation can be highly significant in close campaigns:

> *Autopac (Auto Dealers and Drivers for Free Trade PAC) and a small group of other PACs specialize in so-called independent expenditures. They wait until the closing days of the campaign and then dump potentially decisive amounts of money into a few closely contested races. As long as the PACs operate independently of the candidates they support, the PAC expenditures aren't subject to Federal spending limits. In 1988, Autopac spent $1.3 million to aid five GOP senate candidates. (Abramson 1990f, p. A16)*

An interesting aspect of this case concerns allegations that Autopac is heavily dominated by Japanese automakers. U.S. law prevents foreign corporations and organizations from operating PACs, but their U.S. subsidiaries can. Those who are worried about foreign influence on the U.S. political system are pressing the FEC to outlaw PACs sponsored by concerns that are over 50 percent foreign-owned (Olen 1990). This response may be an example of "concentrated benefits and diffused costs" described earlier. It is interests representing U.S. producers who are pressing for restrictions on Autopac PACs. Though consumers would lose from such restrictions as they are an impediment to free trade, they cannot mount political pressures because of problems with size and free riders.

Politicians distinguish between "hard money" and "soft money." The former is raised according to the strictures of federal election law. In addition to those discussed earlier, provisions in the law limit party organizations from taking more than $20,000 per year from any one person or $15,000 per year from any PAC, and require that donations be fully disclosed.

The party election campaign committees, however, also receive large quantities of "soft" money from unions, rich contributors, and some corporations. Soft money contributions to political parties are supposed to be used for general party-building activities. Thus, these moneys are not designated for any specific elections. In fact, technically these funds are illegally used in federal elections, but the law is so full of loopholes and so poorly enforced that such sources have been extremely important in reelecting incumbents (Jackson 1988, p. 8). Furthermore, the sources and recipients of soft money do not have to be disclosed.

Data for the fifteen months ending in March 1990 indicated that the three major committees of the Republican party raised a total of $113 million in soft money, compared with $24 million for the three Democratic National Committees (Abramson 1990c). Among the top contributors to the Democratic National Committees was Archer-Daniels-Midland Corporation, a large midwestern grain firm that also manufactures ethanol, which contributed $55,000 (1990c).

Soft money from big business has been used heavily to aid recent presidential candidates. For example, in 1988, George Bush, through soft money contributions to the Republican party and a fund-raising effort known as Team 100 (where individual donors and companies each gave $100,000 to the GOP), enjoyed a huge fund-raising advantage over the Democrats. In 1992, although the GOP was again favored in the soft money game, the Democrats closed the gap and even pulled ahead in the critical fund-raising period of July 1 through October 14 (Abramson 1990c), no doubt reflecting the increasing expectation that Governor Clinton would defeat President Bush in the November election.

Another important loophole in the law is known as "bundling" (Jackson 1988, p. 10). It permits a PAC to give up to $15,000 per year to party organizations such as the Democrat and Republican campaign committees. It works this way: Party officials collect the funds, but they then "bundle" them and send them on to the candidates, at the same time making sure that the PACs write the checks directly to the candidates rather than to the party. That way the money will not be credited to the party's bank account and will not count against its legal limits. In this way, more money can be funneled to candidates supported by the party.

Making checks out to the candidate and not to the party campaign committee is critically important. A *Wall Street Journal* article reported Judge Gerhard Gesell ruling that the FEC did not comply with the law by not taking action against the National Republican Senatorial Committee, which deposited funds in its own account first before sending them on to candidates as is the accepted practice with bundling (Jackson 1990a). The committee was assessed a fine because of making excessive donations to candidates.

Another practice akin to a loophole permits legislators to give $1,000 contributions from their own PACs to other candidates. This practice can be quite significant. Jackson reports that in 1986 then chairman of the Democratic Campaign Committee in the House Tony Coelho of California provided $513,600 to other candidates from his personal PAC (1988, p. 17).

Another loophole allows election campaigns to use corporate and union facilities open to the general public for electioneering purposes, and campaign committees are allowed to use private airplanes and other facilities to claim lower costs than those actually incurred (Jackson 1988, p. 17). The effect of this practice is to increase the resources available under the imposed limits.

Jackson describes another mechanism for getting around the limitations of the law:

> *Coelho set up the Speaker's Club. Membership was purchased by making large gifts: $5,000 per year for an individual, $15,000 for a PAC. A brochure used to court new members explained what these big donors got for their money: "Members of the Speaker's Club serve as trusted, informal advisors to the Democratic Members of Congress." Club members were promised they would "gain valuable information" during "exclusive" briefings on tax, budget, and regulatory matters. "You get the real story," the brochure said. They also could "obtain personal assistance in Washington." The Republicans had a similar organization called the "Eagles" club. (1988, p. 98)*

Two additional loopholes are commonly utilized by political parties. Polls of prospective voters can reveal tight races and thus indicate where funds can be expended to have maximum impact on election results. But these polling funds are not charged to specific candidates and are not limited under the law. Also, generic advertisements commonly directed against the other party do not count against the limits of specific candidates because no candidates are named in the ads (Jackson 1988, p. 182).

Finally, the FEC permits state political parties to mix hard dollars and soft dollars in conducting voter drives designed to support both federal and state candidates. Federal funds are regulated by the FEC, but state moneys are not. If state-level candidates run in the same elections as federal candidates, these unregulated state resources could be funneled to drives supporting federal as well as state candidates (Jackson 1988, p. 146).

This is not the whole story by any means. A peculiar situation arose with the Republican Campaign Committee. Party committees were restricted to the $5,000 limit per election just as though they were PACs. After the 1976 election, the party had accumulated a large amount of small-donor funds. If the party supported every House race to the maximum it could spend $4.35 million. But the party had raised $14 million for the 1978 campaign and $29 million for the 1980 campaign (Jackson 1988, p. 146).

To spend the funds, the committee used an obscure provision in the rules to make an additional $10,000 contribution in "coordinated expenditures" to candidates in the general election. Party lawyers believed that this provision gave the party the right to pay political bills incurred by the candidates. The rules also permitted an inflation adjustment for coordinated spending. When all was added up, the committee spent an average of $21,810 for House candidates in 1980 (Jackson 1988, p. 146). By 1986, Republicans had expanded the $5,000 limit in practice to $53,620 for House candidates. The Democrats, who had a much smaller fund for such purposes, took the issue to court but lost in a Supreme Court decision; they thereafter joined the Republicans in the practice.

A demander of political favors need not *give* resources to political candidates; it may loan them. Because elections have become very expensive, it is not uncommon for candidates to incur debts of hundreds of thousands of dollars if not millions. Lenders may even demand more influence than donors because they have larger amounts involved, and candidates who find it necessary to take on debt are probably short on campaign resources and may be politically vulnerable (Abramson 1991).

A variety of institutions have arisen to profit from the business of peddling influence. Entrepreneurial activity always follows when economic rents are available, either by government edict or by private, potentially profitable opportunities. One of the most prominent is the "Washington Campus" (Abramson 1990b). Corporate executives pay from $1,300 to $2,500 each to learn the ways of Washington in seminars lasting from two to six days. The seminars are taught by lobbyists, members of Congress, and congressional staff. These "faculty" are paid honoraria. It is significant, however, that members of Congress do not have to disclose the attendees of these seminars, but it is well known that there is a close correspondence between the congressional committee assignments of the "faculty" and the special interests of the "students." Abramson reported that in 1990 the Washington Campus expected to run seminars for thirty different corporate groups. Senator Donald Riegle, chairman of the Senate Banking Committee, is alleged to have received more than $90,000 from 1987 to 1992 from the Washington Campus for making essentially the same speech every year (Abramson and Rogers 1991).

The Republicans created a similar device called the Republican Senatorial Inner Circle 1990. It was administered by the National Republican Senatorial Committee (NRSC), although Inner Circle paid its own overhead and kept its fund-raising separate. Donors were asked to give $1,000 and were brought to Washington for issue briefings and social events with GOP lawmakers (Abramson 1990d). The NRSC raised $52 million in the 1990 election cycle, greatly exceeding the $13 million raised by its counterpart on the Democratic side.

Honoraria

The taking of honoraria by members of Congress has been another device that interest groups commonly utilized to curry favor and influence legislation. In 1990, however, the House voted to ban honoraria in return for a pay raise, beginning January 1, 1991. On May 21, 1991, the Senate also voted to eliminate honoraria (Abramson 1991a). Although Congress eliminated this one mechanism by which special interests influenced legislators, there is some value in seeing how the payment of these fees operated in the past just in case pressure is mounted to resurrect this practice or something similar.

"'Honorarium' means a payment of money or anything of value to a Member for an appearance, speech, or article, by the Member."[11] As much as $2,000 could be paid for a single appearance, and before the ban was imposed up to 30 percent of the honoraria of House members could be kept for personal use, up to 40 percent for senators.[12] Any excess taken above the limits had to be contributed to charity.[13] Such honoraria soared in the 1980s as PACs and lobbying groups proliferated.

Table 8-1 lists the ten highest recipients of speaking fees in each house

TABLE 8-1 Major Honoraria Recipients, 1989

	Honoraria earned	*Honoraria kept*
Senate		
Robert Dole (R-KS)	$108,900	$35,750
Orrin Hatch (R-UT)	92,499	35,399
Alan Simpson (R-WY)	90,600	35,500
Ernest Hollings (D-SC)	73,450	35,605
John Chafee (R-RI)	66,000	34,554
Dave Durenberger (R-MN)	62,185	35,785
Thomas Daschle (D-SD)	60,500	35,540
Richard Lugar (R-IN)	55,600	35,591
Bob Packwood (R-OR)	54,400	35,765
David Boren (D-OK)	53,650	35,800
House		
Dan Rostenkowski (D-IL)	285,000	26,850
William Gray (D-PA)	164,098	25,000
Pat Schroeder (D-CO)	160,517	26,313
Willis Gradison (R-OH)	105,300	20,586
Bill Frenzel (R-MN)	70,250	25,250
Newt Gingrich (R-GA)	67,491	26,787
Henry Waxman (D-CA)	60,000	26,808
John LeFalce (D-NY)	50,750	26,650
Robert Michel (R-IL)	49,000	30,000
John Dingell (D-MI)	43,800	26,850

Source: Abramson and Pound (1990).

of Congress for 1989 (Abramson and Pound 1990). Several interesting inferences can be drawn from these data. Those who are on the list were influential leaders in both houses, and many hold the top leadership positions. The three top recipients were in the House; Rep. Rostenkowski was far and away the top recipient. Most kept amounts less than the total prescribed by law, and the amounts kept were remarkably similar among members within each house regardless of the amounts actually received. It is difficult to explain this on grounds other than some unwritten understanding as to how much it would be ethical to keep. Such an understanding probably resulted from unfavorable publicity of abuses in the political system connected with PAC and honoraria contributions. In fact, thirty-four senators didn't keep any honoraria at all (Abramson and Pound 1990).

Several of the top-ten senators are on the Agriculture, Nutrition, and Forestry Committee: Dole, Daschle, Lugar, and Boren. In the House, however, not a single one of the top ten was a member of the Agriculture Committee. Of course, the table data do not reveal who contributed the honoraria, although some must have been agriculturally related groups. The Tobacco Institute, a trade association of cigarette manufacturers, shows up repeatedly on the disclosure forms, however (Abramson and Pound 1990).

There were also abuses with honoraria. To increase their income from honoraria, members of Congress collected honoraria above the allowed limit during the course of a year and then deposited them in an interest-bearing bank account until the end of the year. Then, to avoid exceeding the limit established by law, the honoraria not kept were given to charity. But, of course, the member pocketed the interest (Jackson 1988, p. 210).

Another device for capturing real income by members of Congress is accepting perquisites from lobbyists and pressure groups. Members accept meals, gifts, and athletic tickets, travel in vehicles, and visit vacation facilities—all at the expense of pressure groups. Interest groups also use phone banks, mailings, and advertisements to persuade citizens to pressure the government for various favors (Abramson and Rogers 1991).

Potential Reforms in Laws Governing Election Finance

The American public has become increasingly aware of the abuses of influence peddling in politics, especially in elections. Brooks Jackson has recommended that political parties finance all elections, that massive public subsidies be made available to the parties, that PAC contributions be banned, and that honoraria be abolished (1988, p. 311). Pressures for reform have increased to the point that Congress is considering legislation to curb some of the abuses of current practices and establish campaign-spending limits. As already reported, honoraria have now been abolished.

However, it is feared that legislation to curb spending would dramatically favor incumbents. Spending limits would make congressional elections less competitive for the simple reason that closely contested political races cost more than those that are safe (Schotland 1990). Thus, if a challenger is to have any chance of success he or she must normally outspend the incumbent. Between 1982 and 1988, thirty Senate races were considered to be highly competitive (6 percent margin or closer) and sixty-five were considered landslides (20 percent margin or greater.) In the competitive races, more than 60 percent of the candidates spent more than the limits then being proposed in Congress. In the landslides, only 15 percent of the candidates spent more (Schotland 1990). The implication is that spending limits would seem to make only a minor difference in uncompetitive races, where incumbents are safe, but would have a major negative impact on the challengers in competitive races.

When Congress adjourned in late November 1993, the House had passed a campaign reform measure that would set voluntary limits on campaign spending, provide government-funded advertising vouchers for those who comply with those limits, and curb the amount of money candidates can receive from PACs and large contributors (Harwood and Rogers 1993, p. A18). The Senate later passed a similar bill. A conference committee of both houses of Congress came up with a bill that reconciled the differences, but as of October 1994 the conference committee bill had not passed both houses. The probability is now high that any final action will be postponed until a new Congress meets in 1995, at which time developing a campaign reform bill must begin anew. It would be pure speculation at this point to appraise the chances for success of such legislation.

Notes

1. To some extent, the terms of trade between politicians and their constituents are constrained by the ideology of the political parties. But ideology is constantly evolving as perceived social and economic goals and constituencies change.
2. U.S. Code, Title 2, Section 433(b) (1988).
3. To qualify as a multicandidate committee, the PAC must be registered with the FEC for at least six months, have received contributions from at least fifty individuals, and have made contributions to at least five federal candidates.
4. U.S. Code, Title 2, Section 441a(a)(4) (1988).
5. Ibid., Section 441a(a)(2)(B) (1988).
6. Ibid., Section 441g (1988).
7. Ibid., Section 441a(a)(4) (1988).
8. Ibid., Section 439a (1988).
9. Ibid., Section 439a, 170(c) (1988).
10. Brooks Jackson writes: "One of the charities from which Sen. Cranston apparently benefitted was the America Votes project, later renamed USA Votes. The intent of the America Votes was explained by its manager Robert Stein in a 1986 memo: 'As Democrats, we are trying to regain control of the Senate, to increase our majority in the House and, in general, to help strengthen the capacity of state and local groups to motivate voters favorable to Democrats this year and in 1988.'. . . Mr. Stein's memos say the money was used not only to register minority voters, but to push environmental and farm issues where that would be helpful to Democratic Senate candidates." Jackson then shows how very close races were tipped in favor of the Democrats in North Dakota, Washington, and Cranston's own race in California. See Jackson (1990c, p. A14).
11. U.S. Code, Title 2, Section 31-1(a)(2) (1988).
12. Ibid., Section 31-1(b)(1) (1988).
13. Ibid., Section 31-1(c) (1988).

9

The Buying of Subsidies by Agricultural Interest Groups

Political action committees (PACs) are big spenders on the current political scene, and their involvement in election campaigns has been growing in recent years. But are they an important influence on agricultural and resource policy, and if so, how do they make their influence felt? What variables are significant in explaining their patterns of giving? Besides the influence of PACs, what other factors are important to the legislative process affecting agriculture? These are the principal questions addressed in this chapter.

Federal policy affecting the agricultural sector is generated by many congressional committees and subcommittees. In fact, there is scarcely a committee in either house that does not have some impact on agriculture. However, it is the House Agriculture Committee and the Senate Agriculture, Nutrition, and Forestry Committee that are responsible for the preponderance of agricultural legislation.

Congressional Committees and the Activities of Pressure Groups

A wide variety of agriculturally related pressure groups are active in the political arena.[1] Zulauf has identified the major actors who attempted to influence the 1990 farm bill along with their stated objectives on support prices and other policy measures (Table 9-1) (Zulauf 1990). These groups interact with members of Congress and staffs primarily through lobbying, by providing honoraria to members (before 1991), and by attempting to influence elections by establishing and administering PACs.

The two branches of Congress have quite different committee structures, but the question is whether structure makes a difference in how

TABLE 9-1 U.S. Farm Actors and their Major Policy Objectives: 1990 Farm Bill Debate

Actor	*Program commodity* *Prices*	*Quantity*	*Major objective*
Program commodity producers	High	High	High farm income
Input suppliers	High	High	High farm input purchases
Output handlers, users, and processors	Low	High	High output volume and low commodity input prices
Consumers	Not high	High	Safe food at a reasonable price
Food aid advocates	Low	High	Food access by the poor
Taxpayers	Not low	Not high	Low government costs
Environmentalists	—	—	Resource sustainability
Exporters to the U.S.	—	—	Access to U.S. markets
Rural development advocates	—	—	Increased funding
U.S. Export competitors	—	—	No U.S. export subsidy

members are approached by those seeking political favors and in the policy that emerges? The Senate Agricultural Production and Stabilization of Prices Subcommittee is responsible for price and income support policy, and the majority of the members of the general committee (fifteen of nineteen) have membership on this subcommittee.[2]

The House is organized quite differently, with a focus on commodities as well as function.[3] To determine how the contributions of PACs feed into this congressional structure, data were obtained from the Federal Election Commission (FEC) covering PAC contributions to members of Congress serving on the agriculture committees and two other congressional committees that have relationships to agriculture. Specifically, the FEC data are the PAC contributions to candidates for House and Senate seats who ran in 1988 or who were in office after the 1988 elections.[4] A very few members running in 1988 were defeated, and they are also included in these data. The difference in length of the terms of office (six years for Senators and two years for House members) probably is the reason why PAC contributions to Senators were larger on average than those in the House. All subcommittee members

TABLE 9-2 Contributions of PACs in the 1988 Election Cycle

Name	*Spending*
Associated Milk Producers	$1,261,119
National Rural Electric	1,001,833
Dairymen, Inc.	824,475
Independent Insurance Agents	797,059
Chicago Mercantile Exchange	668,529
Mid-American Dairymen, Inc.	663,633
National Rural Letter Carriers	550,166
Alabama Farm Bureau	463,673
American Crystal Sugar	404,566
Food Marketing Institute	392,572
FMC Corporation	390,894
National Restaurant Association	364,781
Chevron Corporation	346,450
Eli Lilly and Company	247,281
National Cattlemen's Association	227,330
Deere & Company	209,795
American Sugarbeet Growers	208,606
Wine and Spirit Wholesalers	207,502
Independent Bankers Association	205,293
Archer-Daniels-Midland Co.	202,848

Source: Federal Election Commission.

were also identified so PAC contributions could be analyzed by subcommittee as well.

Some data showing contributions of the largest agricultural PACs to the 1988 election campaigns will be reviewed first. Then data on specific commodity-related PACs will be presented and analyzed.

Agricultural PAC Contributions to the 1988 Election Campaigns

Table 9-2 lists the contributions of agricultural PACs that each spent over $200,000 in the 1988 election cycle. An agricultural PAC is defined simply as any PAC that contributed to members serving on the agriculture committees in each branch. Remember from Chapter 8 that, among PACs, those in agriculture were not the largest contributors by any means. However, the largest agricultural PACs (listed in Table 9-2) can hardly be considered insignificant.

The diversity of PACs contributing to agricultural committees may be surprising. Rural electric, insurance, and rural letter carrier associations were among the largest contributors. Given congressional committee structure, however, particularly in the House, it is reasonably obvious where any of these groups would focus their lobbying and election campaign efforts. A given subcommittee has clear responsibility, usually explicit in its title, for producing legislation that would affect the identified pressure group. Clearly, changes in congressional structure, especially the relative strengthening of subcommittees over the past two decades, have facilitated the funneling of PAC funds to members of Congress.

Where PAC Contributions Went

All PACs in the FEC data set making contributions to members of the agriculture committees were identified by name and amount contributed. In general, individual PACs could be classified as either special interest or public interest organizations, depending on whom they appeared to represent. The distinction is important in understanding the influence of PACs, since it is not always clear whose interest is being served by a public interest PAC. For example, it would be reasonable to suppose that a PAC sponsored by the sugarcane or beet growers would be interested in high domestic sugar prices, which might be produced by a sugar import quota. But a so-called public interest group could be lobbying for high or low sugar prices depending on whether it was promoting interests of sugar consumers, sugar growers and refiners, or producers of substitute sweeteners. The problem of identifying PACs with commodities is exacerbated because some groups attempt to hide their real interest behind a name that appears to serve the public interest.[5] Since there are thousands of PACs making contributions to members of the agriculture committees, insufficient time and resources were available to investigate each one thoroughly. When interests being represented were not clear, that PAC was omitted from the analysis. It is clear, however, that the vast bulk of the total PAC contributions was included in the sample.

Excluding some PACs from the sample produced an important consequence. The total contributions from agricultural PACs in the sample to each legislator will understate the total support received from all agricultural PACs. Thus, these data should not be interpreted as representing total financial support to legislators, even from agriculturally related PACs. It is not obvious, however, that this procedure for selecting PACs in the sample will bias the empirical analysis to be reported later.

Moreover, many PACs represent more than one commodity class, as with firms dealing in several commodities. Also, contributions from a given PAC may be spread across many legislators. Therefore, the contribution to a given member of Congress by a specific PAC cannot indicate other or total contributions made by that PAC.

The Hypotheses

The purpose in analyzing these data is to test the general hypothesis that PAC contributions are directed to those legislators who are most likely to produce political favors of benefit to the PAC constituents. It could be argued that the hypothesis is a mere tautology; after all, what else could motivate PAC expenditures? However, the rhetoric sometimes heard from both interest groups and politicians is that PAC activity promotes voter participation and serves constituents, both essential to effective democracy. Thus, it is argued that PACs are socially useful institutions that support democratic ideals rather than special interests.

Even if the evidence supports the notion that PACs are attempting to buy political favors, it is frequently denied by politicians that legislative decisions are affected. Both arguments are unconvincing. If PACs are not successful in gaining political influence, why is PAC giving so large and why does it not only persist but increase? Moreover, if PAC contributions are directed disproportionately to key legislators identifiable by a priori criteria as being in positions to benefit interest groups rather than randomly distributed among members of Congress, then the case is even stronger that significant political favors have been produced by PAC activity.

Operationally, however, the hypothesis might be difficult to test without intimate knowledge of the political maneuvering that inevitably accompanies each piece of legislation. It is not always obvious who key legislators are, at what point the influence is brought to bear, and even what form it takes. For example, PAC influence could be directed toward: (1) the "leadership" in the Congress, since committee and subcommittee chairs and ranking members in each party are positioned to control legislative agendas, determine allocations of public expenditures, and sway the votes of other legislators, or (2) specific subcommittee members who might have the power to fashion the legislation in the interests of a pressure group or vote for or against a specific bill in committee. If contributions target either leadership or subcommittee members, a strong case can be made that political decisions are being influenced by PAC contributions.

As indicated, the Senate subcommittees are not organized along commodity lines as is the House. It has only the Agricultural Production and Stabilization of Prices Committee (APSPS), which is responsible for legislating policy for all commodities that receive direct income support. The House, in contrast, has four subcommittees specifically responsible for commodity policy. It is not completely apparent a priori which subcommittee structure can be expected to generate the agricultural bills most favorable to producers, although a hypothesis would be that the House structure does since agricultural policy tends to be commodity specific. If so, the hypothesis that contributions are targeted to subcommittees should be more strongly supported in the House than in the Senate.

Empirical testing may be complicated by the fact that each house of Congress constructs its own farm bill, and then differences between them are reconciled by a conference of members in both houses. Also, sometimes amendments are added when the legislation is offered for passage to the entire membership of each house, although it is relatively rare that such an amendment passes that does not originate in committee.

Another problem in constructing empirical tests is that the Senate APSPS has fifteen of the nineteen members from the general agriculture committee serving on it if Committee Chairman Leahy (D-VT), and the ranking Republican, Lugar (R-IN), are counted as members. Given the smaller Senate committee, it is easier for a greater proportion of the broader membership to serve on a given subcommittee if members desire it; it is also easy to understand why members would want to serve on the APSPS, where the real power to initiate price and income policy resides. However, if any of the four members of the broader committee not on the APSPS have great influence and thus receive strong PAC support, the subcommittee-targeting hypothesis would not be supported by the evidence.

Any comparison of *total* contributions targeted to subcommittee members and to nonsubcommittee members will not be very meaningful, especially in the Senate where the APSPS contains most of the members of the general committee. Rather, a comparison of *average* contributions to those on and off the subcommittee will provide a much stronger test for the subcommittee- and leadership-targeting hypotheses.

To better understand the role of PACs in influencing policy, specific commodity PACs will be presented and analyzed first. Then, a brief section will analyze general farm organization PACs that support the interests of the entire agricultural sector. The intent is to determine if their contribution patterns are different from the commodity PACs and why.

Regression analysis will also be utilized to test the hypothesis that subcommittee targeting is a significant influence on PAC contributions.[6] The dependent variable to be explained is the expenditures of the PACs on various members of the agricultural committees. Other explanatory variables besides subcommittee membership of theoretical interest, as discussed in Chapter 7 and defined in Table 9-3, are also tested for association with PAC expenditures. Table 9-4 lists the states utilized in the test of the "regional" variable and explains the criteria for inclusion. Separate regressions were run for each branch of Congress and for several of the commodities with price support programs. Then, both Senate and House members

TABLE 9-3 Variables Used in Regression Analysis and the Expected Signs of the Regression Coefficients

Variables	*Expected sign*
Dependent (explained) variable	
Contribution Dollars[1]	
Independent (explanatory) variables	
Subcommittee[2]	Positive
Leadership[3]	Positive
Party[4]	—
Regional[5]	Positive
Branch[6]	Positive

Notes: [1] Dollar contributions made to an individual member of Congress by commodity PACs over the 1988 election cycle.

[2] Tests whether a legislator is a member of the subcommittee responsible for initiating legislation for the commodity. The value of this variable is 1 if the member serves on the subcommittee and 0 if not.

[3] Indicates whether the committee member chaired the general committee or relevant subcommittee or was the minority party's ranking member on the committee or subcommittee. The value is 1 if the member qualifies as a leader as indicated and 0 if not.

[4] Indicates whether the member is a Republican or a Democrat. The value is 1 if the member is a Republican, 0 if a Democrat. The expected sign of the coefficient is indeterminate on theoretical grounds; the Democrats control both houses of Congress and therefore might be individually more influential, but Republicans are thought to represent rural areas more than Democrats do, especially outside the South, and thus might be expected on this criterion to have more influence.

[5] Indicates whether the member of Congress represents a state where the commodity is important relative to its importance in other states. The value is 1 if the member is from the state representing the commodity in question and 0 if not. Table 9-4 lists the important states for each commodity and further explains the qualifying criteria for determining an important state.

[6] Indicates in which branch the member of Congress serves. The value is 1 for a senator and 0 for House members.

TABLE 9-4 Top Producing States by Commodity

Wheat, feed grains, soybeans	*Sugar*	*Rice*	*Cotton*
Iowa	Florida	Arkansas	Texas
Illinois	Hawaii	California	California
Nebraska	Louisiana	Louisiana	Mississippi
Minnesota	Minnesota	Texas	Arizona
Kansas	California	Mississippi	Louisiana
Indiana	Idaho	Missouri	Arkansas
Ohio	N. Dakota		Tennessee
N. Dakota	Michigan		Alabama
Missouri	Texas		Oklahoma
S. Dakota	Nebraska		Missouri

Peanuts	*Tobacco*	*Dairy products*
Georgia	N. Carolina	Wisconsin
Alabama	Kentucky	California
N. Carolina	Tennessee	New York
Texas	S. Carolina	Minnesota
Virginia	Virginia	Michigan
Florida	Georgia	Ohio
Oklahoma	Pennsylvania	Texas
New Mexico	Maryland	Indiana
S. Carolina	Florida	Washington
	Ohio	Missouri

Note: The criterion used for choosing important states for each commodity was the contribution of the state's output of a given commodity as a percentage of the total national value of that commodity. This amounts simply to a ranking of the states by the value of production of a given commodity. Another decision was how many states to choose for each commodity group. The ten top-ranked states from each commodity group were selected as long as all ten states had "significant" production, where significant was arbitrarily set. Only in the case of rice (six states) and peanuts (nine states), however, were ten states not chosen. This procedure suffers from the fact that all states have the same influence in the regression analysis regardless of differences in the value of production of the various commodities.

Sources: U.S. Department of Commerce, Bureau of the Census (1989), *Statistical Abstract of the United States* (Washington, DC); U.S. Department of Agriculture (1989), *Agricultural Statistics* (Washington, DC).

were lumped together into one combined regression analysis for each commodity analyzed.

Tobacco PACs

Table 9-5 lists contributions from top tobacco PACs to members of Congress on the agriculture committees. Topping the list were two large corporations and a producer organization. RJR Nabisco's PAC more than doubled the receipts from employees in 1989 over 1987, to a total of $323,549 (Abramson and Jackson 1990). "The external environment has become so supercharged on tobacco issues that more of our employees want to get politically involved," said a spokeswoman for the company (1990, p. A20). The Tobacco Institute, lobbying against further increases in cigarette taxes, paid $1,000 per House member for just an hour having breakfast with their lobbyists (Jackson 1988, p. 209).

Every tobacco PAC that gave more than $5,000 contributed more to subcommittee than to nonsubcommittee members. Thus, the tobacco PACs confirm the subcommittee-targeting hypothesis: $304,491 was contributed to political candidates, with $211,741 (69.5 percent) targeted to the subcommittees and $92,750 (30.5 percent) given to other members of the agriculture committees in both houses. Of the total, $158,450 of tobacco PAC contribu-

TABLE 9-5 Contributions of Tobacco PACs, 1988

	Targeted	*Unrelated*	*Total*
Phillip-Morris	$72,175	$37,050	$109,225
RJR Nabisco, Inc.	69,600	26,900	96,500
Tobacco Institute	30,066	16,900	46,966
Brown and Williams Tobacco Corp.	21,600	5,500	27,100
U.S. Tobacco Executives (U.S. Tobacco Company)	5,200	2,500	7,700
Loews Corporation	5,250	1,750	7,000

Note: "Targeted" includes contributions given to members of the Tobacco and Peanuts Subcommittee in the House and to the Agriculture Production and Stabilization of Prices Subcommittee in the Senate. "Unrelated" refers to contributions made to members of the broader agriculture committees in both houses who were not members of the relevant subcommittees.

Source: Federal Election Commission.

tions went to the House, of which $88,200 (55.7 percent) was targeted to the subcommittee. On average, House subcommittee members received $6,785 each, whereas an average of only $2,342 was given to other members of the House Agriculture Committee.

Table 9-6 indicates that the regression coefficients on the "subcommittee" variable are sizable and statistically significant.[7] If the legislator was a subcommittee member, the regression coefficient is interpreted as being worth $2,438 in contributions from tobacco PACs in the House (the value of the subcommittee regression coefficient in Table 9-6 for the House) and $4,376 in the Senate.[8] The F and R^2 statistics are both high.[9]

The chairman of the House subcommittee, Congressman Rose (D-NC) received the most PAC money, followed by Congressman Tallon (D-SC) and ranking Republican Hopkins (R-Ky). Both Carolinas and Kentucky are very important tobacco states suggesting that both leadership and regional variables can be expected to be significant in the regression analysis and indeed they are.

In the Senate, the ranking Republican on the APSPS, Jesse Helms (R-NC), received $15,500 from the tobacco PACs.[10] In total, $146,041 went to the Senate Agriculture, Nutrition, and Forestry Committee, of which $123,541 (84.6 percent) was targeted to members of the APSPS. On average, $8,236 was given to subcommittee members, while members of the broader committee received $5,625. This relatively high average for senators not on

TABLE 9-6 Regression Coefficients, t Values, R^2, and F Values for Tobacco PACs

	House		*Senate*		*Combined*	
	Regression	*t value*	*Regression*	*t value*	*Regression*	*t value*
Intercept	1897.4	3.707*	3631.9	1.421***	1650.0	2.426*
X_1 (Subcommittee)	2437.8	2.558*	4376.0	1.565***	3724.9	3.327*
X_2 (Leadership)	3056.7	2.242*	-3192.4	-1.168	-362.4	-0.261
X_3 (Party)	473.1	0.670	3986.2	1.811**	1491.0	1.750**
X_4 (Regional)	3092.9	3.302*	-1234.6	-0.405	2156.1	1.886**
X_5 (Branch)					2542.0	2.390*
F		13.76*		1.55***		9.98*
R^2		0.59		0.32		0.48

Note: * Significant at 5 percent or lower probability level. ** Significant at 10 percent or lower probability level. *** Significant at 25 percent or lower probability level.

the subcommittee suggests that the tobacco industry had a few other favorites on the Senate agriculture committee.

The subcommittee variable in the regression analysis for the Senate has a coefficient that is only weakly significant, however. Neither the leadership nor the regional variable coefficients are statistically significant for the Senate. Republican senators received significantly more than their Democratic counterparts, however.

In the combined regression analysis, all of the coefficients are significant at the 10 percent probability level except the leadership variable, whose coefficient has the unexpected sign. The F and R^2 statistics are larger than for any of the commodities analyzed except for the grains and soybean group.

Peanut PACs

The peanut PACs are really "peanuts" in their contributions compared to the other commodities, and subcommittee targeting is much weaker than for tobacco (see Table 9-7).[11] In total, only $21,225 was given to House members, and $12,975 (61.1 percent) was targeted to subcommittee members. On average $998 was targeted to subcommittee members with nonsubcommittee members receiving an average of only $275. However, the regression results do not confirm subcommittee targeting in the House to a significant extent.[12]

It is apparent from Table 9-7 that regional representation is important, but the contributed amounts are small. The regression results (Table 9-8) confirm the importance of the regional variable in the House, but the coefficient on the leadership variable is even more significant. Qualifying as

TABLE 9-7 Contributions of Peanut PACs, 1988

	Targeted	*Unrelated*	*Total*
Southwest Peanut Membership Org.	$15,050	$3,000	$18,050
Peanut PAC of Alabama (Alabama Peanut Producers Association)	6,550	2,750	9,300
Peanut Butter and Nut Producers	7,000	2,000	9,000
Southeastern Peanut Membership	5,525	1,500	7,025
Gold Kist, Inc.	6,450	—	6,450
Virginia–Carolina Peanut Membership PAC	1,000	500	1,500

Source: Federal Election Commission.

TABLE 9-8 Regression Coefficients, *t* Values, R^2, and *F* Values for Peanut PACs

	House		*Senate*		*Combined*	
	Regression	*t value*	*Regression*	*t value*	*Regression*	*t value*
Intercept	312.0	2.096*	285.0	0.392	118.3	0.577
X_1 (Subcommittee)	61.5	0.203	613.4	0.697	57.9	0.165
X_2 (Leadership)	1187.3	3.122*	2819.6	3.365*	2012.3	5.027*
X_3 (Party)	-216.2	-1.045	359.8	0.518	-7.1	-0.027
X_4 (Regional)	494.6	1.715**	908.5	0.972	621.6	1.780**
X_5 (Branch)					989.1	3.104*
F		6.43*		4.33*		12.18*
R^2		0.40		0.57		0.53

Note: * Significant at 5 percent or lower probability level. ** Significant at 10 percent or lower probability level.

a "leader" was worth nearly $1,200 in PAC contributions in the House, whereas being from a district in a peanut region was worth slightly less than $500. Peanut PACs provided House Democrats more on average than Republicans, but the regression coefficient on party is not significant.

Approximately the same results hold for the Senate; only the leadership variable has a significant coefficient.[13] In total, $30,600 was given to senators, $29,100 (95 percent of the total and $1,940 on average) to the APSPS, and $1,500 (5 percent of the total and $375 on average) to others. In the combined regression analysis, the leadership, regional, and branch coefficients are statistically significant.[14] Perhaps something of importance is beginning to emerge here. PACs representing commodities that are very significant in a very limited region of the country may not be targeting contributions to subcommittee members as much as to powerful legislators from the limited region.

Each peanut PAC gave more money to subcommittee members than to nonmembers, however. The Southwest Peanut Membership Organization gave $18,050 of which $15,050 went to subcommittee members. And the Alabama Peanut Producers Association gave $9,300, $6,550 to subcommittee members.

Cotton PACs

The cotton PACs consist of some large trade organizations such as the National Cotton Council, American Textile Manufacturers, the American

Cotton Shippers Association, and Calcot, as well as a very large individual California cotton grower, J. G. Boswell (Table 9-9). All of these PACs gave the bulk of their funds to subcommittee members consistent with the subcommittee-targeting hypothesis.

The regression model has significant explanatory power in the House but does not do so well in the Senate (Table 9-10). The regression coefficients for both leadership and regional variables are significant, corroborating the point made in the section on peanut PACs that these variables might be expected to be more significant for crops that are confined to small regions. The subcommittee-targeting hypothesis in the House is supported both by average contributions received ($3,714 compared with only $1,215 for non-subcommittee members) and by the highly significant regression coefficient.

Jerry Huckaby (D-LA), chairman of the House Cotton, Rice, and Sugar Subcommittee received the most cotton PAC contributions, $8,586.[15] In the Senate, an average of $7,317 was given to members of the APSPS, while only an average of $2,400 was given to nonmembers. The top recipient was Jesse Helms (R-NC), the ranking Republican on the subcommittee.[16] It is difficult to discern strong patterns in cotton PAC contributions in the Senate, however. In the regression analysis, only the party and regional coefficients are weakly significant, although all coefficients have the expected signs.

The combined House and Senate results show all regression coefficients to be at least weakly significant. And the combined model (as represented by the *F* statistic) has highly significant explanatory power.

TABLE 9-9 Contributions of Cotton PACs, 1988

	Targeted	*Unrelated*	*Total*
National Cotton Council	$60,232	$19,000	$79,232
American Textile Manufacturers Institute, Inc.	25,900	10,500	36,400
J. G. Boswell	29,800	1,050	30,850
American Cotton Shippers Association	23,950	5,000	28,950
Calcot Ltd.	11,156	2,900	14,056
West Point Pepperell	4,650	2,350	7,000
Cotton Warehouse Association of America	2,650	—	2,650
Producers Cotton Oil Co.	1,600	—	1,600
Plains Cotton Cooperative	1,560	—	1,560

Source: Federal Election Commission.

TABLE 9-10 Regression Coefficients, t Values, R^2, and F Values for Cotton PACs

	House		*Senate*		*Combined*	
	Regression	*t value*	*Regression*	*t value*	*Regression*	*t value*
Intercept	929.8	2.452*	-881.6	-0.251	-65.5	-0.083
X_1 (Subcommittee)	1330.3	2.156*	4453.8	1.198	1782.5	1.544***
X_2 (Leadership)	2125.6	2.311*	2881.6	0.731	2106.1	1.389***
X_3 (Party)	327.7	0.655	4290.5	1.450***	1649.8	1.760**
X_4 (Regional)	1293.7	2.252*	4545.5	1.286***	2171.4	2.032*
X_5 (Branch)					3413.7	3.074*
F		8.44*		1.70***		7.48*
R^2		0.47		0.34		0.40

Note: * Significant at 5 percent or lower probability level. ** Significant at 10 percent or lower probability level. *** Significant at 25 percent or lower probability level.

Rice PACs

The rice PACs are also relatively small contributors to political campaigns. Six sugar PACs each gave more to members of congressional agriculture committees than any of the rice PACs. Contributions to individual members of Congress by the rice PACS were also much lower than was the case for the sugar PACs. Interestingly, however, the explanatory power of the regression model for the rice PACs is consistently higher in both houses than is the case for dairy PACs in both houses and for the sugar PACs in the Senate. The reason is undoubtedly the less complex government programs for rice and the narrower geographic focus of rice pressure on the agriculture committees compared with the same for dairy products and sugar. All the individual rice PACs observed targeted more money to subcommittee members than to nonsubcommittee members in the 1988 election cycle and by a considerable margin (Table 9-11).

Representative Herger (R-CA) received $6,000 from rice PACs in the data set, by a large margin the most given to any subcommittee member. California is the largest rice-producing state after Arkansas, and the House Cotton, Rice, and Sugar Subcommittee had no members from Arkansas. The chairman of the subcommittee, however, Jerry Huckaby (D-LA), received the second largest contribution, and he represents the third most important rice state. An ex officio member of the subcommittee, E de la Garza (D-TX), chairman of the House Agriculture Committee, received $1,500. These data account for why the leadership variable was weakly significant in the regression analysis in the House.

Of the eight legislators receiving more than $1,000 in contributions from rice PACs, seven were members of the Cotton, Rice, and Sugar Subcommittee. Other members of the Agriculture Committee not on the subcommittee received only very small amounts. Rice PACs targeted an average of $1,053 to subcommittee members and only $165 to nonsubcommittee members. These data, therefore, strongly support the subcommittee-targeting hypothesis.[17] The regression analysis for the House (Table 9-12) shows that the regional variable is significant, suggesting that contributions to members on the committee from important rice states (Arkansas, California, Louisiana, Texas, Mississippi, and Missouri) were significantly greater than for non-rice-producing states.[18]

Senators receiving the most from the rice PACs were Republicans Cochran (R-MS), $4,000, and Helms (R-NC), $3,500. Both received more than the subcommittee chairman John Melcher (D-MT), who did not represent a rice-producing state. Senator Dole (R-KS) and Senator Pryor (D-AR) received $2,000 each. Senator Breaux (D-LA), one of the four senators not a member of the subcommittee, received more than any subcommittee member; however, following him in order were five members of the subcommittee. The average contribution to nonmembers of the subcommittee exceeded the average contribution to subcommittee members, $1,950 to $1,565, not a large difference, but one reflecting the relatively large contribution to Senator Breaux (D-LA) ($4,750). From these data, it is not possible to find strong corroboration for the subcommittee-targeting hypothesis in the Senate.

These conclusions are generally supported by regression results. The

TABLE 9-11 Contributions of Rice PACs, 1988

	Targeted	*Unrelated*	*Total*
American Rice Inc.	$11,500	$1,000	$12,500
Nestle Enterprises	6,050	4,300	10,350
Riceland Food Inc.	5,100	1,000	6,100
Farmers' Rice Co-op Fund	6,000	2,500	8,500
Rice Growers Association	400	250	650
Rice and Soybean PAC	6,500	3,000	9,500

Source: Federal Election Commission.

TABLE 9-12 Regression Coefficients, t Values, R^2, and F Values for Rice PACs

	House		*Senate*		*Combined*	
	Regression	*t value*	*Regression*	*t value*	*Regression*	*t value*
Intercept	-40.7	-0.178	1405.3	1.956**	9.2	0.039
X_1 (Subcommittee)	364.8	1.023	-1187.3	-1.559***	-94.6	-0.286
X_2 (Leadership)	900.0	1.622***	1566.2	1.939**	1081.3	2.430*
X_3 (Party)	225.3	0.748	181.6	0.300	243.3	0.877
X_4 (Regional)	776.5	2.208*	1765.6	2.437*	1131.4	3.538*
X_5 (Branch)					799.3	2.469*
F		4.16*		2.13***		5.90*
R^2		0.30		0.40		0.35

Note: * Significant at 5 percent or lower probability level. ** Significant at 10 percent or lower probability level. *** Significant at 25 percent or lower probability level.

subcommittee coefficient has the "wrong" sign and is significant at the 25 percent probability level, weakly contradicting the subcommittee-targeting hypothesis. Both leadership and regional coefficients have the expected signs and are statistically significant, confirming the notion that these variables would be important for a crop from a limited geographic region. The coefficient on the regional variable indicates that regional representation on the committees in the case of rice is important, despite the fact that only six states had significant production of the crop.[19] The combined regression results contain a wrong sign for the subcommittee variable (although it is not statistically significant), whereas both the leadership and regional variable coefficients have the expected sign and are significant. The *F* statistic is also significant, indicating the model's explanatory power. As expected, senators received significantly more than did House members.

Wheat, Feed Grain, and Soybean PACs

Because price support programs for wheat, the feed grains (corn, barley, oats, and sorghum), and soybeans are similar to each other, and because legislation affecting them is the responsibility of a single subcommittee in the House as well as in the Senate, the PACs representing these program

TABLE 9-13 Contributions of the Wheat, Feed Grain, and Soybean PACs, 1988

	Targeted	*Unrelated*	*Total*
Con Agra	$57,350	$30,450	$87,800
Archer-Daniels-Midland	47,300	26,500	73,800
Cargill	43,800	19,000	62,800
Land O' Lakes, Inc.	34,800	12,750	47,550
A. E. Staley	31,650	14,250	45,900
Pillsbury Inc.	24,397	14,159	38,556
National Association of Wheat Growers	29,450	6,550	36,000
Farmland Industries	17,250	7,250	24,500
Feed Industry PAC	15,600	7,969	23,569
Ag Processing, Inc.	9,500	6,500	16,000
American Soybean Association	9,550	6,200	15,750
Tyson Foods	5,490	5,850	11,340
Continental Grain Company	7,250	3,750	11,000
Quaker Oats Company	8,500	1,000	9,500
Ralston Purina Company	6,525	2,000	8,525
Rice and Soybean PAC	5,500	3,000	8,500
Central Soya Company	7,300	900	8,200
Gold Kist, Inc.	5,250	1,200	6,450

Source: Federal Election Commission.

crops have been analyzed together. Hereafter, this group will be referred to as the WFGSB (wheat, feed grains, soybeans).

The WFGSB PACs listed in Table 9-13 show the relative importance of corporate PACs compared with commodity-oriented PACs. In fact, the top six are corporate PACs. Only the National Association of Wheat Growers and the Feed Industry commodity PACs contributed over $20,000. Con Agra ($87,800), Archer-Daniels-Midland ($73,800), and Cargill ($62,800), all large firms, contributed much more.

The empirical results for the WFGSB are impressive. In the House, WFGSB PACs gave $153,040 to members of the subcommittee ($8,054 on average per member) and $82,400 to members not on the subcommittee ($3,433 on average) (see Table 9-13). The top eight House members receiving contributions were subcommittee members, with the chairman of the subcommittee ranking fifth. Supporting this subcommittee-targeting result, the regression coefficient on the subcommittee variable is statistically significant (see Table 9-14). Thus, the evidence is compelling that contributions of the WFGSB PACs support the subcommittee-targeting hypothesis.

Of the five congresspeople receiving contributions over $10,000 from the WFGSB PACs, four are Republicans, all from midwestern states where these commodities are very important. This would lead to the expectation that the regression coefficients on party and regional variables would be significant, and indeed they are. The F and R^2 statistics reveal that the model has good explanatory power.

The three senators receiving the most contributions from the WFGSB PACs (Boschwitz [R-MN], Karnes [R-NE], and Lugar [R-IN])[20] were not subcommittee members (although Lugar is ex officio), and each received over $33,000. However, all represent important grain-producing midwestern states.

The next ten senators in order of contributions received were subcommittee members, and contributions varied from $13,000 to $33,647 each. Recall, however, that all but four of the senators on the agriculture committee are members of the subcommittee. With the WFGSB PACs, regional representation would be expected to be important since these crops have such large values, and as expected, the regional coefficient is statistically significant. The average contribution to senators on the subcommittee was $14,381, compared with $22,095 on average to nonsubcommittee members, which probably explains the negative sign of the subcommittee coefficient in the Senate.

TABLE 9-14 Regression Coefficients, t Values, R^2, and F Values for Wheat, Feed Grains, and Soybean PACs

	House		*Senate*		*Combined*	
	Regression	*t value*	*Regression*	*t value*	*Regression*	*t value*
Intercept	1986.0	2.257*	5980.6	1.150	646.7	0.453
X_1 (Subcommittee)	2487.3	1.755**	-4567.7	-0.915	-2133.5	-1.147
X_2 (Leadership)	1044.8	0.484	10419.7	2.166*	5469.5	2.084*
X_3 (Party)	3088.5	2.908*	12773.4	3.264*	6190.3	3.920*
X_4 (Regional)	2748.6	1.872**	12969.6	3.086*	8305.6	4.654*
X_5 (Branch)					9905.2	5.469*
F		6.89*		7.95*		17.66*
R^2		0.42		0.71		0.62

Note: * Significant at 5 percent or lower probability level. ** Significant at 10 percent or lower probability level.

The party, regional, and leadership regression coefficients are significant, as is the F statistic for the Senate. In the combined analysis, all coefficients except for the subcommittee variable are highly significant. As expected, senators received significantly more than members of the House. The F and R^2 statistics are the highest of all the commodities analyzed.

Senator Dole and Archer-Daniels-Midland

Of course, all PAC contributors have their own reasons for supporting given political candidates. By referring to an example that has received considerable publicity, the intent is not to excoriate specific politicians or to imply that any impropriety has been committed. Specific examples, however, provide useful knowledge of how the political system works in supplying favors.

Reports indicate a link between the large agribusiness corporation Archer-Daniels-Midland (ADM) and its chairman, Dwayne Andreas, and Senator Robert Dole, minority leader in the Senate and a member of the Agricultural Production and Stabilization of Prices Subcommittee (see Birnbaum and Abramson 1990). ADM produces about 70 percent of the nation's ethanol, the principal use of which is to mix with gasoline to yield gasohol. Gasohol is burned in internal combustion engines as a substitute for straight gasoline and is alleged to produce fewer environmental damages than does gasoline. The government has subsidized gasohol production for many years.

By 1980 Mr. Andreas, his relatives, and ADM's PAC had contributed \$81,000 to Senator Dole's political efforts as well as more than \$300,000 to an array of Republican and Democratic members of Congress (Birnbaum and Abramson 1990). These politicians generally support tax breaks for the ethanol industry, which uses surplus corn alcohol as a substitute for scarce domestic and imported oil. In response to the *Wall Street Journal* article pointing out his link with ADM, Senator Dole wrote that he did not deny the contributions but indicated that not one penny of the ethanol subsidy goes to ADM, but instead goes directly to oil companies, which blend ethanol with gasoline (Dole 1990). But this disclaimer seems to miss the important point that the subsidy is designed to increase the attractiveness of ethanol as a fuel made from corn, and ADM produces ethanol and handles tremendous quantities of corn. So even though ADM may not receive the direct subsidy, it certainly profits from the enhanced demand for ethanol that the subsidy makes possible.

Another *Wall Street Journal* writer reports that Senator Dole was primarily responsible for maintaining the tax breaks to producers of ethanol in the final deficit-cutting accord between Congress and the administration passed on October 27, 1990 (Calmes 1990).

Another important contributor to political campaigns of members of the agricultural committees was Cargill, a very large privately held grain exporter. In his book *Merchants of Grains,* Dan Morgan relates that representatives of Cargill, working through Senator Hubert H. Humphrey, were instrumental in persuading the USDA to put surplus government grain up for sale at inland as well as port locations (see Ruttan 1990), thus increasing the volume of business for grain handlers.

It must not be inferred that all the political pressures brought by agribusiness firms produce inefficient outcomes. Agricultural economist Vernon Ruttan points out:

> *The agribusiness sector, however, has generally opposed farm programs that have been responsible for surplus accumulation. They have been more favorable to programs that partially or fully "delink" commodity prices and payments to farmers. Cargill was, for example, particularly active in the mid-1960s and again in the 1980s with proposals to delink U.S. farm commodity prices and farm program payments and thereby reduce the role of government in international trade. The shipping industry was successful, in the FSA of 1985, in forcing an increase in the portion of food aid shipped on U.S. vessels from 50 to 75 percent. (1990, p. 14)*

Here was a case in which the political interest of Cargill was to promote decoupling (see Chapter 13), a policy innovation that produces a more efficient allocation of resources and a more efficient agricultural sector than do alternative price support policies, and at the same time improve its own position as a handler and trader of grain.

Dairy PACs

The dairy PACs were huge contributors to election campaigns compared with the PACs of other agricultural commodities. One reason is the sheer size of the dairy industry compared with most other commodity sectors, and thus much more wealth is affected by dairy policy. Individual dairy farmers on average command large quantities of resources and sell more product than most other types of farmers. Most are full-time operators and thus individually have a large stake in a profitable industry. And perhaps most importantly, the dairy industry is tightly regulated by a host of government policies at both federal and state levels: federal price supports on raw milk; federal marketing orders that set prices for different classes of milk and often establish marketing quotas for fluid milk sales; milk-class price systems in some states accompanied by production quotas; tough federal controls on imports; a federal dairy herd buy-out program designed to reduce supplies of milk reaching the market, and stringent sanitation and quality requirements.

Because of these extensive government regulations, the dairy industry, probably more than for any other commodity group, has a greater incentive to control the free-rider problem, which is the principal barrier to collective action in the political arena. The big dairy cooperatives have been authorized to withhold political donations from checks they send to farmers to pay for collectively marketed milk (see Jackson 1988, p. 303).

In addition, the dairy industry is important in all major regions of the country, suggesting that a wider geographic distribution of PAC contributions among politicians might have a more significant political payoff than would be true for many other commodities with more regional production patterns. This would lead to the expectation that subcommittee and leadership targeting might be somewhat less significant than with some other commodity PACs that are more focused politically.

Indeed, the data indicate that in the House dairy PAC expenditures are distributed quite broadly among the membership of the Agriculture Committee and among the members of the Livestock, Dairy, and Poultry Subcommittee. The big winner on the subcommittee was ranking Republican James Jeffords (R-VT).[21]

In total, $247,036 was targeted to subcommittee members in the House, while $214,986 was not (Table 9-15). But members of the subcommittee received an *average* of $13,724, compared with $8,599 given to members of the broader committee not on the subcommittee, data supporting the subcommittee-targeting hypothesis.

Among the dairy PACs, the big contributors were the large dairy cooperatives: Associated Milk Producers, Inc., Mid-America Dairymen, Inc., Dairymen, Inc., and Land O' Lakes, Inc. (see Table 9-15), which are truly major players in the PAC and lobbying game. Every single PAC on the list targeted more contributions to subcommittee members than to members of the overall committee, although contributions to the latter group were also very substantial.

Seventeen representatives received contributions in excess of $10,000, both a broader distribution of support and bigger amounts than for other commodity PACs. Also, unlike other commodity PACs, the average contribution to Democrats was more than that to Republicans. Rank appears to be important, but representation from big dairy-production states like Wisconsin and California does not seem to carry much weight.

These findings are supported generally by the regression results in Table 9-16. For the House, the coefficient for subcommittee membership has the expected positive sign and is statistically significant. Although the

TABLE 9-15 Contributions of the Dairy PACs, 1988

	Targeted	*Unrelated*	*Total*
Associated Milk Producers, Inc.	$158,700	$116,700	$275,400
Mid-America Dairymen, Inc.	125,400	70,750	196,150
Dairymen, Inc.	103,600	59,550	163,150
Land O' Lakes, Inc.	40,000	20,050	60,050
Ice Cream and Milk PAC (Milk Industry Foundation)	16,750	14,850	31,600
Milk Marketing, Inc.	11,000	3,550	14,550
Southland Corporation	7,678	6,450	14,128
Political Action Trust (Mountain Dairymen's Association)	10,430	1,000	11,430
Western United Dairymen's Association	6,856	1,000	7,856
Agri-Mark, Inc.	7,000	550	7,550
Borden, Inc.	4,500	1,750	6,250
Budd Foods	4,000	1,500	5,500
Dairyman's Co-op Creamery	5,000	—	5,000

Source: Federal Election Commission.

TABLE 9-16 Regression Coefficients, t Values, R^2, and *F* Values for Dairy PACs

	House		*Senate*		*Combined*	
	Regression	*t value*	*Regression*	*t value*	*Regression*	*t value*
Intercept	7287.5	3.723*	20585.7	2.886*	8196.0	3.879*
X_1 (Subcommittee)	4532.9	1.835**	-4382.9	-0.574	2564.0	0.995
X_2 (Leadership)	4603.6	0.952	5329.4	0.697	4440.4	1.133
X_3 (Party)	742.0	0.307	2307.5	0.321	989.6	0.403
X_4 (Regional)	2544.2	1.052	56.1	0.006	2085.1	0.804
X_5 (Branch)					7392.2	2.689*
F		1.80***		0.20		3.24*
R^2		0.16		0.06		0.23

Note: * Significant at 5 percent or lower probability level. ** Significant at 10 percent or lower probability level. *** Significant at 25 percent or lower probability level.

coefficient for the leadership variable has a positive sign, it is not statistically significant. Therefore, a significant relationship between leadership and PAC contributions to House members cannot be claimed. The coefficient for party is positive, indicating that Republicans received more than Democrats, contradicting the results of the simple averages previously reported, but it is not statistically significant. The regional variable also has the expected positive sign but is not statistically significant. The *F* statistic is only weakly significant, while the R^2 indicates that about 16 percent of the variation in dairy PAC contributions to individual members of the House on the Agriculture Committee is accounted for by the independent variables. The one significant finding is that membership on the subcommittee is important.[22]

The dairy PACs gave $264,578 to the Senate subcommittee members and $87,014 to the four nonsubcommittee members. However, the average contribution to nonsubcommittee members exceeded that to subcommittee members: $21,754 compared with $17,832. This result is confirmed by the negative coefficient on the subcommittee variable in the regression analysis, although it is not statistically significant. The larger average contribution to noncommittee members was due in large part to the heavy contributions made to Senator Rudy Boschwitz (R-MN), representing a very important dairy state and a powerful force on the general Agriculture, Nutrition, and Forestry Committee.[23] He was the top recipient of contributions from the dairy PACs with a total of $39,764. The subcommittee chair, now also out of the Senate, John Melcher (D-MT), received $31,500, but he did not represent an important dairy state.[24] Perhaps the Boschwitz and Melcher data help explain the finding that the leadership regression coefficient has the expected sign but is not statistically significant. In fact, none of the regression coefficients is statistically significant, and neither is the *F* statistic.

Even though the regression results are quite weak for both branches of Congress, the model for the dairy PACs explains more for the House than for the Senate, confirming an earlier expectation that PAC contributions would be more focused on the subcommittee in the branch of Congress in which the subcommittees have a more narrow commodity focus. In the combined regression, all variables have the expected signs, but only the branch coefficient is significant, indicating that senators received more than did House members. The *F* statistic is also significant, indicating that the model as a composite explains a significant amount of the variation in PAC contributions.

An interesting characteristic of the dairy PACs is the large difference between sums of money received by the number one and number two members in both houses ranked by contributions. In the House, almost a $15,000 difference exists; in the Senate, over $8,000. This suggests that these two members are expected to have crucial influence in representing the dairy cause in Congress.

Summing up, subcommittee targeting was significant in the House but not in the Senate. Also, as expected, senators received larger contributions on average than House members did. No other variables were strongly significant in explaining PAC contributions. Given the nature and location of the dairy industry, however, these weak empirical results are not really surprising. (A later section comparing the empirical findings of the different commodity PACs will further explain this point.)

Sugar PACs

Among agricultural groups, the sugar PACs are also big contributors to election campaigns. In the sample data, total contributions of the sugar PACs to House committee members were $337,725, a relatively large amount, given that the number of sugar producers in the nation is only just over 10,000. Another important factor is the way the sugar industry is organized; like dairy producers, sugar refiners are few and large in scale, which makes the free-rider problem more manageable. Thus, the hypothesis that groups having concentrated and large individual interests will have strong incentives to bring political pressure is supported. Of the total contributions, $111,450 (33 percent) was targeted directly to the Cotton, Rice, and Sugar Subcommittee members.

Individual sugar PACs follow the pattern of targeting more to subcom-

TABLE 9-17 Contributions of Sugar PACs, 1988

	Targeted	*Unrelated*	*Total*
American Crystal Sugar PAC	$81,935	$42,250	$124,185
American Sugarbeet Growers	36,250	29,500	65,750
American Sugar Cane League of the USA	34,050	14,850	48,900
Southern Minnesota Beet Sugar Co-op	22,350	19,250	41,600
Florida Sugar Cane	20,700	10,950	31,650
Hawaiian Sugar Planters	19,100	11,800	30,900
Great Lakes Sugar Beet Growers	5,000	6,875	11,875
United States Beet Sugar PAC	7,437	3,950	11,387
California Beet Growers Association	4,000	1,900	5,900

Source: Federal Election Commission.

mittee members than to nonmembers, although as indicated earlier, totals are not so meaningful as committee member averages (Table 9-17).[25]

The ranking Republican on the subcommittee, Arlan Stangeland (R-MN) received $25,550 from the sugar PACs, by far the most of any committee or subcommittee member. Following Stangeland was the chairman of the broader Agriculture Committee, E de la Garza (D-TX), an ex officio member of the subcommittee with $11,250, and the subcommittee chair, Jerry Huckaby (D-LA) with $9,850. These data account for why the leadership variable in the regression analysis is statistically significant (Table 9-18).

Many contributions in the range of $5,000 to $8,000 were given to committee members not on the subcommittee, with Ron Marlenee (R-MT) receiving the most ($8,300). However, the *average* contribution to members of the general committee not on the subcommittee was only $4,524, while those members on the subcommittee received an average of $6,556. The subcommittee regression coefficient has the expected positive sign but is not statistically significant. It is, therefore, imprudent to claim strong empirical support for the subcommittee-targeting hypothesis.

None of the variables except leadership has a significant coefficient in the regression analysis, although all have the expected positive signs. In the House, however, the *F* statistic is significant, indicating the explanatory power of the leadership variable. This is also reflected in a relatively high R^2 coefficient.

In the Senate Agricultural Production and Stabilization of Prices Sub-

TABLE 9-18 Regression Coefficients, t Values, R^2, and F Values for Sugar PACs

	House		*Senate*		*Combined*	
	Regression	*t value*	*Regression*	*t value*	*Regression*	*t value*
Intercept	3873.3	5.157*	2989.6	0.721	3659.0	4.117*
X_1 (Subcommittee)	210.6	0.186	3605.3	0.900	703.1	0.608
X_2 (Leadership)	7949.9	4.503*	4333.8	1.239***	5925.9	3.706*
X_3 (Party)	1024.9	1.082	696.7	0.253	1020.2	1.013
X_4 (Regional)	1154.8	1.019	4216.1	1.107	1800.0	1.632***
X_5 (Branch)					1743.4	1.482***
F		8.04*		0.74		5.97*
R^2		0.46		0.18		0.35

Note: * Significant at 5 percent or lower probability level. ** Significant at 10 percent or lower probability level. *** Significant at 25 percent or lower probability level.

committee, Bob Dole (R-KS) topped the list with $23,000 in PAC contributions.[26] The leadership variable has a weakly significant coefficient in the regression analysis of Senate contributions (Table 9-17).

In terms of *average* contributions, subcommittee members received $8,331, while nonmembers received $6,500. The subcommittee regression coefficient has the expected positive sign but is not quite significant at the 25 percent probability level. The sign of the party coefficient favors the Republicans but the coefficient is not significant. The same is true for the regional variable, which has the expected sign but is not significant. The conclusion must be that except for a weak relationship between leadership and PAC contributions, the regression model does not have much explanatory power for the sugar PACs in the Senate.

Across both houses, the sugar PACs gave a total of $380,047 to the agriculture committees and targeted $236,422 (62.2 percent) to subcommittee members. In the combined regression analysis, only the leadership variable and the *F* statistic are significant at the 5 percent probability level, but both the regional and branch variables are weakly significant.

Sugar PAC Contributions to Other Related Committees

Data were acquired also from the FEC on agricultural PAC contributions to some other congressional committees that directly affect the agricultural sector. The objective was to ascertain if contributions to these committees were "large" compared with those given to the agriculture committees. In general, the answer is negative.

It was the sugar and dairy PACs, however, that were the most generous contributors to other committees, confirming the broad congressional focus of these commodity PACs. Only the contributions of the sugar PACs are analyzed here, however. Total contributions to the House Agriculture Committee from the sugar PACs were $229,075, while those to the Appropriations Committee were only $64,900. Of this latter amount, $42,000 was targeted to the Agricultural Subcommittee and $22,810 to the Energy and Interior subcommittees combined. Contributions from the sugar PACs to the Interior and Insular Affairs Committee were $43,750, probably reflecting the sugar industry's interest in continuing water and electric power subsidies from federal agencies overseen by this committee.

In the Senate, $83,004 from sugar PACs was given to the subcommittee members of the Appropriations Committee: $47,354 to the Agriculture Subcommittee and $35,650 to the Energy Subcommittee. Members of the Senate Energy and Natural Resources Committee, however, received $101,416 from the sugar PACs.

An intriguing question is why the dairy and sugar PACs gave more to committees and subcommittees outside of the agricultural committees than did the PACs of other commodities? The reason is probably different for the two industries.

Domestic sugar prices were supported in the 1985 Food Security Act by nonrecourse loans to producers via sugar refiners at the rate of 18 cents per pound. World prices have been much lower, making it highly profitable to import sugar. To protect domestic producers and to prevent government accumulation of huge stocks of homegrown sugar, domestic market prices have been held up by import quotas to about 22–23 cents per pound.[27] The sugar interests appear to have supported politicians on several congressional committees in the belief that broad support was needed to continue these quotas in the face of consumer and foreign producer opposition.

However, while domestic sugar production is fairly localized, (sugarcane production occurs only in the southern states of Florida, Hawaii, Texas, and Louisiana, and significant sugar beet production in only a few additional states), the dairy industry is relatively large in every region and in the majority of states. In fact, dairy sales are the highest of any agricultural product in many states. It is expected, therefore, that the dairy PACs would contribute to a broader geographical distribution of members of Congress to maintain favorable dairy prices than would be true for most other supported commodities. Besides, the income support to dairy producers comes through a variety of policies, previously enumerated. Some of these programs are outside the jurisdiction of the Livestock, Dairy, and Poultry Subcommittee of the House Agriculture Committee.[28] Therefore, the political contributions of the dairy PACs might be expected to be more broadly based and they are.

PACs of General Farm Organizations

Because general farm organizations are not commodity specific, their PAC contributions could not be identified with a specific subcommittee. These organizations represent a broad spectrum of commodity and producer interests (Table 9-19). Many, such as the American Farm Bureau Federation, have state and local branches that support members of Congress representing the states and districts in which the branches are located. There were a few exceptions—the Election PAC of Alabama Farm Bureau and the Minn-Dak Farmers Cooperative, to name two, did not support only local members of Congress. Also, the national organizations appear to have given very broadly with no obvious patterns.

Given that all but four members of the Senate agriculture committee were members of the Agricultural Production and Stabilization of Prices

TABLE 9-19 General Farm Organization Contributions, 1988

National Council of Farmer Cooperatives	$93,969
Election PAC of Alabama Farm Bureau	42,079
National Farmers Organization	22,750
Missouri Farm Bureau (six different districts)	22,600
Minn-Dak Farmers Cooperative	15,650
Western Growers Association	13,500
California Farm Bureau Federation	12,950

Source: Federal Election Commission.

Subcommittee, a general purpose organization could be expected to contribute more heavily to individual Senate political races than to House races, where the candidates would be more narrowly focused geographically. Of the general organizations that qualified for the sample, the total given to Senate races was $128,273, while that given to House races was $160,633. But since there were so many more House than Senate races, the latter were supported more generously. Of the contributions made to identified committee members in each branch, $6,751 was given on average to Senate candidates, $3,736 to House candidates.

For decades, the general farm organizations, especially the Farm Bureau, have been strong lobbyists for agricultural research and extension because these activities were perceived to benefit agriculture broadly. Pressure is brought at both federal and state levels, which is significant because the agricultural experiment stations and cooperative extension services are increasingly being funded by state and local governments. In addition, the Farm Bureau has been promoting market expansion policies for many years, whereas commodity organizations have been much more likely to support subsidies that benefit their own producers. Market expansion includes food stamps, school lunch programs, and foreign food aid. The initial proposals for the sale of agricultural commodities abroad through Public Law 480 was strongly promoted at the 1952 American Farm Bureau convention (Ruttan 1990).

Some Comparative Findings for the Commodity PACs

What conclusions can be drawn from analysis testing some of the hypotheses developed in Chapter 7? Table 9-20 shows the total value of production by commodity class, the total contributions by PACs in various commodity

TABLE 9-20 Value of Production, PAC Contributions, and Producer Subsidy Equivalents for Supported Crops, 1986–87

	Average value of production		*PAC contributions*					
Commodity	*Total (in millions)*	*Rank*	*Total (in thousands)*	*Rank*	*Per million of sales*	*Rank*	*Average PSE*[1]	*Rank*
WFGSB	$44,140	1	$539.5	2	$12.2	7	41.9%	5
Rice	1,546	6	47.6	7	30.8	6	61.0	2
Cotton	3,502	3	214.1	5	61.1	3	49.5	4
Peanuts	1,052	7	51.8	6	49.3	4	—	—
Tobacco	1,822	5	304.5	4	167.2	2	—	—
Sugar	1,832	4	380.0	3	207.5	1	66.5	1
Milk	17,644	2	813.5	1	46.1	5	60.0	3

Note: [1] PSEs are essentially the subsidies captured as a percentage of value of market production.

Source: U.S. Department of Commerce (1989), Bureau of the Census. *Statistical Abstract of the United States, 1989* (Washington, DC).

classes, PAC contributions per million dollars of sales, producer subsidy equivalents (PSEs) where available, and the number of farmer cooperatives involved in sales in each commodity grouping.[29] These data will permit some further tests, albeit primitive ones.

Wheat–feed grains–soybeans (WFGSB) was easily the largest commodity class in value of production in 1986–87, followed in order by milk (a proxy for dairy products), cotton, sugar, tobacco, rice, and peanuts. In total PAC contributions from these commodity groups, the ranking was milk, WFGSB, sugar, tobacco, cotton, peanuts, and rice. The correlation between the two rankings is clearly positive, indicating that the commodity sectors with the most income at stake also contributed the most money to election campaigns through their PACs. However, the rank correlation is not perfect, implying that sector size is not the only important variable affecting contributions.

In fact, contributions per million dollars of commodity sales reveal a quite different ranking. By this criterion, sugar leads the list, followed by tobacco, cotton, peanuts, milk, rice, and WFGSB. Sugar is also the most heavily protected of those commodities for which PSEs are available, and WFGSB is the least protected. Therefore, there is a clear tendency for commodities that are the most heavily subsidized (protected) per dollar of sales to be the ones that gave the most to their PACs.

It was hypothesized earlier that commodities with low (inelastic) price elasticities of demand would have an incentive to bring more pressure for income support policies, especially involving supply reductions, than those with more elastic demands. The idea is that if supply can be curtailed via government policy such as acreage controls or import quotas, the lower quantity (higher price) would generate more revenues the more inelastic the demand. This hypothesis is strongly confirmed by the data in Table 9-20. The ranking by PSEs are sugar, rice, milk, cotton, and WFGSB. The ranking by the degree of inelasticity of demand[30] are sugar, milk, rice, cotton, and WFGSB, obviously very close to the ranking by PSE.

The hypothesis concerning group size is weakly supported by the data. This may be partly due to limitations in finding a suitable definition of group size. Because of the free-rider problem, the expectation is that small groups will be more active in bringing political pressure than will large groups. To surmount the free-rider problem in the agricultural sector, assessments are often mandated for individual producers. These payments are generally made to larger member entities, such as cooperatives and commodity promotion organizations, which then organize PACs to push the political interests of member producers. Data presented in tables earlier in the chapter showed the largest PAC contributors in each commodity class. Many of these were cooperatives, and in the case of some commodities like milk, were predominantly so. Thus, the number of cooperatives in each commodity grouping in 1986–87 was used as a proxy to indicate the severity of the free-rider problem.

The correlation between the ranks of contributions per million dollars of sales and the number of cooperatives is negative and moderately close (Table 9-21). WFGSB ranks first in the number of representing co-ops and last in the PAC contributions per million dollars of sales. Rice and milk rank low in contributions per million dollars of sales (sixth and fifth respectively) but are in the middle in terms of the number of co-ops (fourth and third, respectively.) Sugar and tobacco rank first and second in contributions but fifth and seventh in the number of farmer co-ops. Thus, there is some support for the hypothesis that political pressure is inversely proportional to group size.

Regression results presented earlier generally confirm the hypothesis that subcommittee targeting is more strongly supported in the House than in the Senate because the House structure gives subcommittees closer identification with specific commodities. In the House, the coefficient of the subcommittee variable was significant at the 25 percent or lower probability level for cotton, WFGSB, dairy products, and tobacco, whereas in the Senate similar confirmation for the hypothesis existed only for rice and tobacco.

In contrast, the leadership-targeting hypothesis was confirmed in the House for cotton, peanuts, sugar, tobacco, and rice, whereas in the Senate this was true for only peanuts, sugar, WFGSB, and rice. Only sugar and rice appear on both lists. In the House, the regional variable was significant for cotton, peanuts, WFGSB, tobacco, and rice, whereas in the Senate it was

TABLE 9-21 Number of Farmer Cooperatives for Supported Crops, 1986–87

Commodity	*Average*	*Rank (per $ million)*
WFGSB	2,027	1
Rice	56	4
Cotton	417	2
Nuts	36	6
Tobacco	33	7
Sugar	42	5
Dairy products	330	3

Source: U.S. Department of Agriculture (1989), *Agricultural Statistics* (Washington, DC), Table 608, p. 437.

significant for only cotton, WFGSB, and rice. In the House, Republicans received significantly more than Democrats from the cotton and WFGSB PACs, and in no case did Democrats receive significantly more than Republicans. In the Senate, Republicans received significantly more than Democrats from the cotton, WFGSB, and tobacco PACs, and in no case did Democrats receive significantly more than Republicans. No theory purports to explain these party findings beyond the conventional one that Republicans represent rural constituencies disproportionately.

In the House, the complete regression model explained a significant proportion of the variation in contributions by the PACs to members of Congress for all commodities, although only weakly so for the dairy industry. In the Senate, however, this was true only for WFGSB and peanuts, although weakly for cotton, tobacco, and rice. This finding also confirms that PAC targeting is tighter in the House where the subcommittee structure is more conducive to targeting than in the Senate. In the combined House and Senate regressions, the *F* statistic was significant for all commodity groups.[31] This finding suggests that the attempt to model political favors, identify important explanatory factors a priori, and establish significant empirical relationships between the explanatory variables and PAC contributions has been successful.

To summarize, in general commodity PACs do not randomly distribute their contributions to politicians, but carefully target funds to where they have the highest payoffs for the interest group represented. In most cases, it is to subcommittee members and leaders of the general congressional agriculture committees. It is not always precisely the same variables that account for contribution patterns, but in every case patterns do emerge.

Notes

1. They can be classified as producer organizations, producer/agribusiness organizations, agribusiness/middlemen organizations, supplier/facilitator organizations, public interest groups and related organizations, and food firms. See William Browne (1988, p. 44).

2. The Senate Agriculture, Nutrition, and Forestry Committee has subcommittees carrying the titles of Agricultural Credit; Agricultural Production and Stabilization of Prices; Agricultural Research and General Legislation; Conservation and Forestry; Domestic and Foreign Marketing and Product Promotion; Nutrition and Investigations; and Rural Development and Rural Electrification.

3. The House Agriculture Committee has forty-two members and has subcommittees entitled Cotton, Rice, and Sugar; Livestock, Dairy, and Poultry; Tobacco and Peanuts; Wheat, Soybeans, and Feed Grains; Conservation, Credit, and Rural Development; Department Operations, Research, and Foreign Agriculture; Domestic Marketing, Consumer Relations, and Nutrition; and Forests, Family Farms, and Energy.

4. Only about one-third of senators run in any given two-year election since their term is six years. PACs, however, contribute to the political war chests of senators even though they may not be running in a given election. The assumption made here is that the rate of giving to senators does not depend on whether they were candidates in the 1988 election cycle. This assumption may be heroic in cases where close elections were expected in 1988. Commodity PACs would then be expected to join other contributors to participate more heavily in support of those running than those who were not. If this is true, some downward bias may be present in the data for those not running in the 1988 races.

5. It is clear that all PACs have interests of some kind that are being promoted, else why would they be established? But sometimes these interests are difficult and therefore costly to ferret out. With most PACs, however, the classification as special or general interest was quite obvious.

6. Regression analysis is a statistical tool that reveals association between variables of interest. Technically, it explains the variation among observations in the dependent (explained) variable by observed changes in the independent (explanatory) variable or variables. Observations number nineteen in the Senate and forty-two in the House, the number of individual members on the agricultural committees. Variation in the dependent variable is roughly measured as the square of the deviations from a least-squares regression line. The coefficients on each independent variable describe how much the dependent variable changes for each unit change in the independent variables.

7. A statistical distribution known as "Student's *t*" is used to test whether or not the independent variable has statistically significant explanatory power in the regression analysis. In technical terms, the *t* value is the regression coefficient divided by its standard error. If the coefficient is significant only at the 25 percent probability level, it is described here as weakly significant.

8. It must be repeated that not all PACs could be clearly identified with specific commodities, and therefore those in our sample underrepresent the total population of PACs giving to political candidates. Therefore, the regression coefficients will understate the value of subcommittee membership. This same point is equally valid for the other regression coefficients.

9. The *F* statistic indicates whether the complete regression model has statistically significant power in explaining PAC contributions. R^2 indicates the percentage of the variation in the dependent variable (PAC contributions) that is accounted for by changes in the independent variables as a composite.

10. Senator Helms was followed by Pryor (D-AR), Wilson (R-CA), Bond (R-MO), Dole (R-KS), Cochran (R-MS), and Daschle (D-SD). The chairman of the subcommittee (Melcher, D-MT) was far down the list, and Leahy (D-VT), the chairman of the Senate Agriculture, Nutrition, and Forestry Committee received nothing at all. The ranking Republican of the committee, Richard Lugar (R-IN), got only $2,000.

11. In the House, Charles Rose (D-NC), Tobacco and Peanuts subcommittee chair, received the most money, $3,250. Charles Hatcher (D-GA), received $2,075, and ranking Republican Larry Hopkins (R-KY) received $1,550. Claude Harris (D-AL), who is not on the subcommittee, nonetheless received $2,750. All other House members received less than $1,000.

12. What could explain this apparent anomaly? Only twenty of the forty-three House committee members received contributions from peanut PACs—ten of thirteen subcommittee members received contributions while ten of thirty nonsubcommittee members received contributions. With the small divisor of the subcommittee, average targeted contributions appear high ($998); likewise, average contributions to nonsubcommittee members ($275) appear low because of the large divisor. Some targeting would appear to be occurring. However, the regression results, which include as observations all members of the committee, reflect the fact that many members received no contributions at all.

13. Senate Agriculture, Nutrition, and Forestry Committee ranking Republican Richard Lugar (R-IN) tops the list with $6,000 compared with committee chair Patrick Leahy (D-VT), who received only $2,000. Obviously, regional factors are not very important since Indiana and Vermont are not important peanut states and the regression analysis confirms the conclusion that the regional variable is not significant. The subcommittee chair, John Melcher (D-MT) received $4,500, and Jesse Helms (R-NC), ranking Republican on the

subcommittee, got $4,000. Howell Heflin (D-AL) received $4,600, while Wyche Fowler, a Democrat from the important peanut state of Georgia, received nothing.

14. The *F* and R^2 statistics are also large, indicating the model's explanatory power.

15. Wally Herger (R-CA) was next with $7,650, while Arlan Stangeland (R-MN), ranking Republican on the subcommittee, received $5,900, and Claude Harris (D-AL) received $5,800. In fifth place was the ex officio member of the subcommittee E de la Garza (D-TX), chairman of the House Agriculture Committee, who received $4,800. Charles Hatcher (D GA) was the top-ranked nonsubcommittee member at the ninth rank, and only two nonsubcommittee members received more than $1,500 from cotton PACs.

16. Senator Helms was followed by three fellow Republicans, Dole (R-KS), Cochran (R-MS), and Wilson (R-CA). Howell Heflin (D-AL) was the top Democrat, but he ranked below the four Republicans. The subcommittee chair, Melcher (D-MT), and the chairman of the overall Agriculture Committee, Leahy (D-VT), and the ranking Republican on the overall committee, Lugar (R-IN), received only "small" contributions.

17. It is somewhat surprising, therefore, that even though the sign of the regression coefficient on the subcommittee variable is positive as expected, it is not even weakly significant.

18. Also, the *F* statistic is significant at the 5 percent probability level, indicating that the complete model explains a significant portion of the variation in contributions received from rice PACs by House members.

19. The *F* statistic is significant, but only at the 25 percent probability level, although the independent variables account for 40 percent of the variation in the dependent variable.

20. Senator Lugar is the ranking Republican on the Senate Agriculture Committee and as such is an ex officio member of the APSPS.

21. Jeffords was followed by Campbell (D-CO), Stangeland (R-MN), Volkmer (D-MO), Nagle (D-IA), and Gunderson (R-WI). In the House, twelve members of the Agriculture Committee who were nonmembers of the Livestock, Dairy, and Poultry Subcommittee received more PAC money than did the subcommittee chair, Charles Stenholm (D-TX). Also, twelve members of the subcommittee received more money than he did.

22. There are several reasons why these dairy results are not entirely unexpected, and they will be discussed shortly.

23. Boschwitz is perhaps best known for his sponsorship of decoupling, which

was first legislated in the 1985 FSA. Senator Boschwitz was defeated in his bid to retain his seat in the 1990 election.

24. Senator Melcher was defeated in his bid to retain his seat in the 1988 election.

25. The one exception was the Great Lakes Sugar Beet Growers, which targeted $5,000 to members and $6,875 to nonmembers. For some reason, this PAC targeted most of its money to regional candidates: for example, $2,075 to William Schuette (R-MI) and $1,000 to Tim Johnson (D-SD), although the amounts are not very large.

26. Next was John Melcher (D-MT), the subcommittee chair at the time, with $15,708. Others were Jesse Helms (R-NC), the ranking Republican on the subcommittee, $13,400; Pete Wilson (R-CA), $12,579; and Rudy Boschwitz (R-MN), who, as indicated earlier, is not on the subcommittee, at $11,000.

27. U.S. Senate (1990a), *Food, Agriculture, Conservation, and Trade Act of 1990*, Report no. 101–357 (Washington, DC: July 6), p. 135.

28. Ibid., p. 28.

29. Essentially, producer subsidy equivalents include direct government payments to farmers and indirect transfers through policies such as input subsidies, marketing assistance, or exchange rate distortions. Definitions and discussion of PSEs were presented in Chapter 2.

30. Estimates of own-price elasticity for various commodities are: dairy products, -.513; poultry, -.205; red meats, -.407; cotton, -.997; food grains, -.956; feed grains, -.1.021; sugar crops, -.044; oilseeds, -.793; other crops, -.350. (See Hertel 1990, p. 159.)

31. One of the reasons for this finding is the greater statistical power resulting from the greater sample size in combining members from both houses.

PART 3

The Environmental Consequences of Agricultural Support Programs

10

Agricultural Policy and Environmental Quality: Soil and Wetland Issues

The rise of the environmental movement since World War II is familiar to most Americans, and some see it as one of the most important and fundamental developments of our modern era. Two environmental concerns seem to be of special importance: dangers to human and animal health stemming from natural and man-made toxic substances in the living and working environment, and the aesthetic quality of our physical and natural environment. Both concerns are linked to the agricultural sector in the following ways:

- Farmers' decisions about growing crops and managing animals influence the visual appearance of the nation's landscapes and the quality of waterways and are an important determinant of the habitat for many wild animals.
- The technological and crop choices of farmers have an important influence on the stability of soil resources and have complex and significant effects on the quantity and quality of water resources.
- Chemicals used as agricultural fertilizers, herbicides, and pesticides are believed to be important contaminants of the environment, especially of ground and surface water. Many of these chemicals are thought to be carcinogens and are toxic to both humans and animals.
- Air quality is often influenced by agricultural production through the use of airborne chemicals to fertilize crops and control pests and by the burning of agricultural residues. In addition, the chemical composition of the atmosphere worldwide is affected by agricultural production, especially by the encroachment of crops on the world's forests, especially in the tropics.

It is important to understand that, to a large extent, the food, fiber, and waste products that reduce environmental quality are joint outputs of agricultural production. Using available technologies, it is impossible to have meat, milk, and wool without at the same time producing manure. And it is impossible to produce crops without utilizing environmental resources that are critical to the photosynthetic process.

In most cases, however, agricultural output and environmental by-products are not produced in fixed proportions. The technology of the production process will determine what quantities of each are produced in any given situation. In some cases, moreover, agricultural goods and environmental amenities are not competitive but complementary. For example, many people value the sight of plowed ground, growing crops, and grazing animals. And crop residues may provide indispensable habitats for wild animals and birds.[1]

When agricultural goods and environmental quality are competitive in production, potential trade-offs become inevitable if optimal combinations are to be reached. An optimum will depend on the relative values of what may be produced, and these values often will be location specific. Income elasticities are probably much higher for environmental goods than for food and fiber in the rich economically advanced countries. Hence, as incomes rise, the demand for agricultural products weakens relative to that for environmental quality. Indeed, it is generally in high-income countries that environmental concerns receive high priority relative to increases in the production of food and fiber, and it is likely just the opposite in low-income countries. Therefore, in affluent countries we observe government policy for agriculture that considers environmental concerns along with those of feeding and clothing people.

Of course, there are wide differences among various groups within society as to the value trade-offs between producing food and improving environmental quality. Many farm groups see the recommended regulations of environmentalists-preservationists as a threat to maintaining an efficient agricultural sector, while, increasingly, environmental groups view modern large-scale agriculture with its heavy dependence on fossil fuels and chemicals as a serious menace to health and safety.

The environmental community was very active in the political milieu that produced both the 1985 Food Security Act (FSA) and the 1990 Food, Agriculture, Conservation and Trade Act (FACTA). Many perceive this influence as growing through time.[2] It is noteworthy, in fact, that in the 1990 FACTA the word "conservation" appears in a farm bill title for the first time in the long history of federal agricultural legislation.

Strong lobbying by environmental organizations produced two measures in the FSA with profound environmental implications: "sodbuster" and "swampbuster" provisions, the violation of which made a farmer ineligible to receive a wide variety of program benefits specified by the act including deficiency payments, and subsidized, acreage retirement provisions of the Conservation Reserve Program (see Kennedy and Visser 1990, pp. 43–44). Both measures will be discussed and evaluated later in this chapter. In the 1990 FACTA, environmental regulations were changed modestly from those in the FSA, and the sanctions that may be taken against farmers who commit "environmental sin" were expanded.

Most of the connections between agricultural policy and environmental quality can be divided conveniently into two parts: soil and wetland issues and chemical contamination issues. This chapter deals with the first, Chapter 11 with the second. The focus will be on how price support policy affects environmental quality and, in turn, how policies designed to mitigate the most critical environmental problems have affected the efficiency of producing food and fiber.

Conservation Issues in the FSA and the FACTA

The 1985 FSA broke new ground in its concerns for environmental quality compared with previous agricultural acts. The FSA was enacted almost a decade ago, and some evaluation of its environmental provisions is both possible and desirable. Where relevant, environmental provisions of the FACTA will also be reviewed.

A number of new programs in the FSA were aimed at the conservation of farmland and preservation of wetlands. FSA contained both "carrots" and "sticks." The carrots were government offers to make payments to farmers who agreed to follow practices ranging from adopting conservation measures to the retirement of land from farming (Kennedy and Visser 1990, p. 43). The sticks were government sanctions taken against violators of environmental regulations and those who failed to comply with submitting and following a conservation plan. If compliance did not occur and farmers engaged in practices alleged to be environmentally destructive, they were denied the benefits of commodity programs.

Conservation compliance required producers who planted an agricultural commodity on erodible land to develop and begin actively applying an approved conservation plan by December 31, 1989. They have until December 31, 1994, however, to have the plan fully implemented.[3] At the end of 1991, compliance plans had been fully implemented on about half of the nation's highly erodible cropland.[4]

The Conservation Reserve Program

The FSA also initiated a long-term Conservation Reserve Program (CRP). The original goal was to take 45 million acres of erodible land out of production by 1990. The total cropland base of the country is approximately 350 million acres, so 45 million acres would be about 13 percent of the total base. By September 1993, 36.4 million acres were in the reserve.[5]

The 1990 FACTA sets the enrollment goal in the conservation and wetland reserve at 40 to 45 million acres through calendar year 1995.[6] Obviously, Congress has not expanded the goal of acreage to be placed in the reserve since the 1985 act was passed, and it may even be backing off because of the effects on local economies when cropland is removed from production.

The stated objectives of the CRP are to reduce water and soil erosion, protect the long-term capability to produce food and fiber, reduce sedimentation, improve water quality, create better habitat for fish and wildlife through improved food and cover, curb production of surplus commodities, and provide needed income support for farmers. It is now apparent that the CRP has not been very effective in achieving these objectives, with the exception of the last one of transferring wealth from the taxpayers to farmers. The program is *very* effective in meeting this objective, and this is why it is so popular with members of the Congress who, as demonstrated in Chapter 9, are in the business of making such transfers.

At first blush, the CRP has some attractive features when compared with other government subsidy programs. One is the quasi-market way in which the program works. Owners and operators of cropland classified as "highly erodible" submit bids for enrollment of their eligible acreage in the reserve. If the bid is accepted, the government establishes a ten-year contract with the landowner or operator. The contract prohibits haying, grazing, or commercial harvest of any crop and requires that the land be placed in a conservation use with adequate grass or tree cover existing on it. The government pays the annual rent specified in accepted bids and, in addition, provides half the cost of establishing the vegetative cover (Kennedy and Visser 1990, p. 14). The big-bid states so far are Iowa, Texas, Missouri, North Dakota, Kansas, South Dakota, and Montana, most of which are located in the Plains region.

Public Law 100-102 stipulates that funds made available for the CRP may not be used to enter into new contracts that are in excess of the prevailing local rental rates for an acre of comparable land. Maximum acceptable rental rates (MARR) are established on a poolwide basis at the county level. Agricultural Stabilization and Conservation (ASC) county committees determine the MARRs for their respective counties. For submitted bids that are equal to or lower than the county MARR, the local county ASC committee determines whether the bid exceeds the prevailing local rental rate for comparable land (Phipps 1988).

The annual budgetary costs to the federal government of removing acreage from production via the CRP is about $55 per acre (Conley 1990). On October 30, 1990, the secretary of agriculture announced that fiscal year 1991 payments to about 330,000 producers participating in CRP would be $1.6 billion, or an average of $4,848 per participant.[7] Thus, given the size of these payments and the cost-share of establishing plant cover, the CRP is an important mechanism for transferring income to agricultural producers.

Supporters of the CRP program argue that reductions in soil erosion have produced significant off-farm environmental benefits. However, as will be demonstrated later, soil erosion per se may not be a serious national problem, in which case the loss of 13 percent of our cropland to the CRP at a cost of $55 per acre may not be such a good bargain.[8] A water-quality problem, however, that the CRP is also designed to ameliorate, appears to be much more serious, and the targeting of conservation programs to water quality in the 1990 FACTA offers some substantial possibilities for environmental improvement.

Supporters of the CRP also point out that of land then in the program, approximately 21.8 million acres were "base" acres (to be defined later) that could not receive commodity program subsidies while they are under contract in the CRP.[9] Thus, it is claimed that the CRP has reduced government price support payments as well as crop surpluses. This claim may have some validity. But what of the other 12.1 million acres then in the program costing the taxpayers $55 per acre that were not part of the price support base and, therefore, would not have received program benefits? In any case, the removal of 40 to 45 million acres from crop production, the ultimate goal, can hardly be considered costless in terms of economic efficiency.

A study was made of CRP performance in 1986. Three rounds of bidding resulted in an enrollment of 8.9 million acres, with an annual average of twenty-five tons of soil saved per acre. These results were achieved at an annual total rental cost of $408 million, or approximately $46 per acre (Reichelderfer and Boggess 1988).

On the surface, the CRP appears to be successful in reducing erosion, but it is doubtful whether it does so in a cost-effective manner. The USDA's choice of bid selection criteria maximizes both the acreage enrolled in the CRP and the income transfer to farmers. It does not maximize the reduction in soil erosion, its alleged principal intended purpose. That is, the acres enrolled do not represent the subset of submitted bids that would have contributed the most erosion reduction. Performance could be greatly improved by the adoption of bid selection criteria that directly relate desired performance measures to cost-effective erosion control (Reichelderfer and Boggess 1988, p. 7).

Any cropland that is eroding at more than three times the average level for the region is considered to be eligible for the reserve. Received bids from farmers are prioritized within each region on the basis of the bid in dollars per acre. This is tantamount to ensuring that, with a given budget, the least productive land will be placed in the reserve, since bids to take unproductive land out of production will presumably be less than bids for productive land. Significantly, these procedures ensure that total commodity production will be larger than would be the case if more productive land were placed in the reserve. Thus, consumers benefit from lower commodity prices. Producers in the aggregate may lose from the larger production if prices were free to fall proportionately more than the increase in the quantity produced. Fortunately for them, however, producer prices for much of the production is guaranteed by government price supports.

As for preventing soil erosion, the rub is that the least productive land is not necessarily the most erodible. The goal of preventing soil erosion has been sacrificed to the political motivation to supplement farmer incomes. But, of course, this is exactly why politicians favor current land selection criteria.

If erosion reduction were really the overriding objective, bids per acre would be divided by the tons of topsoil preserved before being ranked by dollars per acre. Even more importantly, since soil transport to off-farm sites is the most important problem with erosion, first consideration should be given to the off-site benefits generated in each region per ton of topsoil preserved. This type of program targeting would produce maximum net benefits from any erosion prevention policy.

Some of this criticism of CRP policy seems to have penetrated the halls of Congress as the 1990 farm bill was being fashioned. The FACTA mandates that CRP acres may be targeted for water-quality problems as well as soil erodibility.[10] Also, highly erodible land criteria have been tightened, and marginal pastureland now can be eligible for the CRP under specified conditions. While this broadening of the criteria for inclusion in the program may produce some environmental benefits, more political constituents will be given a claim on the budgetary resources of the government. The result could be that an even greater proportion of the program budget will be politically allocated rather than targeted to the most critical environmental damage.

Another political development protects the program funds from manipulation by the executive branch: the sequestration possibilities that arise from the budget reconciliation agreements enacted in late 1990 to reduce the federal deficit. The 1990 FACTA foresaw such a possibility and explicitly provides an exemption from sequestration for all payments due under CRP contracts.[11] Of course, this congressional action could have been motivated either by an increased concern for the environment or by an interest in protecting funds to reward constituents. In any case, the experience with the CRP proves that there is a wide disparity between identifying important social problems, and even reciting socially worthwhile objectives, and fashioning a set of rules that actually achieve the stated objectives.

One final point about the CRP. Even if soil conservation were a legitimate aim of public policy, far cheaper alternatives are available to conserve soil than CRP land retirement. Of the roughly 101 million acres eligible for the CRP, all but an estimated 25 million acres could be farmed with erosion at or below tolerable soil-loss levels if farmers adopted less erosive cropping practices (Sinner 1990). Subsidizing these changes would be far less costly than retiring cropland from production. A $200 million cost-sharing subsidy to farmers to induce them to utilize soil-conserving practices would have approximately the same effect on erosion as spending $2 billion for CRP land retirement (Sinner 1990, p. 12).

Don Leal (1990) of the Political Economy Research Center in Montana provides a realistic perspective:

> *But after five years, the Conservation Reserve program is an expensive disappointment. The cost to taxpayers approaches $1.49 billion per year—to pay farmers not to grow crops on erodible land—with a one-time outlay of an added $1.15 billion to assist them in planting cover. In the absence of farm supports, much of the highly erodible cropland would have been uneconomical to farm in the first place.*
>
> *Furthermore, according to USDA figures, only three million to four million out the 30 million CRP program acres provide enough diversity of vegetation to help wildlife survive the elements.*
>
> *The CRP is an example of a well-intentioned but misguided effort to accomplish soil and wildlife conservation. It is based on the contradictory principle of rewarding the biggest offenders of conservation (those who sod-busted erodible soils) with the highest government payments. Those who practiced good conservation and did not plant on highly erodible soils are out of luck as far as government payments are concerned. (p. A16)*

Sodbuster and Swampbuster Programs

The FSA stipulated that any person who produces crops on highly erodible land ("sodbusting") or who grows crops on designated wetlands[12] ("swampbusting") will be ineligible to participate in most government assistance programs, including price and income supports, crop insurance, loans to store program commodities on-farm, disaster payments, and FmHA loans (Kennedy and Visser 1990, p. 14).

It is significant that about 80 percent of the nation's 2 million farmers receive benefits from farm programs of some description. Thus, it is clear that penalties in the FSA for sodbuster and swampbuster violations were very harsh for farmers. Thousands of dollars of program benefits could have been sacrificed by most affected farmers if sodbuster and swampbuster violations were detected and penalties imposed. If agricultural producers really have the political clout to change legislation not to their liking, as was alleged in Chapter 9, the expectation is that the 1990 FACTA would have provided some weakening of the sanctions, and this is precisely what happened.

The 1990 FACTA provides for penalties ranging from $500 to $5,000 for each inadvertent sodbuster violation over a five-year period. It is not exactly clear what is meant by "inadvertent," but it appears to refer to those situations where the violator did not intend to break the rules. But it may be difficult to know what motivated the violation. If it turns out that these fines are used to avoid the complete forfeiture of benefits, as required in the FSA, then violations are likely to increase. The FACTA also provides for numerous exemptions to the forfeiture of program benefits.[13]

The penalties are even more severe for inadvertent swampbuster violations: $750 to $10,000 for each violation over a ten-year period.[14] The law also provides for on-site reviews prior to imposing any penalties whenever requested by a producer or when a wetland determination is appealed.[15] It appears that these exemptions and reviews provide a means that many farmers will exploit to escape environmental regulations. In addition, farmers will spend much time and financial resources to access the exemptions. Of course, environmentalists will be actively attempting to persuade the office of the secretary of agriculture to fend off the requests for exemptions. The final result will be high expenditures on both sides to affect both policies and bureaucratic regulators.

The new Wetland Reserve Program mandated in the FACTA calls for an enrollment goal of 1 million acres.[16] This would be included as part of the updated 40- to 50-million-acre conservation reserve goal. Further, the 1990 law establishes an Environmental Easement Program, which requires establishing a program for easement agreements with owners of eligible lands to ensure long-term protection of environmentally sensitive lands.[17] Eligible lands would include, but not be limited to, those under CRP and so-called Water Bank contracts with the exception of CRP timber stands and pasturelands planted to trees.[18] Existing CRP and Water Bank contracts, however, will be terminated upon enrollment into the Environmental Easement Program.

Landowners in the wetland reserve, however, must provide thirty-year or perpetual easements and agree to implement a wetland restoration and protection plan.[19] Payments to a participant may be made over a five- to twenty-year period or in a lump sum if the easement is perpetual.

The federal share for restoring these wetlands will be 50 to 100 percent of cost depending, in part, on the length of the easement. Priority must be given to offers that provide permanent wetland protection and that protect and enhance habitat for migratory birds and wildlife.

The problem with sodbuster and swampbuster programs is not that violation penalties are not severe enough to deter environmental violations. Rather, the dilemma is that the programs are not tightly targeted to the most critical environmental problems. In fact, the violation penalties impose huge costs on farmers, who, by poor luck more than anything else, find themselves trying to make a living in areas designated as wetlands or on soils defined as highly erodible. Thus, affected farmers find the programs unfair and onerous since they take their property rights.[20] Naturally, these programs have aroused heavy political opposition.

Representative of the feelings from the farm community, a North Dakota farmer, Victor Legler (1990) writes:

> *If a landowner stays out of the farm programs as a matter of principle and goes ahead with some drainage, he nevertheless has his land devalued because he cannot get back into the farm program unless he forgoes production on the drained land or goes back and plugs drains. If he sells or conveys his land to another party, the same rules apply. A government agency now tells a farmer if his land is highly erodible or is wetland and how he shall farm and manage it.*
>
> *Governments and government agencies are not the best stewards of the land, wildlife, or other resources. The issue of preserving wetlands through the use of leases and contracts is ignored. If wildlife and environmental groups really want soil and wildlife preservation—honor the deeds to our land—roll back restrictive laws like swampbuster, and come to us with leases, contracts, and yes, with your money—we'll then have grounds for a new spirit of cooperation and all of society will benefit.*

The Subsidization of Soil Erosion

Soil erosion is one of the most emotionally charged and yet least understood issues of our time.[21] The USDA reports that 185 million acres of cropland are eroding fast enough to "eventually impair productivity."[22] The states ranked by acreage of designated highly erodible cropland are Texas, Kansas, Montana, Iowa, Nebraska, Missouri, Colorado, Oklahoma, and Illinois.[23]

The Relationship between Income Support Policy and Soil Erosion

It is not difficult to find linkages between soil erosion and government subsidy and related income support programs. To become eligible for target prices and production loans, farmers must agree to meet certain regulations. One of the most important of these is to set aside from production a prescribed percentage of an established base acreage of a program crop. These land removals are referred to as set-asides or, more recently, acreage reduction programs (ARPs).[24]

How is base acreage determined? In the 1985 FSA, base acreage for a given program crop was defined as the average acreage planted and considered planted to the program crop during the past five years.[25] The 1990 FACTA sets the same average five-year base for wheat and the feed grains, but for cotton and rice the base is the average of the acreage planted and considered planted for the previous three years.[26]

In the case of most program crops, such as wheat, rice, cotton, and the feed grains, incomes are supported by the government chiefly by making deficiency payments to farmers. The basic deficiency payment rate per unit of production is the difference between the target price (the support price set by Congress) and the higher of the loan rate (the rate at which the government will provide a loan to farmers to hold their crops for sale at some later date) and the actual market price. In the case of cotton and rice, the FSA provided for an additional marketing loan deficiency payment rate, which essentially represents the difference between the world price and the loan rate. The deficiency payment for the farm is the deficiency payment rate times the base or permitted acreage. Thus, the aggregate size of the deficiency payment a farmer receives will be directly proportional to his or her base acreage. Therefore, under these price support regulations, farmers have a strong incentive to maximize land planted in program crops to establish acreage bases at the highest levels possible.[27]

These regulations for determining deficiency payments have negative environmental consequences, especially if program crops are associated with high levels of soil erosion. Two high-acreage and erosion-prone program crops are corn and cotton. They are usually planted in rows, which makes them susceptible to both wind and water erosion. This helps to explain the high erosion rates in the Corn Belt and the Cotton Belt.

A study of conservation and commodity programs on the Southern High Plains indicated that participation in government price support programs increased farm net returns by over 100 percent compared with nonparticipation (Lee 1990). This largely explains why over 90 percent of the farmers in the region were enrolled. The problem was that the effects of farm programs (that is, both high payments and the need to maintain acreage base) encouraged the production of cotton year after year without rotation. The average annual wind erosion for continuous dryland cotton was estimated to be two to six times greater than that for other multiple-crop rotations. In fact, a rotation that includes wheat can reduce wind erosion rates in this area by more than 80 percent. The conclusion was that with existing base acreage provisions so restrictive and payments so attractive, farmers could not afford to do what was environmentally benign.[28]

The 1990 FACTA does not alter the definition of base acreage but does change the ARP requirements significantly to give farmers more options. The general surplus situation for most program crops is not so burdensome as it was in the mid-1980s, and thus the ARP requirements have been reduced at the discretion of the secretary of agriculture (see Chapter 2).

Both the 1990 FACTA and the 1990 Budget Reconciliation Act (BRA) also give the secretary discretion to change the ARP set-asides in exchange for income options for farmers. To reduce the budgetary costs of farm programs, the BRA specifies that deficiency payments will not be paid on 15 percent of base acres. This 15 percent is called "normal flexible acres." On these flex acres, a farmer may plant other crops, including all other program crops, any oilseed crop, any industrial or experimental crop, and any other nonprogram crop except fruits and vegetables without the loss of acreage base.[29] The FACTA authorizes base protection for an *additional* 10 percent of optional flex acres to be imposed at the discretion of the secretary.[30] Therefore, up to 25 percent of base acreage plus the acreage in the mandatory ARP will not receive support payments under the BRA.

This shift in policy could have two important impacts on environmental quality. First, participation in government programs might be far less attractive than under previous legislation leading to a withdrawal of many farmers from support programs. Farmers would then be completely free to plant whatever they wish on all their acreage with whatever environmental consequences would ensue. Second, for those who remain in the programs, more flexibility exists to change cropping patterns in response to pure market forces. The environmental impact will depend on the change in total cropped acreage, which crops are grown, and whether or not production is environmentally benign.[31] The implications for chemical use might be significant if more or less fertilizers and pesticides are used on the substituted crops.

In some areas of the country, especially in the Great Plains and Rocky Mountain states, much of the land brought into production because of high price supports is marginal for producing crops and highly erodible. No one knows how many fewer acres of highly erodible land would have been cropped in the absence of price support programs and base acreage requirements, but the cropland base would likely have been substantially smaller.

Price support policy is not the only factor affecting erosion. Production techniques are also very important. In recent years, soil erosion has been sharply reduced on a significant amount of acreage by planting crops without tillage.

But what has this to do with policy? One study found that the way yield is calculated for purposes of determining deficiency payments in the FSA had a detrimental effect on soil erosion by discouraging the use of no-tillage practices. A change in base acres and program yield permitted by an approved conservation plan does not provide sufficient incentive for using a no-tillage system (Williams et al. 1990, p. 180). The essential point is that FSA regulations that fixed base acres and program yields, both of which were strongly advocated by environmental lobbyists, actually discouraged farmers from using soil-saving rotations of crops.

The Location of Highly Erodible Land and the Distribution of Conservation Payments

Some 114 million acres of existing cropland are considered highly erodible, approximately 30 percent of the nation's base. But these 114 million acres account for nearly 60 percent of all erosion that occurs on cropland, suggesting that the erosion problem is highly concentrated in certain geographic regions.[32] Significantly, however, nearly every important agricultural county in the nation claims to have some erodible land. It is this curiosity that explains why existing programs are so inefficient in coming to grips with whatever real soil erosion problems exist.

Despite the concentration of highly erodible land in certain areas, the funds are distributed broadly among all states and regions of the country. Why? Because, since the 1930s conservation payments have been one of the principal instruments for transferring income from taxpayers to farmers.

This can be clearly demonstrated by looking at the origins of the program. In October 1935, President Roosevelt issued a statement outlining his administration's overall agricultural policy. The New Deal farm program had two objectives: to increase farm income and to give farmers incentives for conservation of the nation's soil resources (Reilly 1984). The 1930s were noted for extensive wind and water erosion. As long as farm incomes needed to be supported as a Depression-era measure, why not do it in such a way as to get some conservation benefits? The resulting program was one example among many of good-intentioned policies that ultimately had consequences that were largely unforeseen and became very costly (see B.D. Gardner 1985).

Farmers approve of conservation programs, especially when they are accompanied by high levels of government cost sharing (Esseks and Kraft 1984). Who could object to government subsidies for maintaining and protecting the productive resources on which the nation's health depend? Farmers have always resisted the idea that they are welfare recipients and have strongly favored programs that appear not to be government handouts. This is one reason why artificially high prices produced by import quotas or other foreign trade restraints have been more popular with farmers than the same amount of income support received by direct government payments. Conservation payments are even more palatable. If someone is going to be subsidized, particularly if they pride themselves on their independence, the medicine goes down easier if it appears to support a worthy cause like saving precious soil (Olson 1990, p. 8).

Conservation programs and cost-sharing payments are delivered through soil conservation districts, represented in Washington, D.C., by the National Association of Conservation Districts. This effective lobbying organization applies political pressure ensuring that each district in the nation will gain some portion of available soil conservation funds (Crosson 1984, 1986a). Politicians in both houses of Congress are anxious to cooperate, since they receive political benefits from bestowing favors on constituents. This no doubt explains why targeting conservation funds to serious erosion locations simply has not happened. Congress has stoutly resisted all such efforts by the USDA.

The basic political nature of the CRP is reinforced by another provision of the FSA that remains unchanged in the 1990 FACTA. The secretary of agriculture can enroll acreage in the reserve above 25 percent of a county's cropland base only if this action will not have an adverse impact on the local economy.[33] It is possible to have too much of a good thing after all. On the one hand, members of Congress want a share of conservation payments for their constituents, but on the other, they don't want so much land removed from crop production that the local economy is damaged. Given the complexity and cost of the technical information needed to evaluate this tradeoff, and the conflicting interests involved, deciding what the optimal amount of conservation for each county is must be a formidable task. This is another reason why it is not surprising that targeting serious erosion problems does not happen.

Federal disaster programs are also significant from an environmental point of view and illustrate the difficulties that arise when funds are haphazardly thrown at alleged problems. If farmers can be bailed out of financial difficulty whenever drought, flooding, hail, or even insect infestations occur, then incentives exist to locate in more risky environments than would occur if farmers had to bear the full risks of production themselves. Zinsmeister says:

> *Established in 1973, federal disaster aid allows growers whose harvests are stunted or who are prevented from planting by "conditions beyond the control of the producer" to collect payments that frequently total many hundreds of millions of dollars. The easy availability of free insurance encourages more exploitation of dicey lands, riskier planting decisions, and less care in management. Disaster aid can be characterized as an anticonservation policy. (1989, p. 23)*

Thus, disaster payments are yet another example of moral hazard and adverse selection discussed in Chapter 4.

In the final analysis, are these costly programs really needed to maintain soil productivity and ultimately lower food prices, one of their designated purposes?[34] Or are they simply another political vehicle used to transfer resources to interest groups without any significant environmental value? The question is intriguing since it is not only agricultural producers who strongly favor soil conservation programs. Conservation and environmental organizations have also been very vigorous in lobbying Congress for them.

The Cost-Effectiveness of Soil Conservation Programs

The appropriate question is whether or not soil conservation programs are cost effective in preserving soil?[35] Pierre Crosson of Resources for the Future, a preeminent research organization that conducts studies of natural resource issues, estimates that the annualized costs of yield losses from erosion over the next hundred years will be only about 1 to 2 percent of current costs of crop production. Thus, Crosson argues that continuation of present rates of erosion would not likely impose significantly higher costs of food and fiber on future generations of consumers (1986a, p. 35).

Supporting Crosson's view, the USDA concluded that if present levels of wind and water erosion continue for another hundred years, productivity on the soils with the most severe erosion problems nation-wide would decline only about 4 percent.[36] A host of scientific developments increasing yields will likely much more than offset these erosion losses, although their timing is uncertain. The effects of modern biology alone are expected to have tremendous impacts on yields and livestock output and ensure the continuation of commodity surpluses over the indefinite future, unless, of course, worldwide food and population conditions change radically world-wide because of adverse weather or armed conflict.

If government policy were a reliable indicator of public preferences, farm policies themselves would reveal something about whether there is a shortage of prime agricultural land. For most of the past two decades, however, at the same time that it is alleged that the nation has had a critical shortage of agricultural land that justifies costly programs reducing erosion and preserving prime land, the likewise costly set-aside requirements of farm legislation have removed from 15 to 35 percent of the acreage bases for wheat, the feed grains, rice, and cotton. It would appear that the country cannot make up its collective mind whether or not it really has a land shortage. These sorts of policy contradictions must be a nightmare for those who believe that government actions are produced by some collective "will" of the people.

But to frame the issue this way misses the essence of why agricultural programs, including those for erosion prevention, exist in the first place. As demonstrated in previous chapters with respect to other policies, no one is calculating precisely the benefits and costs of soil conservation programs and designing national programs according to what will increase national wealth or well-being. To the contrary, soil conservation programs, like price support subsidies, exist primarily because of pressures to transfer income from consumers and taxpayers to specific interest groups. Farmers are paid to remove land from production and paid again to conserve soil. The contradiction in such costly policies must be duly noted, but there should be no surprise in discovering this in a world where resource allocations are often political. Those who advocate regulations to reduce soil erosion argue that individual farmer's decisions relating to land use and care are suboptimal when considered from the view of society as a whole. Clearly, a priori, if farmers cannot be trusted to manage their resources in ways that benefit the community as a whole, a case can be made for either governmental regulations or subsidies to induce them to do better.

The Alleged Shortsightedness of Farmers' Decisions

Even if the costs of soil erosion were higher than they are, it is not obvious that government intrusion in farmers' decisions is desirable. Another way to frame the issue is to ask what ways farmers' decisions with respect to the treatment and care of land are likely to be wasteful and inefficient.

The distinguished Nobel laureate in economics Professor T. W. Schultz of the University of Chicago has written persuasively on this question:

> *The dynamics and success of agriculture in the U.S. is ample proof that farmers are competent entrepreneurs; they do not shed their entrepreneurial ability when it comes to investments to improve and maintain their soil resources. They calculate the value of their soil resources to a fine degree, and the value of their land is not so small a detail as to be overlooked. Retired farmers who retain ownership or other investors are not indifferent to soil losses. . . The self-interest and the large stake that farmers have in the economic value of their soil resources hold the key to soil conservation. Let us not sell short the self-interest of farm people in their resources. (1984, pp. 45–58)*

Is it even logical to believe that farmers would abuse their own productive capacity in the long run were it not for conservation subsidies? If they knowingly destroyed the land's productive potential, they must realize that this would make them and their heirs less wealthy. The price of agricultural land is primarily determined by expected future profits from putting that land to productive use and, therefore, to abuse it would reduce its price. No available evidence supports the idea that landowners intentionally forfeit their wealth by running down their land. To the contrary, ample evidence exists that farmers take positive steps to accumulate wealth in land resources by sound investment and management practices. Landowners, primarily farm operators, amass fortunes in land, which they productively use and then ultimately sell or bequeath to their heirs.

A Wisconsin study attempted to identify those factors that explain farmers' investment in erosion prevention (Saliba and Bromley 1984). Broad classes of variables were defined: physical factors such as the percentage of land with erosion hazard and slope, attitudinal factors, and financial and farm-type factors, such as age, ownership, and crops produced. Findings indicate that farmers with real erosion problems knew it and took ameliorative measures. Farmers understand that soil erosion has a detrimental effect on both crop yields and land values. Those who stood to benefit most from erosion control were those who practiced it. Farm-type and financial variables, such as constraints on income, did not significantly explain the extent of erosion control activities.

It is sometimes alleged that farmers plan only for the remainder of their lifetimes and that the public's interests in land use extend far beyond those relatively few years. If this reasoning were valid, farms operated by the elderly and about to be sold or bequeathed to heirs would be in a lower state of productivity than those operated by younger farmers. No available evidence supports this view, and the Wisconsin findings already referred to are inconsistent with it. Indeed, because land is a convenient vehicle for accumulating wealth and, for the most part, property rights in land are well defined and divestible, land markets provide incentives for maintaining the stock of land in a highly productive state.

Some evidence has been uncovered that tenants who do not own property rights in land tend to exploit the soil and other productive capital resources as the expiration date of the lease is approached (Kraft 1978). But, as long as a high degree of competition exists among tenants for land parcels to rent, no rational wealth-maximizing landowner would lease to those who have a reputation for abusing and despoiling the land. Thus, landowners carefully monitor the activities of tenants and insist they responsibly care for the land. Otherwise, they find a new tenant.

The combination of efficient capital markets and nonattenuated property rights guarantees that those competitors most optimistic about the future will control resources such as land (Baden and Stroup 1981). Since the offer price for land in the market will depend on the bidder's expectations of profit potentials in the future, those seeing the more profitable future will outbid those who are less optimistic. Obviously, those who envision a profitable future relative to the present will also keep their resources in a highly productive state to compete more effectively when that future arrives. This reasoning suggests that capital markets and private property rights are generous to future generations in protecting productive resources for their use.

The conclusion is that as long as farmers capture the full benefits from their production decisions and bear the full costs of their mistakes, they will make efficient decisions with respect to land use and conservation. But what if this assumption is not valid? What if costs (or benefits) exist that are not borne (or captured) by the decision maker? This takes us to the core of the *real* environmental problems that exist on U.S. farms.

Subsidies and the Destruction of Wildlife Habitat

The destruction of U.S. wildlife habitat is a phenomenon as old as the settlement of Europeans on the American continent, if not before. The problem stems both from conversion of wetlands and wildlands into cropland and from conversion of agricultural lands used also for wildlife habitat into developed uses.

Wetlands, mostly ponds and potholes containing water for part or all of the year, are of value primarily because they provide important breeding, staging, and wintering grounds for waterfowl and other wildlife. The essential problem is that under U.S. laws, farmers do not own the wildlife and, therefore, do not take the impact of their decisions on wildlife fully into account. When wetlands are drained to produce crops, the wildlife habitat is no longer available. It has been argued that wetlands are also important for providing improved water quality, erosion control, floodwater storage, timber production, and recreational opportunities, but scientific evidence for some of these claims has been challenged (Jessen 1991).

A Senate Agriculture, Nutrition, and Forestry Committee report prepared for the 1990 farm bill puts the acreage in wetlands during the colonial period in the contiguous forty-eight states at 221 million acres.[37] Over half (117 million acres) has since been converted to other uses. The majority of the remaining 104 million acres are now in private hands, although sizable acreage is located on public lands as well. Another estimate places the quantity of the nation's wetlands at about 76 million acres, of which some 5.1 million acres have the potential of being converted to cropland (Lamb 1986). It is not clear why these estimates diverge or which is nearer the truth. The largest recent conversions of wetlands to crops are in the Prairie states of the Midwest, and pintail and mallard ducks and blue-winged teal have declined markedly there since the 1970s (Smolko 1989).

Of course, historically most conversions of wetlands were for cropland. Until recent years, swampland was thought to have little value and converting it to cropland was entirely consistent with the national interest and was even an avowed objective of national policy. The expansion of cropped agriculture across an entire continent was seen as an important component of U.S. development.

Agricultural yields could be increased sharply with appropriate drainage, and insect damage could be mitigated if breeding grounds in standing water could be eliminated. The Senate study already cited estimates that from the 1950s to the 1970s, approximately 12 million acres of wetlands were converted, 87 percent of which went for agricultural purposes.[38] This substantial loss of wetlands provoked wildlife and environmental interests to support strong measures preventing further loss. The results were the cavalier swampbuster provision of the 1985 FSA and the amendments contained in the 1990 FACTA Act already discussed.

Although no precise estimates have been made, it seems clear that subsidies for program crops that made them more profitable at the margin have had a major influence on the conversion of wetlands into cropland since the 1930s, when price supports were first introduced. The base acreage provision of agricultural law also contributed to the loss of wetlands since it encouraged farmers to put the maximum acreage in supported crops that might otherwise have remained in a wild condition. In addition, subsidized crop insurance and disaster bailouts have protected farmers against yield losses from a variety of natural causes and thus have encouraged cropping in areas where it might have never otherwise occurred, including on wetlands. Flood, hail, and drought disaster bailouts are particularly noteworthy in this respect.

Don Leal, quoted earlier, has stated the issue well:

> *Small game animals once thrived on the farms of the Midwestern U.S. In the early 1960s a boy could hunt the ringnecked pheasant as well as ducks, cottontail rabbit and bobwhite quail. These animals made their homes in the shelterbelts between grain fields, the weeds and shrubs growing along the fencerows, and the thick growths of cattails found along streams and marshes.*
>
> *Such a landscape is becoming harder to find today, a victim of fencerow-to-fencerow farming. Farmers are growing the same crop year after year, draining the remaining wetlands, converting upland cover to row crops, and drenching their farms with pesticides and herbicides to maximize the subsidies they get from the U.S. taxpayers.*
>
> *Federal agricultural programs compel farmers to maximize production and virtually wipe out wildlife habitat. In some cases, such as wetland drainage, the government has directly subsidized the conversion of millions of acres of good bird habitat to cropland. (1990, p. A16)*

Leal believes that the annual land set-aside requirements do virtually nothing for wildlife. Much of the idled cropland is without vegetation, so it provides no protection for animals and no nesting habitat. If the land does have cover, it is frequently disturbed by early summer mowing, often during the critical nesting period for pheasants (Leal 1990).

An excellent empirical study by Stavins and Jaffe (1990) shows the impact of federal "conservation" policy on the destruction of wetlands. For at least twenty years, preserving and protecting wetlands has been a prominent goal of environmental policy. The study focuses on the Lower Mississippi Alluvial Plain, one of the largest remaining wetland habitats in the continental United States: "Originally covering 26 million acres in seven states, this resource was reduced to about 12 million acres by 1937. Since then, another 6.5 million acres have been cleared, primarily for conversion to cropland" (1990, p. 338).

A model of forestry and agricultural production was constructed to simulate landowner decisions under a regime of yields, prices, and government policies available:

> *The owner of a wetland faces an economic decision involving revenues*

> *from the parcel in its natural state (primarily from timber), costs of conversion (the cost of clearing the land minus the resulting forestry windfall), and expected revenues from agriculture. Agricultural revenues depend on prices, yields, and, significantly, the drainage and flooding frequency of the land. Needless to say, landowners typically do not consider the positive environmental externalities generated by wetlands; thus conversion may occur more often than is socially optimal. (Stavins and Jaffe 1990, p. 338)*

The flood control and drainage policies of two government agencies, the U.S. Army Corps of Engineers in the Defense Department and the Soil Conservation Service in the USDA have made a major impact on wetlands. The subsidy to agricultural conservation investments (generally a 50-50 cost sharing) makes crops more attractive and thereby induces the conversion of wetlands into cropland. Stavins and Jaffe show that landowners have indeed responded to economic incentives provided by federal policy and that more wetlands have been converted as a result. Of the factors considered in the econometric model, flood protection and drainage provided by federal projects (much if not all of it subsidized) had the largest impact on net changes in forested acreage. Stavins and Jaffe conclude:

> *If there had been no federal flood-control or drainage projects constructed in the 36-county area after 1934, approximately 1.15 million fewer acres of forested wetlands would have been converted, 31 percent of total depletion. Long-term (steady state) depletion due to federal projects (constructed through the year 1984) is estimated to amount to more than 1.23 million acres, about 32 percent of estimated long-term depletion. (1990, p. 349)*

This study also shows that agricultural policies are often contradictory in their effects and have unintended consequences. They may have meritorious aims and yet produce undesirable effects. Even "conservation" investment in flood control and drainage have had severely negative environmental effects by providing incentives for the removal of wetlands. This occurred despite the fact that the Bush administration endorsed a policy of zero net loss of wetlands.

Policies to Mitigate Damage

This may be an appropriate juncture for raising a partly political and partly economic issue that probably contributes significantly to resource misallocation and waste—mitigation policy. It is generally applicable across a broad spectrum of resource and environmental issues but can be illustrated clearly in the case of lost wetlands.

It has been pointed out that government policy was instrumental in the conversion of wetlands into cropland. The construction of federally subsidized irrigation projects is a notorious example. Damming up streams and rivers destroys marshlands that serve as wildlife habitat. This phenomenon has occurred over many decades, and the aggregate effect of many such projects has been to create the critical shortage of wetlands duly noted by environmental groups. The government is then pressured by groups interested in wetlands to mitigate the effects of previous policy. In this context, mitigate means to reduce the "cost" of previous policy by attempting to restore or replace the lost wetlands. This mitigation is often viewed as a moral obligation and may be reinforced by legislative statute and judicial decision. The issue is removed from the realm of tough-minded economic analysis. Mitigation measures are promoted regardless of any rigorous assessment of benefits and costs. The expectation is that such approaches will result in economic boondoggles. Research is needed to determine if such expectations materialize.

Wetland Conversion Is Slowing

The widespread perception of declining wetlands, however, must be revised given the availability of recent data. If they are reliable, the highest rates of wetland conversion have probably already occurred. On October 4, 1990, Secretary of Agriculture Clayton Yeutter reported that wetland losses on private lands slowed significantly during the mid-1980s. Total wetland losses were between 100,000 and 200,000 acres annually from 1982 to 1987, significantly less than losses previously estimated.[39]

The information comes from the 1987 National Resources Inventory (NRI) conducted by the Soil Conservation Service (SCS) and is based on over 300,000 sample sites from across the country. The NRI shows 82 million acres of wetlands on nonfederal rural land in 1987, down from 83.2 million acres in 1982. The SCS estimates the loss of wetlands to agricultural and development uses at about 500,000 acres over the period, a rate of 100,000 acres per year. The remaining change was due to other factors: 300,000 acres changed from private to federal ownership—still likely remaining in wetlands but not included in the SCS nonfederal lands inventory—and over 400,000 acres changed to open water, primarily adjacent to Utah's Great Salt Lake and in southern Louisiana. In the Utah case, the Great Salt Lake has receded sharply in recent years to near its pre-1980 level, and thousands of acres of shore wetlands have returned.

Further, the NRI data do not reflect increases in wetlands that may have resulted from the Conservation Reserve Program (CRP), which was just getting under way at the time of the inventory. The Agricultural Stabilization and Conservation Service reports more than 400,000 acres of cropped wetlands have been enrolled in the CRP.

What these data appear to suggest is that wetland losses are not continuing on a scale that was previously thought. In recent years, there actually may have been no net loss of wetlands at all, in which case the heavy-handed swampbuster provisions of the FSA are more difficult to justify, and the exemptions provided in the 1990 FACTA make more sense.

While the wetland and land easement initiatives of the FACTA might have beneficial environmental consequences, they are also sure to be utilized for income transfers to participants that are not justified by environmental benefits. The fact that the federal government may be willing to pick up the entire cost of these programs is to invite abuse.

There is also concern that ardent environmentalists opposed to economic development in any form will feel that they now have government reinforcement to block costly development projects. For example, in November 1990, in Provo, Utah, activists tried to block an apartment house development in the middle of town on the grounds that it destroys wetlands. Great pressure was brought on government officials to disapprove this development, and it is possible that the case could be tied up in the courts for years.

As a final point, agricultural subsidies are not the major culprit inducing the conversion of wetlands to developed uses. Rather, it was federal income tax law that gave breaks to land developers that was the crucial factor. Land-clearing costs can be deducted from net farm income in the year of the clearing, subject to an upper limit of the lesser of $5,000 or 25 percent of net farm income. Further, deductions for soil and water conservation costs (including drainage) of up to 25 percent of gross farm income are also allowable in the year the costs are incurred, as long as the land is cropped in that year. Expenses in excess of this limit can be deducted in subsequent years. There can be little doubt that the effect of this favorable tax treatment was to induce land conversion to development before it would otherwise have been economic to do so (Kramer and Shabman 1986).

Conclusions

The data and arguments presented support the following conclusions. First, since the benefits of on-farm soil conservation are small, it is doubtful that costly conservation programs can be justified unless their promoters can make a much stronger case for their need and efficacy than has heretofore been made. Second, American farmers have the incentives, ability, and knowledge to manage their soil resources and protect the productivity of the cropland base without the huge government subsidies they have been receiving. Third, government subsidies that produce surplus commodities and ostensibly conserve soils should be eliminated unless they are carefully targeted to ameliorate harmful off-farm sedimentation and chemical pollution damages, discussed in Chapter 11.

If the American public insists on paying tribute to farmers, the decoupling of subsidy payments from production would permit equitable payments to be paid without influencing costs and prices, including export prices. It is the distortion of prices and costs that cause inefficiency and environmental degradation.

Most of the nation's wetlands have been lost to cropland and developed uses over nearly three centuries. It could be that those remaining have high marginal value, although no persuasive proof has been brought forward. Most environmental amenities are simply assumed to be desirable with no effort made to estimate opportunity costs. Their promoters insist that they have unique "spiritual" value and therefore do not have to be justified by economic feasibility. Conservation policy based on this premise would appear to lead down a road to inefficiency and loss of national wealth.

Evidence suggests that the rate of wetland conversion has slowed sharply in the recent past, at least throwing some doubt on the advisability of programs that force farmers operating in some areas to bear such high compliance costs. Wetland easements purchased by the government may be a promising alternative to the heavy-handed forfeiture of all governmental program benefits as well as fines for those who convert wetlands into cropland.

Notes

1. The complexity of agricultural production, quality of the environment, and policy interventions by government have led some observers to conclude that "reality is far too complex to allow generalizations about the environmental impacts of agricultural policies." See Just and Antle (1990, p. 202).

2. An assistant secretary of agriculture, and a former dean of the College of Agricultural and Environmental Sciences at the University of California at Davis, Dr. Charles Hess reported that a coalition of environmental groups drafted its own version of 1990 farm legislation. He does not say how their bill may have differed from the final version passed by the Congress since he spoke at the conference before the final version of FACTA was passed. See Charles Hess (1990, p. 45).

3. Conservation plans include specific, practical, and allegedly cost-effective conservation practices that allow farmers to produce crops without excessive erosion. The plans are developed by the farmer or landowner with consultation and assistance from the USDA's Soil Conservation Service.

4. U.S. Department of Agriculture, Office of Public Affairs (1991), "Conservation Work Completed on Half of Highly Erodible Land," *Selected Speeches and News Releases* (Washington, DC: December 12–18), p. 11.

5. U.S. Department of Agriculture, Office of Public Affairs (1993), *News Releases and Other News Material*, no. 9493 (Washington, DC: September 27–October 1), p. 6.

6. Ibid., U.S. Senate Bill 2830, Title XIV, Subtitle C—Agricultural Resources Conservation Program, Section 1431.

7. U.S. Department of Agriculture (1990), *Selected Speeches and News Releases* (Washington, DC: October 25–November 1), p. 13.

8. On April 16, 1991, Secretary Madigan announced tentative acceptance of 564,899 acres of cropland into the CRP, at an average cost of $53.96 per acre. This acreage was based on bids of 2,453,686 acres of environmentally sensitive and highly erodible cropland submitted during the tenth CRP sign-up. See U.S. Department of Agriculture, Office of Public Affairs (1991), "AR, IFM, and CRP Final Rules Announced," *Selected Speeches and News Releases*, (Washington, DC: April 11–17), p. 8.

9. U.S. Senate (1990), *FACTA*, Senate Report no. 101-357, p. 199.

10. U.S. Senate Bill 2830, Title XIV, Subtitle C, Section 1432(b).

11. Ibid., Section 1434(e).

12. As far back as 1977, wetlands were defined as areas flooded or saturated

with ground water and supporting vegetation typically adapted for life in saturated soil conditions. Normally, wetlands were limited to swamps, marshes, or bogs. These guidelines were incorporated into the *Federal Manual for Identifying and Delineating Jurisdictional Wetlands.* Now, however, wetlands are defined by more technical factors: the wetness of the soil, its chemical properties, and the varieties of plants that grow there. The manual also says that soil that is inundated for as little as one week per year qualifies as wetlands, and this expanded definition has contributed to inflated estimates of wetland losses.

13. U.S. Senate Bill 2830, Title XIV, Subtitle A, Section 1412(d).

    Provisions in the FACTA grant exemptions for people who cannot comply with the sodbuster program. For example, grace periods are provided to those who are in violation providing they make an honest effort to comply. Also, any person whose benefits are reduced in any crop year shall continue to be eligible for all the benefits for any subsequent year if a conservation plan is prepared. Subtitle A, Subtitle XIV—Highly Erodible Land Conservation.

14. Ibid., Title XIV—Conservation, Subtitle A—Highly Erodible Land Conversion, Section 1412(d), and Subtitle B—Wetland Conservation, Section 1422(h).

    Many exemptions are also provided for wetland violations. These have to do with when the wetland conversion occurred and if the wet area is used for irrigation. Also, a producer can convert wetland without penalty if he or she restores acre-for-acre an area to wetland that was previously cropped. If the actions of an unrelated person or public entity, outside the control of, and without the prior approval of, the landowner or tenant, result in a change in the characteristics of cropland that would cause the land to be determined to be a wetland, the affected land shall not be considered to be wetland for purposes of forfeiting payments.

15. Ibid., Title XIV, Subtitle B, Section 1422(c).

16. U.S. Department of Agriculture, Economic Research Service (1990b), *The 1990 Farm Act and the 1990 Budget Reconciliation Act,* Miscellaneous Publication no. 1489 (Washington, DC: December), p. 34.

17. In return for the granting of an easement by an owner, the secretary of agriculture shall: (1) share the cost of carrying out the establishment of conservation measures and practices if the secretary believes such cost sharing is appropriate and in the public interest, and (2) over a period not to exceed ten years make annual easement payments in the aggregate not to exceed the lesser of (a) $250,000 or (b) the difference in the value of the land with and without an easement. The secretary may pay up to 100 percent of the cost of establishing these conservation measures and practices. If so, this can hardly be called cost sharing.

18. Land eligible under the Water Bank Act (16 U.S.C. 1301) contains riparian corridors, is an area of critical habitat for wildlife (especially threatened or en-

dangered species), or contains other environmentally sensitive areas as determined by the secretary. (See S.L.C., Title XIV, Subtitle C, Section 1440: 14–28.)

19. U.S. Senate Bill 2830, Title XIV, Subtitle C, Section 1438.

20. Once a wetland has been designated as such, if the owner wants to do anything with it he or she must get a permit from the Army Corps of Engineers. Corps regulators have complete discretion as to whether they will issue a permit and whether the owner must set aside other property to make up for the lost wetland. People who fill wetlands without obtaining a permit face fines and prison sentences. The Corps gets this authority from Section 404 of the 1972 Clean Water Act. See Henderson (1991).

21. Some of this section contains material that the author used for a debate at three sites in Indiana in 1985. See B. D. Gardner (1985).

22. USDA (1987a), "Soil Erosion: Dramatic in Places, But Not A Serious Threat to Productivity," *Agricultural Outlook* (Washington, DC: Economic Research Service, April).

23. U.S. Department of Agriculture (1988), "Highly Erodible Land Conservation Provision of the Food Security Act of 1985," *Backgrounder* (Washington, D.C., April 8).

24. For most of the period under the 1985 FSA, the ARP for most program crops ranged between 20 and 35 percent of base acreage. Efficiency aspects of these programs were discussed in Chapter 2.

25. Definitions of base acreage and considered planted may be found in Chapter 3, note 7. Also see U.S. Senate Bill 2830, Title X—General Commodity Provisions, Subtitle A—Acreage Base and Yield System, Section 1101, amended Sec. 503(c).

26. The 1990 FACTA gives farmers more planting flexibility in maintaining program crop bases than was available under the FSA. Farmers now can devote set-aside acres to the following purposes without jeopardizing their base in a given crop: (1) any other program crop, (2) any oilseed (including soybeans unless the secretary estimates that the price of soybeans will be less than 105 percent of the loan level, in which case the crop acreage base that producers may plant without suffering a reduction in the base is limited to 15 percent), (3) any industrial or experimental crop designated by the secretary, and (4) any other crop except any fruit or vegetable crop not designated by the secretary as (a) an industrial or experimental crop, or (b) a crop for which no substantial production or market exists. U.S. Senate Bill 2830, Title X, Subtitle A, Section 1101, amended Sec. 504(b)(1).

27. The FACTA changes some of procedures for calculating deficiency payments, but they are unimportant for the discussion here. Also, the Budget Reconciliation bill passed in early November 1990 allows deficiency pay-

ments to be paid on only 85 percent of the base rather than 100 percent. The bill also gives farmers flexibility on how the other 15 percent of the base may be used: in the program crop but without deficiency payments, or in other alternative crops. This change should conduce to greater economic efficiency, since farmers will consider market prices and costs of alternative crops carefully before deciding how to use 15 percent of the acreage base. USDA (1990), *The 1990 Farm Act,* p. 8.

28. Lee suggests that one policy option that could assist producers in maintaining crop production profitability while promoting soil conservation would be a flexible acreage base wherein a producer would be able to allocate established base acreage among different crops and thus promote erosion control and effective chemical use while remaining eligible to receive program benefits.

29. The FACTA specifies that if the USDA determines that soybean price will be below $5.27 (105 percent of the loan rate of $5.02), it must prohibit soybeans on the 10 percent optional flex acres. See USDA (1990), *The 1990 Farm Act,* p. 27.

30. These acreage idling programs mandated by the 1990 Budget Reconciliation Act have been referred to as the "triple base" for cereals and cotton. In effect, a given farm is divided into one part that is eligible for full program payments, another part that must be idled to comply with the mandated ARP, and a third part that can be planted in any crop (other than fruits and vegetables) or applied to other approved uses providing earnings not subject to government subsidies. The triple base has the effect of decoupling production at the margin from government payments.

31. Preliminary 1991 estimates from the USDA have indicated, for example, that farmers were intending to plant more of every major crop in 1991 than in 1990, except wheat. Corn acreage was expected to be up 4 percent, and cotton acreage up 18 percent. These two crops are associated with higher levels of erosion. See Ingersoll (1991).

32. USDA, "Soil Erosion," p. 29.

33. U.S. Senate, *FACTA,* Senate Report no. 101-357, p. 202.

34. Pierre Crosson (1986b, p. 35) notes that from the 1930s to 1980 the federal government spent roughly $21 billion (in 1977 prices) for erosion control programs and that state and local governments and private landowners, often with government assistance, spent another $22 billion.

35. A most useful review of soil conservation issues and programs is Crosson (1991).

36. USDA, "Soil Erosion."

37. U.S. Senate, *FACTA,* Senate Report no. 101-357, p. 215.

38. Ibid.

39. U.S. Department of Agriculture (1990), "Secretary of Agriculture Yeutter Reports Wetland Losses Down During 1980s," *Selected Speeches and News Releases* (Washington, DC: October 4–11), p. 2–3.

11

Agricultural Policy and the Environment: Chemical Contamination

At least since the publication of Rachel Carson's *Silent Spring* in 1962, the public has been bombarded with information about the potential dangers of toxic agricultural chemicals, primarily pesticides and fertilizers that are put into the natural environment. In recent years, the contamination of domestic water supplies, especially ground water aquifers, has been labeled a critical national problem (Powledge 1982). Some evidence exists that these problems have been overstated, but at least the public perception is that chemical contamination is something to worry about and that agriculture is one of the prime sources of the problem.

Sometimes the harmful chemicals are transported off farm in eroded soil, and sometimes they enter the environment directly, percolating down into ground water. It is generally conceded that the Conservation Reserve Program (CRP) and conservation compliance requirements discussed in Chapter 10 contribute only marginally to any solution. This chapter discusses what is known about the extent of the problem, and the principal connections between the environment and agricultural production and policy.

Sedimentation and Chemical Contamination of Water

It is not land productivity costs that are the most urgent problem associated with soil erosion. Rather, the off-farm costs of erosion resulting from sediment transport are substantially higher than losses in crop yields. "Most of the environmental problems associated with agriculture may be traced to two physical processes: rain or irrigation water runoff that carries sediment, adsorbed or dissolved nutrients, pesticides, and salts from the land to rivers and lakes; and the percolation of dissolved nutrients and pesticides into ground water" (Phipps and Crosson 1986, p. 5). But until the 1990 FACTA made modest progress in targeting these problems, costly soil conservation programs simply have not made much of an impact.

Economist Tim Phipps (1988) has looked specifically at the principal defects in the CRP:

> *The CRP is a positive response to the recognition that soil erosion is actually concentrated geographically, and is much superior to the soil bank which was spread uniformly across all cropland. The CRP, however, still falls short in dealing with the environmental externalities associated with agricultural land use—water pollution, provision of wildlife habitat, and other environmental services. It falls short because these values are not directly accounted for in either the selection of eligible land, or in the determination of the maximum annual rental payment the government is able to offer.*
>
> *By concentrating on the productivity of the land in determining maximum bids, the government is looking at the wrong side of the equation. It should concentrate on the net social value of taking land out of production. The way the CRP is currently administered, all eligible land is treated pretty much uniformly.*

Phipps and colleagues at Resources for the Future (RFF) developed a model that suggests what would happen if the CRP program were targeted to environmental externalities. Effective targeting of the acres reserved could lead to substantial water-quality improvements without an increase in program costs.[1] And why does the targeting not occur? The reason is the same as suggested time and again throughout this book: congressional broad-based income redistribution to special interests who effectively exert political pressure.

But encouraging winds of change may be blowing. In preparing for the 1990 FACTA that amended and extended the 1985 FSA, Congress at least recognized the importance of chemical contamination as part of the erosion problem. The Senate Agriculture, Nutrition, and Forestry Committee suggested:

> *The Committee believes there are two other primary objectives for the conservation reserve during these next five years. First, to the extent possible, it should be used as a management tool to help owners and operators reduce erosion on their croplands, without necessarily removing such croplands from production. And second, it should be used specifically to reduce costly sedimentation and other water quality problems, even if the lands enrolled are not themselves highly erodible land.*[2]

Obviously, the committee has not backed away from costly erosion prevention or from the perceived need to keep the economic base healthy, but at least off-farm water-quality problems were explicitly recognized as being important.

The Bush administration announced late in 1990 that it had begun a major effort to reduce the risk of agricultural chemical pollution of ground and surface water.[3] This program is designed to improve coordination among the USDA's broad array of water-quality programs and to encourage voluntary adoption of agricultural practices that will protect and enhance the nation's ground and surface water. The strategy calls for putting USDA's Soil Conservation Service (SCS) and extension personnel from all of the 3,000 agricultural counties of the country through an intensive training course in methods of preserving water quality. Field guides are being rewritten to assist farmers in keeping agricultural chemicals out of the water, and USDA's funding includes eighty-five state-level projects in which USDA experts are working with state officials to solve water quality problems. It is nitrogen and phosphorus compounds from pesticides, herbicides, and fertilizers that have been getting into the ground and surface water, and it is alleged that good scientific research can be used to "help sustain a high level of productivity while also preserving the environment."[4]

I cannot help wondering, however, whether yet another USDA research and educational program will contribute much toward solving this problem. The problem is not so much scientific ignorance about what is actually happening on U.S. farms. Rather, the essence of the problem concerns property rights, externalities, and incentives. Farmers simply are not accountable for practices that impose off-farm environmental costs. Unless this can be changed, even an extensive and costly program is not likely to make an impact.

The FACTA also established an Agricultural Water Quality Incentives Program: a voluntary program to enroll 10 million acres of farmland through 1995.[5] The secretary of agriculture has been authorized to enter into agreements with landowning participants in eligible areas to implement water-quality plans developed by the SCS. These plans are comprehensive and will focus on agricultural and water-quality production practices that promote an efficient use of crop nutrients and pesticides and that ensure safe storage, mixing, and handling of agriculture chemicals and animal waste. The carrot includes incentive payments to farmers of up to $3,500 per year to be paid out over three to five years, not more than an additional $1,500 per person per contract in the form of cost-share assistance, and a lump sum payment to a landowner or operator of incentive payments if such lump-sum payment is necessary for a producer to implement a practice.[6] Technical assistance, through the SCS, would also be provided to program participants. Additional cost-share payments for wildlife and wetland preservation are also authorized under this title.[7] Criteria that will qualify eligible areas are specified, and priority will be given to regions where agricultural production has been determined to be a major factor in an area's failure to meet applicable water-quality standards.[8] Outlays, subject to appropriations, were estimated to be $115 million through 1995.

On November 26, 1990, the secretary of agriculture announced that the USDA would implement forty-five new projects in thirty-four states in fiscal 1991 to accelerate improvement of water quality in agricultural areas. Along with 45 similar projects begun in 1989, these projects were to provide assistance to farmers under the administration's water-quality initiative.[9]

Another subtitle in the 1990 act is "Water Quality Research, Education, and Coordination," which focuses on the need to increase coordination of water-quality programs, both within the USDA and between the federal and state governments. The act directs the secretary to establish a water-quality coordination program within each state.[10]

But recognizing water-quality problems is one thing. A workable program to deal with them in a cost-effective manner is another. In fact, efforts to deal with the off-farm damage of soil movement are very difficult to implement effectively. Sediment moves through watersheds in a slow and complicated manner. The amount of sediment delivered each year at various points in the watershed may have left farmers' fields upstream many years earlier and bears little relationship to current erosion on those fields (Crosson 1986a). It is therefore difficult and costly to monitor sediment transport and affix responsibility.

Certainly the water-quality–agricultural interface is complicated because national policy on water quality is administered primarily by the Environmental Protection Agency (EPA) and is therefore outside the domain of the USDA where many of the programs are.[11] Much of the legislative authority for pollution control resides outside the agricultural committees of Congress. Water-quality policies that have an impact on the agricultural sector are defined by the Safe Drinking Water Act and the Clean Water Act, both administered by the EPA. The EPA also sets general water-quality standards, but it has delegated responsibility for water-quality improvement to the states (Reichelderfer 1990). This is not all bad since state policy can better accommodate local variation in problems and concerns than can a national policy with identical requirements for all states and regions. However, inconsistency in requirements imposed from state to state can create equity problems for farmers and other agricultural suppliers who must compete with each other nationwide if not worldwide.

Subsidizing Excessive Fertilizer and Pesticide Use in Agriculture

Fertilizers

As indicated, nitrogen and phosphorus fertilizers are the principal villains in chemical contamination of the environment by agriculture:

> *Nitrogen is the more soluble of the two and is mainly carried in a dissolved form, though some is also carried by sediment. Phosphorus, less soluble, is more readily carried by sediment. . . . While both nutrients are naturally present in soil, most of the phosphorus and nitrogen reaching waterways originally was applied as fertilizer. . . . Excessive nutrients in water contribute to eutrophication, a process that reduces the ability of a water body to support animal life and as well makes water less attractive for many forms of recreation. (Phipps and Crosson 1986, p. 6)*

Perhaps the most comprehensive study of the damages caused by sediment and pollutants is by Clark et al. (1985) for the Conservation Foundation. They estimate the annual off-farm damages of sediment and dissolved and sediment-borne pollutants to be in the range of $4.2 to $16.9 billion, which far surpasses any on-farm damages from soil erosion.[12]

Regional studies have also been made. One from California finds that at given locations throughout the Central Valley, nitrates in ground water have exceeded the drinking-water standard by a factor of two to three (Tanji 1990a, p. 61). When ingested, nitrates convert into nitrites, which then can react with other substances to produce cancer-causing compounds known as nitrosamines. Nitrates in drinking water have also been implicated in the "blue baby syndrome." Unfortunately, no quantification of the health damages was reported in the study.

Pesticides

Pesticides in water may be an even greater threat to human and animal health than is fertilizer contamination. Because they are poisons, pesticides may directly harm aquatic organisms and those who ingest them. They may enter drinking water directly by getting into available surface water or by percolating through the soil until they reach underground aquifers. About half of the nation's drinking water comes from underground sources so this problem is potentially very serious. It is not accurately known how pesticides move through the soil and how rapidly they spread once they enter an aquifer, however. Clearly it would be very costly to remove these pollutants in situ once an aquifer has been contaminated. The water is not easily accessible for treatment until it is pumped out of the ground.

A study by the EPA suggests that water aquifers may be contaminated more than was realized, but that current levels of contamination may not be very dangerous. The EPA tested a total of 1,347 wells in all fifty states, finding that 10 percent of the wells serving urban or suburban areas and 4 percent of rural wells contain at least one pesticide, although concentrations were too low to be dangerous to human health in most cases. Nitrates were found in 52.1 percent of the urban wells and in 57 percent of the rural wells. The EPA claims it has notified well owners whenever it found unsafe levels of either pesticides or nitrates (Gutfeld 1990).

A prominent example of a contaminating pesticide is the chemical used for killing nematodes, DBCP. It has been identified as a carcinogen in animals and thus is suspected to be the same in humans. DBCP has been found in 24 percent of the wells tested in Tulare County, 16 percent of those in Kern County, and 43 percent of those in Fresno County, all in California's San Joaquin Valley and three of the ten most important agricultural counties in the entire nation (Tanji 1990a, p. 63). California banned the use of DBCP in 1977, but contaminated wells are still being discovered, and more undoubtedly will be in the future since DBCP moves through the soil profile at a very slow rate.

But how is chemical contamination connected to agricultural policy? Does government action contribute to the problem, and if so, how and to what degree? The answers to these questions are more complex than first meets the eye.

Property Rights and Off-Farm Costs of Chemical Use

If property rights in environmental resources utilized and affected by the agricultural sector, such as airspaces and watersheds, were well-defined and enforced such that all beneficial and harmful impacts of agricultural production were clearly captured by and became the responsibility of the producer, no significant environmental problem would likely exist. Producers could charge for beneficial effects conferred on others and would be accountable to pay for harmful effects. Hence, financial incentives would generate the "optimal" level of valuable production as well as any harmful by-products that reduce environmental quality.

Unfortunately, the requisite property rights often do not exist or have been attenuated in some way, especially for so-called fugitive resources like water and air. In reality, producers are not fully liable for their actions affecting others. They often freely use "common property" resources as sinks for disposing of their waste products, such as toxic chemicals. In turn, these contaminants can cause health problems and damage the flora and fauna in the natural environment.

The problem here is clearly one of institutional failure. The farmer captures the bulk of the direct benefits associated with applying chemicals but may or may not share the environmental costs with all other consumers of the air and water affected by chemicals. Information costs are at the root of the difficulty. If individual farmers' contributions to environmental degradation could be clearly identified, they could be required to pay the damages, which would induce responsible use of chemicals. But acquiring this information is economically, if not technically, infeasible because of the number of polluters and the complexities of monitoring and measuring the total effects of chemical use. It appears that heavier taxation of agricultural chemicals or regulating quantities may be necessary to curb use to efficient levels. But information costs are even a problem for a regulator in knowing what tax to charge or at what level of use to regulate (Reichelderfer 1990, p. 2). Both taxes and imposed ambient chemical standards are also bound to be economically inefficient, however, since these blunt instruments do not take into account local variations in the costs and benefits of the polluting activity.

Agricultural Policy and Chemical Use

But to return to the main issue—the relationships between the use of environmentally degrading agricultural chemicals and agricultural policy—the thesis advanced here is that governmental price support policy has contributed to excessive use of chemicals in the agricultural sector.

Program crop support prices higher than those that would clear unregulated markets provide farmers with incentives for expanding production. The accumulation of large surplus stocks that cannot be sold at existing prices is evidence that support prices that drive production decisions have been above equilibrium levels. The expansion of output can result from farming more land (if that is permitted under the regulations), the employment of output-increasing technology, and more intensive use of variable inputs including agricultural chemicals.

In considering the quantity of any variable input to employ, a farmer will add another unit as long as the expected return from its use exceeds its price or cost. However, increasing input use generates diminishing returns in output production. Clearly, if the output price is higher under a price support system than would exist without it, the returns from a given variable input will be higher. For example, if the target price of wheat is $4 per bushel, unless somehow constrained the farmer could be expected to use more fertilizer to grow wheat than if the support or market price were $3 per bushel. The fertilizer simply has more value at the margin if wheat brings a higher price.

However, not all farmers choose to enroll in government programs. For those who do not enroll, land is not regulated by government programs, and output decisions are not driven by target prices.[13] In these situations, the market price rather than the target price motivates production decisions. But government policy also affects the market price through the nonrecourse loan program.

Since the 1930s, for many program crops such as wheat, the feed grains, cotton, rice, and soybeans, the farmer's crop is used as collateral for a government loan. The loan rate is the per unit price at which the government will loan to farmers to hold their crops for sale at some later date. The average period of the loan is approximately nine months. The 1985 FSA directed loan rates to be set at the discretion of the secretary of agriculture at 75 to 85 percent of the average market price for the preceding five years, exclusive of the highest and lowest of these annual prices.[14]

The nonrecourse feature of the loan program is important in supporting market prices. If the market price is greater than the government loan rate, farmers simply sell their crop in the market and pay off their loans. However, if the market price is lower than the loan rate, the nonrecourse feature of the loan program comes into play, and farmers forfeit their crops to the government and thereby discharge their loan obligations. As a result, when market prices are weak and below the loan rate, the government accumulates stocks of the price-supported commodity.[15]

These surplus stocks are costly to store, whether in public or private bins. Of course, removing part of the commodity supply from the market via the nonrecourse loan increases the market price and thus reduces the differential between the market price and the loan rate. Consequently, the loan rate has tended to serve as a floor under domestic market prices and therefore "supports" market prices. For farmers not enrolled in government programs, the loan rate serves as the guide to what market prices might be. Therefore, loan rates as well as target prices drive production decisions and affect the utilization of variable inputs such as agricultural chemicals. The higher the loan rate, the greater the commitment of variable inputs. This combined impact of target prices and loan rates on chemical use might be called the "price" effect of government programs.[16]

Another determinant of chemical use by farmers might be called the "input substitution" effect. The logic of this effect is straightforward, but the empirical relationships are complex. Given the deficiency payment program where farmers are paid the difference between the target price and the higher of the market price and the loan rate, federal budgetary costs are nearly proportional to crop production that the government commits to support. As explained, the acreage supported is affected by the mandatory set-asides—the 15 percent removal of base acreage from deficiency payments required by the 1990 Budget Reconciliation Act and the 10 percent discretionary reduction given to the secretary of agriculture by the FACTA. The problem for the government is to support prices so that budgetary costs can be held to acceptable levels.[17]

It was argued in Chapter 3 that resource misallocation costs associated with production decreases induced by government programs would be lower if labor inputs were reduced rather than land taken out of production, since labor has valuable alternative employments in the economy. Unfortunately, it appears to be politically infeasible to reduce labor because that component of the agricultural labor force most vulnerable to market forces would be the operators of small and inefficient farms. But these are exactly the farms that the American public seems most eager to protect. Consequently, the politically expedient strategy for Congress has been to find an output-reducing mechanism that would induce as few farmers to leave the sector as possible—the removal of cropland.

For approximately half a century, especially in times of crop surpluses, the government has attempted to reduce total inputs by requiring land set-asides when farms are planted in program crops. Up to and including the 1985 FSA, the principal mechanism was the Acreage Reduction Program (ARP), discussed in Chapter 3.[18] The FSA established limits on the ARP for various crops, depending on the surplus stocks on hand, but generally the required acreage set-aside ranged from 0 to 35 percent and was left largely to the discretion of the secretary of agriculture.[19] However, the 1990 FACTA mandates a generally lower ARP for most crops. The salient point is that by utilizing required land set-asides for determining eligibility for deficiency payments, the government has, unwittingly or not, exacerbated the toxic-chemical contamination problem.[20]

Despite intentions, the ARPs have never been very successful in reducing output for at least two reasons. First, farmers naturally set aside their least productive land in order to minimize the costs of the required set-aside. This means that the percentage of acreage reduction is always larger than the percentage decrease in total output. Second, farmers have rather good input substitutes for land, in the form of labor and purchased capital, which are not regulated. As acreage declines, therefore, farmers have incentives to use these purchased inputs more intensively to compensate for the loss of producing land, especially if support prices are favorable.

A significant instrument for increasing yields has been more intensive use of chemical fertilizers, herbicides, and pesticides. Consequently, the greater the land set-aside requirement, the greater the incentive to use chemicals because they are a substitute for land in maintaining productivity. As indicated, damage to the environment naturally results because the residues of these chemicals move into the watersheds and airspaces utilized by everyone. In the absence of restrictions on program yields, the higher the support price and per acre revenues, the greater the incentive for utilizing chemicals that do environmental damage.

Still another way that farm programs encourage chemical use is the need to build program yields (to be defined shortly) and acreages for future subsidy payments. Increasing yields can be accomplished directly by more intensive use of fertilizers, herbicides, and pesticides. In addition, building base acreage in a given program crop might discourage crop rotation, thereby increasing pest populations and consequently leading to more pesticide use.

This impact of current farm programs has been clearly recognized by the environmental community. Heavy lobbying produced efforts to mitigate the damage. The 1985 FSA directed that deficiency payments could be paid only on "eligible" production, defined as a farm's program acreage base multiplied by its program yield. Recall the earlier discussion that the acreage base for a given crop is the average acreage planted and considered planted to the program crop during the past five years. Farmers who exceed their program-acreage base are ineligible to receive government support payments on any of their production of that crop. Hence, strong incentives exist not to exceed the allowable acreage.

"Program yield" is defined as the average yield for a program crop on the farm from 1981 to 1985, excluding the highest and lowest annual yields (Kennedy and Visser 1990, p. 28). Farmers are not prohibited from exceeding their program yields, but any excess production is not eligible for government deficiency payments. In short, deficiency payments are paid on program yields rather than actual yields. And if actual yields exceed program yields, which is normally the case, this implies that at the margin it is the market price rather than the target price that drives the bulk of use of agricultural chemicals and other variable inputs. Theoretically, these regulations on base acreage and program yields would appear to reduce incentives for increasing yields by applying purchased inputs, including agricultural chemicals. Whether they have done so, however, is an empirical question.

Although the secretary of agriculture has the authority to update program yields on the basis of new information, this authority has not been exercised to date, no doubt with the strong encouragement of the environmental community. As a result, program yields have not increased as rapidly as actual yields since 1986.

What can be concluded? The profitability of growing crops under price supports set above the cost of production (the price effect) has probably induced more chemical use in agriculture than would have been the case without the price support system.[21] However, regulations that limit price support deficiency payments to program yields have just as surely retarded chemical use compared to what it would have been if deficiency payments had been based on actual yields. No studies from the United States have thoroughly sorted out the complex net effects on the use of pesticides, herbicides, and fertilizers of these government programs.[22]

However, there is very strong evidence from international comparisons that countries that support agricultural incomes the most are those that use the most chemicals. In per acre fertilizer use, the ranking of selected countries is Japan (427 kilograms per hectare (ha.), South Korea (255 kilos/ha.), the United States (94 kilos/ha.), Canada (50 kilos/ha.), New Zealand (30 kilos/ha.), Australia (24 kilos/ha.), and Argentina (4 kilos/ha.) (Anderson 1992). The *Economist* refers to an OECD study that ranks countries by the percent of farm income received as a direct transfer from taxpayers and consumers as follows: Japan 66 percent, Austria (52 percent), the EC (40 percent), Canada (49 percent), the United States (30 percent), Australia (15 percent), and New Zealand (4 percent). The strong positive, although not perfect, correlation between agricultural subsidy and fertilizer use of those countries appearing in both lists is quite striking (*Economist* 1992).

It must be emphasized in conclusion, however, that the policy to idle land makes little sense from the viewpoint of either economic efficiency or protecting the environment. The U.S. land base is so extensive that except at the urban fringe where it may have some recreational value, if it is not used in agriculture once it has been cleared for use, it will yield almost nothing in wildlife habitat or other amenities (Leal 1990).

Some Data on U.S. Chemical Use in Agriculture

Two questions about chemical use in agriculture appear to be relevant to this discussion. The first is how to describe chemical use in a way that is most meaningful for looking at environmental quality. This could be done in two ways: by noting the total quantity of chemicals utilized in the agricultural sector, and by noting the chemicals utilized per acre.

Second, what would have been the use of chemicals in agriculture had there been no income support policies and accompanying regulations? To show that chemical use is actually increasing, constant, or declining in the policy environment that exists says nothing definitive about what would have been the situation without such programs. Unfortunately, there appears to be no way to solve this dilemma without modeling the sector with and without the relevant agricultural policies.[23]

Table 11-1 contains data that give a rough indication of chemical use through time in the United States. Many chemicals are used on a single farm, and in the sector as a whole hundreds of fertilizers, herbicides, insecticides, and fungicides are employed. Any aggregation, such as tons of fertilizer utilized, is certain to be simplistic. Besides, various individual chemicals impose highly disparate environmental costs since some are much more toxic and persistent than others. The purpose here, however, is to provide a very rough idea of chemical use. In Table 11-1, all fertilizers have been aggregated into one category as have the various pesticides. Heavy chemical use in agriculture is a fairly recent phenomenon so the data begin in 1960 and are shown at five-year intervals until 1975, after which, beginning in 1978, annual observations are shown through 1988.

It is worth noting that changes in the cropland base are fairly small over the period. Most of the year-to-year variation is likely to be due to changes in the large acreage set-asides involved with the payment-in-kind (PIK) program in 1983 and the ARPs established in the 1985 FSA. Cropland acreage peaked in 1981 at about 366 million acres and has fallen substantially since.

No data were available to show which acres of the cropland base have received fertilizers and pesticides and which have not. Some crops require a number of chemical treatments if yields are to be maintained at a high level, and some do not. Treatments also vary by geographic area depending on climate, moisture availability, soils, and production technology.

A sharp increase in total tonnage of fertilizers (primarily nitrogen, phosphorus, and potassium derivatives) occurred from 1960 to 1970. Increases thereafter were small with tonnage peaking in 1981, after which there was some decrease. Fertilizer applied per cropped acre shows a large increase from 1960 to 1970, and has been fairly stable since. In fact, the peak occurred in the latest year covered by the data, 1988, although the rate of use is almost identical to that in 1980.

Year-to-year increases in total fertilizer use are roughly associated with increases in use per acre, but the percentage changes in total use are greater than those for per acre use. For example, in the PIK year of 1983, total use was down approximately 18 percent from 1982, but use per acre hardly changed. These data, therefore, are not inconsistent with the hypothesis that restrictions on program yields (and perhaps other factors to be considered

TABLE 11-1 Cropland and Chemical Use in U.S. Agriculture, 1960–1988

Year	*Cropland (mil. acres)*	*Fertilizers*		*Pesticides*	
		Total (thous. tons)	*lbs./acre*	*Total*[1] *(mil. lbs.)*	*lbs./acre*
1960	324	7,463.7	46.07	—	—
1970	293	16,068.3	109.68	430	1.47
1975	336	17,560.9	104.53	620	1.85
1978	338	20,586.9	121.82	620	2.30
1979	348	22,565.1	129.68	848	2.47
1980	352	23,083.3	131.16	850	2.41
1981	366	23,677.7	129.39	865	2.36
1982	362	21,427.9	118.39	880	2.43
1983	306	18,095.9	118.27	720	2.35
1984	348	21,790.1	125.23	840	2.41
1985	342	21,702.6	126.92	870	2.54
1986	325	19,654.9	120.95	815	2.51
1987	302	19,054.3	126.18	908	2.67
1988	297	19,530.3	131.52	—	—

Note: [1]Pesticide quantities are approximated from a graph.

Sources: U.S. Bureau of the Census. Statistical Abstract of United States (Washington, DC: 1988 and 1990), p. 655; Harry Vroomen (1989), *Fertilizer Use and Price Statistics, 1960–88* (Washington, DC: U.S. Department of Agriculture), p. 24; Craig D. Osteen and Phillip I. Szmedra (1989), *Agricultural Pesticide Use Trends and Policy Issues* (Washington, DC: U.S. Department of Agriculture), p. 11.

later in this chapter) have been significant in stabilizing fertilizer use on U.S. farms.

A rapid increase in total pesticide use occurred from 1970 to 1980, after which it was reasonably constant except for the PIK year of 1983, when there was a sharp decrease, again reflecting the decrease in acreage planted. In terms of pounds utilized per acre, the trend is rising slightly. The peak was reached in the latest year observed, 1987. Thus, despite all the national attention to health problems attributable to pesticides, the amount used per acre has remained roughly constant, perhaps partially because of increasing skepticism about information on the effects of pesticides on health. It cannot be proved that this result is due to the restrictions on acreage bases and program yields already discussed, but at least the data are not inconsistent with the view that these restrictions are important deterrents to increased chemical use.

A significant development is that scientific research has produced pesticides that have a much shorter half-life than those previously used and are, therefore, less dangerous to human and animal health.

> *In the 1960s, about 50 percent of insecticides were chlorinated hydrocarbons such as DDT, which are very persistent in the environment. By the early 1980s, they represented only about 5 percent of all pesticides used, with the remaining 95 percent largely the more toxic-to-pests but less persistent organophosphates and carbamates. Some other relatively new materials, such as synthetic pyrethroids, require low application rates (10 percent less than other chemicals). These have low mammalian toxicity but are highly toxic to fish. (Antle and Capalbo 1986, p. 158)*

A near consensus exists among scientists that serious long-run agricultural productivity problems could stem from pesticide use. Pests develop genetic resistance to pesticides after a certain period of use. And the pesticides destroy the natural enemies of pests as well as the pests themselves. This means that new and increasingly more toxic pesticides must be devised and applied simply to maintain a given level of effectiveness. Some scientists question whether we can stay even over the long haul (Antle and Capalbo 1986, p. 155). It is therefore clear that the search for new pesticides must continue.

A development that could have very favorable environmental impacts is the recent adoption on a large scale of integrated pest management (IPM). This effort attempts to combine chemical use with biological control of pests—the use of beneficial insects to prey upon those that reduce yield. The USDA and state agricultural experiment stations have spent millions of dollars researching and promoting IPM. The focus of the USDA effort is at the Agricultural Research Center in Beltsville, Maryland, and emphasizes biocontrol that finds natural alternatives to chemical pesticides.[24] This same emphasis on IPM has been occurring in several states for well over a decade.[25]

Some On-Farm Health Issues Relating to Chemical Use

It was suggested earlier that the most severe environmental problem arising from agricultural production is off-farm contamination of water. But there are some significant on-farm concerns as well. Farmers are not immune from the barrage of public information ostensibly relating chemicals to cancer and other diseases. Pollsters discovered that nearly three of every four Iowa farmers believe that agriculture depends too much on commercial chemical fertilizers and pesticides (Kilman 1990). Nearly half of all farmers in the entire nation indicate they are concerned about their own safety and that of their families and workers.

Fertilizer use per acre of corn planted on Iowa farms dropped 8 percent from 1988 to 1989, and local farmers and government officials predicted that it would continue down, anywhere from 2 to 10 percent (Kilman 1990). In historical terms, this decrease in use is somewhat surprising since relative prices for commercial fertilizers have been falling. Apparently the demand curve has shifted downward because of these new concerns about the alleged dangers of chemical use.[26]

Still, manufacturers anticipated nation-wide fertilizer consumption would rise about 3 percent from 1990 to 1991. The reason is that the area in corn was estimated to be up 4 to 5 percent in 1991, and corn is the crop on which nearly half of the nation's commercial fertilizer is used (Kilman 1990).

It must not be forgotten that chemicals account for a significant portion of the recent growth in U.S. agricultural productivity, which increased 50 percent in the 1967–1987 period (Parnell 1990, p. 4). Chemicals are also an important expense in the production of most crops, and farmers have incentives to use them sparingly to reduce costs and increase profits.

Conservation technology also is becoming increasingly important in changing chemical use. As explained in the preceding chapter, under rules imposed by the FSA, the government requires farmers on erodible land to adopt conservation techniques if they wish to continue receiving price support payments. One way of conserving soil is to construct conservation ridges. Farmers have found it most profitable to fertilize only the ridges, thus conserving on fertilizer use as well as soil (Kilman 1990).

Another recent technological innovation is to place fertilizer nearer the growing plants and thus improve its efficiency. And as soil tests get more precise, farmers can avoid overfertilizing. University of Nebraska researchers have concluded that American farmers could cut fertilizer and pesticide use by 10 percent over four years with little impact on yields (Kilman 1990).

Water-quality and toxic-element problems are clearly on the minds of rural as well as urban residents. Kilman states:

> *Farmers are concerned not only about the water but about inhaling the chemicals as they apply them. Of 800 U.S. farmers polled in August by Jefferson Davis Associates, a Cedar Rapids firm, about half said they worry that their use of crop chemicals is dangerous to themselves. At the same time, they're concerned about how it all plays among city-dwellers. Some 83% said they fear that townspeople blame them for polluting the environment.* (1990, p. A1)

It is therefore much too simplistic to portray farmers as uncaring about environmental quality as is sometimes charged. But this does not mean that conflict over agricultural chemical use does not or will not exist between rural and urban Americans. The individual stakes are quite different for the two groups. A livelihood at risk makes a difference in how problems are perceived. But there do seem to be significant changes in attitudes and technologies that make predictions of chemical use hazardous purely on the basis of past use.

Besides, some new developments are occurring on the information and education fronts. On November 1, 1990, the USDA announced the availability of the first computerized database that references the physical and chemical properties of pesticides.[27] The database covers sixteen different chemicals in ninety-two widely used pesticides. USDA specialists hope to assist farmers to manage pesticide applications under specific soil conditions to avoid contaminating water.

It is difficult indeed to sort out the net effect on chemical use of these various forces operating in both directions simultaneously. If recent history is any guide, positive forces are approximately offsetting negative ones since the volume of chemical use is not changing much through time. However, this conclusion does not negate the effect of government programs, particularly price supports and acreage set-asides, which result in greater chemical use than would occur without them.

Agricultural Policy and the Greenhouse Effect

The so-called greenhouse effect is receiving increased attention by scientists and policymakers in many countries,[28] although some scientists believe that the phenomenon is of little consequence or has been exaggerated.[29] The greenhouse effect is a gradual warming of the earth's atmosphere, alleged to be primarily attributable to the presence of various gases produced by human activity, especially the burning of fossil fuels in internal combustion engines. By trapping long-wave radiation near the earth's surface, these gases are alleged to lead to an increase in the earth's temperature. The warmed atmosphere will produce a melting of the polar ice caps causing a rise in the level of the oceans by one to three feet, which, in turn, would produce tremendous damage to coastal cities and recreation areas and a general worsening of conditions for comfortable human habitation (Adams 1990). Some see significant effects on agriculture brought about by greenhouse processes as precipitation patterns change and drought becomes more likely. Others expect the warming to increase water evaporation and precipitation, thus benefiting agriculture (Gardner 1993). Some scientists see agriculture as a major contributor of the gases producing the greenhouse effect. The clearing of forests for crop production, the fertilization of crops, and the worldwide increase in livestock populations are other major factors in global climate change arising from the greenhouse effect (Adams 1990).

The damaging gases are carbon dioxide (CO_2), primarily the result of burning fossil fuels, and methane and nitrous oxide (N_2O), both of which are produced by some agricultural practices:

> *Fertilization with anhydrous ammonia and spraying nitrogen are contributors. Feed lots, where cattle are closely confined and fed high energy diets, are sources of methane. Rice production also produces methane. These sources may contribute up to 50 percent of atmospheric methane produced annually. Agricultural burning also releases CO_2 and N_2O into the atmosphere. (Adams 1990, p. 9)*

Few international institutions and control mechanisms exist to cope with the greenhouse effect. No better illustration exists anywhere of the classic externality problem. Millions of automobile drivers the world around are the principal contributors of CO_2, but in the absence of emissions regulations or much higher gasoline prices, there is little incentive for individual drivers to reduce their emissions. Converting cropland to forests might be quite helpful, but it would have to occur on a large scale. And who is to pay for such conversion when the problem extends across international boundaries? Much of the loss of tropical forests occurs in less developed countries where the incentives to increase cropland by poor farmers are very powerful. If it is to be stopped, who is to pay? Much more research attention needs to be given to whether the problem is serious, what is economically feasible to do about it, and to institutions that can facilitate action.[30]

Conclusions

The 1990 FACTA makes some modest progress in targeting the problems of chemical contamination, but effective programs have yet to be conceived and implemented. Whatever their final form, it is probable that these programs will turn out to be like the CRP in that they are more effective in transferring real income to the agricultural sector than they are in producing cost-effective environmental improvements.

Current regulations freeze program yields at 1985 levels for the purpose of determining deficiency payments, and thus to some extent payments are already decoupled from yields. This has produced a beneficial impact on environmental quality. Deficiency payments are also paid on average yields for a certain area rather than for the individual farm. This also has beneficial environmental consequences since if this were not the case, farmers would have even more incentive to pile on chemicals to increase base yields and payments. If price support payments are retained in legislation, at least these features of current law should be kept intact to minimize environmental costs.

Notes

1. For example, there could be a ninefold increase in the number of water-quality model observation points that would meet the reference phosphorous standard. In addition, there could be an improvement by a factor of two in the reduction in average phosphorous concentrations. Average sediment loadings could be reduced by a factor of between 2.75 and 3.
2. U.S. Senate (1990a), *Food, Agriculture, Conservation, and Trade Act of 1990,* Report no. 101-357 (Washington, DC: July 6), p. 203.
3. U.S. Department of Agriculture, Office of Public Affairs (1990), "Statement of Secretary of Agriculture Clayton Yeutter at the Farm Progress Show, Amana, Iowa, September 26, 1990," *Selected Speeches and News Releases* (Washington, DC: September 20–27).
4. Ibid.
5. U.S. Senate, *FACTA,* Title XIV—Conservation, Subtitle C—Agricultural Resources Conservation Program, Section 1439, amended Sec. 1238B(a)(11).
6. Ibid., Section 1438, amended Chapter 2, Sec. 1238B(a)(6)(C).
7. Ibid., Section 1439, amended Sections 1238B(a) and 1238D.
8. Ibid., Section 1439, amended Sec. 1238C.
9. U.S. Department of Agriculture, Office of Public Affairs (1990), "Yeutter Announces 45 Water Quality Projects," *Selected Speeches and News Releases* (Washington, DC: November 22–29), p. 6.
10. U.S. Senate, *FACTA,* Title XIV, Subtitle G—Water Quality Research, Education, and Coordination, Section 1483(a).
11. Some observers express concern that agricultural producers have some advantages in regulatory actions taken against them by the EPA compared with polluters in other sectors of the economy. Much agricultural pollution is considered to be "non-point," which means that it is very difficult to identify the source of the pollution and to punish offenders enough to deter harmful activity.
12. One estimate is that about 50 million people rely on ground water in areas identified as vulnerable to agricultural ground water pollution. Lee and Nielsen (1988).
13. And even for those farmers who do enroll, as explained earlier, the 1990 Budget Reconciliation bill requires that 15 percent of program acreage be exempted from receiving deficiency payments of the price support program, and the FACTA permits the secretary of agriculture to exempt another 10 percent.

14. Kennedy and Visser (1990, p. 30). The FSA placed limits on the maximum amount by which the loan rates for grains could drop from year to year. Minimum loan rates were specified for soybeans, cotton, and rice. These limits resulted in loan rates that were higher than the formula price.

15. As an alternative to holding stocks itself, the government has subsidized the private holding of stocks called the farmer-owned reserve.

16. The 1990 FACTA changed the method of determining loan rates for grains, soybeans, and other oilseeds but kept them the same for rice and upland cotton. The FACTA sets the basic loan rate for wheat and feed grains at 85 percent of market price, before adjustments. The new method first determines the "basic loan rate" and then makes adjustments according to stocks-to-use ratios. The FACTA also gives the secretary of agriculture discretion in adjusting the loan rate to maintain competitiveness of American farmers in world markets.

    The 1990 FACTA adds mandatory marketing loans for soybeans and other oilseeds and leaves them discretionary for wheat and the feed grains. Marketing loans permit the repayment of loans at less than the loan rate to prevent the loan rate from being a floor under the market price. When the world price is low, the marketing loan avoids crops being held under loan, isolated from the market, and forfeited to the government. See U.S. Department of Agriculture, Economic Research Service (1990b), *The 1990 Farm Act and the 1990 Budget Reconciliation Act,* Miscellaneous Publication no. 1489 (Washington, DC: December).

17. Another change made by the 1990 Budget Reconciliation Act was the way that market price is to be calculated in the process of determining deficiency payments. The 1985 FSA required that market price be the average over a five-month period after harvest when prices tend to be "low." The 1990 act requires that the average be calculated over a twelve-month period, which normally will yield a higher market price and a smaller deficiency payment, thus reducing government outlays for support programs.

18. The Soil Bank Program initiated during the first Eisenhower administration was an earlier and significant cropland reduction program.

19. The secretary was charged with the delicate task of managing the costs of holding stocks, the budgetary costs of support prices, and the competitive position of American farmers in world trade. See Kennedy and Visser (1990, p. 28).

20. Paradoxically, government price support policy has also increased the acreage of environmentally fragile land in cropland use and has accelerated soil erosion, particularly in the Great Plains and Rocky Mountain states.

21. This conclusion is strongly supported by New Zealand evidence that indicates that when New Zealand went off price supports in the late 1980s, the application of fertilizer fell by 55 percent. *Economist* (1992, p. 15).

22. A strong beginning in modeling these relationships has been made by Professor Gerald A. Carlson and his associates at North Carolina State University. Although papers are at this point unpublished, Carlson et al. have developed a crop production model focusing on corn to determine how government program provisions affect crop rotation and how well rotation substitutes for insecticide use. Preliminary findings suggest that rotating corn increases with program participation rates, leading to a reduction in per acre insecticide use. This work also finds that irrigation acts as a barrier for crop rotation and therefore leads to increased use of pesticides.

23. Thomas Hertel has attempted a very limited modeling effort. He asks the hypothetical question: If the price of agricultural output were raised 10 percent by set-aside programs similar to the ARP, what would be the effect on chemical use even with the smaller acreage growing crops? He finds that chemical use would increase by 0.2 percent, not a large but still a positive response. See Hertel (1990, p. 164).

24. U.S. Department of Agriculture, Office of Public Affairs (1990), "USDA Posts New Road Sign for Agricultural Research," *Selected Speeches and News Releases* (Washington, DC: July 19–26), p. 9.

25. Recent reports from the USDA indicate an experimental program on actual commercial farms that may in time produce useful cost-benefit evidence. In the 1990 field season, the Agricultural Stabilization and Conservation Service tested a cost-share program for reducing chemical use. The trial program was designed to encourage adoption of environmentally benign integrated pest and fertilizer management practices recommended by the federal government. Trials were limited to twenty farms in each of five counties per state. Participants were required to enroll at least forty acres of small grains, forage, hay, or row crops and follow a written integrated crop management plan designed to reduce pesticide or fertilizer use by at least 20 percent. See Carter and Nuckton (1990, p. 49).

26. In fact, falling prices are the dominant factor explaining the increasing use of fertilizers on U.S. farms since World War II. It was increasing fertilizer use, mainly anhydrous ammonia, that enabled farmers to grow corn on the same land year after year, increasing total corn production and net income.

27. U.S. Department of Agriculture, Office of Public Affairs (1990), "New USDA Database Will Help Protect Rural Water Supplies," *Selected Speeches and News Releases* (Washington, DC: October 25–November 1), p. 25.

28. A very balanced and penetrating discussion of the subject has recently been authored by a past president of the American Economic Association. See Schelling (1992).

29. For example, S. Fred Singer believes that global warming lacks scientific support but is being promoted by environmental activist groups and by political

leaders to "place natural resources and even national economies under international control, preferably theirs." See Singer (1992, p. A16).

30. Perhaps an important beginning by the U.S. government has been made in the FACTA by the appropriation of $25 million for conservation of forests in Latin America. The concept is a debt-for-nature swap, in which the U.S. government would buy the Latin American debt owed to U.S. banks. This debt can be purchased for only a few cents on the dollar. The debt would then be sold back to Latin American countries for local currency, which would then be used for in-country conservation purchases such as buying up forests and game parks. This is also being done by organizations like the Nature Conservancy. See Sawhill (1991).

12

*Irrigation Subsidics and their Economic and Environmental Consequences**

The increase in irrigated agriculture over the past 150 years, particularly in the arid regions of the West, has been a significant factor in the growth of the agricultural sector in the nation as a whole. Large federal projects have become a very important part of western irrigation, and federal water has been heavily subsidized by American taxpayers. The question raised in this chapter is whether these irrigation subsidies make economic sense in terms of increasing living standards and raising the quality of life in the nation as a whole.

At the time of settlement, water was diverted from rivers and streams and applied to arid lands to grow crops for human and livestock consumption. Without irrigation, agriculture consisted only of livestock grazing and some "dry" farming of small grains and forages. Developers used their own labor and capital resources, and where credit was available, it was borrowed from private lenders.

The mutual irrigation company was the principal organizational vehicle utilized in most areas before the law permitted creation of the public water districts. Shares of stock in the mutual company, generally in proportion to irrigated acreage, were issued to water users, who then participated in the governance of the company based on the number of shares owned. The majority of these irrigation companies still exist today and have delivered water to users for over a century. Water was also impounded in storage facilities where it could be collected during the season of nonuse or high flow and then released when the natural flow of the stream would be insufficient to meet desired uses. The discovery and use of ground water by private users also increased at a rapid rate during the first part of the twentieth century.

During the settlement period, these private water projects were small by modern standards, but generally profitable. If they had not been expected to enhance the wealth of those who paid to build them, these projects could not have generated development resources and would not have been built. There were no governmental subsidies available from outside the region.

But this was not to last. At about the beginning of the twentieth century, under the impetus of President Theodore Roosevelt's progressives and preservationists, the federal government became heavily involved in protecting and managing western resources. Many forests and watersheds were reserved by the federal government and placed in the national forest system, where grazing and timber production could be regulated. They were thus protected from sales to private users who had been able to purchase or homestead public lands for more than a century. National parks were established beginning with Yellowstone. And in 1902, the National Reclamation Act was passed, initiating federal participation in building and managing large irrigation projects in the West. The Bureau of Reclamation was established to promote, plan, and build water projects. These federal projects furnished water to arid lands that did not have enough and drained water from swamps that had too much.

Along with federal sponsorship of water projects ultimately came water subsidies and excessive and premature water development. The Reclamation Act established the revolving Reclamation Fund, which provided money for surveying, constructing, and maintaining irrigation works in the western states. Settlers using the irrigation water were expected to repay these funds, without interest, over a ten-year period (Wahl 1989, p. 21). A highly centralized water allocation system became competitive with and gradually displaced most new development by the decentralized system of private mutual companies. Why should irrigators employ their own scarce capital resources when heavy subsidies could be obtained from the U.S. Treasury?

Watering the arid lands of the West by government projects was very attractive politically. Half the continent of a growing nation was virtually empty, and populating it was a way of expanding the frontier. The nation was anxious to fortify the western lands with a larger and economically viable population to make it inviolate against any ambitions possessed by their Mexican, Russian, and Canadian neighbors. Cheap land and water provided a living for eager migrants and foreign immigrants. As soon as it was realized that the financial resources of the federal government could be tapped to transfer income and wealth from the taxpayers of the nation to the western region via irrigation development, a tremendous burst of political activity to make such transfers occurred.[1] In 1900, both the Republican and Democratic platforms favored federal assistance for irrigation (R. Robbins

1976, p. 330). New and emerging territories and states furnished the political constituencies that could bring pressure on the federal government to undertake the construction of larger water projects than had hitherto been attempted with private resources. Some areas of the West, especially those along the Pacific Coast, had ideal climates and soils for growing the fruits, nuts, and vegetables desired by Americans. With the coming of the railroad and later refrigerated transportation, these commodities could be marketed in all parts of the country at times of the year not previously available. These developments only enhanced the power of the irrigation lobby attempting to get cheap water for the region.

Still, the pace of federal water development was slow (see Table 12-1). Irrigable acreage in bureau projects was about 3.5 million acres in 1934, but only 2.84 million acres were served with water. By 1944, there were 4.147 million irrigated acres. Over the next decade, there were over 6 million irrigated acres in bureau projects, and, by 1964, over 7.5 million acres. The rate of increase then slowed as the best dam sites had already been developed, but the peak acreage was reached in 1982 with 10.635 million irrigated acres. Since that time, irrigated acreage has been slightly less than 10 million acres.

Table 12-1 also shows the percent irrigable acreage actually serviced. On many projects, it required several years to put the project facilities in place before designated land actually received water. Serviced acreage is from 66 to 73 percent of the irrigable acreage.

The total irrigated acreage in the region for selected years from 1934 to 1987 is also shown in Table 12-1. Total irrigated acreage peaked around 1978. The percentage of total regional acreage in bureau projects rose slowly from 1939 to 1982 and has been roughly constant since. However, these data understate the importance of bureau water in the region as a proportion of *surface* water supplies. Much of the increase in irrigated acreage since the 1930s, reflected in the regional total, has utilized ground water.[2] Because most underground aquifers were accessible to several pumpers and there were only loose controls on pumping, many aquifers were overused and water tables declined. This is significant from the viewpoint of water policy because much of the political pressure for development of new federal surface water supplies arose from the alleged "need" to replace ground water that was being pumped from declining aquifers.

A system of discretionary administrative law and regulations employed on bureau projects also partially superseded the appropriation law historically utilized by the states as the doctrinal basis for water rights. The law of prior appropriation, which relied on the principle "first in time, first in right," was extremely important in providing security of tenure for early

TABLE 12-1 Irrigable and Irrigated Acreage Serviced by the Bureau of Reclamation and Total Irrigated Acreage in Seventeen Western States, 1934–1987

Year	*Bureau irrigable acreage for service (mil. acres)*	*Bureau total irrigable acreage (mil. acres)*	*Percent irrigable acreage serviced*	*Bureau irrigated acreage (mil. acres)*	*Total Irrigated acreage 17 western states (mil. acres)*	*Percent irrigated acreage by the bureau*
1934	3.495	n/a	n/a	2.837	n/a	n/a
1939	3.890	n/a	n/a	3.141	17.244	18%
1944	4.490	n/a	n/a	4.147	19.430	21
1949	5.679	n/a	n/a	4.821	24.261	20
1954	7.232	n/a	n/a	6.126	26.971	23
1959	8.101	n/a	n/a	6.803	30.841	22
1964	9.037	n/a	n/a	7.523	30.209	23
1969	9.904	15.033	66%	8.387	34.784	24
1974	11.037	16.369	67	9.418	36.648	26
1978	11.409	16.015	69	9.576	43.629	22
1982	12.592	17.497	72	10.635	41.284	26
1987	12.494	17.034	73	9.798	37.777	26

Sources: U.S. Department of Agriculture, *Agricultural Statistics* (Washington, DC: various years); U.S. Department of the Interior, Bureau of Reclamation, *Summary Statistics* (Washington, DC: various years).

water users. But this principle lacked flexibility to meet the needs of a changing economy in more recent years and has, therefore, impeded the transfer of water to higher valued uses and users. Also, federal administrative regulations associated with water allocation have significantly prevented the transfers of water to higher valued uses and, therefore, have reduced water productivity (B. D. Gardner 1986). Because federal development was premature, the government had large quantities of unsold water on its hands. Thus, the principal purpose of rules preventing private exchanges was the need of federal agencies to market water that otherwise could not have been sold.

As a historical note, as early as 1880 the commissioners on public lands appointed by the president to review federal policy were skeptical of government development:

> *The general government or State government may itself construct the hydraulic works necessary to the reclamation of these (arid) lands, and own and control them in such a manner as to derive a revenue from the sale of the water. Such is the method often adopted by other governments, but such a method is not in consonance with the traditions of the American people, but is utterly opposed to the prevalent theories of wise legislation. It would require the establishment of a vast irrigating department with an extensive retinue of officers and the appropriation of many hundreds of millions of dollars. It would seem therefore wiser to invite enterprise to these undertakings, and indeed capitalists have not shown an unwillingness to undertake the redemption of these lands.*[3]

The recommendations of the commissioners notwithstanding, the huge and costly federal bureaucracy to promote and administer irrigation development is exactly what the American people got. The question is, can it be justified on either efficiency or equity grounds?

Efficiency Impacts of the Irrigation Water Subsidy

Subsidized irrigation projects impose large net costs on the economy, even though as with most investments there are some gainers.[4] The problem is not just that the federal government spends hundreds of millions of taxpayer dollars each year to supply water to farmers at "low" prices. If this subsidy simply represented a transfer of equal value from taxpayers to farmers, little net efficiency loss and perhaps no environmental damage might occur. But in actual fact, subsidized reclamation projects squander valuable capital and environmental resources, as well as benefit farmers far less than what taxpayers pay.

Public understanding is deplorably meager concerning the nature of the irrigation water subsidy, who gains and who loses from it, and what the size of the aggregate efficiency loss is. "Subsidy" is generally construed to mean the difference between societal costs for some economic activity and what beneficiaries pay for it. The source for most of the ignorance about the water subsidy is the perception that beneficiaries collect the full subsidy, that is, the full difference between taxpayer costs and what the farmers pay for their federal water. This perception is surely wrong.

The Subsidy and Efficiency Losses

Some data from California's San Joaquin Valley, where the bureau's Central Valley Project supplies irrigation water, will illustrate the relationship between water costs, values, and producer prices. The precise numbers for other subsidized projects in the region will be different, of course, but the patterns are similar.

Water project costs may be classified into two groups: joint costs for facilities such as dams, which contribute to many project uses such as electric power, recreation, flood control, and irrigation; and separable costs, which are identified solely with a given use such as irrigation. Roughly, the separable costs for irrigation (that is, construction and operation and maintenance [O&M] costs for canals, ditches, pumps) for the newer projects built and proposed by the bureau are $250 to $500 per acre-foot of water delivered.[5] (An acre-foot is the volume of water one foot deep over one acre of land, or about 326,000 gallons.) Of course, these costs include appropriate interest charges on the original capital investment.[6] These costs, however, do *not* include many of the negative environmental consequences of water development such as loss of wild rivers, forests, and wildlife (discussed later in the chapter).

To obtain access to federal water on a long-term contract, the typical California irrigator repays the government less than $20 per acre-foot, some much less (B. D. Gardner 1983, p. 94; P. Davis 1992b, p. 531). In many instances, even the project O&M costs, ranging from $5 to $9 per acre-foot, exceed what farmers pay.[7] Thus, there is a huge deficit in the government's water accounts (Huffaker and Gardner 1986). It was this fact that was perhaps the principal motivation for the 1982 Reclamation Reform Act, which increased water prices to those irrigators who operate more than the limit of 960 acres.

But what is water worth to irrigators? Studies show that the value of water to a typical farmer in the San Joaquin Valley averages around $50 per acre-foot, although great variation exists among farmers and geographic areas (Noel et al. 1980). Thus, on average, farmers capture a net benefit of about $30 per acre-foot, the difference between what water is worth and what they pay. Assume a conservative water cost to the taxpayers of $300 per acre-foot and an average water value of $50. Therefore, it costs federal taxpayers a *net* $280 ($300 less the $20 farmers repay the government) per acre-foot to supply this average value of $30 of net benefit to the irrigators.

What are the principal efficiency implications of these subsidies and pricing policies? Most of the taxpayer investment has been sunk into physical capital—dams, canals, ditches, pumps— that cannot be economically recovered and converted to other uses. Therefore, taxpayers must accept the fact that these sunk costs on existing projects that represent the bulk of the irrigation subsidy simply are gone forever. They are the consequence of uneconomic political decisions that have produced economically infeasible projects. Without the subsidy, it is apparent that much irrigation development could not have been viable and thus many fewer resources, including land, would have been devoted to agricultural production.

Some irrigation apologists contend that the construction of irrigation facilities has benefited particular local economies so that the $280 per acre-foot loss is not actually wasted from the national point of view. This contention is almost wholly erroneous. While there are some local gains in employment and output from building and operating irrigation structures like dams and canals, generally these gains are fully offset by losses in other areas where taxpayer resources would have created similar benefits in alternative purposes. Or alternatively, if the government had collected the taxes but used them in alternative public projects, the resources could be expected to yield secondary benefits approximately equal to those generated by the water project. Hence, there is little if any net gain to the nation's economy as a whole.

Still, it is undoubtedly these local economic gains, especially increases in land values, that produce much of the political pressure for subsidized water development. Members of Congress who vote for such projects do not have to satisfy a national constituency to get elected; they must only promote the interests of their local constituencies in a state or congressional district. The water lobbies—such as the American Water Resources Association, the Irrigation Districts Association, many grass-roots organizations of water users such as the California Westside Farmers operating in the Westlands Water District, and general farm organizations like the American Farm Bureau Federation, as well as many others—are very effective in Washington in promoting water development and in perpetuating water subsidies (Taylor 1975, p. 15).

An example from recent congressional hearings. A fascinating example of political maneuvering in Washington is provided by 1990 hearings before the Senate Water and Power Subcommittee, Energy and Natural Resources Committee, chaired by Senator Bill Bradley (D-NJ). The topic of the hearing was the completion of the Irrigation and Drainage System (I&D) of the Bonneville Unit of the Central Utah Project (CUP). Senate Bill 2969 then under consideration, the Central Utah Project Completion Act, would have authorized $150 million in federal funds for construction of the I&D. No construction work had yet begun. Senator Bradley had requested the General Accounting Office (GAO) to prepare a benefit–cost analysis on this anticipated activity.

Originally, the CUP was to be built by the bureau under authority of the 1956 Colorado River Storage Project Act. There were to be five units; two relatively small ones had already been constructed, two were deferred, and the large Bonneville Unit, begun in 1966, is presently still under construction. The Bonneville Unit is divided into six systems that are designed to collect water in the Uintah Basin in northeastern Utah, part of the Colorado River drainage, and transport it through the Wasatch Mountains through a complex system of aqueducts, tunnels, and canals to the Bonneville Basin, a part of the Great Basin. This will enable Utah to use more of its entitlement under the Colorado River Compact, negotiated in the 1920s:

> *According to the Bureau, about 40 percent of the I&D system's water will provide supplemental irrigation to presently irrigated land to offset an existing water shortfall, and thereby stabilize agricultural production. Most of the remaining I&D system water will be used to irrigate presently unirrigated land to offset land being taken out of agricultural production by urbanization and industrialization.*[8]

The bureau had not calculated a benefit–cost ratio on the I&D system, per se. To do so the GAO extracted from the bureau's 1988 benefit–cost analysis of the entire Bonneville Unit only those benefits and costs associated with the I&D system. The benefit–cost ratio was 0.8. (This number means that the national economy will benefit by 80 cents for every dollar of assigned cost to the system. Recall, however, that these separable costs do not include any interest costs and therefore are only a fraction of the actual costs of the system.)

Using standard economic principles, GAO analysts found what they considered to be errors in the bureau data that overstated the benefit–cost ratio. The bureau had included as benefits the indirect profits earned by food processors, transporters, and retailers for delivering increased farm production to final consumers. The GAO correctly surmised that these secondary benefits should not be considered a benefit to the economy as a whole since they would have also been earned if the project funds had been spent alternatively. The bureau had not counted the labor of the farmers as a cost of the project, which assumes that farmers would have no alternative employment over the 100-year life of the project had it not been built. This assumption is clearly fallacious since farmers have moved out of agriculture to other and perhaps even better employments for decades. And finally, the GAO increased the annual costs to deal with increased salinity impacts downstream resulting from the I&D system. By diverting water from the Colorado River, the salt concentrations in the remaining water would be higher, imposing costs on downstream users in both the United States and Mexico. These various adjustments made by the GAO resulted in a $5 million annual decrease in benefits, a $5.4 million annual increase in costs, and a benefit-cost ratio reduced to 0.3.[9]

The reactions of western senators at the hearings for the GAO report were hostile and hardly surprising. They did not dispute the GAO data or conclusions; they simply found them irrelevant. In fact, Senator Garn (R-UT) argued that he and the other politicians knew all along that some components of the CUP were infeasible but contended that the whole project was economically sound.[10] Besides, the federal government had promised this project to the people in poor rural counties and the credibility of the government was now at stake.[11] It was not fair for the government to change the rules and fail to deliver on its promises.[12] In other words, any tough economic analysis on how the government uses its resources at this point in time is irrelevant. The bill to complete the CUP was favorably reported out of committee and President Bush signed the bill before leaving office.[13]

Restrictions on Irrigation Water Use

To complicate the efficiency problem, the value of water in federally subsidized reclamation projects is lower than it could be were it not for governmental restrictions on the volume of subsidized water that can be legally used. There is a mandated limitation on acreage that may receive subsidized water. To limit the per farmer subsidy in the belief that small farms supporting the farmer and his family would be promoted, the 1902 Reclamation Act restricted the amount of land per qualified recipient to a maximum of 160 acres. A 1926 amendment interpreted the act to mean 320 acres for a husband and wife farming together. However, farmers were permitted to expand their actual operated acreage beyond 320 acres by leasing land from other landowners who also qualified to receive subsidized water. By renting land, farmers could benefit from size economies (such as larger and more efficient machinery) that became available after World War II and still meet the acreage limitation on owned land.

Whether the acreage limitation has been adequately enforced has always been a hotly contested issue. Opponents of large-scale agriculture in the West have argued for tighter enforcement of the limitation (Taylor 1975). Proponents have held that the technical requirements of the law were being met by the leasing option already discussed. The matter was finally resolved by the 1982 Reclamation Reform Act (RRA), although many issues remain controversial. The RRA changed the law to increase the maximum acreage that could receive subsidized water to 960 acres. But the limit was applied to leased as well as owned land. Any water applied to land that exceeds the acreage limitation will not be available at the subsidized price. Full cost will be charged and would include an interest charge for capital investment, one that is waived in calculating the subsidized price. The effect of this rule change is that full-cost water will generally be priced at a much higher rate than the subsidized price. The ultimate impact of the 1982 act will be to reduce the size of many efficient western farms and thus raise costs of production to the detriment of consumers of fruits, nuts, and vegetables nation-wide.

In terms of economic efficiency, the important point is that water will almost certainly be worth less to farmers when there are restrictions on its use that prevent the most efficient farm size and structure (Huffaker and Gardner 1986b). But even if such restrictions reducing water value did not exist or were removed, there is little likelihood that the water value in irrigation would even remotely approach the separable federal costs of water development, to say nothing of covering irrigation's share of the joint costs. As a consequence, irrigation water subsidies have seriously misallocated resources in producing excessive water development.

Some Equity Effects of Water Subsidies

The equity impacts of subsidizing water are somewhat complex, but the principal effect is on landowners.

Gains to Landowners

Even a relatively small net benefit to the farmer, such as the $30 per acre-foot of water delivered as already postulated, will push land prices up sharply. It is ownership of land that provides entitlement to the subsidized water since contracts are made with eligible landowners. The acreage limitation requires that subsidized water be tied to eligible project acreage. Furthermore, it is the land that is essentially fixed in supply and, therefore, captures the bulk of the economic rents associated with the subsidy, especially in the long run. The owners of other factors of production, such as labor and purchased inputs like agricultural chemicals, will fairly quickly adjust to any above-normal returns by increasing their supplies, thus driving returns down to the normal competitive level.

A typical contract with the bureau might provide three acre-feet of water annually per acre of eligible land over a period of forty years. Using the numbers in the previous example for illustrative purposes, land is likely to increase in value about $1,500 an acre. By providing three acre-feet of water per year, the contract creates an additional annual return of $90 ([$50 water value - $20 repayment charge] x 3 acre-feet per acre = $90) for each acre of land for forty years. Assuming a real interest rate of 5 percent, the present value of a forty-year flow of real net benefits of $90 per year is $1,544.

Under government contract, renewal policies that respond to the political pressures brought by subsidy-receiving groups, the best expectation is that contracts will be renewed at terms not far different from those under the initial contract when the current one expires. If so, the capitalized value of the annual flow will be even higher since the subsidy period can be expected to extend beyond forty years. But government policy is notoriously risky, and therefore landowners may use a higher interest rate for discounting the annual rents. If so, the present value of the flow of rents will be lower than indicated earlier. Regardless of the exact numbers used, the wealth gains in land will be substantial as "economic rents" resulting from the expected subsidy are quickly capitalized into land prices. Thus, the principal beneficiaries of pricing water below its value are the initial owners of land that benefit from project water. To receive entitlement to subsidized water, however, subsequent eligible purchasers of land must pay market prices that reflect the capitalized future value of the water subsidy. Thus, their wealth gains from the subsidy will be much more limited, if they exist at all.

These expected windfalls to landowners have been the most controversial aspect of federal water policy. Promoters of the 1902 act wanted to encourage settlement of farm families on the land and to prevent large landowners and "speculators" from capturing the benefits from the water subsidy. The populists of the time argued that the land speculators were exploiting farmers right along with middlemen, bankers, and railroads. Fears of land monopolists are expressed everywhere in the rhetoric of the times and are the principal reason the 160-acre limitation was imposed. Landowners receiving subsidized water were required by the government to enter into recordable contracts to sell owned land in excess of the eligible acreage within ten years and, further, to sell it at a "pre-project" land price approved by the government. Supposedly this would limit the wealth windfall in increased land prices. One thing seems obvious. If landowners agreed to dispose of their excess land under these harsh terms, the expected windfall gains on the land kept and receiving subsidized water must have been very substantial.

Equity for the Taxpayers

But what about the interests of taxpayers who foot the bill for the water subsidy? One way to make existing reclamation projects—such as California's Central Valley Project, Washington's Columbia Basin Project, or the Central Arizona Project—more equitable to the taxpayers would be to raise the price of irrigation water to its full separable cost, a policy commonly advocated by environmental and conservation organizations. But for projects already constructed, this policy makes no economic sense, either from efficiency or equity points of view. Priced to the farmer at $300 per acre-foot, little water would be demanded since it would be far more costly than it would be worth under any conceivable irrigation regime. If the developed water were not used, even the $50 of water value—the $30 worth of net benefits to farmers and the $5 to $35 repaid to the government that currently exist—would be lost. It is better to recoup small gains from irreparable mistakes than none at all. Some environmental gains, such as an improvement in fisheries if water flowed unrestricted to the oceans, may be captured, but many environmental amenities were also irrevocably lost when water development occurred. Taxpayers and consumers must also write off these lost benefits.

This is not to suggest, however, that nothing can be done to more efficiently allocate already-developed water. Prices of water on existing projects should be renegotiated to more current values when contracts come up for renewal every forty years or so. Price cannot accomplish its resource allocating task efficiently if it is not periodically free to equate supply with demand. Also, the contract period might be shortened to provide more opportunity for updating prices as economic conditions change.

The price, as administered by the government, should be set at or near the market-clearing level to do the least damage—the price at which all water available could be sold—as long as the price covers the O&M costs of the project (something approximating the average variable costs). If the water value were not high enough to cover the avoidable O&M costs, then wealth would be greater if the water were not used at all. Through time, the price could be tied to some suitable price index representing the movement of aggregate prices, and thus inflation would not reduce the real water price over the period of the water contract as now occurs. Of course, this pricing policy would reduce the economic rents (defined as the difference between water's value and the user's repayment to the government) derived from subsidized water use. Raising the repayment rate would cause land prices to fall, just as underpricing water caused land prices to rise. Many farms have changed ownership since underpriced water was first delivered, however, and the current owners paid for the expected net benefits in the form of higher-priced land. Naturally, these landowners would lose wealth if water prices were increased, and they could be expected to lobby hard for a continuation of present pricing policies.

A Market Approach to Efficiency and Equity

An alternative is available that would be at once more equitable to current landowners than simply raising the water repayment price and certainly more efficient. Rather than allocate water for long periods by inflexible contracts between government and water users at a fixed price as now happens, the government would simply permit contractors to rent or sell water at prices that would be freely negotiated between the affected parties. If the market system allocated water, demand could be reduced, supply could be increased efficiently, and no water shortages could exist (Anderson 1983, p. 8). If transfers of water were unrestricted, as long as other existing water rights were not impaired by the transfer,[14] markets would arise to move water to higher-valued uses and users. Without restrictions on eligible acreage and with complete freedom of transfer, the value of water could be expected to increase, perhaps sharply, creating wealth for both buyers and sellers.

But under these arrangements, what about the obligation to taxpayers who provided the funds to build existing projects? At a minimum, the water users should be obligated to reimburse the federal government for project O&M costs to ensure that further taxpayer losses are avoided. If it were deemed politically expedient that taxpayers should receive an even larger share of the economic rents available from market transfers, a transfer tax of some kind could be imposed. However, increasing government revenues is not the same thing as reimbursing taxpayers, as everyone knows, if other ways are found to spend the revenues. In any event, a transfer tax would increase the cost of making the transfer and would impede water movement to more valuable uses and would therefore be allocatively inefficient. To reduce the institutional risk of changes in policy that would constrain otherwise economically efficient transfers, the important thing would be for all negotiating parties to know in advance what the government would take off the top and then to make as few policy changes thereafter as possible. This would provide institutional stability needed for efficient markets to function.

It is significant that bill HR 429, signed by President Bush just before leaving office, contains some very important breakthroughs that economists supporting water markets have been advocating for years. Individuals or water districts are authorized to transfer all or a portion of water received under the Central Valley Project to other California water users or agencies. Any purpose that meets beneficial use criteria is acceptable, and the terms of transfer shall be set by mutual agreement between the transferee and the transferor. Only the historic consumptive use, rather than the diverted quantity of water, however, may be transferred, thus protecting third-party owners of water rights. If used for irrigation, all water under contract shall be repaid at the greater of the full cost of service rates or, if necessary, by the ability to pay of the irrigators. If the water is used for municipal and industrial purposes, however, repayment will be subject to a three-tiered system whereby the repayment price on the last units received will be higher, thus giving incentives for water conservation.[15]

Water Subsidies and Environmental Degradation

The natural environment in the West has been significantly altered by federal reclamation projects and water subsidies, mostly for the worse: the loss of free-flowing rivers and streams to water impoundments and water transportation facilities, causing an irrevocable loss of scenic beauty and valuable fisheries; the extension of irrigated agriculture to areas that were once wildlands and habitat for wild animals; the saline and chemical contamination of streams and aquifers, which now threaten human and animal health, reduce productivity, and destroy animal habitat; a loss of air quality resulting from burning agricultural residues; a variety of adverse effects on Native American tribal grounds and burial plots, places of historical interest, and natural genetic diversity.

In addition, if water were not used for irrigation, it could be available for the repulsion of salt encroachment in some freshwater bodies near the oceans or for unregulated outflow that would benefit fish, wildlife, and some forms of recreation. Toxic-element contamination of drainage water is of increasing concern in some areas and has been prominent in the public eye since the Kesterson Reservoir problem with dead fish and deformed birds surfaced in California in the early 1980s (discussed briefly ahead).

Not all of the environmental impacts have been negative, however. Federal projects have also reduced flood damages, with mixed economic effects, and have produced a variety of recreational benefits: boating, waterskiing, swimming, sailing, and fishing. Recreationists also use riparian land near water projects for hiking, camping, and picnicking.

Salinity and Waterlogging of Soils

Salinity is the accumulation of various salts in soil or water in concentrations that interfere with the growth of plants and therefore animals as well. The salts include the chlorides, sulfates, and bicarbonates of sodium, calcium, magnesium, and potassium. Soils almost always contain salts, and with irrigation more salts arrive to the land already dissolved in the water. Since plants absorb nearly pure water, the dissolved salts remain behind in the soil. Unless the salts are ultimately removed, the time must come when the soil will no longer support crops (Biggar et al. 1984).

Salinity is perhaps the most pervasive and most costly environmental problem resulting from irrigation. The only effective remedy available is to leach salts from the soil by applying low-salt water in excess of the quantities needed by plants. Of course, prevention can be achieved by applying low-salt irrigation water if available and by avoiding soils where a salt buildup can occur.

Stream flow reduction that results from irrigation water diversions will normally increase the salt concentrations in the remaining water. This can have deleterious impacts on the flora and fauna in the watercourse itself and on riparian lands. If natural waterways and marshes are used for water storage and transport, and if the salt is at toxic levels, the contaminated water must be diluted by higher-quality water if damage is to be avoided.

Warren Hall, a noted water expert, has written:

> *Salt problems are particularly insidious. They do not come charging at you with trumpets blowing and battle flags flying, a sight to set stirring the heart of activists in any century. Rather, they slip in almost unnoticed. They invariably seem to promise to step aside and behave themselves in return for small additional concessions. Then one day, as witnessed by many dead civilizations, they assert their supreme command of the situation. Time is of no concern, for they are supremely confident of their ultimate victory. History is on their side, as are the laws of physics, chemistry, and biology. They have quietly destroyed, without fuss or fanfare, more civilizations than all of the mighty armies of the world. (1974, n.p.)*

Waterlogging is the rising of the water table into the root zone of plants, thus destroying their ability to grow and even live. Unlike salinity, waterlogging is often due to heavy applications of irrigation water. For example, some parts of California's San Joaquin Valley, generally along the bottom and west side, are underlain by nearly impervious layers of clay at various depths. This clay virtually stops the downward movement of water, which then accumulates on top of the layer, forming what is called a "perched" water table. Capillary action and evaporation concentrate the salts at the top of the underground water.[16] Eventually, generally after a period of years, the top of the perched water table reaches the root zone of the plant, and damage to the crop ensues. Since the salt no longer can be flushed downward, a way must be found to remove it from the root zone. One way is to install perforated pipes below the root zone to collect the water, which can then be moved to some salt sink.

Salinity and waterlogging are interconnected in some locations. Water is needed to flush salts through the soil by leaching. But the water has to go somewhere, and it either reaches an underground aquifer or an impermeable layer of rock, ultimately leading to waterlogging, or it drains into a surface watercourse. Ultimately, any of the three dispositions can become a problem for subsequent water users.

An excellent example of the problem is the saline waters in the lower Colorado River that cost farmers in the Imperial Valley and Mexico millions of dollars annually. Most of the salt loading is in the Upper Basin states of Colorado and Utah, whereas most of the costs are borne in the Lower Basin. This presents some difficult institutional problems of how contamination can be reduced and who should pay for it.

Both salinity and waterlogging are examples of incomplete property rights of the sort discussed in Chapter 7. Since salty water produced by irrigation on one farm becomes a problem for users downstream or for others using groundwater aquifers, salinity is a classic externality. So is waterlogging, since normally many water users contribute to the rising water tables of a given aquifer. Thus, in both instances market failure will lead to resource misallocation and some public action will probably be considered necessary to limit the damage.

The subsidizing of irrigation water has exacerbated both salinity and waterlogging. Given the existing subsidies and the absence of water markets, few incentives presently exist for irrigators to limit water use to socially efficient levels. In many areas of the West, some of the federal water is supplemental to existing private supplies. This supplemental water is generally the cheapest water available to farmers since it is priced with an "ability-to-pay" rule that produces very low prices. Farmers, like all other rational managers of resources, consider their marginal water cost in determining water use on both the extensive and intensive margins. Thus, these low marginal subsidized prices will determine the extent of irrigated acreage (the extensive margin) as well as the amount of water applied per acre (the intensive margin). Therefore, these "low" subsidized prices are a major factor in producing some of the most critical environmental problems, such as waterlogging of soils and chemical contamination of aquifers.

The enormous subsidies provided by federal irrigation projects have especially contributed to the expansion of irrigated acreage. Acreage expansion alone increases salinity by reducing the natural water flows available to dilute salts and by contributing return flows from irrigation that are much saltier than withdrawal flows.

Unless severe controls are placed on water quantity, the subsidy will also contribute to excessive applications of water, potentially leading to waterlogging if drainage is poor. The combination and intractability of salinity and waterlogging problems have raised the question of whether irrigated agriculture is even viable in the long run. As Hall suggests in an earlier quote, civilizations long since dead seem to have been victims.

Water-conserving irrigation practices, such as sprinkler and drip systems, generally are the most effective means of reducing water contamination associated with irrigated farming. Water conservation reduces runoff that not only causes erosion but also carries with it the salts and agricultural chemicals that damage water sources. With many farmers treating water as essentially a free resource because of the subsidy, water application rates and runoff tend to be well in excess of optimal levels (Frederick 1986).

Nor are salinity and waterlogging the only serious environmental problems created and exacerbated by water subsidies. Almost half of irrigation water comes from groundwater aquifers. Data collected by the USDA's Economic Research Service suggest that groundwater tables underlying more than 14 million irrigated acres in the United States are declining from one-half to more than five feet per year (B. D. Gardner 1979). As the groundwater table declines, pumping costs increase, well yields decline, pumping efficiency falls, and land subsides, often with severe impacts on the environment. Land subsidence occurs when water is pumped, creating a space in the earth that is then filled as the overlying ground collapses.

Water Subsidies and Agricultural–Urban Interactions

Many interfaces exist between farmers and nearby urban dwellers. Odors, chemicals, smoke, and noise originate in the agricultural sector that affect the quality of life of neighbors in the urban sector. Originating in urban areas are ozone, carbon monoxide, and other toxic chemicals, transportation bottlenecks, and crop and livestock thievery, which impose costs on agricultural producers. One of these problems will be discussed here to illustrate how these interactions produce higher costs for growing rice and higher rice prices for consumers.

The burning of crop residues, primarily grain straw, is a controversial environmental problem in many areas around the country. Primarily it is particulate matter left over from burning that enters the atmosphere where it is breathed by humans and animals causing a variety of health problems, the most severe being respiratory infections. Agricultural burning also releases CO_2 and N_2O into the atmosphere (Adams 1990). The most frequently suggested remedy is a ban on burning. Unfortunately, no one has estimated what the social gains from enhanced health from a ban on burning would be. It is quite clear that the impact on crop producers could be significant. A good example of the problem is the rice-growing industry in California's Sacramento Valley (B. D. Gardner et al. 1990).

Difficult equity problems are usually associated with such situations. No one owns property rights to the airspace. The rice industry has existed in California for over half a century, far longer than most of the urban residents have lived there. The rice farmers wonder why they should be penalized for utilizing production methods they have employed for decades. They argue that urban dwellers should have taken the air-quality problem into account when they decided to locate in the valley. Urbanites see the problem quite differently: People have a right to clean air, and rice farmers should not be permitted to use the common-property airspace as a dump for their wastes.

Rice production in the Sacramento Valley antedates federal reclamation projects and would probably continue at some level even if surface water subsidies were reduced. In fact, were it not for the federal Central Valley Project, which moved subsidized water from the Sacramento River to the San Joaquin Valley, even more water might have been available for water-intensive crops like rice. However, now the rice industry is growing in some areas of the San Joaquin Valley as well. This development depends largely on federally subsidized water, since without the subsidy it is doubtful that rice could compete with more water-efficient crops.

Tax Subsidies and Water Quality

Both water and commodity subsidies have been instrumental in bringing increased quantities of land under irrigation. But so has tax policy. Tax breaks have made investment in center-pivot irrigation farming attractive to landowners, especially to absentee investors lacking a deep concern for the land (Lichtenberg 1989). Center-pivot irrigation has been particularly important in the Great Plains states and the Columbia Basin of the Northwest.

Critics of irrigation have argued that lower-quality lands have been converted to irrigated farming, particularly in traditional rain-fed regions, leading to greater erosion hazard and groundwater contamination by agricultural chemicals. Center-pivot irrigation, a technology that permits very large tracts to be irrigated from a single well, has also overridden concern for land quality and has been most rapidly introduced on sandy soils that are more erosion prone as well as more vulnerable to groundwater contamination. The rate of adoption of this technology has been quite sensitive to the cost of capital, which is determined in part by tax policies. During the period 1966 to 1980, investment tax credits, interest deductibility for income tax purposes, and accelerated depreciation reduced the real user cost of capital by 10 to 20 percent. Reductions of this size in the cost of capital accelerated irrigation development on sandy soils between 13 and 40 percent and contributed significantly to soil erosion (Lichtenberg 1989, p. 193).

The Kesterson Debacle

One of the most visible and startling examples of environmental degradation associated with subsidized irrigation is the chemical contamination of Kesterson Reservoir in California's San Joaquin Valley.[17] Other sinks utilized to store drainage water in the West are also beginning to suffer similar problems. Kesterson will be described in some detail because the situation is a prototype of many other chemical contamination problems that will probably arise in the future, the resolution of these types of problems is very costly, and the political fallout in the form of public disillusionment and frustration arising from inability to find a satisfactory solution is very serious.

The Nature of the Problem

High concentrations of selenium, chromium, and mercury have been found in the shallow ground water in some areas of the West, including the San Joaquin Valley.[18] Selenium is one of the essential trace elements for animal and human survival. In humans, selenium increases the potency of vitamin E and is a possible inhibitor of cancer (Pauling 1982, p. 149). A deficiency of selenium is expressed in livestock as "ill-thrift" disease or as the more severe "white-muscle" disease occurring in both lambs and calves (Burau 1985).

But there can be too much of a good thing. Selenium is toxic to wildfowl and animals, including humans, in high concentrations. Toxic effects of selenium on birds and rodents include death, reduced growth, reduced reproductive success, and deformities in hatchlings (Deverel et al. 1984). The observed disappearance of fish and the deformed birds and dead embryos in coot eggs observed at Kesterson were caused by selenium poisoning. Much less is known about selenium toxicity in humans, although linkages have been made with depression, intestinal disturbances, nervousness, convulsions, diarrhea, and respiratory failure.[19] Human exposure could be caused by drinking water contaminated with drainage water containing selenium and eating selenium contaminated food, especially waterfowl and fish (Deverel et al. 1984). Like many other toxins, it concentrates first in lower organisms, such as algae, which are then ingested by higher organisms, such as fish and waterfowl that feed on the lower organisms.

Irrigation water draining into Kesterson is supplied primarily by the San Luis Unit of the federal Central Valley Project (CVP) via the Westlands Water District, by far the largest irrigation district in the United States. Deep subsurface seepage of groundwater into Kesterson also has heavily contributed to selenium loading (L. Carter 1985b). All of the federal water is heavily subsidized. However, the farms in the district are some of the largest and most efficient in the entire country and grow cotton, much of it for export, alfalfa, tomatoes, other vegetables, melons, and garlic.

The soils of the area are underlain by an impermeable layer of clay. Without subsurface drainage, irrigation raises the water table and produces waterlogging, as described earlier in the chapter. The San Luis Drain, authorized by Congress in 1960, was intended to convey the brackish drainage water out the west side of the San Joaquin Valley and to the San Francisco Bay and the Pacific Ocean.

From 1968 to 1975, the bureau constructed eighty-five miles of the drain, which carried water to what was intended to be a temporary terminus at Kesterson Reservoir. Even though the reservoir is now managed as part of a National Wildlife Refuge, its main purpose was to be a temporary repository for agricultural drainage flows (Hancock 1984).

What the Benefit–Cost Analyst Can Say

Selenium contamination presents a very difficult challenge for benefit–cost analysis. It is not just a matter of ignorance of the scientific questions such as the source of the selenium and its infiltration into water courses. It is also estimating benefits and costs that impinge on societal welfare. What are the losses suffered when birds are deformed and waterfowl populations are reduced? Markets do not exist that price wildlife directly. Estimates of part of the loss could be obtained from observing the decreases in the value of memberships in numerous private gun clubs in the area since selenium poisoning has become well publicized. These values could be expected to reflect the capitalized amount of annual benefit losses associated with hunting waterfowl under regulated conditions at a given club. But the loss in value due to selenium contamination of such estimates would undoubtedly understate the entire loss, since many waterfowl are migratory, and hence losses would be suffered by others outside the local clubs.

Human life and health values are even more difficult to estimate, although not impossible (Mishan 1976, cps. 45 and 46). It is likely that toxicity must reach some threshold level and remain there for some time before a serious threat to health exists. Far too little is known about what these threshold levels are. Because of these serious knowledge gaps and the difficulty of closing them, strict safety standards and regulations on environmental quality have commonly been applied.

Meanwhile, what is to be done about the perceived severe environmental problems surrounding Kesterson? Several proposals have been made to mitigate the worst of the risks. But it has not been decided who will bear the costs of the alternative options, always the most severe stumbling block to any solution. Consider some of the proposals that have been made.

Some Technological Options for Dealing with the Problem

The Interagency Drainage Program (IDP) was initiated by the federal government in 1976 to study various policy options for coping with toxic wastes in the San Joaquin Valley (Beck 1984). Five alternatives were considered by IDP: no action, evaporation ponds within the valley, discharge of wastes to the San Joaquin River, discharge to the Pacific Ocean, and discharge to the western edge of the Sacramento–San Joaquin Delta. The option recommended by the IDP was a gravity-flow, concrete-lined canal from Bakersfield to Suisun Bay in the upper reaches of San Francisco Bay. Waterfowl marshes within the valley would delay the discharge peak from summer to winter and spring when the waste water would receive maximum dilution with waters flowing into San Francisco Bay.[20]

Beyond the lack of any cost–benefit analysis, the IDP proposal had three critical drawbacks, mostly of a political nature: It was not clear who would pay for the drainage canal; no politician wanted the discharge of the toxic waters in his or her district; and the Kesterson problem made it clear that holding reservoirs and marshes could be dangerous, so no others have since been constructed. In any event, because of political opposition, little has been done to implement the IDP recommendation.

The bureau suggested some solutions of its own: no action (state regulations on discharge to the San Joaquin River would determine permissible courses of action); delta disposal (the same proposal essentially as the IDP's except that a treatment plant would be added to remove toxic substances); in-valley evaporation ponds (thirteen ponds comprising an area of 108 square miles along the length of the service area, each with twelve cells, where one cell out of twelve would be dried up each year permitting removal of the salts to an ocean-disposal site); and desalting (solar brine ponds using electrical energy to reduce the concentration of salts.)[21] No benefit–cost feasibility analyses have been made of these various options, however. A limited number of inferences can be drawn about some of the options proposed without resorting to extensive analysis.

Cease irrigating the land causing the toxic problems. It is not entirely clear what a cessation of irrigation would mean in terms of how much the toxic wastes would be reduced, but almost certainly they would fall. Suppose that it could be demonstrated that ceasing irrigation on given parcels would permit the toxic-waste problem to be kept below critical threshold levels. What would be the efficiency costs of this option?

One study estimated the direct and indirect economic effects of halting production on some 42,000 acres in the Westlands Water District thought to be the source of most of the selenium problems (Wallace and Strong 1985). The method used to detail the private-sector direct impacts involved estimating the value of agricultural sales lost if irrigation were prohibited. Some large numbers were produced that were alleged to represent the annual costs of ceasing irrigation in the region. The problem with this procedure is that it implicitly assumes that the resources currently used in agricultural production have no valuable alternative uses. Thus, all the sales produced currently could be assumed to be lost to the economy if irrigation ceased. But clearly most of the resources would have alternative employments, albeit of lower value perhaps. The "true" loss is the difference between what the resources earn now and what they would earn in their best alternative employments.

Consider some alternative resource employments for the different resources. Much of the land in the area was producing rain-fed crops before irrigation water was applied and would likely do so again. Some would be used as seasonal pasture. Labor resources are quite mobile in the long run and would ultimately find other employment—perhaps not so remunerative as the present employment. Even much of the capital equipment and machinery is adjustable and mobile and would have some value in alternative areas and uses.

Marketing the water elsewhere appears to be one of the keys to the solution of the environmental problem, but it is institutionally complex. Some water might be reallocated within the Westlands Water District under current water rights arrangements where it would not contaminate the environment. If the water could be sold for the highest-valued alternative uses outside the region, however, most or all of it would probably move and undoubtedly be worth more than in its present use. Some urban areas of Southern California are demanding more water, and it could be transported there through existing State Water Project facilities.[22]

A counterargument might be made that even though this logic is valid, empirical quantification of the necessary values presents a huge problem. Estimating hypothetical values of resources in various uses cannot possibly be reliable enough for policy recommendations. Fortunately, this may not be the case. The land market can reveal much of the value that would be forgone if irrigation ceased. Land prices reflect the capitalization of the flow of expected net profits accruing to the owners of land and water. Thus, a rough approximation to the sum of the discounted net benefits forgone if irrigated land is removed from production is the difference between irrigated and nonirrigated land prices. Because markets for both irrigated and nonirrigated land are active in most areas, representative values could be easily obtained (Heinrichs 1985).

Construct evaporation ponds. Evaporation ponds have been proposed as an alternative to a master drain. If ponds are deep, bottom feeding by waterfowl will be discouraged (Hancock 1984). Uncultivated land would be utilized first to minimize the opportunity cost of land for the ponds.[22] The more impermeable the soil, the less percolation of contaminants into the groundwater aquifers.

But would evaporation ponds turn into mini-Kestersons? Much would depend on the prevalence of toxic salts and their movement as well as pond construction features. Some type of waterfowl protection might be required, such as hazing operations to frighten birds away from the ponds, managing ponds to make them unattractive to waterfowl, and improving the existing nearby habitat to attract waterfowl away from the ponds (Hancock 1984).

Either on-farm evaporation basins or regional facilities require land areas equivalent to about 20 percent of the irrigated land to be drained (Backlund and Hoppes 1984). Costs have been estimated at $695 per irrigated acre in 1983 dollars.[24] It seems quite unlikely at current prices and costs of growing crops, however, that farmers could afford such drainage-water costs without subsidy.

Treatment of waste water by desalting plants. It is also doubtful if desalting of contaminated irrigation water to remove the toxic elements can be done economically. A 1973 Department of Interior study estimated a per-acre-foot cost of $136 to desalinate water in California's Imperial Valley.[25] Applying a conservative inflationary factor would imply a current cost of more than double that amount. A 1986 estimate places the desalination cost at well over $1,000 per acre-foot (CH2M Hill 1986).

A British wastewater treatment firm claims to have found a process for removing selenium and boron from drainage waters, which may prove to be very promising (L. Carter 1985a). The process isolates elements that block the precipitation of selenium from the drainage water and removes them. Once the selenium precipitates it can be filtered out. Apparently the process can work on a large scale for $100 to $150 per acre-foot, or about half the cost of other currently available technologies.

The important issue for both desalination and boron and selenium removal is the value of water in irrigation. No available empirical evidence suggests that the average value of irrigation water in the San Joaquin Valley is as high as $100 per acre-foot. Therefore, if growers must bear the entire cost, it is doubtful that they would prefer to treat the water than to take land out of irrigation. With subsidies, of course, it is a different matter, and farmers will argue that subsidies are justified. But it would appear to be far cheaper for the government to resort to an even more effective treatment: simply buy out landowners operating on the most selenium-tainted and salt-toxic soils.

The Kesterson problem illustrates clearly that many environmental impacts from irrigated agriculture may be unexpected and very costly to correct once they are discovered. The politics of doing something sensible about these problems are very complex. One thing seems to be clear. Without water and drainage subsidies, most of the west side of the San Joaquin Valley would not have been irrigated on a long-term basis, although groundwater may have been utilized until it was no longer economic to pump it from increasing depths. Some kind of drain may have been needed to dispose of the salt-degraded and toxic water resulting from irrigation, but the problem would almost certainly have been an order of magnitude smaller than it has been with subsidized water.

In short, irrigation water subsidies have produced overinvestment in water storage and delivery and agricultural production from irrigated lands. In 1978 dollars, the San Luis Unit of the Central Valley Project has received a subsidy of about $1,422 per acre (Wahl 1986, p. 12). Project water users pay only about 15 percent of actual project costs so the subsidy has been enormous (Wahl 1989, p. 202). The benefits to landowners have been much, much smaller. Without the subsidy an entirely different agriculture, one that would have been much more environmentally benign, would exist today on the west side of the San Joaquin Valley.

Some Distorting Legal and Pricing Concerns

Beneficial Use and the Formation of Water Markets

In most western states, economic waste results from the prevailing law that requires irrigators to use their entitlement of water or risk losing it to other applicants for appropriations. This requirement, known as "beneficial use," forms the basis of water law in every western state. Those who file for a right to appropriate water must demonstrate that the water would be put to some useful purpose before a legal right can be acquired. Beneficial use supposedly prevents speculators from locking up water without using it, a high-priority fear at the time of settlement and the formulation of water law. The problem is that under this doctrine an appropriator cannot use water if it is transferred in a market transaction to another user. Therefore, beneficial use, as it has been traditionally interpreted, precludes full-scale water markets.

At least one state, California, however, has eliminated this problem by passing a law that declares water transfers themselves to be beneficial use.[26] Thus, if water-right owners wish to rent water or even sell their right, they would not be risking a challenge by other appropriators who may wish to condemn the right under the beneficial-use law. Other states need to follow California's example and pass similar legislation to rid themselves of this barrier to water markets.

By allowing farmers and water districts to sell water at a profit, a mechanism would be created for transferring water to those who value it most. In nearly every region of the West, agriculture is the marginal user of water in the sense that water is less valuable in agriculture than in other uses. For this reason, the net sellers of water in free markets would likely be irrigators. The buyers would probably be municipalities or urban water districts or even other irrigators who are looking for cheaper ways to augment existing supplies. As transfers from agriculture to urban uses occur, water values in the two sectors would move closer to equality.

Because the consumptive use of water in agriculture usually exceeds 80 percent of the total in most western states, however, large quantities of water could be transferred to urban and industrial uses without significantly threatening agricultural viability, especially if there were incentives for conservation. One study suggests that about 10 percent of the water used by California agriculture in 1985 would have moved to other uses if free water markets existed, but that this amount could be transferred without taking any farmland out of production since water conservation would increase efficiency (Howitt et al. 1982). Even in-stream recreational and transportation users of water would be able to buy rights to guarantee minimum stream flows.

An example of how markets could work to provide better water allocation and prevent economic waste has been the dickering between the Metropolitan Water District (MWD) and the Imperial Irrigation District (IDD), both in southern California. In 1985, the MWD offered the IDD $10 million per year to fund water conservation measures that would salvage 100,000 acre-feet of water annually for use by the MWD (see Wahl 1989, p. 128). Unfortunately, overcoming the legal and institutional rigidities has proved to be extremely difficult.

If an efficient water market existed, the true opportunity cost of using water is what it would fetch if transferred to a more valuable *alternative* use. Thus, if farmers could transfer water at free market prices, water-conserving irrigation technologies and management practices and new cropping patterns that conserve water would emerge that now are undeveloped and unutilized (B. D. Gardner 1983).

Water Pricing Blunders at District, State, and Federal Levels

It is not only the federal water subsidy per se that is economically inefficient and environmentally destructive. Other water-pricing practices and subsidies at other levels also contribute substantially. If water prices utilized by marketers more nearly reflected the marginal cost of new water, much of the political pressure for new water development would be reduced, and further environmental damage could be avoided.

Public water suppliers manipulate the price in several ways to hide high marginal supply costs, thus making it easier to acquire those supplies. To justify the development of high-cost water, exaggerated water values are claimed. But once the new supplies are available, much lower prices to consumers are needed to dispose of quantities inefficiently and prematurely developed.

A brief enumeration and discussion of some of the pricing practices that militate against efficient water development and allocation follows. First, when it comes to economic efficiency and the effect on the environment, probably the most pernicious of all pricing practices commonly utilized in the public water districts and municipalities, especially those serviced by the bureau, is price averaging. Much lower "older" project water costs are averaged with the costs of expensive "new" project water. Thus, the new expensive project water is never subject to an economic feasibility test by comparing its value (price) to consumers with its cost (Willey 1985, p. 7). The consequence is that more water gets developed than is economically and environmentally efficient.[27]

Second, many western states have statutory prohibitions against public entities such as water districts earning profits. Water districts are not allowed to generate revenues from water sales that exceed their total costs, a condition leading to resource misallocation.[28] Firms have no incentives to economize on their costs.

Third, a common pricing policy used by water districts in California's

Sacramento Valley (and probably many other places) is the imposition of a fixed per acre water charge that varies by crop but not by the quantity of water used.[29] The problem is that there is no obvious relationship of these charges to the quantities of water used by these crops. No incentives exist for irrigators to economize on water use and to choose crops that are water efficient, with more water getting consumed as a result. Negative environmental impacts are aggravated by these pricing policies, since both the intensive and extensive margins of water use are extended.

Fourth, federal ability-to-pay water-pricing policies to irrigators are notorious for subsidizing water use and misallocating resources to water development. Early reclamation law required that water users pay for all project costs, but it was soon discovered that agricultural producers either could not or would not meet these obligations. Interest costs were waived from the beginning, and the rules were changed so that repayment periods were lengthened, scheduled payments were delayed for as long as a decade pending completion of large projects, and the proportion of project joint costs assigned to irrigators for repayment were reduced. All of these measures reduced the effective water price and made it easier for irrigators to meet repayment obligations. Even these significant concessions, however, were inadequate to generate enough water demand to eliminate the excess supply on most projects. Therefore, the bureau concocted an ability-to-pay rule having water prices that cover only a fraction of the construction and interest costs, convincing evidence that federal water projects have been prematurely constructed and overbuilt.[30]

Fifth, most western states have programs that provide subsidized state funding for water development, although the subsidies are generally much lower than those of the federal government.[31]

The effect of every one of these pricing practices is to make water appear cheaper than it really is, thus encouraging inefficient development and use, discouraging conservation, and promoting excessive environmental degradation.

Conclusions

Even if it were desirable, it is impossible to go back to the time before federal irrigation development and water subsidies. The projects are already in place. The mistakes of the past cannot be washed away. The best that can be done on existing projects at this point is to insist that sound economic principles, including market allocations, and careful benefit–cost analysis guide resource allocations. Of course, it is not too late to do something about proposed water projects where resources have not yet been committed. No economic efficiency justification exists for subsidizing new water projects that are far more costly to build than they are worth. Water should be priced at marginal cost to minimize the demands for an extension of irrigated acreage. Even the sensible rule that would require water users to bear the full separable costs of water development and distribution (including environmental costs where they can be clearly identified and evaluated) would prevent much of the environmental degradation on new lands that is now observed in areas of subsidized water development.

It is true, of course, that consumers benefit from the production of specialized products grown under irrigation in the West. California, which depends almost entirely on irrigation to grow these commodities, alone produces between 40 and 50 percent of the nation's production of table vegetables, fruits, and nuts. Pricing water rationally does not threaten the nation with the loss of this produce, however. As already argued, the formation of water markets and pricing at marginal cost would not cripple agriculture, especially the part of it that produces high-valued crops, but would undoubtedly make it more water efficient.

Moreover, it does not appear that the answers to the most critical environmental problems lie in regulatory controls and prohibitions of water and agricultural chemical use by large doses of state action. The "Hayden" or Big Green Initiative in California, considered by voters in 1990, is the wrong way to go about solving the environmental problems created by irrigation and crop subsidies, and California voters were right to reject it.[32]

But if governmental regulations are inefficient and counterproductive, is there nothing that makes economic sense? To the contrary, economic and environmental problems could be substantially reduced by eliminating crop subsidies, rationally pricing water, and eliminating the barriers to the formation of water markets. Markets permit "win–win" situations where all trading parties expect to gain.

What may not be realized by the American public is that irrigation subsidies have also greatly stimulated the production of crops that already receive heavy price support subsidies—cotton, wheat, the feed grains, and rice. From 1929 to 1978, 60 percent of the increase in irrigated acreage went into the production of subsidized program crops, most of which have been in surplus (Zinsmeister 1989, p. 23). Therefore, price-supported crops under federally subsidized water receive a double subsidy. This misallocates resources among regions and means that irrigation subsidies have substantially contributed to the problem of excess resources in agriculture.

What policy prescriptions would produce a more efficient allocation of water and ameliorate associated environmental problems? The following policy changes would move us substantially in this direction, but political opposition will no doubt be intense.[33]

First, property rights in federal water should be created at the level of individual farmers so that markets can be formed to allocate water among potential uses and users. Legal and institutional impediments to market transfers of water must be identified and removed. Rights must be well-defined, enforced, and transferable (Anderson 1983, p. 18). Prices should be freely negotiated between buyers and sellers without governmental intervention and no-profit constraints. This action would also provide incentives for conservation, and much environmental degradation would be ameliorated.[34]

Second, in water planning, including both development and allocation planning, economic efficiency criteria should play a more important role, and water price should be explicitly taken into account in gauging water demand and repayment ability. Water policy should not be used to redistribute income via such vehicles as acreage limitations and interest rate concessions for low-income individuals and communities.[35]

And third, where significant negative externalities exist, such as with chemical pollution, taxes on chemicals and damaging effluents, if they can be measured, will be much more efficient than regulatory devices such as standards and mandated best-management practices (B. D. Gardner 1981, p. 76).

Notes

* Some of the material in this chapter is from my paper, "Irrigation Subsidies: Efficiency, Equity, and Environmental Implications," in *Volume 2, Essays on Agricultural Economics in Honor of D. Gale Johnson*, University of Chicago Press.

1. The National Irrigation Association was established to promote irrigation legislation in 1899. Wahl (1989, p. 19).

2. In California, ground water makes up about 39 percent of the state's applied water. See Tanji (1990b, p. 53).

3. U.S. House of Representatives (1880), *Report of the Public Lands Commission*, Executive Document no. 46 (Washington, DC), p. 13.

4. This section utilizes some material from an earlier publication by the author and a colleague. See B. D. Gardner and Huffaker (1988).

5. In California, new federal water, such as the expansion of Lake Shasta, is generally considered to be available at lower cost than new state water, depending on how interest costs are calculated. One recent estimate is $250 to $325 per acre-foot for federal water. See Coppock et al. (1982).

   Zack Willey points out that the costs of proposed new California state water projects range from approximately $450 to $850 per acre-foot in 1985 dollars. See Willey (1985, p. 26).

6. It is important to note that repayment obligations to the federal government are very different for irrigation than for other water uses such as electric power and municipal and industrial purposes. Capital costs for irrigation are repaid *without* interest, whereas interest is charged for the other uses. In fact, historically about half of the irrigation interest subsidy has been paid by other users of water, especially by electric power. See U.S. Department of the Interior, Bureau of Reclamation (1968), *Summary Report of the Commissioner*, Statistical Appendix Parts I, II, and III (Washington, DC), p. viii.

7. A 1975 U.S. Water Resources Council study estimated that the combined effect of the interest waiver and ability-to-pay repayment policies was to produce a subsidy on bureau projects of 82 percent. At interest rates above 10 percent, which prevailed from 1980 through 1985, the interest subsidy exceeded 90 percent of construction costs of new bureau projects. See Wahl (1989, pp. 33–34).

8. U.S. Senate (1990c), *Central Utah Project Completion Act*, Hearing before the Water and Power Subcommittee, Energy and Natural Resources Committee (Washington, DC: September 18), p. 148.

9. Ibid., p. 147.

10. What Senator Garn and others usually mean when they say that the project is

economically sound is that power users pick up the part of the project cost assigned to irrigation that irrigators do not repay. But this assertion is wrong or at best misleading. Even if revenues from federal hydropower are used to "repay" costs beyond the "ability-to-pay" of the irrigators, there is considerable subsidy involved. This is because the repayment assigned to irrigation is interest free and because the power payment usually occurs after forty or fifty years of irrigation repayment. As Wahl points out, if federal borrowing costs 4 percent annually, then interest-free repayment forty years later returns to the government only 20.8 percent of the true cost of the loan. See Wahl (1989, p. 27).

11. This is a curious argument. Is the credibility of the government supposed to be enhanced by politicians supporting projects that they know are uneconomic from the very beginning and then, when this fact is exposed, arguing that any questioning of the project is breaking a promise?

12. U.S. Senate (1990c), *Central Utah Project Completion Act,* (Washington, DC), p. 154.

13. In fact, the bill was a very large omnibus piece of legislation that contains highly disparate elements. It is officially House of Representatives Bill 429, but has been called the Bradley–Miller bill, named after Senator Bill Bradley and Congressman George Miller, the chief sponsors in the Congress. In addition to the authorization of funds for pork-barrel projects like completion of the CUO, the bill contains some fundamental changes in the federal role in the Central Valley Project in California dealing with water transfers and protection of wildlife habitat in the project area. See U.S. House of Representatives, 102d Congress, Public Law 102-575, 1992, HR 429.

14. This could be accomplished by permitting sellers to transfer only their consumptive use, not the amount they divert from the watercourse.

15. House of Representatives (1992), HR 429, Title XXXIV, Section 3505.

16. U.S. Department of Agriculture, Soil Conservation Service (1984), *Preauthorization Report, South Fork Kings River Watershed* (Washington, DC).

17. Some of the following discussion is contained in B. Delworth Gardner (1987).

18. U.S. Department of Interior, Bureau of Reclamation (1984b), *Information on Kesterson Reservoir and Waterfowl,* Information Bulletin no. 2 (Washington, DC).

19. National Academy of Sciences and National Academy of Engineering (1973), *Water Quality Criteria,* EPA R3 73 033 (Washington, DC: U.S. Environmental Protection Agency), pp. 1–594.

20. U.S. Department of Interior, Bureau of Reclamation, California Department of Water Resources, and California State Water Resources Control Board (1979), *Agricultural Drainage and Salt Management* (Washington, DC). The benefits of meeting the standard by the proposed plan were assumed to be

the cost of the most likely nonfederal alternative, since it was reasoned that if this plan were not adopted, then some other one would have to be. The rationale was that state water-quality standards simply had to be met. But the logic of this approach of estimating benefits is curious: If a low-cost alternative were available, the benefits of the proposed plan would be low, otherwise they would be high. By this kind of calculating legerdemain, any proposal would be economically feasible if the costs of some alternative plan were high enough.

21. U.S. Department of Interior, Bureau of Reclamation (1984), *Information on Kesterson Reservoir.*

22. To indicate the institutional complexity of water allocation and quality control, the following entities would have to be involved in any market solution under present institutions. The bureau must permit affected farmers to sell their contracted water at market value to potential buyers; The Westlands Water District holds the water contract with the bureau and must therefore agree to the transfer and probably would serve as the broker in any market deal; Congress must authorize delivery of the water outside the primary service area of the bureau's San Luis Unit; State Water Resources Control Board of California would also need to approve a change in the point of diversion and location of water use as required in state law; the State Water Project would need to agree to transport the water through its facilities (presumably for a fee.) See Wahl (1989, p. 205).

    This institutional complexity is a serious barrier to the formation of markets and has blocked many economically feasible proposals for water transfers. But with the Kesterson problem perceived to be so serious and with public opinion aroused to a high level, perhaps some institutional reform to facilitate market transfers is now possible.

23. USDA, Soil Conservation Service, *Preauthorization Report.*

24. Ibid.

25. U.S. Department of Interior, Office of Saline Water and Bureau of Reclamation, Colorado River International Salinity Control Project (1973), *Special Reports 19 and 20* (Washington, DC).

26. "The Legislature hereby finds and declares that voluntary transfers between water users can result in a more efficient use of water, benefiting both the buyer and the seller.

    "The Legislature further finds and declares that it is in the public interest to conserve all available water resources, and that this interest requires the coordinated assistance of state agencies for voluntary water transfers to allow more intensive use of developed water resources in a manner that fully protects the interests of other entities which have rights to, or rely on, the water covered by a proposed transfer" (Section 475, Article 2, West's Annotated California Codes, Water Code, Volume 68, p. 26).

27. Federal contracts for New Melones (a federal project in the east foothills of California's San Joaquin Valley) water were negotiated at a melded rate of $3.50 per acre-foot during the 1982–83 period, while the project's separable irrigation costs have been estimated at between $15 and $168 per acre-foot (depending primarily on how interest costs are calculated). See Willey (1985, p. 7).

28. To see the efficiency implications of the no-profit requirement for a water firm, consider the usual situation where the costs of new supplies exceed those of existing supplies. In the jargon of economics, if the price for water (its value in consumption) is set at the marginal cost, the price will exceed average cost and the firm will earn illegal profits. If the price must be set at average cost to avoid profits, then price will be lower than the marginal cost. The value of water in consumption at the margin will be lower than the value of resources being used to bring new supplies on line, and the new supplies will not be economically efficient.

    But assume that high-cost water is provided by hook or by crook. Then the no-profit firm is caught in a dilemma. If the price to customers were raised to the marginal cost of new water supplies, and price discrimination among users (for example, power users charged more than irrigators) is not permitted, it is unlikely that all existing supplies could be sold, precisely the situation encountered by irrigators on the newer federal projects. The water firm must then charge a water price lower than the marginal cost if it is to sell all available supplies. This price will eliminate excess supply, but then the firm must find other ways to cover costs. They usually accomplish this by supplementing per unit water fees with taxes levied on real property within the boundaries of the water district or by levying fixed assessments on water connections to the system. These revenue-generating vehicles are inefficient since they do not relate at all to the quantity of water consumption.

29. As a typical example, one irrigation district that sells large quantities of water to farmers announced water rates effective February 7, 1980, as follows: $17.25 per acre flooded for rice; $12.10 per acre irrigated for sugar beets and tomatoes; $10.35 per acre irrigated for pasture, clover, ear corn, alfalfa, and orchard; and $6.90 per acre irrigated for general crops (barley, vine crops, wheat, milo, other cereal grains, and silage corn). The announcement also specified that the regular rates would apply to three irrigations (except for rice, which gets flooded on a continuous basis for many months). Water quantities delivered are not measured. See B. G. Gardner (1983).

30. Of course, if irrigators paid at their "true" ability to pay, which would be the full net value of the water to them, no remaining economic rents would exist to be capitalized into land values. The fact that land values invariably rise sharply when water is delivered to irrigators at the ability-to-pay price proves that the ability-to-pay calculation must understate the true value of water.

31. Almost all state money loaned out for water development carries rates of interest that are lower than market rates, and some loans are altogether interest

free. Often state projects are funded with bonds that are exempt from state income taxes, and sometimes power users are required to pay for part of the separable costs of irrigation water. All of these forms of subsidy lower the contract price of new water to levels below its supply cost and thus promote excessive development that cannot be justified on economic efficiency grounds. However, these subsidies are politically attractive since many economic interests rally behind political leaders who want to get their share of state resources for their constituents.

Most state departments of water resources also explicitly include equity criteria for allocating water development funds. Interest rate concessions are often given to low-income and rural communities for building potable water systems. It should not be surprising, therefore, that equity criteria come into conflict with efficiency criteria.

32. The initiative would have severely curtailed chemical use in agriculture and driven up the prices of fruit, nuts, and vegetables for all Americans. The late newspaper columnist Warren Brookes pointed out that the best scholars believe that the scientific bases of linking human disease to pesticides and herbicides are very weak indeed. In fact, if the initiative were to have increased the price of fruits and vegetables as much as is feared, the net effects on human health may well have been negative. Brookes points out that it is well established medically that one of the best ways to fight cancer and most other chronic diseases is to increase the consumption of fresh fruits and vegetables. Sharply increasing their prices is a sure way to decrease their consumption. Warren Brookes (1990).

    Besides, governmental regulation always produces "win–lose" situations where any societal gains are achieved at the expense of some losses imposed on those regulated since they are forced into actions that they would rather not take.

33. Wahl points out that in 1982 when federal hydropower contracts were expiring, the president formed a task force to study raising the power rates to market value. Congress passed a resolution that prohibited any federal funds from being spent even to study the proposition, and the task force disbanded. Wahl (1989, p. 128).

34. Because not all water diverted is consumptively used and the remainder returns to the water system to become someone else's right, the quantity transferred must be limited to consumptive use if third-party rights are to be protected. It would appear to be necessary for state water control agencies to perform a regulatory role in recording and monitoring transfers between private parties to be sure that third parties are not injured by market exchanges.

35. Many more efficient income redistribution tools such as food stamps, school lunches, and even standard welfare programs are available to reduce inequities of the economic system.

PART 4

Reform of Agricultural Programs and the Budget Process

13

Prospects for Reform

If valid reasons for governmental income support to agriculture ever existed, they have long since vanished. Even price supports and production controls as devices to stabilize prices now have good substitutes in futures and options markets. The justification for government programs of the kind that exist to promote equity are equally flimsy, given that those receiving the bulk of crop and irrigation subsidies are not poor but have incomes and wealth above the national average.

The best possible outcome to enhance the wealth of the nation (and world) as a whole would be the elimination of the entire gamut of agricultural programs, with the possible exception of federal financial support to basic research and extension, which are public goods.[1] However, there is a strong reservation in exempting from elimination a huge government enterprise that employs academics (including economists) in the agricultural and resource sciences, primarily in the land grant universities. Despite the high rates of return to public investment in agricultural research and extension, there is little question that if the public sector were out of this business, much of the effort would be picked up by the private sector and even perhaps more impressive results might well be forthcoming.

The question is not whether to wean agriculture away from subsidies and controls, but when and how? Arguments can be made for doing it both gradually or in one fell swoop. Adjustments could be painful for some resource owners, particularly agricultural laborers and landowners, as wealth shifts could be substantial, especially in declining land values. Perhaps some governmental programs to assist resource adjustment, particularly for retraining and relocating labor, could be justified on efficiency and equity grounds. At least then the resources of the public sector would be used to move resources in an efficient direction rather than the reverse, as is now the case—where excessive resources are induced into the sector and then subsidized to remain there. Some manpower-training programs are already available at both federal and local levels, but these may need to be supplemented and perhaps more targeted to the agricultural sector.

The United States was on the right track in the General Agreement on

Tariffs and Trade (GATT) negotiations by arguing that income support policies be abolished in ten years in all the advanced countries. The agreement reached in December 1993 was disappointing but was at least a beginning. All countries should now approve the agreement. But if a few refuse to go along, particularly the largest trader, the United States, the temptation will be strong for none of the major international competitors to act unilaterally and a stalemate could eventuate. Despite its rhetoric, it is not even absolutely clear that the United States is serious about free trade in agricultural commodities. The executive branch, from the president to the U.S. trade representative, has argued for trade liberalization, as well they should, but there is no way of knowing whether Congress will cooperate by passing legislation to reduce protection for domestic producers. It is clearly in the Congress that the most powerful constituency interests are brought to bear in continuing protection. The principal theme of this study is that what is economically desirable for the country as a whole may be difficult to achieve under our political system. But unless the costs of continuing under the present policies are clearly understood by those bearing these costs, mainly taxpayers and consumers, there will be little likelihood of arousing public support for change.

Also receiving public attention are two other classes of political reform that, if implemented, may help correct the problems in the agricultural sector. They are reforms of the budgetary process and election campaigns, including term limits for elected officials. However, it is doubtful that they will eliminate subsidies in agriculture or in countless other places. As long as the political system countenances the transfer of economic rents (subsidies) from taxpayers to interest groups, politicians will have an incentive to find ways to do it. But the chances of agricultural policy reform will be enhanced by what is likely to occur on the budgeting and election reform fronts.

Reforming Agricultural Policies Toward a More Efficient Sector

Two salient characteristics of the agricultural sector have been demonstrated in previous chapters. First, for decades the sector has contained excess resources; too much productive capacity exits at prevailing prices for markets to clear, given the restrictions on international trade. Thus, immense political pressures are generated to provide governmental programs that will protect income and wealth in agriculture. Second, instead of moving the sector toward an efficient equilibrium by freeing resources to move to more productive employment outside the sector, these policies have impeded efficient resource allocations that would improve the well-being of consumers, taxpayers, and even labor resources in agriculture over the long run.

The principal policy tool to limit supplies of supported commodities has been the idling of land, which has few valuable uses outside the agricultural sector. Thus, the sacrificed rent from this land is a deadweight social loss. In addition, supply control policies have attracted more nonland resources into the sector, such as chemicals and water, which have high opportunity costs, and their excessive use creates environmental problems, mostly off the farm. Another finding of major significance is that it is principally landowners and original recipients of supply control devices such as milk, tobacco, and peanut quotas, grazing permits, and sugar-producing contracts, as well as foreign consumers who have gained significantly from U.S. agricultural policies. But it has not all been a one-way street. In the early to middle 1980s, landowners in particular suffered large wealth losses from which some have not fully recuperated.

In the absence of some world catastrophe that will sharply increase demand or reduce supply of agricultural products, or a complete eradication of barriers to trade, a chronic problem of surplus capacity will likely exist for American farmers in the years and even decades ahead. What are the factors producing this prediction?

Perhaps most important are technological advances on the horizon that have the potential to dramatically increase crop yields and animal productivity and therefore decrease costs: gene splicing, recombinant DNA, new fertilization techniques in animals, and growth hormones to name a few. While there are problems to be solved before many are commercially feasible, given the history of technological advance since World War II, few agricultural scientists seriously doubt that such advances will be significant in the near future. And they will ultimately be available in developing as well as the advanced countries, compounding surplus problems.

As has always been the case, the prosperity of American farmers depends importantly on developments in trade policy. If GATT negotiations could eliminate export subsidies and import quotas, as well as reduce tariffs in the advanced countries, U.S. exports of agricultural products would undoubtedly increase. No other country has such a favorable combination of a highly productive land base and climate conducive to growing crops. High labor costs could be a problem, but U.S. agriculture is very efficient in its use of labor. At current energy prices, U.S. agriculture probably has a comparative advantage in the production of many basic agricultural products demanded worldwide, especially wheat and the feed grains. But other advanced nations are very protective of their farmers, and there is some evidence that developing countries are seeing that exploiting their farmers is counterproductive. Both of these phenomena will increase competitive pressures on American farmers.

Compelling evidence indicates that if the protection of U.S. agriculture were reduced or eliminated, the consequences would not be catastrophic. Fisher and de Gorter model U.S. agriculture using a dynamic optimization framework.[2] The main policy conclusion emerging from this work is that abolishing price support programs would increase U.S. exports and lower world prices of corn, rice, cotton, and wheat. A second conclusion is that tightening supply controls in land set-asides may not decrease output, a conclusion reached earlier in this book.

Despite the benefits that would occur if subsidies and supply control programs in agriculture were eliminated completely, the likelihood of this happening is not great given the political climate documented in earlier chapters. However, some less extreme policy measures might be politically feasible, even though they are poor substitutes for a complete demolition of existing programs and policies.

Decoupling

Decoupling severs the relationship between payments to farmers and the quantity of production and has been strongly advocated by academics and several government units including the Council of Economic Advisers and the USDA. Decoupling involves a complete separation of income support from production decisions and price formation. Farmers would not be induced to increase production and overuse scarce resources because market prices would fall to equilibrium levels. Farmers would be freed from production controls; national income would be increased as the efficiency of the sector improved; and consumers of food and fiber would benefit from lower prices. At the same time, farmers would be compensated in the form of direct cash payments as a supplement to their market sales to reach some predetermined level of income support.

Some elements of the decoupling idea are contained in the 1985 Food Security Act, for example, the so-called 50-92 provision. Deficiency payments may be made on 92 percent of permitted acreage if only 50 percent or more of eligible land is planted. Because farmers can collect payments on 92 percent of permitted acreage, the only reason to plant more than 50 percent would be if the market price or the loan rate exceeded variable production costs. Therefore, the support or target price does not stimulate excessive production.

Another example of partial decoupling is the freezing of historical program yields in the determination of deficiency payments. Farmers no longer have an incentive to increase their yields in current and future years simply to increase the level of production on which deficiency payments are determined.

The USDA seems now to be favoring a 0-92 provision: Farmers receive payments based on 92 percent of their historical base acreage without a requirement to plant any program crop on those acres. Of course, this amounts to complete decoupling on 92 percent of the acreage base. There can be little doubt that such a policy would be effective in reducing supply and, thus, decreasing resource use in the sector. On efficiency grounds, therefore, complete or partial decoupling has much to commend it and would be strongly superior to the target-price, support-price policies now in vogue.

But such a policy would create major public relations problems for farmers, and this is why adoption of complete decoupling may be difficult to implement politically. Imagine farmers receiving a government check covering deficiency payments from 92 percent of permitted acreage without putting a seed in the ground. This would make explicit what most subsidy policies are implicitly: direct income transfers, a form of welfare. But neither farmers, taxpayers, nor politicians presently appear to regard them as such. When subsidies are incorporated into prices, the welfare payments are largely hidden because transfers appear to be market determined. Farmers who take pride in their independence and self-reliance and capture huge public benefits because of the residues of the agrarian myth still extant in American society do not want to forfeit these benefits and think of themselves on the public dole. This attitude accounts for their adamant opposition to decoupling, despite its efficiency advantages when compared with price supports. Confirming this view, many farm organizations have stoutly advocated price supports based on "parity," where the price farmers receive is ostensibly equated to their costs and thus is fair.[3] Also, taxpayers are not accustomed to thinking of support prices to farmers as welfare payments, and were they to do so, the political acceptability of subsidies to agriculture might be substantially weakened.

Of course, deficiency payments likely would not be unlimited under a decoupling scheme. In some of their news releases, the USDA proposes to make the $50,000 per farm payment limitation apply to all deficiency payments, including marketing-loan payments. However, the combination of the 0-92 program and a more rigidly enforced $50,000 payment limitation might well place the entire farm program apparatus in jeopardy. With such a "low" payment limitation, it is doubtful that the large-scale farmers who produce the bulk of marketed production would participate in government programs. Another likely prospect is that uncompetitive small-scale farmers would cease production and draw their government checks under the 0-92 decoupling program while large-scale farmers, mainly opting out of the government programs, would produce everything. Perhaps this would not be such a bad outcome from an economic efficiency point of view, but those who support the small-scale farmer would not like it.

Getting Target Prices and Loan Rates "Right"

In the event that neither complete elimination of subsidies nor decoupling are politically feasible, some progress toward improved efficiency could be made by leaving the current structure of policies in place, but move the discretionary prices and controls to more efficient levels. The following constitute a minimum response to making current policy more efficient.

First, keep loan rates at expected world market prices so as not to erect an impediment to world trade for American farmers. With the nonrecourse loans in place, loan rates tend to serve as a floor under domestic market prices. If domestic prices are above world market levels, American farmers must be protected against imports by imposing restrictions, or exports must be subsidized. Loan rates at world market prices would allow American farmers to compete freely in world markets, as is now the case with cotton and rice. If this policy were adopted in all advanced countries, farmers in less developed nations would also have access to world markets without the export dumping now being perpetrated by rich countries. Progress toward this goal was made with the marketing-loan provisions of the 1985 FSA for cotton and rice and the potential implementation of marketing loans for soybeans, oilseed crops, wheat, and the feed grains authorized in the 1990 FACTA.

Second, ratchet down target prices for wheat, the feed grains, cotton, and rice and support prices for milk even further. Target prices represent the marginal returns farmers receive for their program crops. As demonstrated in Chapters 2 and 3, if support prices are set above equilibrium levels, they cease being only a stabilization tool but also attract excess resources into the agricultural sector. The government must be given credit for the slight ratcheting down of support prices mandated by the 1985 act. However, this downward trend ceased in the 1990 FACTA, and target prices are to be held at 1990–91 levels throughout the period 1991 through 1995 for wheat, the feed grains, cotton, and rice. Of course, because of inflation, the real target prices will fall slightly, but it is unlikely that this will be enough to eliminate excess production in the sector. It must be remembered that for many decades technological progress has reduced the real costs of agricultural production. If this trend continues, and it almost certainly will, the difference between fixed support prices and cost will widen, giving rise to incentives for increasing production.

Third, it is difficult to find a convincing rationale for government disaster and subsidized crop insurance programs, given the risk-reducing insurance programs available in the private sector that would arise if it were not for competition of government programs.[4] These programs simply encourage farmers to produce in inherently risky and costly environments and, at the same time, to shift much of the risk costs to taxpayers.

Fourth, eliminate the conservation payments. The country does not need costly income transfers to already rich farmers to conserve resources that are not in short supply and do not threaten productivity. Of course, given the long-term nature of Conservation Reserve Program contracts, these contracts will need to be phased out slowly as contracts expire.

Fifth, no new input subsidies should be paid. The water subsidy is a case in point. No new federal development should be undertaken that prices water to irrigators at below full development costs including interest. Existing project water prices should be adjusted to cover variable O&M costs or be placed at market-clearing levels, whichever is higher, when contracts come up for renewal. This reform would have a favorable impact on environmental quality in the West.

Sixth, federal credit policies in the agricultural sector badly need reform. There is no national purpose served by subsidizing agricultural and rural community loans. And perhaps even more important, the FmHA and other creditors must be weaned away from congressional dictates to keep farmers in business regardless of efficiency consequences. Free capital markets should be permitted to move resources to higher valued employments. Reforms suggested recently by the USDA on the need for a market-oriented industry rather than a welfare program, the need for better loan application and reporting procedures, the need of stronger tests for determining eligibility for limited-resource loans, and a need for much stronger financial discipline in administering loans are moves in the right direction. However, no efficiency case can be made for limited-resource farmers to receive special consideration, and if incomes need to be supplemented on equity grounds, let other government transfer programs available to other citizens take care of the problem.

Seventh, investment in human capital, such as expanded education and job retraining and loans for moving expenses, which would induce labor to move in efficient directions, should be considered a replacement for price supports that immobilize resources in the sector. Decoupling could also be helpful in this regard if payments could be linked to relocation, education, and retraining.

Reforming Federal Fiscal Policies

The perceived need to decrease the federal budget deficit has ultimately produced some real reduction of transfer payments to agriculture in recent years and promises more to come. This is perhaps the most hopeful development on the political horizon as both major political parties have strongly advocated reducing the federal deficit. The pressure for deficit reduction affecting the agricultural sector was evident in the 15 percent reduction in acreage that would be eligible for deficiency payments mandated by the 1990 Budget Reconciliation Act (BRA), the first major reduction in subsidies legislated in several decades. President Clinton made deficit reduction a major issue in the 1992 presidential campaign, and in 1993 Congress passed the largest tax increase in U.S. history. Expenditure decreases have been promised by both the executive and legislative branches, but it is not at all clear that they will be forthcoming in significant amounts, especially considering that a costly government program in health care is presently in limbo. However, the deficit has been reduced in the past two years and appears to be receding as a critical political issue. There may be continuing pressures for reducing expenditures such as agricultural subsidies, but there undoubtedly will be fierce opposition in the Congress for reasons amply demonstrated in earlier chapters.

Public choice theorists have recommended several measures to curtail federal spending: requiring Congress to identify a specific source of revenue for any legislation that establishes a new spending program; tax indexing that would prevent taxation increases beyond the basic rate of inflation; balanced-budget legislation with stronger potential enforcement, a constitutional amendment requiring a balanced budget; a line-item veto given to the president; changing the incentives for bureaucrats by allowing several government agencies to supply the same service thus stimulating competition; promoting fees by users of services as a substitute for financing from the general Treasury; leaving as much regulation and supplying public services as possible to local government; putting more economic proposals requiring government spending on the ballot through referenda rather than spending via public districts that does not require citizen approval; and privatizing government operations. Some of these items have already been seriously considered, while others seem to be simply a "wish" list. Perhaps the most likely is the construction of devices to reduce the budget deficit.

Balanced-Budget Alternatives

Mandates for a balanced federal budget have taken two forms: legislative action, such as the 1985 Gramm–Rudman–Hollings Act and its precursors; and a constitutional amendment, such as was proposed as early as 1982 and again in 1990 in the House of Representatives. Both proposals have strong and weak points.

Some economists argue that mandated balanced budgets would be a serious mistake since an important discretionary stabilization tool would be taken away from policymakers (Courant and Gramlich 1986; Savage 1988). In addition, neither a balanced-budget law nor a constitutional amendment may actually solve the perceived deficit problems. The budget process is complex and relies heavily on correctly forecasting economic conditions. Unexpected changes in the national income can radically affect revenues and, therefore, can also produce unexpected deficit spending. In the 1980s when budget-control statutes were on the books, the actual deficit exceeded published expectations of various administrations by an average of $40.2 billion per year (Rasky 1990). The latest permutation in this litany was the revelation claimed by President Clinton about the time of his inauguration as he announced that the budget deficit was much worse than he had believed it was during the presidential campaign.

Deficit-reduction laws. Serious and chronic deficit spending has plagued the economy for at least two decades and episodically from the time of the founding of the republic. Before 1974, responsibility for a federal budget was highly dispersed throughout Congress. Because of this fragmentation, Congress lost its fiscal authority for the budget mainly because of the impoundment of funds by the executive branch. To help reclaim its perceived constitutional power to establish spending priorities, Congress passed the 1974 Budget Reform Act.[5] By establishing centralized budget committees in each house and by founding the Congressional Budget Office, the act gave Congress increased informational and analytical resources; it also established timetables and outlined procedures for the development of the budget, outlined information to be included in the president's budget submission, and established procedures for congressional review of presidential impoundment actions. Despite these ostensibly strong measures, the act that was supposedly created to curb spending had, by 1990, been waived 398 times by Congress (*Wall Street Journal* 1990d).

Nearly everyone recognized that the budget process itself has been a shambles. It was supposed to be completed by the beginning of each new fiscal year, now October 1, so the government could legitimately spend resources. But budgetary timetables were largely bypassed, and resolutions that extended funding from the preceding year were commonly employed to fund the federal government (Savage 1988, p. 242). With a Congress that could not or would not conform to its own budgetary rules, other spending restraints became necessary.

The famous Gramm–Rudman–Hollings budget-balancing act was passed in 1985. It originally stipulated that the federal budget deficit must be incrementally reduced each year until 1991, when a balanced budget would be required by law. However, when this goal proved unattainable, the law was revised to stretch out debt ceilings through 1993 (Rosenbaum 1990).

In 1990, Congress faced a budget crisis. Not counting the costs of bailing out the savings and loan institutions, the Office of Management and Budget estimated the 1991 deficit would be between $123 and $138 billion. The revised Gramm–Rudman–Hollings act required a deficit limit of only $64 billion. The first response of Congress was simply to ignore the required timetable. Almost five months past the May 15 deadline, a deadlocked Congress still had no budget for the new fiscal year. The government shut down over the Columbus Day weekend while Congress fussed over who should take the cuts or face the required sequestration.[6]

With this sort of congressional performance even with the strong statutory mandates, legislative action hardly appears to be a reliable antidote to deficit spending. The principal problem is that laws enacted to balance the budget are simply ignored or amended by congressional action as needed.

Yet it has been argued that Gramm–Rudman–Hollings has not completely failed. "In some ways, it is working the way it was supposed to work, by threatening a train wreck and bringing all sides to the bargaining table."[7] Perhaps Gramm–Rudman's most important impact, for good or ill, is that it has forced negotiations between executive and legislative branches, as occurred prior to the passage of the 1990 BRA. Moreover, it is widely believed that Gramm–Rudman has forced at least some discipline on government spending. Compared with the size of the GDP, the deficit has been cut in half under Gramm–Rudman. Supporters also point out that amending the law is simply plugging the original loopholes and making the bill fit the realities of a changing economy (*New York Times* 1990).

A balanced-budget amendment. As early as 1792, Thomas Jefferson foresaw the potential problems that debt financing could produce. In a letter to President George Washington, he observed, "This exactly marks the difference between Colonel Hamilton's views and mine, that I would wish the debt paid tomorrow; he wishes it never to be paid, but always to be a thing wherewith to corrupt and manage the Legislature" (quoted in Savage 1988, pp. 106–107).

Three balanced-budget amendments to the U.S. Constitution have been proposed in Congress in the recent past. The first, in 1982, won a majority vote but didn't get the required two-thirds. The first of two amendments in 1990 was proposed by Congressman Barton (R-TX) and mandated a balanced budget unless three-fifths of the Congress voted to run a deficit. The rate of growth in government spending would be limited to the rate of growth of the national income; to raise this limit would also require a three-fifths vote. Barton lost by a vote of 244 to 184 in the House (*Wall Street Journal* 1990d).

The second 1990 version was proposed by Charles Stenholm (D-TX) (a member of the Agricultural Committee) and Larry Craig (R-ID). It carried 279 to 150, barely short of the required two-thirds majority. The Stenholm–Craig amendment also required a balanced budget unless three-fifths voted to run a deficit; however, to raise taxes to balance the budget required only a majority vote. This tax-raising feature apparently was very attractive to Congress. After the vote was taken, the *Wall Street Journal* published the names of House members who voted for Stenholm–Craig but against Barton. The *Journal* claimed, in effect, that these members were trying to have it both ways: "Those members wanted to be recorded as supporting a balanced budget, but at the same time make certain they buried the amendment that would have put a real crimp in the spending habits that create deficit spending."[8]

Only time will tell whether other versions of a balanced-budget amendment will surface and whether one of them might eventually be approved and enacted into law. From all indications, it does not appear that the administration of President Clinton will support the idea as strongly as did the Bush administration.

Reforming the Political Election Process

Brooks Jackson has opined that "the true predicament [of our political system] is that perverse incentives twist the behavior of ordinary legislators. The system doesn't require bad motives to produce bad government. America is becoming a special-interest nation where money is displacing votes" (1988, p. 295). To correct this ailment, Jackson makes a number of recommendations:

> *Congress should outlaw PAC donations outright, just as past reforms have forbidden the use of corporate money and funds from labor-union treasuries. It should also banish out-of-state donations. Candidates ought to accept money only from their party or from individuals who live in their home state. Limits on individual donations to candidates should remain at $1,000 per election. Annual limits on gifts to parties should be reduced to $1,000 per person, from the present $20,000. Otherwise, operations like the Speaker's Club will continue. The limit on what the*

PACs may collect from individuals should be reduced to $1,000 per year, from the present $5,000. (1988, p. 304)

Jackson further argues that political parties are the only instruments available to impose collective responsibility on legislators. Therefore, he would attempt to strengthen their role in elections at the expense of individual supporters and special interest organizations. Current restrictions, however, allowed party campaign committees in 1988 to furnish financial aid of only $56,100 for a House candidate, amounting to little more than one-tenth of what a typical contestant needed to win an election. The limit for Senate candidates was between $109,700 and $1.9 million depending on the size of the state (Jackson 1988, p. 301). But since parties do not raise the necessary funds, Jackson believes that the solution is to provide massive public subsidies for the major political parties. He estimates that it would cost just under $109 million per party during each two-year election cycle to provide $250,000 for candidates in all 435 House districts. Funding competitive Senate races in each of the thirty-three or thirty-four states that have seats up for election in a given year would cost roughly $60 million per party, given current rates of spending by successful candidates. Also, Jackson argues that members of Congress should be brought under the special prosecutor provision of the Ethics in Government Act, from which they are currently exempt.[9] What can be said about Jackson's proposals?

Spending Limits on Elections

This study has documented the powerful political influence of PACs in campaigns of legislators who are on the congressional agriculture committees. It is tempting, therefore, to agree with Jackson that one approach to confining the influence problem is simply to outlaw PACs. But as long as the U.S. election process is as long and expensive as it is now, it is not clear that other sources of funding would distort the political process less than PACs do. One possible approach to the funding problem, therefore, would be to curtail the amount of money that could be spent on elections.

Campaign reform bills were introduced in the Senate by both major political parties during 1990. The main thrust of the Democratic proposal was to curtail spending on election campaigns, while the Republicans, like Jackson, sought to mitigate the influence of special interests by outlawing PACs.

Senator David Boren (D-OK) was the leading sponsor of the Democrats' proposal, which would make public subsidies available to both challengers and incumbents if candidates voluntarily agreed to limit spending.[10] The limits would apply to both primary and general elections and would range from $1.5 to $8.2 million depending on the voting-age population in various states. Not unexpectedly, however, the proposal favored incumbents. Aside from the advantages to incumbents of free mail and office staffs, the bill also allowed that the "costs of any ordinary and necessary expenses incurred in connection with an individual's duties as a holder of the office of United States Senator" would not count toward spending limits (Berke 1990a). A compromise limited such expenses to the lesser of 15 percent of a candidate's total campaign spending or $300,000 per election. In either case, this would leave incumbents with a wide variety of expenses that could be charged to their campaigns without counting toward their limit. Senators could continue the common practice of charging travel and entertainment expenses of supporters to their campaigns, a practice that challengers could not use to the same extent because their supporters would not be as well defined. Still, the public interest group Common Cause estimated that if the Democrats' proposal had been in effect in 1988, Senate challengers would have had on average $639,924 more to spend, while incumbents would have averaged $1.3 million less (Berke 1990b). These figures, however, do not account for free mailing privileges and current office staff enjoyed by incumbents that are paid for with public funds.

Another feature of Senator Boren's bill was a reduction of the maximum that any one PAC could give, $3,000 per election, down from the present $5,000. However, individuals would be allowed to give more, $1,500 per election, up from $1,000 (Jackson 1988, p. 293).

Opposed to spending limits, the Republicans, headed by Mitch McConnell (R-KY), opted to center their efforts on eliminating PACs altogether. The Republicans argued that PACs perpetuate special interest legislation, dominate political campaigns, and give more often to incumbents who have proven their loyalty than to challengers who have only campaign promises to offer. Two problems, however, existed with the Republican proposal. First, PACs are required to make campaign contributions public whereas if campaign contributions came solely from individuals, as recommended by the Republican version, it would be difficult, if not impossible, to track the influence of "special interests." Second, eliminating PACs could be unconstitutional. The Supreme Court in *Buckley v. Valeo* made it clear that campaign contributions and expenditures are a form of expression protected by the First Amendment (Armstrong 1990).

Neither the Democratic or Republican versions of campaign reform passed in the 1990 session. Modifications were made, and congressional advocates have been trying to pass meaningful election reform legislation ever since. Election reform bills were introduced again in 1994 but were killed by filibuster in the Senate. Even though election reform appears to be gaining strength each year, it is unclear when serious changes in federal law will come about relating to campaign contributions and perquisites received from lobbyists.

Another example of spending-limit legislation was passed by the New York State Assembly in 1991; it would provide matching funds for candidates who agree to spending limits that range from $7 million for gubernatorial general election campaigns to $75,000 for the state Assembly campaigns (Shribman 1991). In the case of gubernatorial races, the bill would also impose contribution restrictions that limit the largest gifts to $4,000, down from nearly $43,000, where they are now.

Perhaps the most drastic reform plan for spending limits was proposed by Governor Lawton Chiles in Florida during the 1990 election campaign. This plan would limit campaign contributions for statewide and legislative races to $500, would ban corporate entities from making more than one $500 contribution in a contested race, would set aside $4 million a year for public financing of statewide races, and provide as much as $2.5 million in taxpayer money for each gubernatorial candidate if both agree to cap their individual spending at $5 million (Shribman 1991). But what if one candidate was unwilling to limit spending? In these cases, the state would provide the participating candidate with funds equal to the amount by which the opponent exceeded the limit. Some critics of the provision think the Chiles plan would skew the political system, perhaps by diverting money to the state's weak political parties or by nudging candidates to appeal to well-organized interest groups that provide organizational help rather than money to their campaigns (Shribman 1991).

It is true that spending limits would produce cheaper elections and therefore make it easier to generate the "needed" funds. It is not at all obvious, however, that they will benefit challengers vis-à-vis incumbents and open up the political system. Spending limits would make congressional races less rather than more competitive for the simple reason that closely contested races cost more than those that are safe (Schotland 1990). Thus, if a challenger is to have any chance of success the incumbent must be outspent. Ten of twelve challengers who replaced incumbent senators between 1982 and 1988 spent two to six times more than the proposed limits in the Boren bill (Schotland 1990). In addition, with population being the only variable that determines limits on spending in various states, no room is left for differences in campaign costs. A study by a nonpartisan research group found that Senator Bob Graham (D-FL) spent 80 cents per eligible voter in Florida to win his seat in 1986, while Senator Tom Daschle (D-SD) had to spend $8 per eligible voter in South Dakota. The same study indicated that for a challenger in California to overcome the advantages of an incumbent, at least $17 million must be spent—nearly $9 million more than the proposed $8.2 million limit (Berke 1990c). Between 1982 and 1988, thirty Senate races were considered to be highly competitive (6 percent margin or closer) while sixty-five were landslides (20 percent margin or greater.) In competitive races, more than 60 percent of the candidates spent more than the limits proposed, whereas in landslides, only 15 percent of the candidates spent more (Schotland 1990). The inference is that limits would seem to make only a minor difference in uncompetitive races where incumbents are safe but would have a major negative impact on challengers in close races.

Spending limits could also change the balance of power in the Senate between states that do and do not have competitive elections in any particular year. In competitive states, incumbents would be constrained from taking advantage of their fund-raising edge, while challengers would have sufficient public funds to mount strong races. Those states might have an unprecedentedly high turnover of senators and would accordingly build little seniority. This would cost states relative bargaining power in Congress.

Spending limits would also have another impact. Every formula proposed for setting spending limits has established state population as the only variable determining the cost of elections. Therefore, for the first time in law, limits would ensure that the population of the state would affect the outcome of Senate races. So limits would appear to prevent serious competition in small states with closely contested elections (Schotland 1990).

More and more public financing of election campaigns is recommended by most observers. What are the disadvantages? Little is done to offset the advantages of incumbency and, therefore, to open up the political system to newcomers. Public financing could lead to a colossal waste of taxpayer money as candidates with no realistic chance of winning get money the taxpayers would have been unwilling to give them voluntarily. Thomas Jefferson said, "To compel a man to furnish contributions of money for the propagation of opinions in which he disbelieves is sinful and tyrannical" (quoted in Fund 1990, p. 19).

In the final analysis, however, with all the proposals to reform campaign-financing laws, perhaps a cure to the wrong illness is being sought. There are problems with Congress that go far beyond campaign financing. The following have been suggested to limit the power of incumbents and abuses in Congress:

- *Limit terms.* Over the past several elections, the House has a reelection rate of about 98 percent of those choosing to run, the Senate, 85 percent.
- *End free mail.* The House sent out mailings costing taxpayers an estimated $79 million in 1990.
- *Cut congressional spending.* It took Congress 191 years to reach

an annual budget of $1 billion in 1980. Just 10 years later, the budget had climbed to $2 billion.

- *Shorten the campaign season.* It has been suggested that fund-raising be deferred to twelve months before any election to free an incumbent's time for consideration of important, pending legislation.
- *Insist on openness.* Full disclosure makes for the greatest accountability. (Armstrong 1990)

Term Limitations for Elected Officials

Limiting the number of terms that elected officials can serve in office seems to be an idea whose time has come. Few political issues in recent times have had the depth of public support that polls show for term limits (Crane 1990a). Polls indicate over 70 percent backing. The rationale is straightforward. The public choice theorists, such as Buchanan and Tullock, have shown that when left unattended by constitutional or legislative constraints, government has a tendency to grow regardless of the desires of the people or the cost that growth imposes (Crane 1990b). Government spending is now approximately 43 percent of the national income. State and local taxes have grown since 1950 from 6 percent of GDP to nearly 11 percent. If this growth in government spending is to be stopped and reversed, something has to be done to curtail incentives that propel that growth. As demonstrated in previous chapters, spending grows because both suppliers and demanders of political favors gain from such growth at the expense of taxpayers and consumers. The theory behind term limits is that if their terms of office were limited, elected officials would be more likely to pass laws that would be good for the community rather than good for themselves:

> *Term limitation could become in the 1990s what tax limitation was in the 1970s—a popular movement politicians abhor, but one to which they must respond. . . . Many practical benefits are to be gained from imposing a limitation on terms: 1) elections would be more competitive, 2) term limits would make ability more important than seniority, 3) term limits would improve the quality of candidates, and 4) term limits would counter the "culture of ruling." (Fund 1990, pp. 19–21)*

John Fund reminds us that term limits are not a new idea:

> *Members thinking of Congress as a career is a new and unfortunate trend in politics. Voluntary term limits were a part of the American political tradition for more than 100 years. At the time of the Civil War less than 2% of the House served for more than 12 years. Today 34% of members have spent more than 12 years in office, and many have been committee chairmen that long. . . . In Virginia, the state called the cradle of*

democracy, half of the residents had no choice for either their congressmen or U.S. senator last year. Five of the 10 House members had no primary or general-election opponents, and GOP Senator John Warner was unopposed. . . . Those opposing term limits argued that this is a "sledgehammer approach to democracy" that will take away the people's right to choose whomever they want. All the term-limit opponents maintained there were better ways to improve competitiveness in congressional elections and open up the political process. Among those mentioned were forcing television stations to provide free time on the air to candidates, campaign-finance reform, an end to gerrymandering and perhaps public financing. But there is not one reform that has helped challengers more than incumbents. Change must come from outside. (Fund 1991)

Led by California's Proposition 140,[11] which passed in the November 1990 election, many states and cities have considered or are considering term limits. In fact, as of June 1993, fifteen state constitutions had set term limits for their congressional representatives: Arizona, Arkansas, California, Colorado, Florida, Michigan, Missouri, Montana, Nebraska, North Dakota, Ohio, Oregon, South Dakota, Washington, and Wyoming (Balzar 1994). Colorado was the first in 1990 to pass such limits, and as of February 1994 term limit proposals were scheduled to land on the ballots of eight more states.

California Assembly Speaker Willie Brown estimated that 40 percent of the current Assembly will retire when their terms are up (Oliver 1991). Apparently, legislative staffs also feel threatened. The *Wall Street Journal* reports that more than 700 of the legislature's 2,500 staffers are retiring, while lobbyists are worried that they are losing their "investments" in longtime incumbents who have become attuned to their interests (Oliver 1991).

James C. Miller III has pointed out a connection between the length of time legislators serve in Washington and their tendency to vote for increased government expenditures. The propensity of congresspersons to spend tends to rise the longer they are in office, except that first-termers tend to be slightly bigger spenders than second-termers (Miller 1991). Miller finds further that in the Senate the spending peaks after sixteen years in office and that in both houses Democrats spend significantly more than do Republicans.

However, given the great advantage incumbents have over challengers and given the Democratic majorities in both houses, the lack of a limit on terms perpetuates more aggressive spending behavior. Moreover, limits on terms would reduce the payoff to lobbyists as well as incumbents from efforts to secure re-election, and this would further level the political competition playing field. (Miller 1990, p. A8)

The most persuasive critique of term limits has come from economist

Robert J. Barro (1991). He argues that in a democratic political system, the voters ought to be free to choose their representatives without restriction just as consumers should be free to choose the bundle of goods they consume. Term limits sound very much like rent controls and minimum wages in their implications. Voters should be free to decide between the freshness of new politicians and the experience of incumbents.[12]

There is some appeal in the Barro position for those who believe in free markets, whether they be economic or political. However, given the potent public choice principles of the rational ignorance of voters and the power of special interests to acquire political favors at the expense of community welfare, it is not obvious that political markets can work efficiently to promote the general welfare.[13]

Still, the fundamental point should not be missed. Despite the fact that recommendations abound for reforming the political system to reduce influence peddling, as long as it is constitutionally permissible for the government to transfer economic benefits to recipient groups, some way will be found to structure the political institutions to accommodate those transfers, and interest groups will find ways to bring their influence to bear on the relevant decision makers.

Conclusions

Despite recurring income crises in agriculture, such as occurred most recently in the early 1980s, current programs do not deal with them efficiently. Rather, they impede reallocations that would eventually correct the problem of excess resources in the agricultural sector. If public funds are to be spent, it is important that they move resources in the efficient direction, not immobilize them in a sector of the economy where they will be condemned to earn submarginal returns, often even with the aid of government subsidies.

None of preceding discussion on the need for reform is meant to denigrate the remarkable accomplishments of American farmers in improving the quality of life in the United States. It is beyond dispute that when reviewed in a historical context, U.S. agriculture has no equal in producing food and fiber at low real costs. The principal beneficiaries have been and continue to be consumers, not only here in the United States but worldwide. American consumers spend a lower percentage of their disposable incomes for food and fiber than do those in any other country. This is due in large part to the creative effort of clever and hard-working individual farmers who are still reasonably free to exercise entrepreneurial talent in a competitive market environment with significant assistance from public and private support institutions. Labor productivity increases in the agricultural sector have been particularly spectacular over the past fifty years, and the world may be on the threshold of a new wave of productivity-enhancing technical advances.

In light of these indisputable facts, some may be tempted to respond to the analysis and arguments of this book by maintaining that "if it ain't broke, don't fix it." But this is a reactionary and defeatist point of view. Agriculture has produced these benefits *despite* the costly regulations laid on it by the government, not because of them. There can be little doubt that agriculture is far less efficient today than it would have been if the policies invoked in the Great Depression had never seen the light of day. What is quite obvious is that this vital and important sector of the economy could contribute much more to standards of living today if it were freed from governmental controls and subsidies that distort prices, impede trade, misallocate resources, and create environmental degradation. It can be stated with confidence that substituting market processes for governmental controls now will not jeopardize the wondrous benefits produced by agriculture but will enhance them.

It is quite clear what needs to be done to correct the most egregious problems: the policy reforms are outlined in this chapter. The most significant deterrent to progress is a political system that will not yield easily to such reforms. Terry Anderson has discussed this issue with respect to water policy:

> *The real problem in effecting institutional change is in getting from here to there. There is little hope that politicians living in a rent-seeking society will actively support the decentralization of water policy. Politicians and bureaucrats currently work within a system that gives them the discretionary power necessary to reward their constituencies. If the coalition between politicians/bureaucrats and water users is to be opposed, the opposition must come in the form of a competing coalition.... The evidence and arguments presented... suggest the possibility for such a coalition among environmentalists, fiscal conservatives, and persons who value individual freedom. (Anderson 1983, p. 116)*

What potential coalitions exist to demand reform of agricultural policy? They appear to include the same groups as Anderson cites for water reform: environmentalists, fiscal conservatives, and those who value freedom. All of them have just as much at stake, and probably even more, in the case of agricultural policy as they do for water policy. And because the costs of agricultural and water subsidies are so high for consumers and taxpayers, these groups should be added to the list, although it will not be inexpensive to organize them because of free-rider and rational ignorance problems. However, one must be cautiously optimistic since the political climate appears to be changing.

Ordinary citizen disapproval of political graft that wastes resources is beginning to show itself in referenda, poll results, and such legislation as term limits. Solid information and analysis as to the nature and costs of current policies should help mobilize public opinion against them. This is no time for pessimism that might retard further efforts to produce the needed reforms.

Notes

1. Investment in agricultural research and the dissemination of its findings has produced extraordinary technical advances in U.S. and world agriculture. Returns to this investment have been far higher than the average return to capital investment in the economy as a whole. Studies show annual rates of return of 20 to over 100 percent, depending on location and commodity. See Nuckton and Gardner (1980).

2. Fisher and de Gorter (1992) describe six hypothetical policy scenarios and use dynamic programming to show their effects on the markets for the major U.S. export crops: corn, cotton, rice, and wheat. The first policy replicates the status quo. The second eliminates subsidies entirely. The third freezes base acreages at 1987 levels. The fourth halves the level of protection for each crop by reducing target price and diversion payments. The fifth doubles payments for land left fallow, and the sixth policy doubles acreage set-aside requirements.

3. Those familiar with history, however, know that the periods chosen for parity calculations were those when net incomes were especially favorable to the agricultural sector, such as 1910 through 1914. Primarily because of productivity changes, current "parity" prices have little relationship to current costs. If farmers received support prices at 100 percent of parity as defined traditionally, prices would exceed costs by a large margin, and the effect would be to draw even more excess resources into the agricultural sector.

4. Leo Mayer has proposed programs that could protect farmers from both overproduction and crop losses. "Such a concept might work as follows: Each year, a target yield would be established for each crop that is covered by a target price/deficiency payment program. With unfavorable weather and yields that are less than the target yield, target prices would be raised with the amount determined by the difference between the target yield and the actual yield. With favorable weather and yields that exceed target yields, target prices would be lowered. This adjustment would increase income protection for farmers in drought years. It would also provide some budget savings for the government in years of unfavorable weather" (Mayer 1991, p. 30).

5. U.S. House of Representatives (1986), "The Congressional Budget Process: A General Explanation," Serial no. CP-9 (Washington, DC).

6. Sequestration (automatic formula reduction of budgetary resources) was written into Gramm–Rudman–Hollings to provide Congress and the president with enough incentive to achieve deficit reductions through the regular budget process. "The sequester was to be to budget politics what the atom bomb was to the Cold War—a deterrent too horrible to contemplate." See du Pont (1990).

If the budget process fails, the law allows the president to initiate a sequestration order as soon as September 1. Some programs are completely or partially exempt from sequestration, however.

7. Stanley E. Collender, a budget specialist in the firm of Price Waterhouse, quoted in Rosenbaum (1990).

8. *Wall Street Journal* (1990d). It is of special interest to this study that fourteen of the ninety-five members who voted for Stenholm–Craig, but against Barton, sit on the House Agriculture Committee, including the committee's chair, Congressman E de la Garza (D-TX).

9. Jackson (1988, p. 301). Executive branch officials are under tight rules that forbid them from accepting a free lunch from a contractor, a lobbyist, or even a newspaper reporter. But members of Congress allow themselves practically unlimited free travel, food, and drink from lobbyists. Recent proposals to eliminate these perks have been unable to muster the required votes for passage.

10. Congress enacted spending ceilings in 1974 for both presidential and congressional campaigns. The limits were challenged in court, however, and in 1976 the Supreme Court ruled in *Buckley v. Valeo,* that statutory limits on campaign contributions are constitutional, but that limits on overall spending are not. However, the court did allow spending limits to be used as a condition for public funding of campaigns. See Schotland (1990).

11. Proposition 140 limits California statewide officeholders in the executive branch and state senators to two four-year terms and members of the state Assembly to three two-year terms. Proposition 140 also cuts the budget of the legislature by nearly 40 percent, to about $1 million for each legislator. See Crovitz (1991).

    In California, a lawsuit was brought by legislators to prevent the budget restriction, and the justices of the State Supreme Court have issued a restraining order preventing the budget cuts pending a full review of the statute. In the suit, the legislators claim that the voters must be protected from their decision to limit terms because this deprives the voters of a constitutional right to be represented indefinitely by the same legislator. The legislators also claim that their constitutional rights are also at stake. There is a "fundamental right to be candidate for public office," which they say is among the "associational rights" in the First Amendment.

12. Thus, Barro (1990) argues, "The main inference from a 95% re-election rate is that the political process is working and that officeholders are conforming to the wishes of their constituents. If we ever see a 50% re-election rate, then there really would be reason to worry."

13. These arguments are developed in Chapter 7 and its appendix.

References

Abramson, Jill. 1990a. "PAC Contributions to Senators Totaled $96.3 Million in "83–88, Group Says." *Wall Street Journal* (New York: April 24), A16.

______. 1990b. "Washington Campus Pays Legislators, Lobbyists to Teach Executives the Ins and Outs of Influence." *Wall Street Journal* (New York: May 7), A16.

______. 1990c. "GOP War Chest Surpasses by Far Democrats' Sum." *Wall Street Journal* (New York: May 25), A14.

______. 1990d. "GOP Group Finds New Way to Raise Funds." *Wall Street Journal* (New York: August 27), A12.

______. 1990e. "While Foe, Duke May be Aiming to Fund National Right-Wing Machine." *Wall Street Journal* (New York: August 29), A10.

______. 1990f. "Autopac's Spending Late in Campaigns Is Bane of Many Democratic Candidates." *Wall Street Journal* (New York: November 2), A16.

______. 1991a. "Senate Votes Ban Against Honoraria for Its Members." *Wall Street Journal* (New York: May 22), A4.

______. 1991b. "If You're a U.S. Lawmaker, the Important Thing Really Isn't What You Owe, It's Who You Owe." *Wall Street Journal* (New York, June 26), A12.

______. 1992. "Crowd of Usually Stalwart Pro-GOP Industries Stopped Feeding Elephant as Clinton Surged, *Wall Street Journal* (New York: November 19), A12.

Abramson, Jill, & Jackson, Brooks. 1990. "Debate over PAC Money Hits Close to Home As Lawmakers Tackle Campaign-Finance Bill." *Wall Street Journal* (New York: March 7), A20.

Abramson, Jill, & Pound, Edward T. 1990. "Lawmakers Continue to Rake in Speaking Fees, with Senators More Cautious Amid Inquiries."*Wall Street Journal* (New York: May 31), A18.

Abramson, Jill, & Rogers, David. 1991. "Five Are on the Grill, but Other Lawmakers Help Big Donors Too." *Wall Street Journal* (New York: January 10), A4.

Ackerman, Susan Rose. 1989. "Small Bribes Are Still a Big Scandal." *Wall Street Journal* (New York: December 30).

Adams, Rich. 1990. "Agriculture and the Greenhouse Effect." In *Implementing Agricultural Policies to Achieve Environmental Objectives: Lessons for the 1990s*, Stephen B. Lovejoy & Kenda M. Resler, eds. (West Lafayette, IN: Resource Policy Consortium, Purdue University, July), 9–10.

Alchian, Armen A., & Demsetz, Harold. 1972. "Production, Information Costs, and Economic Organization." *American Economic Review, 63* (5) (December), 777–795.

Alston, Julian, & Carter, Colin. 1989. "Causes and Consequences of Farm Policy," Unpublished paper prepared for the sixty-fourth annual meeting of the Western Economics Association, Lake Tahoe, June 18–22.

Alston, Julian M., & Hurd, Brian H. 1990. "Some Neglected Social Costs of Government Spending in Farm Programs." *American Journal of Agricultural Economics, 72* (1) (February), 149–156.

Alston, Lee J. 1984. "Farm Foreclosure Moratorium Legislation: A Lesson from the Past." *American Economic Review, 74* (3) (June), 445–457.

Alston, Lee J., & Hatton, T. J. 1991. "The Earnings Gap Between Agricultural and Manufacturing Laborers, 1925–1941." *The Journal of Economic History, 51* (1) (March), 83–100.

Anderson, Kym. 1992. "Effects on the Environment and Welfare of Liberalizing World Trade: The Cases of Coal and Food," In *The Greening of World Trade Issues,* Kym Anderson & Richard Blackhurst, eds. (Ann Arbor: University of Michigan Press).

Anderson, Kym, & Hayami, Yujiro. 1986. *The Political Economy of Agricultural Protection* (Sydney: Allen & Unwin).

Anderson, Terry L. 1983. *Water Crisis: Ending the Policy Drought* (Baltimore: John Hopkins University Press).

Anderson, Terry L. & Leal, Donald R. 1991. *Free Market Environmentalism* (Boulder, CO: Westview Press).

Antle, John M., & Capalbo, Susan M. 1986. "Pesticides and Public Policy: A Program for Research and Policy Analysis." In *Agriculture and the Environment.* Tim. T. Phipps, Pierre R. Crosson, & Kent A. Price, eds. (Washington, DC: National Center for Food and Agricultural Policy and Resources for the Future), 155–174.

Armstrong, Bill. 1990. "Campaign Unreform." *Wall Street Journal* (New York: June 8), A10.

Atlanta Journal. 1990. "Giveaway Farm Bill Proves Congress Has No Discipline." Editorial (Atlanta: July 27), A10.

Backlund, V.L., & Hoppes, R. R. 1984. "Status of Soil Salinity in California." *California Agriculture, 38* (10) (October), 8–9.

Baden, John, & Stroup, Richard L. 1981. "Transgenerational Equity and Natural Resources: Or, Too Bad We Don't Have Coal Rangers." In *Bureaucracy vs. Environment,* John Baden and Richard L. Stroup, eds. (Ann Arbor: University of Michigan Press), 203–216.

Ballenger, Nicole. 1988. "PSEs: What They Are and Their Role in Trade Negotiations." *Choices* (First quarter), 36.

Balzar, John. 1994. "Congress Term Limits Set by Initiative Voided," *Los Angeles Times* (February 11), A24.

Barkley, Andrew P. 1990. "The Determinants of the Migration of Labor out of Agriculture in the United States, 1940–85." *American Journal of Agricultural Economics, 72* (3) (August), 567–573.

Barnaby, G.A., & Skees, Jerry. 1990. "Public Policy for Catastrophic Yield Risk: An Alternative Crop Insurance Program." *Choices* (Second quarter), 7–9.

Barro, Robert J. 1991. "A Free Marketeer's Case Against Term Limits." *Wall Street Journal* (New York: December 24), A14.

Barry, Peter J. 1980. "Capital Asset Pricing and Farm Real Estate." *American Journal of Agricultural Economics, 62* (3) (August), 549–553.

______. 1985. "Needed Changes in the Farmers Home Administration Lending Programs." *American Journal of Agricultural Economics, 67* (2) (May).

Baumes, Harry S., Jr., & Spitze, R. G. F. 1990. "Current U.S. Economic Environment for Agriculture and Food Policy Development." In *Agricultural and Food Policy Issues for the 1990s* (Urbana: University of Illinois Press, April).

Baumol, William J. 1982. "Contestable Markets: An Uprising in the Theory of Industry Structure." *American Economic Review, 71* (2) (March), 1–15.

Beck, L. A. 1984. "Case History: San Joaquin Valley." *California Agriculture, 38* (10) (October), 16–17.

Becker, Gary S. 1983. "A Theory of Competition Among Pressure Groups for Political Influence." *Quarterly Journal of Economics, 98,* 371–401.

Becker, Geoffrey S. 1986. *Farm Support Programs: Cost Considerations,* 86-1012 ENR (Washington, DC: Congressional Research Service, Library of Congress, November).

Belongia, Michael T., & Gilbert, R. Alton. 1990. "The Effects of Federal Credit Programs on Farm Output." *American Journal of Agricultural Economics, 72* (3) (August), 769–773.

Berke, Richard L. 1990a. "Altered Campaign Bill Aids Senators." *New York Times* (New York: May 11), A20.

______. 1990b. "Senate Campaign Reform vs. a Senate Campaign." *New York Times* (Section 4) (New York: May 13), 4.

______. 1990c. "Study Criticizes Proposed Election Spending Limits." *New York Times* (New York: May 19), A24.

Biggar, J. W., Rolston, D. E., & Nielsen, D. R. 1984. "Transport of Salts by Water." *California Agriculture, 38* (10) (October), 10–11.

Birnbaum, Jeffrey H., & Abramson, Jill. 1990. "Dole, Despite Budget-Cutter Image, Seeks Tax Break Aiding Company Tied to Him." *Wall Street Journal* (New York: September 28), A18.

Blandford, David, & Dewbre, Joe. 1994. "Structural Adjustment and Learning to Live without Subsidies." Paper presented at the annual meeting of the American Agricultural Economics Association, San Diego, CA, August 8.

Bolling, Christine, Caplan, Lois, Coyle, William, & Deaton, Larry. 1990. "Japan." In *Estimates of Producer and Consumer Subsidy Equivalents,* Statistical Bulletin no. 803, Alan J. Webb, Michael Lopez, & Renata Penn, eds. (Washington, DC: U.S. Department of Agriculture, Economic Research Service, April), 160–176.

Bonnen, James T. 1984. "U.S. Agriculture, Instability and National Political Institutions: The Shift from Representative to Participatory Democracy." In *United States Agricultural Policy for 1985 and Beyond* (Tucson, AZ: Department of Agricultural Economics, University of Arizona).

Bosworth, Barry P., Carron, Andrew S., & Rhyne, Elisabeth H. 1987. *The Economics of Federal Credit Programs* (Washington, DC: Brookings Institution).

Bovard, James. 1989. *The Farm Fiasco* (San Francisco: Institute for Contemporary Studies Press).

______. 1990a. *Update 7* (Washington, DC: Competitive Enterprise Institute, July).

______. 1990b. "Our Disastrously Archaic Farm Policy." *New York Times* (Section 3) (New York: July 8), 11.

______. 1991a. "The Great Dairy Heist." *Free Market, 9* (5) (May), 6–7.

______. 1991b. "America's Suicidal Farm Export Subsidies." *Cato Policy Report, 13* (6) (Washington, DC: Nov./Dec.), 1, 10, 11, 12.

Brabenstott, Mark & Morris, Charles. 1989. "New Sources of Financing for Rural Development." *American Journal of Agricultural Economics, 71* (5) (December), 1314–1320.

Brookes, Warren. 1990. *Revenge of the Killer Watermelon: California's Big Green Initiative.* Speech given before the Pacific Research Institute for Public Policy (San Francisco: July 26).

Browne, William. 1988. *Private Interest, Public Policy, and American Agriculture.* (Lawrence: University Press of Kansas).

Browne, William P., & Bonnen, James T. 1989. "Why Is Agricultural Policy So Difficult to Reform?" In *The Political Economy of U.S. Agriculture: Challenges for the 1990s,* Carol S. Kramer, ed. (Washington, DC: Resources for the Future).

Buchanan, James M. 1959. "Positive Economics, Welfare Economics, and Political Economy." *Journal of Law and Economics, 2* (October), 1125–1138.

Buchanan, James M., & Tullock, Gordon. 1965. *The Calculus of Consent: Logical Foundations of Constitutional Democracy* (Ann Arbor: University of Michigan Press).

Burau, R. G. 1985. "Environmental Chemistry of Selenium." *California Agriculture, 39* (7–8) (July-August), 16–18.

Burton, Thomas M. 1990. "Many Farmers Harvest Government Subsidies in Violation of Law." *Wall Street Journal* (New York: May 8), A1.

Calmes, Jackie. 1990. "Dole Secures Key Role in Bargaining as Gringrich Deals Himself Out in House." *Wall Street Journal* (New York: October 29), A5.

______. 1991. "Despite the Lure of a Lucrative Legal Loophole, For Senior Lawmakers Likely to Retire Next Year." *Wall Street Journal* (New York: March 28), A16.

Carson, Rachel. 1962. *Silent Spring* (Boston: Houghton Mifflin).

Carter, Harold O., & Nuckton, Carol Frank (eds.). 1990. *California's Central Valley—Confluence of Change* (Davis: University of California Agricultural Issues Center).

Carter, Hodding III. 1990. "Limits on Congressional Terms: A Cure Worse Than the Disease." *Wall Street Journal* (New York: October 4), A21.

Carter, L. G. 1985a. "Process Removes Selenium." *Fresno Bee* (September 4).

______. 1985b. "Seepage May Be the Source of Selenium in Canal." *Fresno Bee* (September 15).

Chavas, Jean-Paul, & Holt, Matthew T. 1990. "Acreage Decisions under Risk: The

Case of Corn and Soybeans." *American Journal of Agricultural Economics, 72* (3) (August), 529–538.

Chicago Board of Trade. 1986. *Agricultural Options: A New Direction in Risk Management and Marketing for Farmers* (Chicago).

______. 1990. "Ag Options Pilot Program Update." *Commodity Futures Profession,* 3–4.

CH2M Hill, Inc. 1986. "Reverse Osmosis Desalting of San Luis Drain." *Conceptual Level Study, Final Report* (Emeryville, CA).

Clark, E. C. II, Haverkamp, J. A., & Chapman, W. 1985. *Eroding Soils: The Off-Farm Impacts* (Washington, DC: The Conservation Foundation).

Conley, Howard. 1990. "Federal Budget Implications for 1990 Agricultural and Food Policy." *Agricultural and Food Policy Issues for the 1990s* (Urbana: University of Illinois Press, Agricultural Experiment Station, April).

Coppock, Ray, Hagan, Robert, & Wood, William. 1982. Introduction. In *Economic Development and Environmental Quality,* Ernest A. Engelbert, ed. (Berkeley: Institute of Governmental Studies, University of California).

Courant, Paul N., & Gramlich, Edward M. 1986. *Federal Budget Deficits: America's Great Consumption Binge* (New York: Prentice-Hall).

Crane, Edward H. 1990a. "Should Terms in Office Be Limited?" *Arkansas Gazette* (September 30).

______. 1990b. "Term Limits for a Citizen Legislature." *Vital Speeches of the Day, 62* (5) (December 15).

Crosson, Pierre R. 1984. "New Perspectives on Soil Conservation Policy." *Journal of Soil and Water Conservation* (July-August), 222–225.

______. 1986a. "Soil Conservation, It's Not the Farmers Who Are Most Affected by Erosion." *Choices* (Premier issue), 33–36.

______. 1986b. "Soil Erosion and Policy Issues." In *Agriculture and the Environment,* Tim T. Phipps, Pierre R. Crosson, & Kent A. Price, eds. (Washington, DC: National Center for Food and Agricultural Policy and Resources for the Future), 35–74.

______. 1991. "Cropland and Soils: Past Performance and Policy Challenges." *America's Renewable Resources,* Kenneth D. Frederick & Roger A. Sedjo, eds. (Washington, DC: Resources for the Future), 169–204.

Crovitz, L. Gordon. 1991. "Lawmakers Sue for Their Jobs—Another Reason for Term Limits." *Wall Street Journal* (New York: June 19), A15.

Davis, Bob. 1991. "GATT Talks Resume, with France and India Calling Many of Shots." *Wall Street Journal* (New York: Monday, January 13), A8.

______. 1992b. "Tough Trade Issues Remain as EC, U.S. Agree on Agriculture," *Wall Street Journal* (New York: January 13), A8.

Davis, Bob, & Ingrassia, Lawrence. 1993. "After Years of Talks, GATT Is at Last Ready to Sign Off on a Pact," *Wall Street Journal* (New York: December 15), A1.

Davis, Phillip A. 1992a. "An Agency in Transition," *Congressional Quarterly* (Cover story, Government and Commerce: March).

______. 1992b. "Congress Seeks to Rechannel Flow of Water in the West," *Congressional Quarterly* (Cover story, Government and Commerce: March 7).

De Gorter, Harry & Zilberman, David. 1990. "On the Political Economy of Public Good Inputs." *American Journal of Agricultural Economics, 72* (1) (February), 131–137.

De Jouvenel, Bertrand. 1952. *The Ethics of Redistribution* (Cambridge: Cambridge University Press).

Deverel, S. J., Gilliom, R. J., Fujii, R., Izbicki, J. A., & Fields, J. C. 1984. "Areal Distribution of Selenium and Other Inorganic Constituents in Shallow Ground Water of the San Luis Drain Service Area, San Joaquin Valley, California: A Preliminary Study." *Water Resources Investigation Report 84-4319* (Washington, DC: U.S. Department of the Interior, Geological Survey).

Dole, Bob. 1990. "Same Old Hatchet Job." *Wall Street Journal* (New York: October 4), A21.

Downs, Anthony. 1957. *An Economic Theory of Democracy* (New York: Harper & Row).

Du Bois, Martin & Wolf, Julie. 1992. "EC Revamps Its Farm Policy on Subsidies." *Wall Street Journal* (New York: May 22), A3.

Du Pont, Pete. 1990. "Shoot the Sequester Arrow, Mr. President." *Wall Street Journal* (New York: October 12), A14.

Economist. 1992. "A Survey of Agriculture" (December 12), 3–18.

Esseks, J. Dixon, & Kraft, Steven E. 1984. "Farmers' Attitudes on Policies to Control Soil Erosion: Results of an Attitudinal Survey in Six Diverse Areas." Unpublished paper presented at the meeting of the American Agricultural Economics Association, Ithaca, NY, August 5.

Fabre, Raymond, & Rucker, Randal R. 1978. "Lease Rates and Sale Prices for Peanut Poundage Quota: 1978–1987," *Economics Information Report,* no. 78 (Raleigh: North Carolina State University, February).

Feltenstein, Andrew. 1989. "Agricultural Policies and the U.S. Federal Budget and U.S. Trade Deficit." In *Macroeconomic Consequences of Farm Support Policies,* Andrew B. Stoeckel, David Vincent, & Sandy Cuthbertson, eds. (Durham, NC: Duke University Press), 200–221.

Fisher, Eric, & de Gorter, Harry. 1992. "The International Effects of U.S. Farm Subsidies," *American Journal of Agricultural Economics, 74* (2), 258–267.

Fort, Rodney D., & Baden, John. 1981. "The Federal Treasury as a Common Pool Resource and the Development of a Predatory Bureaucracy." In *Bureaucracy vs. Environment,* John Baden & Richard L Stroup, eds. (Ann Arbor: University of Michigan Press), 9–21.

Frederick, Kenneth D. 1986. "Comment and Discussion" of paper by Young and Horner. In *Agricultural and the Environment,* Tim T. Phipps, Pierre R. Crosson, & Kent A. Price, eds. (Washington, DC: National Center for Food and Agricultural Policy and Resources for the Future), 117–122.

Fund, John H. 1990. "Term Limitation: An Idea Whose Time Has Come." *Policy Analysis,* no. 141 (Washington, DC: Cato Institute, October 30).

______. 1991. "There's No Debate—The Career Congress Lives." *Wall Street Journal* (New York: April 11), A14.

Galper, Harvey and Dennis Zimmerman. 1977. "Preferential Taxation and Portfolio Choice: Some Empirical Evidence." *National Tax Journal, 30,* 387–397.

Gardner, B. Delworth. 1962. "Transfer Restrictions and Misallocation in Grazing Public Range." *Journal of Farm Economics, 44* (1) (February), 50–64.

______. 1979. "Economic Issues in Ground Water Management." *Proceedings, Twelfth Biennial Conference on Groundwater.* Report no. 45 (Davis: Water Resources Center, University of California).

______. 1981. "The Water Management Crunch: An Economic Perspective." In *Economics, Ethics, and Ecology: Roots of Productive Conservation,* Walter E. Jeske, ed. (Ankeny, IA: Soil Conservation Society of America), 67–77.

______. 1983. "Water Pricing and Rent Seeking in California Agriculture." In *Water Rights,* Terry L. Anderson, ed. (San Francisco: Pacific Research Institute), 83–114.

______. 1984. "The Market Allocation of Land to Agriculture." In *The Vanishing Farmland Crisis,* John Baden, ed. (Lawrence: University Press of Kansas), 17–30.

______. 1985. "Government and Conservation: A Case of Good Intentions but Misplaced Incentives." In *Government and Conservation: What Should Be the Role of Government.* Proceedings from a public policy education program sponsored by the Indiana Association of Soil and Water Conservation Districts and the Indiana Cooperative Extension Service at Purdue University (West Lafayette: February).

______. 1986. "Institutional Impediments to Efficient Water Allocation." Symposium: Water Resources and Public Policy. *Policy Studies Review, 5* (2), 363–365.

______. 1987. "Assessing Salinity and Toxic-Element Disposal Problems in the San Joaquin Valley." *Applied Agricultural Research, 2* (1), 20–31.

______. 1989. "A Proposal for Reallocation of Federal Grazing—Revisited." *Rangelands, 11* (3) (June), 107–111.

______. 1991. "Rangeland Resources: Changing Uses and Productivity." *American's Renewable Resources,* K. Frederick and R. Sedjo, eds. (Washington, DC: Resources for the Future), 123–165.

______. 1993. "Environmental Crises in Perspective," *Family Perspectives, 27* (3), (Provo: Center for Studies of the Family, Brigham Young University), 195–214.

Gardner, B. Delworth, & Howitt, Richard E. 1986. "Modeling Production and Resource Interrelationships Among California Crops in Response to the 1985 Food Security Act." In *Impacts of Farm Policy and Technological Change on U.S. and California Agriculture,* Harold O. Carter, ed. (Davis: Agricultural Issues Center, University of California), 271–292.

Gardner, B. Delworth, Howitt, Richard E, & Goodman, Charles. 1990. *Impacts on California Agriculture of a Ban on Rice Straw Burning.* Giannini Foundation Information Series no. 90-1. (Berkeley: Division of Agriculture and Natural Resources, University of California: October), 1–23.

Gardner, B. Delworth, & Huffaker, Ray G. 1988. "Cutting the Loss from Federal Irrigation Water Subsidies." *Choices* (Fourth quarter), 25–27.

Gardner, B. Delworth, & Nuckton, Carole Frank. 1979. "Factors Affecting Agricultural Land Prices." *California Agriculture* (Berkeley: University of California Division of Agricultural Sciences, January), 4–7.

Gardner, Bruce L. 1977. "Commodity Options for Agriculture." *American Journal of Agricultural Economics, 59* (5) (December), 986–992.

______. 1981. *The Governing of Agriculture* (Lawrence, KS: Regents Press of Kansas).

______. 1987a. "Causes of U.S. Farm Commodity Programs." *Journal of Political Economy, 95,* 290–310.

______. 1987b. *The Economics of Agricultural Policies* (New York: Macmillan).

Gray, John. 1990. "Forward." In *The Ethics of Redistribution,* Bertrand de Jouvenel (Indianapolis, IN: Liberty Press), xvii.

Green, Robert, & Baumes, Harry. 1989. "Supply Control Programs for Agriculture." *Agricultural-Food Policy Review: U.S. Agricultural Policies in a Changing World,* Agricultural Economic Report no. 620 (Washington, DC: U.S. Department of Agriculture, Economic Research Service, November).

Gugliotta, Guy. 1990a. "House Retains Crop Subsidies for Rich." *Washington Post* (Washington, DC: July 26), A6.

______. 1990b. "Down on the Farm: The Other Depression in Rural America." *Washington Post* (Washington, DC: November 18), A18.

Gustafson, Cole R. 1989. "Credit Evaluation: Monitoring the Financial Health of Agriculture." *Journal of Agricultural Economics, 71* (5) (December), 1145–1151.

Gutfeld, Rose. 1990. "EPA Says Over 50% of U.S. Wells Contain Nitrate." *Wall Street Journal* (New York: November 14), A16.

Gwartney, James D., & Wagner, Richard E. 1988a. "Public Choice and the Conduct of Representative Government." In *Public Choice and Constitutional Economics,* James D. Gwartney & Richard E. Wagner, eds. (Greenwich, CT: JAI Press).

______. 1988b. "The Public Choice Revolution." *Intercollegiate Review, 23* (2) (Spring), 17–26.

Halcrow, Harold G. 1984. *Agricultural Policy Analysis* (New York: McGraw-Hill).

Hall, Warren A. 1974. "Statement: Salty Solutions to Salty Problems." *Salinity in Water Resources* (Boulder, CO: Merriman).

Hancock, L. F. 1984. *Testimony, Hearings, California Water Resources Control Board* (Sacramento: U.S. Department of the Interior, Bureau of Reclamation, October).

Hardin, Clifford M. 1986. "Congress Is the Problem." *Choices* (January), 6–10.

Harwood, John, & Rogers, David. 1993. "House Clears Campaign Rule Changes, but Skirts New Curbs on Lobbyists' Gifts," *Wall Street Journal* (New York: November 23), A18.

Hatcher, Charles. 1991. "There's No Dearth of U.S. Peanuts." *Deseret News* (Salt Lake City, UT: April 27), A6.

Hayek, F. A. 1945. "The Use of Knowledge in Society." *American Economic Review, 35* (4) (September), 519–529.

Heinrichs, T. 1985. "Land Values May Have Hit Bottom." *California-Arizona Farm Press, 7* (47) (November 23).

Henderson, Rick. 1991. "The Swamp Thing." *Reason* (April), 30–35.
Hertel, Thomas W. 1990. "Ten Truths about Supply Control." *Agricultural Policies in a New Decade* (Washington, DC: Resources for the Future and National Planning Association), 152–169.
Hess, Charles. 1990. Statement in *California's Central Valley—Confluence of Change,* Harold O. Carter, & Carole Frank Nuckton, eds. (Davis: University of California Agricultural Issues Center).
Heyne, Paul. 1980. *The Economic Way of Thinking* (Chicago: Science Research Associates).
Higgs, Robert. 1987. *Crisis and Leviathan: Critical Episodes in the Growth of American Government* (New York: Oxford University Press).
Hoffman, Elizabeth, & Libecap, Gary D. 1991. "Institutional Choice and the Development of U.S. Agricultural Policies in the 1920s." Unpublished paper presented at Brigham Young University.
Horwich, George. 1990. "Disasters and Market Response." *Cato Journal, 9* (3) (Winter), 497–530.
Houck, James. 1990. "Stabilization in Agriculture: An Uncertain Quest." *Agricultural Policies in a New Decade* (Washington, DC: Resources for the Future and National Planning Association), 173–199.
Howitt, Richard E., Mann, Dean E., & Vaux, H. J., Jr. 1982. "The Economics of Water Allocation." In *Competition for California Water,* Ernest A. Engelbert & Ann Foley Scheuring, eds. (Berkeley: University of California Press), 133–162.
Huffaker, Ray G., & Gardner, B. Delworth. 1986a. "The Distribution of Economic Rents Arising from Subsidized Water When Land is Leased." *American Journal of Agricultural Economics, 68* (2) (May), 306–312.
______. 1986b. "The 'Hammer' Clause of the Reclamation Reform Act of 1982." *Natural Resources Journal, 26* (1) (Winter), 41–68.
Ingersoll, Bruce. 1990a. "Peanut Quota System Comes Under Attack for Distorting Market." *Wall Street Journal* (New York: May 1), A1.
______. 1990b. "Senate Adopts 5-Year Farm Bill of $54 Billion." *Wall Street Journal* (New York: July 30), A12.
______. 1990c. "U.S. Pays Record Subsidies to Boost Grain Sales to Counter EC Competition." *Wall Street Journal* (New York: Monday, September 17), C12.
______. 1991. "Nation's Farmers to Expand Production of Most Major Crops in 1991, U.S. Says." *Wall Street Journal* (New York: February 12), A2.
Ingrassia, Lawrence. 1993. "Developing Nations Feel Shortchanged by GATT," *Wall Street Journal* (New York: December 15), A6.
Irwin, Scott H., Forster, D. Lynn, & Sherrick, Bruce J. 1988. "Returns to Farm Real Estate Revisited." *American Journal of Agricultural Economics, 70* (3) (August), 580–588.
Irwin, Scott H., & Hanson, Gregory D. 1989. "Farmland: A Good Investment." *Choices* (Fourth quarter), 22–23.
Jackson, Brooks. 1988. *Honest Graft* (New York: Knopf).
______. 1990a. "Republicans Panel Illegally Funneled Funds, Judge Says." *Wall Street Journal* (New York: January 26), A16.

______. 1990b. "Senate Takes Turn in Ethics Hot Seat with Sticky Case of the 'Sorry Seven.'" *Wall Street Journal* (New York: January 30), A20.

______. 1990c. "Cranston's Use of Voter-Registration Charities to Benefit Campaign Highlights Gray Legal Area." *Wall Street Journal* (New York: March 1), A18.

Jaroslavsky, Rich. 1990. "Washington Wire." *Wall Street Journal* (New York: October 5), A1.

Jessen, E. James. 1991. "The Truth About Wetlands," *Pennsylvania Landowner, 4* (1) (February), 4–5.

Johnson, D. Gale. 1973. *World Agriculture in Disarray* (London: Fontana/Collins).

Jordan, Brenda & Tweeten, Luther. 1987. "Public Perceptions of Farm Problems," *Research Report P-894* (Stillwater: Agricultural Experiment Station, Division of Agriculture, Oklahoma State University, June), 1–10.

Just, Richard E., & Antle, John M. 1990. "Interactions Between Agricultural and Environmental Policies: A Conceptual Framework." *American Economic Review, 80* (2) (May), 197–202.

Kennedy, Joseph, & Visser, Jon. 1990. "An Introduction to U.S. Agricultural Programs." *Agricultural Policies in a New Decade* (Washington, DC: Resources for the Future and National Planning Association), 27–46.

Kiewiet, D. Roderick, & McCubbins, Mathew D. 1989. "Parties, Committees, and Policymaking in the U.S. Congress: A Comment on the Role of Transaction Costs as Determinants of Governance Structure of Political Institutions." *Journal of Institutional and Theoretical Economics, 145*, 676–685.

Kilman, Scott. 1990. "Seeds of Change: Farmers, Eyeing Costs and the Environment, Limit Use of Chemicals." *Wall Street Journal* (New York: May 30), A1.

______. 1991. "Agriculture: A New Season." *Wall Street Journal* (New York: April 18), A1.

______. 1992. "U.S. Farmers Get Modest Shot in the Arm from Subsidy Compromise with the EC." *Wall Street Journal* (New York: November 23), A6.

Kilmer, Richard L., & Ambruster, Walter J. (eds.). 1987. *Economic Efficiency in Agricultural and Food Marketing,* Farm Foundation and Institute of Food and Agricultural Sciences of the University of Florida (Ames: Iowa State University Press).

Knutson, Ronald D., Penn, J. B., & Boehm, William T. 1983. *Agricultural and Food Policy* (Englewood Cliffs, NJ: Prentice-Hall).

Kraft, Steven E. 1978. "Macro and Micro Approaches to the Study of Soil Loss." *Journal of Soil and Water Conservation, 33* (5), 238–239.

Kramer, Randall A., & Shabman, Leonard A. 1986. "Incentives for Agricultural Development of U.S. Wetlands: A Case Study of the Bottomland Hardwoods of the Lower Mississippi River Valley." In *Agriculture and the Environment,* Tim T. Phipps, Pierre R. Crosson, & Kent A. Price, eds. (Washington, DC: National Center for Food and Agricultural Policy and Resources for the Future), 175–204.

Ladd, Everell Carll. 1986. *The Ladd Report* no. 4 (New York: W.W. Norton).

LaDue, Eddy L. 1990. "Moral Hazard in Federal Farm Lending." *American Journal of Agricultural Economics, 72* (3) (August), 774–779.

Lamb, Eugene. 1986. "Busters Can Lose Farm Program Benefits." *Choices* (Fourth quarter), 29.

Leal, Don. 1990. "A Bird's-Eye View of Destructive Farm Policy." *Wall Street Journal* (New York: March 1), A16.

Lee, Dwight R., & McKenzie, Richard B. 1987. *Regulating Government: A Preface to Constitution Economics* (Lexington: Lexington Books).

Lee, Dwight R., & Orr, Daniel. 1980. "Two Laws of Survival for Ascriptive Government Policies." In *Toward a Theory of the Rent-Seeking Society,* James M. Buchanan, Robert D. Tollison, & Gordon Tullock, eds. (College Station: Texas A&M University Press).

Lee, John. 1990. "Conservation Compliance: An Answer to Environmental Concerns." In *Implementing Agricultural Policies to Achieve Environmental Objectives: Lessons for the 1990s.* Stephen B. Lovejoy & Kenda M. Resler, eds. (West Lafayette, IN: Purdue University, Resource Policy Consortium, July).

Lee, L. K., & Nielsen, G. 1988. "Groundwater: Is It Safe to Drink?" *Choices,* (3), 4–7.

Legler, Vic. 1990. "Landowner's Rights." Unpublished address to Landowners Association of North Dakota, February 7.

Lichtenberg, Erik. 1989. "Land Quality, Irrigation Development and Cropping Patterns in the Northern High Plains." *American Journal of Agricultural Economics* (February), 187–194.

Long, James E. 1990. "Farming the Tax Code: The Impact of High Marginal Tax Rates on Agricultural Tax Shelters." *American Journal of Agricultural Economics, 72* (1) (February), 1–12.

Lowi, Theodore J. 1979. *The End of Liberalism,* 2d ed. (New York: W.W. Norton).

Luh, Yir-Hueih, & Stefanou, Spiro E. 1991. "Productivity Growth in U.S. Agricultural Under Dynamic Adjustment," *American Journal of Agricultural Economics, 73* (4) (November), 1117–1124.

Luttrell, Clifton B. 1989. *The High Cost of Farm Welfare* (Washington, DC: Cato Institute Press).

Mayer, Leo V. 1991. "Putting Balance in U.S. Commodity Programs." *Choices* (First quarter), 30–32.

McKenzie, Richard B. 1991. "The Retreat of the Elderly Welfare State." *Wall Street Journal* (New York: March 12), A24.

Miller, James C. III. 1991. "Cut Federal Spending—Limit Congressional Terms." *Wall Street Journal* (New York: August 19), A8.

Mishan, E. J. 1976. "Loss of Life and Limb." *Cost-Benefit Analysis* (New York: Praeger).

National Academy of Sciences and National Academy of Engineering. 1973. *Water Quality Criteria,* EPA R3 73 033 (Washington, DC: U.S. Environmental Protection Agency), 1–594.

National Center for Food and Agricultural Policy. 1990. *Gleanings, 1* (3) (Washington, DC: Resources for the Future, Spring).

National Crop Insurance Service. 1990. "Crop Insurance Programs in North Dakota Counties for 1990 Crop Year." Crop Insurance Services no. 760.

Neal, Thomas. 1992. "Agricultural Options-on-Futures: Tools that Can Reduce Your Rish," *Journal of Agricultural Lending, 5* (3) (Spring), 21–24.

New York Times. 1990. "Not to a Balanced Budget Amendment." Editorial (New York: July 17), A20.

Noel, Jay E., Gardner, B. Delworth, & Moore, Charles V. 1980. "Optimal Regional Conjunctive Water Management." *American Journal of Agricultural Economics, 63* (3) (August) 489–498.

Nuckton, Carole Frank, & Gardner, B. Delworth. 1980. "Public Investment in Research: A Lesson from Agriculture." *Journal of the American Society of Farm Managers and Rural Appraisers, 44* (2) (October), 28–31.

______. 1992. "Deficiency Payments More Fair to Some than to Others?" *Choices* (Second quarter), 25.

Oldaker, William C. 1982. "Rules of the Game." In *PACs Americana,* Edward Roeder, ed. (Washington, DC: Sunshine Services), xvii–xxiv.

Olen, Helaine. 1990. "FEC Weighs Outlawing PACs Operated by Concerns Over 50% Foreign-Owned." *Wall Street Journal* (New York: November 7), A16.

Oliver, Charles. 1991. "Cleaning House." *Reason* (May), 20.

Olson, Mancur. 1965. *The Logic of Collective Action* (Cambridge, MA: Harvard University Press).

______. 1982. *The Rise and Decline of Nations* (New Haven, CT: Yale University Press).

______. 1990. "Agricultural Exploitation and Subsidization." *Choices* (Fourth quarter), 8–11.

Osteen, Craig D., & Szmedra, Phillip I. 1989. *Agricultural Pesticide Use Trends and Policy Issues* (Washington, DC: U.S. Department of Agriculture).

Paarlberg, Robert L. 1989. "The Political Economy of American Agricultural Policy: Three Approaches." *American Journal of Agricultural Economics, 71* (5) (December), 1157–1164.

______. 1990. "The Mysterious Popularity of EEP." *Choices* (Second quarter), 14–17.

Parnell, Jack C. 1990. "Food Safety: Some Changes are Needed." *Choices* (Third quarter), 4–7.

Pasour, E. C., Jr. 1989. *Agriculture and the State: Market Processes and Bureaucracy* (San Francisco: Independent Institute).

______. 1990. *Agriculture and the State: Market Processes and Bureaucracy* (New York: Holmes & Meier).

Pattison, Scott. 1991. "End Quota on Imported Peanuts." *Deseret News* (Salt Lake City, UT: April 27), A6.

Pauling, Linus. 1984. "Orthomolecular Nutrition." *Pivot Original Health Book* (New Canaan, CT: Keats).

Peltzman, Sam. 1976. "Toward a More General Theory of Regulation." *Journal of Law and Economics,* 211–241.

Perry, Janet, Schreiner, Dean, & Tweeten, Luther. 1991. "Analysis of Characteristics of Farmers Who Have Curtailed or Ceased Farming in Oklahoma." *Research Report P-919* (Stillwater: Oklahoma Agricultural Experiment Station), 1–33.

Phipps, Tim T. 1982. "The Determination of Price in the U.S. Agricultural Land Market." Ph.D. dissertation (University of California, Davis).

______. 1988. "The Conservation Reserve and Water Quality: Results of a Simulation Study." Unpublished paper presented at the annual meetings of the American Agricultural Economics Association, Knoxville, Tennessee, August.

Phipps, Tim T., & Crosson, Pierre R. 1986. "Agriculture and the Environment: An Overview," In *Agriculture and the Environment*, Tim T. Phipps, Pierre R. Crosson, & Kent A. Price, eds. (Washington, DC: National Center for Food and Agricultural Policy and Resources for the Future), 3–34.

Pope, Arden III. 1987. "Rangeland and Romance." *Choices* (Fourth quarter), 24–25.

Pope, Rulon D. 1986. "Agricultural Factions." *American Journal of Agricultural Economics, 68* (5) (December), 1096–1101.

Powers, Mark J. 1973. *Getting Started in Commodity Futures Trading* (Columbia, MD: Investor Publications).

Powledge, Fred. 1982. *Water: The Nature, Uses, and Future of our Most Precious and Abused Resource* (New York: Farrar, Straus Giroux).

Rasky, Susan F. 1990. "War of Numbers on Budget Reopens." *New York Times* (New York: January 25). B9.

Rausser, Gordon C., & Foster, William E. 1990. "Political Preferences Functions and Public Policy Reform." *American Journal of Agricultural Economics, 72* (3) (August), 641–652.

Rausser, Gordon C., & Zusman, Pinhas. 1992. "Public Policy and Constitutional Prescription," *American Journal of Agricultural Economics, 74* (2), 247–257.

Reichelderfer, Katherine H. 1990. "Agriculture and Water Quality: A Policy Dilemma." In *Agricultural and Food Policy Issues for the 1990s* (Urbana: University of Illinois, Agricultural Experiment Station, April).

Reichelderfer, Katherine, & Boggess, William G. 1988. "Government Decision Making and Program Performance: The Case of the Conservation Program." *American Journal of Agricultural Economics, 70* (1) (February), 1–11.

Reilly, William K. 1984. "Soils, Society, and Sustainability." *Journal of Soil and Water Conservation* (September-October), 286–288.

Rieselbach, Leroy N. 1986. "Reforming Congress: Philosophy, Politics, Problems, Prospects." In *Bureaucratic and Governmental Reform*, Donald J. Calista, ed. (Greenwich, CT: JAI Press).

Robbins, Lionel. 1932. *An Essay on the Nature and Significance of Economic Science* (London: Macmillan).

Robbins, Roy M. 1976. *Our Landed Heritage: The Public Domain, 1776-1970*, rev. ed. (Lincoln: University of Nebraska Press).

Robinson, Sherman, Kilkenny, Maureen, & Adelman, Irma. 1989. "The Effect of Agricultural Trade Liberalization on the US Economy: Projections to 1991." In *Macroeconomic Consequences of Farm Support Policies*, Andrew B. Stoeckel, David Vincent, & Sandy Cuthbertson, eds. (Durham, NC: Duke University Press), 222–259.

Roningen, V. & Dixit, P. M. 1988. "Economic Implications of Agricultural Policy Reform in Industrial Market Economics." Paper prepared for International Agricultural Trade Research Consortium Symposium, *Bringing Agriculture into the GATT* (Annapolis, MD: August).

Rosenbaum, David E. 1990. "Budget-Deficit Law is Facing Change." *New York Times* (New York: May 19), A10.

Rossmiller, George E. 1990. "The Effect of the 1990 U.S. Farm Bill on Agricultural Trade." Paper presented at Allied Social Science Associations Meetings, Washington, DC, December 28.

Rothenberg, Stuart. 1990. "The Year Congress Busts Open." *Wall Street Journal* (New York: July 24), A14.

Rucker, Randal R. 1990. "The Effects of State Farm Relief Legislation on Private Lenders and Borrowers: The Experience of the 1930s." *American Journal of Agricultural Economics, 72* (1) (February), 24–33.

Rucker, Randal R., & Alston, Lee J. 1987. "Farm Failures and Government Intervention: A Case Study of the 1930s." *American Economic Review, 77* (4) (September), 724–730.

Rucker, Randal R., & Thurman, Walter N. 1990. "The Economic Effects of Supply Controls: The Simple Analytics of the U.S. Peanut Program," *Journal of Law and Economics, 33* (October), 483–515.

Rucker, Randal R., Thurman, Walter N., & Sumner, Daniel A. 1991. "Production Rights with Limited Transferability: A Case Study of the U.S. Tobacco and Peanut Programs." Unpublished paper, North Carolina State University, March 27.

Ruttan, Vernon W. 1990. "International Food Aid: Interest Groups and Clients." *Choices* (Third quarter), 12–15.

Sabato, Larry. 1984. *PAC Power* (New York: W.W. Norton).

Saliba, Bonnie, & Bromley, Daniel. 1984. "Empirical Analysis of the Relationship between Soil Conservation and Farmland Characteristics." Unpublished paper presented at the meeting of the American Agricultural Economics Association, Ithaca, New York, August 5.

Sanderson, Fred H. 1990. "Agricultural Protectionism in the Industrialized World." *Resources* 100 (Washington, DC: Resources for the Future, Summer), 6–9.

Sands, Laura. 1991. "High Sugar Subsidies Sour Soybean Farmers." *Farm Journal* central ed. (Mid-January), G8.

Savage, James. 1988. *Balanced Budgets and American Politics* (London: Cornell University Press).

Sawhill, John C. 1991. "Using Debt to Save the Rainforest." Nature Conservancy (January/February), 3.

Schelling, Thomas C. 1992. "Some Economics of Global Warming." *American Economic Review, 82* (1) (March), 1–14.

Schotland, Roy A. 1990. "The Perversity of Campaign Reform." *Wall Street Journal* (New York: May 15), A20.

Schultz, Theodore W. 1945. *Agriculture in an Unstable Economy* (New York: McGraw-Hill).

______. 1984. "The Dynamics of Soil Erosion in the United States." In *The Vanishing Farmland Crisis,* John Baden, ed. (Lawrence: University Press of Kansas), 45–58.

Shaffer, James D., & Whittaker, Gerald W. 1990a. "Average Farm Incomes: They're Highest Among Farmers Receiving the Largest Direct Government Payments." *Choices* (Second quarter), 30–31.

______. 1990b. "The Distribution of Direct Payments to Farm Operators in 1987 and 1988: Some Questions About Policy Objectives." Discussion Paper FAP90-08 (Washington DC: National Center for Food and Agricultural Policy and Resources for the Future, May).

Shribman, David. 1991. "Campaign-Financing Reform, Pushed with Zeal by Gov. Chiles, Attracts Converts in Many States." *Wall Street Journal* (New York: April 4), A16.

Singer, S. Fred. 1992. "Earth Summit Will Shackle the Planet, Not Save It." *Wall Street Journal* (New York: February 19), A16.

Sinner, Jim. 1990. "Soil Conservation: We Can Get More for our Tax Dollars." *Choices* (Second quarter), 10–13.

Smith, Steven S., & Deering, Christopher J. 1984. *Committees in Congress* (Washington, DC: Congressional Quarterly).

Smolko, John F., Jr. 1989. "Impacts of Agricultural Policy on Wildlife." Unpublished paper presented at conference sponsored by the Political Economy Research Center, Bozeman, Montana, December 8.

Sorauf, Frank. 1984. *What Price PACs?* (New York: Twentieth Century Fund).

______. 1988. *Money in American Elections* (Glenview, IL: Scott Foresman/Little Brown).

Sowell, Thomas. 1980. *Knowledge and Decisions* (New York: Basic Books).

Stavins, Robert N., & Jaffe, Adam B. 1990. "Unintended Impacts of Public Investments on Private Decisions: The Depletion of Forested Wetlands." *The American Economic Review, 80* (3) (June), 337–352.

Stigler, George J. 1971. "The Theory of Economic Regulation." *Bell Journal of Economics and Management Science* (Spring), 3–21.

Tanji, Ken. 1990a "Ground-Water Contamination from Nitrates and Pesticides." *The Central Valley—Confluence of Change,* Harold O. Carter & Carole Frank Nuckton, eds. (Davis: Agricultural Issues Center, University of California), 51–63.

______. 1990b. "Water: Stretching the Limits." In *California's Central Valley—Confluence of Change,* Harold O. Carter & Carole Frank Nuckton, eds. (Davis: Agricultural Issues Center, University of California), 53.

Taylor, Paul S. 1975. "California Water Project: Law and Politics." *Ecology Law Quarterly, 5* (1), 1–51.

Thurow, Lester C. 1981. *The Zero Sum Society: Distribution and the Possibilities for Economic Change* (New York: Penguin).

Torell, Allen, & Doll, John P. 1991. "Public Land Policy and the Value of Grazing Permits." *Western Journal of Agricultural Economics, 16* (1) (July), 174–184.

Tullock, Gordon. 1967. "The Welfare Costs of Tariffs, Monopolies, and Theft." *Western Economic Journal*, 224–232.

Tweeten, Luther G. 1980. "Macroeconomics in Crisis: Agriculture in an Underachieving Economy." *American Journal of Agricultural Economics, 62* (5) (December), 853–865.

______. 1989a. *Farm Policy Analysis* (Boulder, CO: Westview Press).

______. 1989b. "The Economic Degradation Process." *American Journal of Agricultural Economics, 71* (5) (December), 1102–1111.

U.S. Department of Agriculture. 1987a. "Soil Erosion: Dramatic in Places, But Not A Serious Threat to Productivity." *Agricultural Outlook* (Washington, DC: Economic Research Service, April), 28–33.

______. 1987b. *Agricultural Resources* (Washington, DC: July).

______. 1988. "Highly Erodible Land Conservation Provision of the Food Security Act of 1985." *Backgrounder* (Washington, DC, April 8).

______. (various years). *Agricultural Statistics* (Washington, DC).

______. (n.d.). Budget Reconciliation Provisions Related to Agriculture (Washington, DC).

U.S. Department of Agriculture, Agriculture and Rural Economy Division, Economic Research Service. 1988. *Economic Indicators of the Farm Sector: National Financial Summary, 1986* (Washington, DC: April).

______. 1989. *Economic Indicators of the Farm Sector: Farm Sector Review, 1987* (Washington, DC: April).

U.S. Department of Agriculture, Economic Research Service. 1990a. *Agricultural Outlook* (Washington, DC: November).

______. 1990b. *The 1990 Farm Act and the 1990 Budget Reconciliation Act,* Miscellaneous publication number 1489 (Washington, DC: December).

______. 1990c. "Cash Rents for Farms, Cropland, and Pasture, 1960–89," *Statistical Bulletin, No. 813* (Rockville, MD), 5.

U.S. Department of Agriculture, Farmers Home Administration. 1982. *Information for Farmers Home Administration County Committees* (Washington, DC: May).

______. 1983. *A Brief History of Farmers Home Administration* (Washington, DC: February).

______. 1988. *FmHA Instruction 1951-S with Attachments* (Washington, DC).

U.S. Department of Agriculture, National Economic Analysis Division. (various years). *Farm Real Estate Market Development* (Washington, DC).

U.S. Department of Agriculture, National Economics Division, Economic Research Service. 1987a. *Government Intervention in Agriculture: Measurement, Evaluation, and Implications for Trade Negotiations,* Staff Report no. AGES 861216 (Washington, DC).

______. 1987b. *Economic Indicators of the Farm Sector: Production and Efficiency Statistics, 1985* (Washington, DC).

______. 1989. *World Agricultural Trends and Indicators, 1970–88,* Statistical Bulletin no. 781 (Washington, DC: June).

U.S. Department of Agriculture, Office of Information. 1988. *Farmers Home Administration* (Washington, DC: November).

U.S. Department of Agriculture, Office of Public Affairs. (various years). *Selected Speeches and News Releases* (Washington, DC).

U.S. Department of Agriculture, Office of Public Affairs. 1993. "USDA Announces 1994 Wheat Program Provisions," *News Releases and Other News Material,* no. 5493 (Washington, DC: May 28), 15.

______. 1993b. "USDA Announces 1993-Crop Sugar Price Support Loan Rates," *News Releases and Other News Material,* no. 7193 (Washington, DC: June 28-July 2), 4.

______. 1993c. "USDA Announces 1994 Feed Grains Acreage Reduction Program Percentages," *News Releases and Other News Material,* no. 9493 (Washington, DC: September 27-October 1).

U.S. Department of Agriculture, Soil Conservation Service. 1984. *Preauthorization Report, South Fork Kings River Watershed* (Washington, DC).

U.S. Department of Commerce, Bureau of the Census. *Census of Agriculture, 1974: Tenure, Type of Organization, Contracts, Operator Characteristics, Principal Occupation* (Washington, DC: September).

______. 1988, 1989, 1990, 1993. *Statistical Abstract of United States* (Washington, DC).

U.S. Department of the Interior. 1980. Acreage Limitation, Draft Environmental Impact Statement. *Westwide Report* (Washington, DC).

U.S. Department of the Interior, Bureau of Reclamation. 1968. *Summary Report of the Commissioner.* Statistical Appendix Parts I, II, and III (Washington, DC), 1–205.

______. 1984a. *Information on Kesterson Reservoir and Waterfowl,* Information Bulletin no. 1 (Washington, DC).

______. 1984b. *Information on Kesterson Reservoir and Waterfowl,* Information Bulletin no. 2 (Washington, DC).

______. (various years). *Summary Statistics* (Washington, DC).

U.S. Department of Interior, Bureau of Reclamation, California Department of Water Resources, and California State Water Resources Control Board. 1979. *Agricultural Drainage and Salt Management* (Washington, DC).

U.S. Department of Interior, Office of Saline Water and Bureau of Reclamation, Colorado River International Salinity Control Project. 1973. *Special Reports 19 and 20* (Washington, DC).

U.S. General Accounting Office. 1986. *Farmers Home Administration Financial and General Characteristics of Farmer Loan Program Borrowers* (Washington, DC: January).

U.S. House of Representatives. 1880. *Report of the Public Lands Commission,* Executive Document no. 46.

______. 102d Congress, Public Law 102-575, 1992, HR 429, Title XXXIV—Section 3405 (a).

______. 1986. "The Congressional Budget Process: A General Explanation." Serial no. CP-9.

______. 1987. *Amending the Food Security Act of 1985, and for Other Purposes,* Report no. 100-497.

______. 1990. *Omnibus Budget Reconciliation Act of 1990,* Report no. 101-964.

U.S. International Trade Commission. 1990. *Estimated Tariff Equivalents of U.S. Quotas on Agricultural Imports and Analysis of Competitive Conditions in U.S. and Foreign Markets for Sugar, Meat, Peanuts, Cotton and Dairy Products,* Publication no. 2276.

U.S. Senate. 1988. *The Administration and Enforcement of the $50,000 Per Person Payment Limitation for Farm Programs,* Senate Hearing 101-595.

______. 1990a. *Food, Agriculture, Conservation, and Trade Act of 1990,* Report no. 101-357.

______. 101st Congress, 2d Session. 1990b. *Food, Agriculture, Conservation, and Trade Act of 1990,* Report no. 101-357. Committee on Agriculture, Nutrition, and Forestry to accompany S. Doc. 2830 (July 6), 1–1282.

______. 1990c. *Central Utah Project Completion Act.* Hearing Before the Subcommittee on Water and Power, Committee on Energy and Natural Resources, 148–168.

Variyam, Jayachandran N., Jordan, Jeffrey L., & Epperson, James E. 1990. "Preferences of Citizens for Agricultural Policies: Evidence from a National Survey." *American Journal of Agricultural Economics, 72* (2) (May), 468–474.

Vroomen, Harry. 1989. *Fertilizer Use and Price Statistics, 1960–88* (Washington, DC: U.S. Department of Agriculture).

Wagner, Richard E. 1989. *To Promote the General Welfare: Market Processes v. Political Transfers* (San Francisco: Pacific Research Institute).

Wahl, Richard W. 1986. "Cleaning up Kesterson." *Resources* (Washington, DC: Resources for the Future, Spring), 11–14.

______. 1989. *Markets for Federal Water: Subsidies, Property Rights, and the Bureau of Reclamation* (Baltimore: Johns Hopkins University Press).

Wallace, L. Tim, & Strong, D. 1985. "Selected Economic Estimates of the Impact of Restricting Irrigation Inflows to Agricultural Lands in the Westlands Water District of California." (Berkeley: Cooperative Extension, University of California, April).

Wall Street Journal. 1990a. Editorial (New York: January 4), A13.

______. 1990b. "Congress v. Campesinos." Editorial (New York: March 5), A14.

______. 1990c. "Balancing Amendment." Editorial (New York: July 16), A12.

______. 1990d. "Balancing Down, Not Up." Editorial *(New York: July 20), A12.*

______. 1990e. "GATT's in the Fire." Editorial (New York: December 3), A14.

Webb, Alan J., Lopez, Michael, & Penn, Renata. 1990. "Government Intervention in Agricultural." In *Estimates of Producer and Consumer Subsidy Equivalents,* Statistical Bulletin no. 803, Alan J. Webb, Michael Lopez, and Renata Penn, eds. (Washington, DC: U.S. Department of Agriculture, Economic Research Service, April), 1–358.

Westcott, Paul C. 1991. "Planting Flexibility and Land Allocation." *American Journal of Agricultural Economics, 73* (4) (November), 1105–1115.

Wicksell, Knut. 1896. *Finanztheoretische Untersuchungen* (Jena: Gustav Fischer).

Willey, Zack. 1985. *Economic Development and Environmental Quality* (Berkeley: Institute of Governmental Studies, University of California).

Williams, Jeffery R., Llewelyn, Richard V., & Barnaby, G. Art. 1990. "Risk Analysis of Tillage Alternatives with Government Programs." *American Journal of Agricultural Economics, 72* (1) (February), 172–181.

Wittman, Donald. 1989. "Why Democracies Produce Efficient Results." *Journal of Political Economy, 97* (6) (December), 1395–1424.

Wooten, H. H. 1950, 1953, and later years. *Supplement to Major Uses of Land in the United States—Basic Land Use Statistics* (Washington, DC: U.S. Department of Agriculture, Bureau of Agricultural Economics).

Yeutter, Clayton. 1990. Statement before the Senate Agriculture, Nutrition, and Forestry Committee. In *Selected Speeches and News Releases* (Washington, DC: February 1–8), 7.

Zinsmeister, Karl. 1989. "*Technology, Ecology, and the American Farmer.*" *Reason* (December), 22–37.

______. 1990. "Cultivating Independence." *Reason* (January), 28–36.

Zulauf, Carl R. 1990. "Policy Trade-offs and the 1990 Food and Agricultural Legislation." In *Agricultural and Food Policy Issues for the 1990s* (Urbana: University of Illinois Press, April).

Index